Aubrey Pascall

Breaking Boundaries

Carol Comfort

California State Polytechnic University, Pomona

Prof. Maxwell
C203

Phillip 495-1665

Prentice Hall, Upper Saddle River, New Jersey 07458

Library of Congress Cataloging-in-Publication Data

Comfort, Carol.
Breaking boundaries / Carol Comfort.
p. cm.
ISBN 0-13-081350-8
1. College readers. 2. English language—Rhetoric—Problems, exercises, etc. I. Title.
PE1417.C63735 2000
808′.0427—dc21 98-47828
CIP

Editorial Director: *Charlyce Jones-Owen*
Editor in Chief: *Leah Jewell*
Senior Acquisitions Editor: *Maggie Barbieri*
Editorial Assistant: *Joan Polk*
Senior Managing Editor: *Bonnie Biller*
Production Liaison: *Fran Russello*
Project Manager: *Marianne Hutchinson (Pine Tree Composition)*
AVP/Director of Manufacturing and Production: *Barbara Kittle*
Prepress and Manufacturing Buyer: *Mary Ann Gloriande*
Cover Director: *Jayne Conte*
Cover Designer: *Bruce Kenselaar*
Marketing Manager: *Sue Brekka*

For permission to use copyrighted material, grateful acknowledgment is made to the copyright holders on pages xix–xx, which are hereby made part of this copyright page.

This book was set in 10/12 ITC Bookman Light by Pine Tree Composition and was printed and bound by Courier Companies, Inc.
The cover was printed by Phoenix Color Corp.

Printed in the United States of America

10 9 8 7 6 5 4 3 2 1

ISBN 0-13-081350-8

Prentice-Hall International (UK) Limited, *London*
Prentice-Hall of Australia Pty. Limited, *Sydney*
Prentice-Hall Canada Inc., *Toronto*
Prentice-Hall Hispanoamericana, S.A., *Mexico*
Prentice-Hall of India Private Limited, *New Delhi*
Prentice-Hall of Japan, Inc., *Tokyo*
Pearson Education Asia Pte. Ltd., *Singapore*
Editora Prentice-Hall do Brasil, Ltda., *Rio de Janeiro*

Contents

PART TWO Writing and Word Processing 69

Chapter 4 Reading, Writing, and Word Processing 71

This chapter addresses using computers in and out of the classroom to aid in the drafting process.

PART THREE The Readings 95

Includes Prereading Journal Questions, Postreading Writing Assignments, Extended Writing Assignments, and Forging Connections.

Allen explores the ways in which American Indian women are struggling to redefine themselves. She discusses tribal definitions of women and analyzes the differences between tribal definitions and non-tribal, non-Indian definitions.

From I Know Why the Caged Bird Sings. *Angelou explores being "Negro and having no control over [her] life." This excerpt is an account of Angelou's graduation; it provides a look at confronting the expectations of others.*

Anzaldúa explores the power of language and the significance of silence. This text is an exploration of issues involving language and bicultural identity.

Atwood's short story presents a glimpse of women discussing serious and not so serious subjects. Her female characters are strong and her writing conveys a sense of feminism.

NANCY MAIRS, Carnal Acts 274

From Carnal Acts. *In this excerpt from her autobiography, Mairs responds to the request: "[Could you talk] on how you cope with your M.S. disability and how you discovered your voice as a writer?" Mairs explores connections between "body" and "written voice."*

BARBARA MELLIX, From Outside, In 287

Mellix discusses working with language in two worlds—private language and academic discourse.

RICHARD RODRIGUEZ, Aria 299

From Hunger of Memory. *Rodriguez, based on his experiences with Spanish and English, proposes the elimination of bilingual classrooms. He explores the differences between public and private language, and reveals the ways in which learning English causes him to lose a certain degree of intimacy with his family.*

LYNN SMITH, Minorities: Alienation and Failure in Academia 310

From the Los Angeles Times. *Smith examines the lives of a number of "minority students" who upon beginning their formal college education experience overwhelming feelings of loss and alienation.*

PART FOUR Thematic Writing Assignments 321

Section I Equal Education: Is Education Fair to Everyone? 323

JONATHAN KOZOL, Savage Inequalities of Public Education in New York

LYNN SMITH, Minorities: Alienation and Failure in Academia

MAYA ANGELOU, Graduation

BELL HOOKS, keeping close to home: class and education

These readings examine the many and varied inequalities some see as inherent in the education systems of the United States. Kozol provides graphic testimony to the inequalities he found in America's schools, inequalities based largely on the socioeconomic status of children's parents. Smith provides a scholarly look at the challenges "minority" students face in academia. Angelou provides a different perspective; in this excerpt from her autobiography, she confronts the low expectations of others. hooks provides a discussion of maintaining ties between her public and private life. Through these readings and the thematic writing assignments, you will be exploring, defining, and redefining your own key experiences in education. Although some of what you read may be difficult for you to relate to (or difficult to read with the grain), try to read with an open mind; be willing, as you read, to see others' perspectives and to find ways to connect what you read with what you already believe to be true. As you work through these texts, reading them with and against the grain, place yourself at the center of the discussions. You are someone with something valuable to say here—an expert, an authority; assert that authority as you write in response to these texts.

Section II The Power of Language 326

RICHARD RODRIGUEZ, Aria

BELL HOOKS, keeping close to home: class and education

BARBARA MELLIX, From Outside, In

GLORIA ANZALDUA, How to Tame a Wild Tongue

Each of these texts presents discourse about the power of language and the ways in which language can be used to include or exclude people from various discourse communities. The essays examine the use of "public" and "private" languages. Rodriguez explores connections between public

and private language; he also argues against bilingual education. hooks provides a different perspective; indeed, in her essay she provides direct rebuttal to Rodriguez's arguments against bilingual education. She also explores maintaining family ties in the midst of academic and professional success. Mellix discusses her use of "cherished" black English and her journey into "academic" English. She also looks at the transforming power of writing. Anzaldua's text will prove problematic. She writes in the many discourses of her life: Spanish, English, Tex-Mex, and Spanglish. Her essay is a powerful testimony to what happens when others try to "tame [her] wild tongue."

These readings provide varied definitions of literacy and education. Rodriguez explores connections between language and intimacy; he also provides a discussion on language and literacy in America's schools. hooks explores maintaining family ties and private language in the midst of academic and professional success. Douglass, in this excerpt from his autobiographical writings, discusses the consequences that he, as a slave, was willing to face in order to learn how to read and write. E. D. Hirsch, in this excerpt from his book Cultural Literacy, *discusses assimilation, acculturation, and his belief that American schoolchildren need to learn a curriculum based on "shared knowledge" and national culture. As you write in response to these readings, you will be asked to see ideas from each writer's perspective, to redefine some of your own experiences, to read one text from another writer's perspective, and to develop your own strong readings of each essay. You may find yourself identifying closely with one writer and reacting strongly against another; remember to read each text closely, trying to see through each writer's lens, understanding her or his point of view, before moving to an "against the grain" reading.*

These autobiographical essays offer glimpses into each writer's life. Are their stories important or worthwhile? Why do people write autobiographies? What do they believe they have to offer their readers? In addition to reading these texts as "stories," you will find that these texts also offer you insight into the act of writing, the empowering quality of writing, and being aware of one's audience.

Nancy Mairs writes about being a woman, finding a written voice and the ways in which her writing empowers her in all areas of life, including "coping" with disability. Harriet Jacobs's narrative explores issues surrounding slavery from a woman's perspective. Black Elk (a holy man of the Oglala Sioux) tells the stories that he does not want to have buried with him, to John G. Neihardt. Frederick Douglass discusses his experiences with learning to read and write as a slave. As you read and respond to each writer's story, keep the following question in mind: does the act of telling one's story empower the writer, the reader, or both?

These essays explore the idea of women's bodies and "ownership" of women. Each text presents a different perspective of how we view women and how society determines in some ways what women should look like and act like. Kingston's story is a retelling of a family story about her aunt and the reason that the family cannot speak her aunt's name. Jacobs's text exemplifies the idea of "ownership" as she presents her story of being a female slave. Mairs writes about being a woman, finding a written voice and the ways in which her writing empowers her in all areas of life, and "coping" with a disabled body in a culture that "demands" women look a certain way. Allen presents "tribal" views of American Indian women and explores the ways in which women come to define and redefine themselves. Dorris's text may appear to be out of place here. Dorris is a man, yet he is writing about an issue that very much affects both men and women and women's bodies. He explores the issue of Fetal Alcohol Syndrome (FAS). Should a woman's right to drink alcohol while pregnant overshadow the rights of an unborn child to be born without FAS? There are no easy answers here, but there are many powerful stories and complex ideas to consider.

One of the intriguing aspects of fiction is that it tells us about ourselves. If a reader takes the time to investigate beyond the entertainment of a story, she or he may be rewarded by discovering rich insights not only into the story but also into the society or culture out of which the story grew. This section explores four diverse short stories. As you read and then write about these stories, you will be looking to discover or uncover the commentaries that they provide about society and culture.

Does gender affect and shape the way people view the world? As you read these texts, notice the ways in which the men and the women tell different stories and how the stories are told differently. Watch for patterns that emerge within the stories, think of ways to categorize each writer's text, and try to establish criteria for ordering and labeling the texts. While gender can be one issue to keep in mind as you interpret and analyze these texts, think of other factors (such as ethnicity, socioeconomic level, and political ideology) that also influence the way that one comes to define reality.

Note to Students

Students often ask, "How can I become a better writer?" My response is, "Read and write a lot." Reading allows you to see and experience the ways in which written language functions. As you read, you internalize the many ways different writers write. You may discover that you learn much more about writing by reading than by being formally instructed in the writing process. If someone tells you that she wants to become a good basketball player, track star, or tennis player, you would probably advise her to practice and practice. My advice to you as you explore the writing process is to read and write as much as possible. In other words, practice.

This textbook invites you to enter into the rewarding experience of reading and writing about ideas, issues, and problems. There are no formulas or shortcuts to writing, but there are strategies that will enable you to become a stronger reader and writer. The reading and writing assignments in this text are designed to help you become effective readers of complex, college-level material and writers of "academic" essays. This textbook doesn't offer easy steps in learning to be a better writer, no magic formulas, or four- (or five- or . . .) step procedures; however, *Breaking Boundaries* does offer strategies to make writing more manageable and more engaging. Writing is a messy process for most of us. Most people, including professional writers, cannot write just one draft and then produce a perfect, polished text; therefore, you need to be willing to revise your drafts.

The title *Breaking Boundaries* suggests breaking the boundaries that supposedly separate freshman composition students from developmental or prebaccalaureate level composition students. The breaking of those boundaries begins with your thinking about yourself. I see college students (including those in Basic Writing courses) as complex, intelligent, capable people who need more practice in reading and writing. What separates developmental writers from freshman composition writers is experience, not ability. The separation between you and someone in freshman composition is probably smaller than you imagine, and your experience this term, if you are willing to work, will prepare you for freshman composition and the writing projects you will be assigned in other college courses.

Another boundary that this book tries to break is the boundary which implies that developmental writers need simple texts. You will discover that the readings in this book are academic and difficult. Developmental writers can and do master college level texts. Challenging readings are more fun to explore than simple straightforward texts because they present an opportunity to examine someone else's serious and interesting ideas and then to respond to those ideas in writing. (I know—this may not sound like "fun" yet, but trust me for a while, and see whether you find certain rewards in this kind of hard work.) Sometimes the hardest texts to understand will become the ones you like the best, the texts that you reread and think about even after you leave this class.

Writing at the college level requires you to learn to manage the discourses, ways of communicating, within the university. At first "academic discourse" may seem foreign to you. You may find yourself lost in what seems to be insider jargon, but you should realize that most newcomers feel this way upon entering a new community. My intent with the readings and the writing assignments provided here is to help you engage in the ongoing discourse of the communities that matter to you, including the discourse of the academy. Academic discourse is a way of communicating that takes place within the communities of the university; it is a way of communicating that you, as a college student, are expected to know and to use. In college, your instructors expect you to know certain terms, to understand allusions, to comprehend fully the complex material that you read in your textbooks, and to respond to the material that you read in competent, analytical prose. In your academic career, you will, through exposure and practice, learn this discourse. This textbook is designed to help you engage in such discourse, to become active participants as readers and writers. Keep in mind as you grapple with new ideas and ways of understanding that what may seem new and strange now will become more common, understandable, and familiar.

Breaking boundaries in your thinking and actions will help you see yourself as part of your academic community. As you become more comfortable in the academic community, this kind of discourse will become less foreign and more accessible to you. Many of the writings in this text examine the use of two languages—the language of the academy and the private language of the individual and his or her community. You need not give up your private language(s) or discourse(s) to participate in the language of the academy. Think of learning academic discourse as adding to your ever-growing ways of communicating; you already communicate differently in various communities. For example, do you speak to your family the same way you speak with your coworkers? Do you communicate in your classes the same way you talk with your friends before or after class—not to mention how you talk while hanging out together on Friday nights? Each of us engages in various kinds of discourse. To participate fully and effectively in college, you will need to learn the language of the academy.

As you become active learners and members of the academy, your dialogue is vital to the classroom environment. Writers and teachers value the input (oral and written) of students and readers; thus, I have included readings that demand dialogue. The readings in this text allow you to become active participants within your classroom and within the larger academic community. The readings also require you to define, explore, and redefine many of your own experiences. Several of these readings are self-reflective; that is, as you read, you will see certain aspects of your own life represented in writing. Thus, many of the writing assignments ask you to redefine your own experiences after reading a particular text. Each reading is followed by suggested topics for essay assignments. Some of these assignments ask you to include a discussion of your own experiences; these assignments ask you to reexamine your own experience as you consider a text you have read. Not only will you discuss your own experience, but you will also explore how reading a particular essay enables you to "see" your experience differently than you saw it before. Other assignments require you to work strictly with essays that you read, exploring connections between texts and themes. The "Thematic Writing Assignments" ask you to make connections between several texts, exploring a particular theme throughout the quarter or semester. Each essay you write builds on the previous essay(s), and the assignments become increasingly more complex as the term progresses.

The readings and the writing assignments in this text require you to become an active, rather than a passive, participant in your education. I'd like to invite you to join the challenging, sometimes frustrating adventure of aggressively seeking knowledge as you read and write. At this point in your academic career, the "rewards" as stated here may not sound worth all this labor; however, it is my hope that the benefits of all this hard work will become more readily apparent as you take responsibility for becoming a stronger reader, more critical thinker, and more accomplished writer.

Note to Instructors

Breaking Boundaries emphasizes writing in response to reading. Many beginning writers, both those in developmental writing and those in Freshman Composition courses, lack reading skills; some enter college never having read a book, and developing strong reading skills is an integral part of becoming a good writer. This book extends an invitation to students to enter into the intensive work of reading and writing and to learn to take part in the rewards of that work. I have included selections that are complex, challenging college-level texts, and have avoided texts that are simple or condescending. Although I see this textbook as aimed primarily at Basic Writing students, I have included a diverse range of reading and writing assignments so that it can also be used for Freshman Composition courses. For students who need intensive reading apparatus, this textbook should be effective. Some of the texts included here may appear to be "beyond" the scope of developmental writers; however, I do have a rationale for including such texts. This book grew from my frustration with the limitations of teaching from "basic writing" textbooks. I know what will be expected of these students when they enter Freshman Composition, and I want to prepare them as much as possible.

My hope is that instructors will work through assigned readings with their students. In class discussion, an instructor can guide students to perform "strong" readings of these texts, to question, probe, and use texts as models for their own writing projects. It is vital that students in prebaccalaureate courses be given the direct instruction needed to engage with complex texts. Far too many students succeed in basic writing only to reach Freshman Composition and fail. If, in basic writing courses, students are asked to read one- to two-page excerpts and write two or three paragraph responses, how then might they be expected to cope with a Freshman Composition textbook like Bartholomae and Petrosky's *Ways of Reading*? There seems to be a huge gap between what we expect of students in Basic Writing and what we demand in Freshman Composition. Perhaps if students in Basic Writing are exposed to scholarly texts, encouraged to participate in academic discourse, and given strategies to write college-level essays, they will find more success in all their courses. We know that if students are taking courses in History, Psychology, Biology, and so on, they are being asked to read, analyze, and respond to complex material. Basic writing courses can be a springboard for students' success in all courses involving reading and writing. As they become stronger readers, thinkers, and writers, they will improve as students.

I see developmental writers as intelligent, capable students who have not fully developed their reading, critical thinking, and writing abilities. Obviously, there are going to be some students who struggle more than others with the demands of a writing course. These students will benefit from intensive reading and questioning activities. If we, as instructors, have low expectations, our students will work at lower levels; however, if we have high expectations, our students will strive to meet and exceed those standards. This ideology is labor intensive for both students and instructors as students learn to grapple with texts that are often difficult for them to read and understand. We can model for our students how to work through difficult texts and ideas, nudging them toward articulating their own complex thinking. Sometimes the first step in this process may be helping students realize that just because they don't fully understand a text doesn't mean that they are not capable of working through the text and gleaning insight and understanding. This might be their first experience in learning to tackle, rather than to dismiss as too difficult, a text they don't readily understand. This is an opportunity to teach the rewarding process of working though a foreign or difficult set of ideas. This is a good time for students to realize that everyone—freshman composition students, upper division students, graduate students, and yes, even instructors—encounters texts that are not easily accessible and need to be worked through. My experience has been that students are willing to put time and energy into this process because they are working with college level texts. They are doing work that matters rather than repeating drills and workbook assignments that don't reflect the kind of work they are doing or will be doing in other college classes.

Because I believe (on the basis of my teaching experience, dialogue with colleagues, and current composition theory) that students learn about writing through successes and failures with their own writing, I have not included fill-in-the-blank or workbook repetition of writing strategies but have instead provided prereading questions and writing assignments that allow students to grapple with complex issues and to write a lot, thereby learning about writing through reading, thinking, and writing. I am sure, though, that students would become discouraged if all texts and assignments for writing appeared overwhelming. To avoid discouraging students, there are a variety of readings, some more difficult than others. Although all the readings are challenging, some texts, writing assignments, and thematic writing assignments are more difficult than others. This feature allows you to develop and tailor a course for your students.

One of the goals of this book is to provide a variety of teaching options for an instructor. Each instructor is unique and has her or his own way of working. An instructor can tailor this text to suit her or his own way of working, teaching, and developing a writing course. The features in this book can be used as they are laid out, or the instructor can custom design a course, using what is helpful and by-passing what is not. I hope to accommodate many instructors' needs and teaching styles as well as accommodating students' needs. Included in this text are prereading journal questions, several postreading writing assignments, options for extended writing projects, essay assignments connecting two or more essays, and thematic writing assignments.

In using this book, you may, of course, choose to develop your own essay questions and/or thematic assignments, or you may want to use the assignments included in the book. Preceding each reading are prereading questions and reading strategies; following each reading are suggestions for postreading writing assignments, extended writing assignments, and thematic assignments. The prereading questions and reading strategies are designed for students who need experience with reading, and they encourage students to read more closely and develop their own reading strategies. (Some students with specific reading and/or learning disabilities may need the guidance of a learning disabilities specialist; however, many of these strategies will prove helpful in addition to any accommodations such students might need.) In the first three chapters of *Breaking Boundaries*, I address reading and writing strategies, recognizing that instructors will have to reinforce and redirect students to incorporate these strategies into their own reading and writing throughout the term. Chapter 1 provides a comprehensive discussion of reading strategies that I have found successful in my experiences as a Reading Disabilities Specialist, Director of Cal Poly Pomona's College Reading Skills Program, and as an instructor of composition at the community college and university level. If you require students to keep a Reader's Journal, there is a discussion in Chapter 2 on journal writing that includes sample student journal entries. Journals are an excellent way to engage students with a text and to encourage closer readings. Chapter 3 is an overview of the drafting process and includes sample student essays for review and discussion. Chapter 4 (written by Stephen Elias) addresses the use of computers to aid in the drafting process. (*Note:* I use a writing handbook to augment the material in *Breaking Boundaries*. This textbook is intended to be coupled with a rhetoric.)

An Instructor's Manual is available and includes sample syllabi, suggestions for class discussion, and ideas for working through several of the writing assignments. I welcome your input, questions, and dialogue. Feel free to E-mail me at: CCOMFORT @CSUPOMONA.EDU

Acknowledgments

No one lives or writes in a vacuum, and I have many people to thank for their input, guidance, patience, and support as I wrote and rewrote this text. My friend and colleague Cora Foerstner (California State Polytechnic University, Pomona) worked with me when the idea of writing a textbook seemed out of reach. This book would never have been written without her assistance. I would also like to acknowledge Professor Kate Massey and Professor Don Kraemer (California State Polytechnic University, Pomona). Both Drs. Massey and Kraemer enabled me to develop and shape my pedagogical beliefs and supported my sometimes "radical" ideas about teaching composition. Drs. Helen Jaskoski (California State University, Fullerton) and Deirdre Lashgari (California State Polytechnic University, Pomona) introduced me to the formal study of Native American and African American Literature. Their influence is evidenced by the texts I have chosen for inclusion in *Breaking Boundaries.* I would also like to thank Steve Elias (California State Polytechnic University, Pomona) for taking the time to write the chapter on computer use for this text. Steve is a good friend and an instructor I admire. I also extend thanks to my friend and colleague Michele Krueper for her assistance with editing and with answering numerous questions on style and mechanics.

My family and friends also deserve recognition for enduring the endless hours I spent at the computer; thus, I'd like to publicly thank my children, Heidi and Josh Comfort, and my fiancé, Christopher Williams, for their support; my mother, Sandra Green, for her belief in me; my sister, Melinda Heise, for always listening; and my colleagues/friends at the Cal Poly Pomona College Reading Skills Program and the Learning Resource Center (special thanks to Lia Gutierrez for her help and to Ricardo Quintero for all those lunches at which he listened to me agonize over revising this textbook). I must send a large thank you to Maggie Barbieri, my editor with Prentice Hall. Her personal touch made the task of completing this text much more humane than it might have been. I would also like to acknowledge and thank the following instructors who took the time to review *Breaking Boundaries:* Charles Wukasch of Austin Community College, Sallyanne H. Fitzgerald of Chabot College, Margo Eden-Camann of DeKalb College and Keith Coplin of Colby Community College. My thanks also extend to Marianne Hutchinson, Production Coordinator with Pine Tree Composition, Inc., and the many individuals who helped coordinate the publication of *Breaking Boundaries.* Most importantly, I cannot forget the students who made this text possible. I have taught "developmental" writing courses at a number of universities and community colleges. Each group of students has taught me the value of their work and the importance of listening to all voices equally. I thank them for their influence in my life and my work.

Credits

PAULA GUNN ALLEN, "Where I Come From is Like This" from *The Sacred Hoop: Recovering the Feminine Side in American Indian Traditions.* Copyright © 1986 by Paula Gunn Allen. Reprinted with the permission of Beacon Press, Boston.

MAYA ANGELOU, Chapter 23 from *I Know Why the Caged Bird Sings.* Copyright © 1969 by Maya Angelou. Reprinted with the permission of Random House, Inc.

GLORIA ANZALDÚA, "How to Tame a Wild Tongue" from *Borderlands/La Frontera: The New Mexico.* Copyright © 1987 by Gloria E. Anzaldúa. Reprinted with the permission of Aunt Lute Books.

MARGARET ATWOOD, "Rape Fantasies" from *Dancing Girls.* Copyright © 1977, 1982 by O. W. Toad, Ltd. Reprinted with the permission of Simon & Schuster and McClelland & Stewart, Ltd.

MICHAEL DORRIS, from *The Broken Cord.* Copyright © 1989 by Michael Dorris. Reprinted with the permission of HarperCollins Publishers, Inc.

FREDERICK DOUGLASS, selections were first published as a tract by the Boston Anti-Slavery Society, Spring 1845.

GABRIEL GARCIA MARQUEZ, "The Handsomest Drowned Man in the World" from *Leaf Storm and Other Stories.* Copyright © 1971 by Gabriel Garcia Marquez. Reprinted with the permission of HarperCollins Publishers, Inc.

SUSAN GLASPELL, "Trifles" was first performed in 1916, and was first published in book form in PLAYS (New York: Dodd, Mead & Co., 1920).

ERNEST HEMINGWAY, "Hills Like White Elephants" from *Men Without Women.* Copyright © 1927 by Charles Scribner's Sons, renewed © 1955 by Ernest Hemingway. Reprinted with the permission of Scribner, a division of Simon & Schuster.

E. D. HIRSCH, excerpt from *Cultural Literacy.* Copyright © 1987 by Houghton Mifflin Company. Reprinted with the permission of the publishers. All rights reserved.

BELL HOOKS, "keeping close to home: class and education" from *Talking Back.* Reprinted with the permission of South End Press, Boston.

MAXINE HONG KINGSTON, excerpt from *The Woman Warrior.* Copyright © 1975, 1976 by Maxine Hong Kingston. Reprinted with the permission of Alfred A. Knopf, Inc.

JONATHAN KOZOL, excerpt from *Savage Inequalities.* Copyright © 1991 by Jonathan Kozol. Reprinted with the permission of Crown Publishers, Inc.

NANCY MAIRS, "Carnal Acts" from *Carnal Acts.* Copyright © 1990 by Nancy Mairs. Reprinted with the permission of Beacon Press, Bobston.

BARBARA MELLIX, "From Outside, In" from *The Georgia Review* XLI, no. 2 (Summer 1987) Copyright © 1987 by The University of Georgia, 8 1987 by Barbara Mellix and The Georgia Review.

JOHN G. NEIHARDT (Black Elk), "Grandmother's Land" from *Black Elk Speaks.* Copyright *1932,* © 1972 by John G. Neihardt. Copyright © 1961 by the John G. Neihardt Trust. Reprinted with the permission of the University of Nebraska Press.

RICHARD RODRIGUEZ, "Aria" from *Hunger of Memory* (Boston: David R. Godine, Publisher, 1981). Copyright © 1982 by Richard Rodriguez. Reprinted with the permission of Georges Borchardt, Inc. for the author.

LYNN SMITH, "Minorities: Alienation and Failure in Academia" from *The Los Angeles Times* (January 6, 1988). Reprinted with the permission of The Los Angeles Times Syndicate.

Part One

Reading, Thinking, Writing, and Revision: The Intertwined Parts of the Writing Process

1

Acts of Reading: Making Meaning from Texts

Reading Strategies

The essays in this book require you to do academic reading and writing. The essay assignments require you to move beyond simple summary-writing to more analytical, scholarly writing. You will grapple with difficult texts and come to terms with ideas that you read about to create your own understanding and reading of the texts that you encounter. The movement toward writing begins with reading.

I would like to make some suggestions about ways to approach your reading. Try the following strategies, and tailor them to fit your particular needs. This section of *Breaking Boundaries* addresses the act of reading and offers ideas for improving both your interpretation and your critical comprehension of texts. These suggestions are not rigid formulas but rather are resources to use as you need them. By using these strategies, you are likely to increase your ability to read closely, to formulate your own ideas, and to express, through dialogue with the text and with your class as well as through writing, your reading of a text. You should discover, as you use and practice these strategies, that they are useful when you approach other reading, thinking, and writing tasks. The more strategies you acquire, the more resources you have for writing situations.

Making Sense of Reading

As you begin reading, several things happen. If you know something about a text you are going to read, your perception, interpretation, and understanding of that text will likely begin before you start to read. Even if you do not know anything about a text, your mind tries to make sense of the material. You may have experienced frustration with trying to read something that you did not understand; you may have tried to tackle it, or you may have given up in discouragement because it seemed too foreign, too inaccessible. A feeling or sense of difficulty or confusion when tackling something new is normal. Most people experience this feeling when confronted with new situations, ideas, thoughts, or concepts.

Making sense of a text often requires a conscious effort on your part that includes paying attention to clues before you begin to read, connecting what you are reading to material you have read before, aiming for a comprehensive rather than a fragmented view of the text, seeing the text from many different perspectives, and working as an active, not a passive, reader. In order to guide you into becoming a more active reader, this text provides reading tips, headnotes, prereading and postreading questions, and writing assignments for each reading. Textbooks and anthologies often include introductions, headnotes, and footnotes to help readers; however, many readers skip these helpful additions and thus miss opportunities to create stronger, fuller readings. Strong readers take advantage of these helps. *Breaking Boundaries* includes more questions and reading strategies than most other textbooks to provide you with many ways to approach a text as well as to model the kinds of questions and strategies that help you wrestle with and gain control of new ideas and concepts and to learn to develop your own questions and interpretations of texts that you read.

Reading as a Process

As you work toward becoming a more aware reader, become conscious of what you do before, during, and after you read. Looking at the physical layout of a text often leads you to begin making some assumptions about its content before you actually begin to read. You may form an opinion or opinions from a text's appearance. A text that has lots of blank spaces and pictures creates a different response than one that is tightly written with little white space and with paragraph after paragraph of writing. A play presents itself differently on the page than does a short story, and an academic essay looks different from a poem. Look at some of the texts included in *Breaking Boundaries*. What do differences in appearance cause you to think about various texts?

Titles also reveal information about texts. Consider, for example, Harriet Jacobs's essay, which is taken from her book *Incidents in the Life of a Slave Girl*; in this case, the title provides specific information. From this title, what assumptions might you make about her or her essay? Taking time to think about a title can help you with your reading. Authors choose their titles and their words with care; one of their goals is to communicate, so paying attention to titles can signal meaning before you begin to read.

If you are familiar with the author's name, this familiarity too might cause you to begin to form early thoughts about a text. What facts or ideas do you know about an author? What do these facts or ideas suggest? Knowing something about the authors helps you as a reader to place essays within a context. Reading the headnote preceding Jacobs's essay can add to your understanding of Jacobs and her text. Knowing a little about the author, what she or he has written, and something about the text adds to your understanding and interpretation of a text. Learning to read and to make meaning by utilizing all possible resources gives you more material with which to work and is part of becoming a stronger reader and writer.

Considering a text's appearance, the author, title, and any other information you can use enables you to begin creating your own reading of a text. Reading, writing, and thinking are all complex parts of a whole process. Being aware of this connection can empower you as a reader, thinker, and writer. Your writing process begins as you make initial assumptions about a text; the writing process evolves as you actively read, perhaps changing some of your early assumptions, adding to your initial view of each text. Becoming a more effective reader and critical thinker equips you to become a stronger writer.

Reading Speed

When you read an essay, try to read without stopping each time you come to a word or phrase you do not understand. Jot down or underline words you do not know, and look them up in a dictionary after you have finished reading. If you interrupt your reading a number of times, it will be difficult to create an understanding of a whole text. There is a temptation to stop each time you encounter an unfamiliar word. Most of us have been taught, somewhere along the line, that we must read and understand every single word in order to make sense of a text. Usually, though, interrupting your reading has the opposite effect and will cause your reading to be fragmented. If you keep stopping, it will be difficult to create an overview of the reading. Starting and stopping make it difficult to remember what you have read. One strategy that often proves more effective than stopping your reading to look up individual words is to determine the meaning of words or phrases "in context." When trying to figure out a word's meaning from the context, look at the function of the word: What does it seem to mean? What does it do in the sentence? What possible meanings would not be possible on the basis of the rest of the sentence or paragraph? By decoding the meaning of words in context, you are more likely to increase your reading speed, comprehension, and vocabulary.

As you attempt to do the required reading for your college courses, a slow reading speed will be a hindrance. On the average, college students read at approximately two hundred words per minute. If you are reading at a significantly lower rate, you will have difficulty finishing assignments, and your comprehension may decrease; when you are reading very slowly, your mind tends to wander—when you notice, for example, that if you have "read" four paragraphs but cannot remember a single thought from the passage, it may be that you are not reading fast enough to concentrate. There are a number of ways to increase your reading speed. One strategy to practice is picking up word groups rather than individual words. When you look at a line of text, your eyes should stop a limited number of times. For example, in this sentence how many times do your eyes stop? Do you see every individual word, or are you able to see word groups? Rather than seeing each word as a separate unit, you should see groups of words as a unit. If you begin to notice that your comprehension is slipping, though, you may be missing too many essential words. Find a pace that is comfortable for you. You also want to be conscious of your eye movements: Do your eyes move consistently and rhythmically as you read? Are you able to move from the end of one line to the beginning of the next without getting "lost"? These are skills you can work on and, with practice, improve.

Keep in mind that your reading speed is determined, in part, by the material you are reading. Most of the texts you encounter in college will be difficult, and to understand them fully, you may find yourself reading more slowly than if you are reading a novel for pleasure. This situation creates an apparent paradox: You need to read fast enough to make meaning from the words but slow enough to grapple with the ideas of a text. Of course, some texts do not require a lot of effort; they can be read quickly and often are read for pleasure. Be prepared. Academic texts are usually more difficult and require a more thoughtful reading.

Visualizing

Visualizing as you read can help to improve your critical comprehension of a text. Visualizing is seeing an essay, a short story, or a play come to life in your mind's eye. You create mental images of events as they unfold. Visualizing will enhance the strategies previously described as you create images based on what you read. If you read Maya Angelou's "Graduation," for example, you create in your mind's eye a representation of your reading: see her in her beautiful yellow dress; imagine the other eager graduates; watch their expressions as the commencement speaker sentences them to lives as farmers and maids; and create new images as the valedictory address of Henry Reed brings them from despair to hope. Visualizing gives you, the reader, further opportunity to interact with the text, to make it more your own. Visual images should be based on the text. For instance, if the text tells you that Angelou is twelve years old, to imagine her as forty-six is not to create your own reading but is to ignore the boundaries of the text. (Visualizing is not the same as fantasizing.) You may find that your images change with subsequent readings or after class discussions. This change happens because your interpretation and understanding of a text or texts evolves: reading complex texts is not a static activity but is a living, growing experience.

If you do not visualize at all, begin the process by visualizing a selected paragraph or short essay. Drama and fiction, of course, lend themselves to visualizing—a story is there for us to see, to imagine. Visualizing becomes more difficult, though, with abstract or very academic texts. For example, visualizing E. D. Hirsch's essay "Cultural Literacy" may present some difficulty for you. Try to imagine him speaking to you; imagine the setting; put yourself into the picture with him; speak back to him and his text; ask questions; and watch yourself move through his writing. Involve yourself, in any way possible, with a text. Doing this will enable you to become part of the picture you create as you read.

Your images will be constantly evolving as you gain more information from a text. Visualizing improves not only your basic comprehension of a text but also your understanding of the way the pieces of an essay work together, and it allows you to make connections between a number of essays. As you visualize, you begin to connect new information to information already stored in your mind, thereby creating points of connection between new and existing information.

NOTE: I was first introduced to the idea of "visualizing" in this kind of formal context by Nanci Bell in her book *Visualizing and Verbalizing*, Academy of Reading Publications, 1991.

Reading and Writing Connections

As you read, you begin to create your own reading, and you also begin your writing process. While reading, take up your pen, and underline ideas that seem important to you or that puzzle you. Do not be reluctant to mark your textbook; this marking is a way to stay actively engaged with the text and will enable you to stay focused on your reading.

Reading is an active process. Mark your text, take notes, and write notes in the margins. Marking or annotating a text is your response to what you are reading, and it might prove valuable to you later as you begin to organize and plan your essay. Marking a text is not the same thing as highlighting or underlining words: marking a text is your way of discovering what you find important, what you want to explore, and/or what puzzles you about a text.

Think of this process as having a dialogue with a text. Although the text cannot speak verbally, the written words communicate—sometimes the meaning is clear, while other times it is not. Your response—talking back to a text—can take place in your mind and also on the pages of text. As you underline, make notes in the margins, and raise questions, you are keeping a written record of your dialogue with the text. If you don't record your reactions, the wonderful, insightful ideas or important questions you have while reading may be lost to you. If you annotate a text, you can return to it later to rethink what you consider important.

There is no one perfect way to annotate a text. Indeed, people will mark a text in different ways. Because each person creates her or his own reading, each person will find different points interesting, complex, or worth noting. Review the following annotated texts. Two different students marked up this selection from bell hooks's essay "keeping close to home: class and education." Note the similarities and the differences—how might a reader use these annotations as a way to come back to the text for subsequent readings?

Before reading the following passage, turn to hooks's text. Read the headnote and skim the essay in order to place the passage in context as you review the annotations.

Studying at Stanford, I began to think seriously about class differences. To be materially underprivileged at a university where most folks (with the exception of workers) are materially privileged provokes such thought. Class differences were boundaries no one wanted to face or talk about. It was [easier] to downplay them, to act as though we were all from privileged backgrounds, to work around them, to confront them privately in the solitude of one's room, or to pretend that just being chosen to study at such an institution meant that those of us who did not come from privilege were already in transition toward privilege. To not long for such transition marked one as rebellious, as unlikely to succeed. It was a kind of treason not to believe that it was better to be identified with the world of material privilege than with the world of the working class, the poor. No wonder our working-class parents from poor backgrounds feared our entry into such a world intuiting perhaps that we might learn to be ashamed of where we had come from, that we might never return home, or come back only to lord it over them.

class differences create boundaries? Why? What kinds of boundaries?

easier for . . . ?

Is education always a transition toward privilege?

Is this a realistic fear? How might Richard Rodriguez respond?

Studying at Stanford, I began to think seriously about class differences. To be materially underprivileged at a university where most folks (with the exception of workers) are materially privileged provokes such thought. Class differences were boundaries no one wanted to face or talk about. It was easier to downplay them, to act as though we were all from privileged backgrounds, to work around them, to confront them privately in the solitude of one's room, or to pretend that just being chosen to study at such an institution meant that those of us who did not come from privilege were already in transition toward privilege. To not long for such transition marked one as rebellious, as unlikely to succeed. It was a kind of treason not to believe that it was better to be identified with the world of material privilege than with the world of the working class, the poor. No wonder our working-class parents from poor backgrounds feared our entry into such a world intuiting perhaps that we might learn to be ashamed of where we had come from, that we might never return home, or come back only to lord it over them.

Is this based on money?

What kinds of boundaries?

Coping & anxiety

Guilt?

How do parents' anxieties influence their children?

Compare the two annotated texts. What does each annotator notice about the text? Are there patterns that emerge from the marking? Are there similarities between the two examples? Differences? What focus does each annotator seem to have? What are some issues that each of these writers might explore in an essay about hooks's text?

Notice that the annotations in each example are marked with specific meaning. Annotating a text is a technique to help you become a more thoughtful reader. There is a danger, however, of marking or highlighting too much. Many students highlight nearly an entire page of a text; doing this does not enable the writer to come back to what was important to him or her, but simply gives the student a yellow (or blue, or . . .) page. Think of the marking up your text as the beginning of your dialogue with a text, which will lead you to an extended writing project. In this dialogue, you will be doing most of the work because as you ask questions, bring up inconsistencies, or try to explore ideas more deeply, you have to rely on the text and your reasoning to respond to your inquiry. If you read a text more than once—and some of these texts will require more than one reading—note the ways in which your annotations change. What seemed so puzzling the first time around may make more sense with subsequent readings, or you may discover why a particular section seemed so important to you. Clearing up one point may lead to another question or to a conclusion. Class or small group discussions may give you insights or raise more questions or spark an interest in something you had not noticed before. This is an exciting process. Marking up your text is an integral part of the process. Thinking about and reviewing your annotations can be crucial as you move on to more extended and sustained writing.

AN ASIDE: Obviously, these suggestions cannot meet the individual needs of all students. For those of you with specific learning and/or reading disabilities, some of these suggestions may not be practical; however, most of them should be beneficial in some way. If you have ever been diagnosed with a specific learning disability, there are many ways for you to work on improving your reading speed and comprehension. Most colleges have an office designed to assist students with disabilities and/or a Learning Assistance Center. A Reading Specialist or a Learning Disabilities Specialist can offer you an individualized plan for becoming a stronger reader.

Reading with and Against the Grain

One reason to become a stronger, more critical reader is to understand how writers write. A strong reader is one who reads actively, interacting with the text in many ways and reading deeply, looking for more than main ideas or answers to simple questions. Understanding ideas, questioning ideas, coming to your own conclusions, reading what words literally say as well as what words imply, and thinking about and considering what writers do not say as well as what they do say are all parts of critical thinking and reading—reading, thinking, and writing are the intertwined parts of the writing process.

As a reader and writer you can make some assumptions about authors: they write for many different reasons; they want to communicate; they have something to say that they think is important, right, and/or worth saying; and they write to persuade readers to their points of view. Just as academic and non-fiction readings have complex meaning and importance, so too do short stories and plays. Fiction was written with purpose and often tells us about what it means to be "human." By reading fiction, we can learn more about ourselves and others.

As you begin to understand an author's ideas, you also can begin to form your own opinion about what she has to say, how she says it, and why she says it in a particular way. When you do this kind of reading, you are actively reading a text; you are trying to understand the ideas and ways of thinking that an author presents, yet you are also analyzing and questioning those ideas and ways of thinking. You are also influenced by an author's rhetorical strategies. Active reading can be laborious; however, it also can be deeply rewarding and satisfying because you are interacting with ideas and exploring new ways of thinking, and are developing as a reader, writer, and thinker. You should be honing these skills throughout your academic and professional life. Your role as a reader, writer, and thinker will not end after the completion of this course. You will keep learning and growing in these areas as long as you actively participate in the process.

I have borrowed two terms, "reading with the grain," and "reading against the grain," from David Bartholomae and Anthony Petrosky.* Understanding the theory behind these terms and applying these ideas to reading have helped students become more active readers.

Although I am going to present these labels and ideas sequentially, when you are reading and writing, you will probably find that sometimes you will be reading "with the grain" and at other times "against the grain." At times this process happens sequentially; at other times you may find that you move between reading "with and against the grain."

Reading to understand a text as an author likely intended it to be understood, seeing through a writer's eyes, through his or her lens, is reading "with the grain." When you read "with the grain," you are seeking to understand an author's point of view. You might imagine that you are walking along in dialogue with an author, considering and examining a text to come to terms with an author's ideas as ways of thinking and seeing. Imagine a scenario in which you are having a conversation with an author; you would give the writer's point of view thoughtful consideration, trying to see as you

*Bartholomae, David, and Anthony Petrosky, eds., *Ways of Reading.* Boston: Bedford Books of St. Martin's Press, 1987.

think the writer would see. In this conversation, you want to make a text live, giving attention to the terms the author uses, looking closely at the words, themes, ideas, images, point of view, or plot of a text. Your goal in reading "with the grain" is to experience a text as much as possible as the author likely intended; even if you disagree with an aspect of the author's perspective, this is the time to work with an author. A thoughtful, careful reading of a text is important.

Good authors choose their words carefully, working with care to convey meaning to their readers. Reading carelessly might cause you to create a poor or incomplete reading. As a college student, you will encounter not only complex academic texts but also texts that use satire and/or humor, subtle ways of writing that require careful, critical reading to understand fully. All these texts rely on carefully chosen words, tone, and style to convey meaning and provide clues about the author's likely intention.

If you read Richard Rodriguez's "Aria" "with the grain," you might acknowledge the difficulties he encounters when he enters kindergarten speaking only fifty words of English; you might attempt to understand his reasons for alienating himself from his family and his private self in order to succeed in public life; you might seek to understand his point of view and his logic. You would consider his word choices, style, tone, and syntax. You might question who his intended audience is. What does he say to this audience? And how does he say it? You work through Rodriguez's essay to see through his eyes or through his lens.

"Reading with the grain" helps you to gain an understanding of a text and the idea that an author is attempting to communicate. Before you can form a fully developed interpretation of a text, you must first come to terms with it and understand it as thoroughly as possible. A careful reader moves from reading a text "with the grain" to reading "against the grain." As you read "against the grain," you again explore a text with the writer, walking alongside her or him, questioning and closely examining the writer's points, ideas, and ways of seeing and articulating the ideas. With this kind of reading, though, you also seek out contradictions, silences, and faulty logic of the text. You begin to ask questions: What does this text tell me about the author, about the author's ideas and biases? What has the author left unsaid? Why? What cultural stance does the author reflect? What does this tell me? What are the limits of the text? What do those limits suggest?

You are no longer looking through an author's lens. Your reading is pushing "against the grain" of what an author has written. Now you see the text through your own lens, trying many ways of reading, seeing, interpreting, and thinking about a text. Imagine that you are in a disagreement with an author. How might the author respond? In what ways can you envision the author's answering your questions? Think of yourself as an expert of the text: questioning, pushing, and testing for inconsistencies and ambiguities.

If you were to read Rodriguez against the grain, imagine questioning him for proof of his assertions, challenging his premise, pointing out flaws in his reasoning. How might he answer you in this dialogue? What might you ask him? What gaps do you see in his arguments? Would you have acted as he did if you had been in his situation? Why or why not?

In some ways, reading in this way is very idealistic because you might find that you identify so closely with an essay that it is difficult for you to read against the grain, but to become a strong reader, you need to learn to read against the grain of a text, even those texts that you like and admire. On the other hand, you might encounter an essay that you react to negatively, finding yourself in strong disagreement with it. You might find it very difficult to read with the grain of such an essay or a story; yet, it would benefit you to work through your objections, disagreements, and frustrations, so that you can develop a with-the-grain reading. You cannot formulate an effective and complete against-the-grain reading until you have a clear understanding of what you think are the author's intentions and point of view. Reading both with and against the grain enables you to engage fully with a text and an author's ideas, moving toward developing your own reading.

Your written project will emerge from your reading of a text; writing your essay becomes your response to the reading you created. You take the ideas and key terms of an author and work with them, forming your own analyses, opinions, and ideas. As you do this, you are creating your own reading, which will evolve and mature as you write in response to a text. Embedded in a text are possibilities for many readings and interpretations. You—as reader, writer, and thinker—are creating your unique reading. You choose how your reading will unfold, and you create your interpretation within the frame of the text. You begin with your reading and understanding of a text, and you make choices, accepting some ideas but eliminating others as you seek to make a complete sense of your reading. This process does not mean that misreading can never occur. You are limited by the boundaries, the frame, of each text. Although there is a lot of room within the frame of a text, there are some limits that you cannot ignore.

If you read Rodriguez's text, you have to come to understand his perspective. You work with his text, accepting what is agreed upon by everyone—for example, his struggle to reconcile his public and private language, or his loss of intimacy with his family. These ideas are central to his essay, and although you may or may not agree with him, he has created a frame from which to work. Within this frame you may choose to read "against" his claims. You will use your reading "with and against the grain" to construct your own reading. Your project is likely to become complex because you have both agreed and disagreed with Rodriguez, so that you can create a written project that reflects your readings, interpretations, and conclusions regarding Rodriguez's text. As you write your essay, placing Rodriguez's text in a context he might not have imagined, you give life to your words, and others can read and respond to you.

2

Moving from Reading to Writing: Reader's Journals

Your reading and writing can improve significantly if you keep some sort of "Reader's Journal." Journals can be a place for you to record your thoughts, questions, images, and reactions to the texts you are reading. As you read, keep your journal handy so that you can copy into it passages that puzzle or intrigue you and record your reactions to these sections. (Your instructor may have some specific guidelines about writing journal entries—for example, they might need to be typed or perhaps kept in a certain kind of notebook.) Your Reader's Journal is an extension of the reading strategies discussed in Chapter 1. In your journal, you can write about a text in order to think through a specific reading. You will discover that writing is a way of thinking—you don't have to know what you want to say before you begin to write. Journals can include summaries of what you read, but you will also want to move beyond summaries to explore ideas, questions, and concepts that puzzle or interest you. You might also write down passages that you find interesting. If something is memorable or seems very important to you, record the passage; it will be there later for you to consider. If you don't write down your responses, you may forget them, and they will be lost.

You will, at some point in your writing course, be asked to do formal and extended writing projects. Your Reader's Journal is where you begin an extended writing project; this is where you discover, in writing, what it is you have to say about a text and where you examine your ideas, questions, and interests. While this discovery may have begun in your "marking up" of a text, your journal becomes an extension of your initial thoughts. Often students avoid beginning their extended writing projects because they don't have a crystal-clear idea of what they want to say; however, if you have already marked up a text and written journal entries in response to a given text, you will have rich resources from which to draw. As you write, give yourself time to discover what is important to you and what you think is important enough to write about. Inevitably, students who invest time and energy in writing thoughtful, thorough journal entries write better essays because they have already spent time thinking and writing about the texts.

You might also think of your journal as a place to do your **prewriting**. Before you begin an essay assignment, prewriting can help you figure out what you have to say in response to the text you read. Although you may not have considered being able to have a dialogue with a text, your journal is a place to do just that. Imagine "talking back" to the text or the author. What is it that you want to say? Put yourself in the position of questioning the author, interacting with the characters in a short story, challenging the points made in academic essays, looking for places you identify with in a text, and finding moments where you can share the give and take of a dialogue with the text.

Your journal is also a place to wrestle with your understanding of difficult or problematic sections of a text. As tempting as it may be to ignore sections of text that are seemingly incomprehensible, try instead to respond to these sections in your journal. Ask yourself the following: "Why is this section so difficult? Exactly what is it that I do not understand? What do I understand about other sections in this text?" You need to be willing to explore various meanings and to propose a number of possibilities regarding the material you read. Because some essays are going to be difficult, it might be helpful early on to acknowledge difficulty rather than ignore it. If you ignore or skip over difficult sections of text, you may be missing out on crucial moments—some of these moments may be meaningful to you after working your way through them. As you read and find complex or puzzling moments in a given text, copy down the particular passages or thoughts, and explore the possible meanings. If a particular section of text continues to be problematic, bring up the problem during class discussion; chances are you are not the only one experiencing difficulty. Many times just hearing others' ideas and perspectives will enable you to develop and extend your own point of view.

All too often, students come to the end of a term and realize that their journals contained insights and ideas that would have been useful in their writing, but they hadn't used the journals when they were drafting their essays. Think of journal writing as an integral part of the writing process, a place to record your visual images, thoughts, and questions, and to return to when developing your ideas, thoughts, and first, second, or third impressions in extended writing. Students who use their journals in this way develop stronger readings and, as a result, stronger writings.

Following are some sample student journal entries in response to various readings. Read through the entries, and analyze what these students were attempting to do as writers and how these journal entries might have led to extended writing projects. You will notice that the writing is not "perfect." There are mechanical errors and undeveloped ideas, yet the writers are beginning to discover their thoughts about the texts that they are discussing:

Sample Reader's Journal Entries

Reader's Journal
Student: Marlene
English 095—Basic Communication Skills
Cal Poly Pomona
Essay: Barbara Mellix "From Outside, In"

After reading "From Outside, In" by Barbara Mellix, I noticed the title contained the main idea of her essay. In her eyes the standard of English was a foreign language used by "others". "Others" meaning "proper" blacks and whites. In the first paragraph Mellix demonstrates the acute differences between "black" Enlgish and "proper" English. She starts off by describing her working environment and being interupted by her daughter. There is a great differnece in discourse between herself and her daughter versus herself and the reader. I believve she begins in this manner to clearly demonstrate what her essay is reflecting on. Mellix describes her acquiring of the English language in a chronological order; her insights vary from a child to present day adult.

As a child Mellix describes her use of "standard" English as a form of writing, which contained simple short expressions. Standard English had a designated time and place. It was used around "others" to prove ones intelligence. She believed using "standard" Englsih was a mask or costume which betrayed her "customary manner of speaking" somehow making it inferior to standard English. The use of "black" English was a comfortable form of discourse, full of personality and expressions. I can relate to Mellix but the boundaries differ, instead of a differnece in language (black English vs. proper Englsih), there is a differnece in how I use the language. There is a great difference in how I would talk to a peer versus how I would talk to an instructor. For example, I am more relaxed, easy going, when talking to a peer, versus feeling self-conscious and stressed when talking to an instructor, not only do emotions differ but the use of language. When I talk to a friend I use slang and I catch myself using curse words and humor. When I talk to an instructor I find myself using different choice of words excluding cuss words.

Going back to Mellix, as she studied the English language she found it difficult to compose her thoughts because she felt she did not own this language thus she was unable to think in standard English. Through time she noticed that the languages were diverse but similar, thus enabling her to express herself in "standard" English. Mellix refrained from using standard English because it was foreign and impersonal. As an adult she is able to use both forms of English in a personalized manner.

Mellix end her essay with a powerful statement, "through writing one can continually bring new selves into being, each with new responsiblities and difficulties. I write and continually give birth to myself." In my eyes writing is an obstacle, it requires time and effort. Each piece of writing requires thought, resposibilities which can be time consuming as well as dificult.. I must agree, writing enables expansion, fulfillment, and is endless in possibilities. The power lies in the individual. They may us it any way to form their expression and idealogies.

Reader's Journal
Student: Carlo
English 095—Basic Communication Skills
Cal Poly Pomona
Essay: Maxine Hong Kingston "No Name Woman"

The essay written by Maxine Hong Kingston, named *No Name Woman*, is very interesting. It is about a girl that gets pregnant from a fellow villager. Everybody in the village disowns her, including her family. She ends up killing her self by jumping into a well. The story is told by a number of people, including Maxine Hong Kingston and her mother. The father acts as though he never had a sister and that she was never born. The father hopes that her sister will be tortured for the rest of her life. Maxine now thinks that her aunt now haunts her and means her harm.

I do not understand why the villagers and the family member disowned her the way they did. The villagers and others believe that their village got attacked because of her. I guess the mentality fifty years ago is not the same as the mentality as we have now. And I do not think the strict Chinese mentality helped her cause either. I think though she should have named the person that raped her. I do not understand why she did not. The entire ordeal was not only her aunt's fault, the guy had a big part to play in it too.

Now I understand why the book is called *No name Women*. The aunt does not exist through the eyes of many, including her father. So if she supposably does not exist, she can not have a name. I think all these people are in their own fantasy world. The reality is that she did in fact lived and caused a big mess, and it is hard to ignore it, but her family is trying to hard to forget it.

Reader's Journal
Student: Charlie
English 095—Basic Communication Skills
Cal Poly Pomona
Essay: Maxine Hong Kingston "No Name Woman"

When I first read the title, I had strong desire to know the story better, the title" no name woman" gave me a strong sense of hidden saddness that have ever been told, I believed the story not only telling the mysterious thoughts of older people in China, but also making powerful interpretation of conflict between the older and young generations. Nevertheless, the aunt's story is the key that tells the romantic and tragic love story, is pretty similar to the "Romeo and Juliet" love story, except that the public influence are more brutally and realistically shown. If we read the first lines of the beginning of story, it quote "You must not tell anyone." It gives be mixed feeling, is this woman a devil-like siner? And what she had done that makes people refused to forgive what she done. Ever since I read the first line, I feel like I'm trapped in the cage of sadness. Is not hard to tell what's the whole story about to reveal after you read the third paragraph, to have a "unknown" baby is a unacceptable sins that should receving the cruelest punishment, yet , the birth of this baby are the hardest thing that the mother and the whole family have to face in the present time.

In the old chinese society, the traditions are the primary pinciple of the people, is like the hardest laws that no men dare to challenge, even though after manys of years, that people emigrants to the other world, they still carry the tradition roles that had been wear since the day they were born. Mr. Kingston did point out reasons for the doing, for one, the Chinese imgrants usually translate their names in unspeakable letters, this might be the expression of the forgiving their idenities and heavy tradition roles from their homeland. They pretty much denied their own culture, seeking for the new life, away from their family, their tradition. They're pursuing another way of freedom, to think and do what ever they wanna do without fear the consequence of breaking the rules. I think Kingston are try to make the connections between traditional roles and how women establish their own future against the realities.

Reader's Journal
Student: Shannon
English 095—Basic Communication Skills
Cal Poly Pomona
Essay: Barbara Mellix "From Outside, In"

In Barbara's essay she focused on the way people speak and how language is used in context. She metions something about two different types of language, black english and standard english. There is a certain time to use the black english and standard english depending upon who you are conversing with. Should there even be two different types of English? Just because Barbara might of grown up in the world around blacks does not mean it is necessary to have a separate language.

In paragraph five Barbara mentions that at her grandmothers house in Greenleyville, South Carolina, when her city relatives are home her whole family thinks twice before talking. I could never imagine having to always rethink what I am about to say because I like to talk about everything when it comes to mind. I think that if Barbara's parents set a better example of conversing the standard english nobody would have to feel uncomfortable at talking at any occasion. To make matters worse when her relatives left they all made fun of the way they talk. This is where I begin to start reading against the grain. If they want to be able to speak comfortably around people in there own language, then they should not make fun of the others speaking the standard language. Barbara's family felt that their relatives made them feel like "country" and to regain their pride in themselves they mocked them. If they have so much pride in the way they tallk then why don't they use it without having to think twice? I think that the reason they only speak around certain people is because they are uncomfortable and feel different about their language, but they have to much pride to admit, and will never use standard english for that reason. If they want respect and want to be able to talk in any language, then they have to learn that to receive respect you have to give respect. This is something I have always lived up to.

The reason I fell that they have to much pride in their language is that throughout the whole essay they try to explain that they only feel right speaking their own type of language. First of all, I did not realize we all have a certain type of language, and I still don't believe that. In

Paragraph seven, when the white officer Toby complimented Barbara on her dress and she says "Thank you very much", and then feels like those words were foreign coming from her mouth. She has heard and spoken of this phrase before, and it is even the same in black english, but she felt like it was an occasion for proper english. Toby was not even grammatically correct to the proper english, and she still felt foreign saying that phrase. Is this because Toby is white? I do not understand why she feels that just becuase he is white he can speak how ever he wants, and that she has to prove herself to people. I think that she does not have to prove herself to anyone, what would she have to prove? It seems to me that nobody was making a big deal of the black english, even if it is grammatically incorrect. If they have so much pride in their language then they should be able to speak freely and not have to feel like it is a big competition, trying to make prove themselves to people when nobody was questioning them. I think that they are just insecure about things in life, and need to look around and observe things before they just jump to conclusions.

Reader's Journal
Student: Marlene
English 095—Basic Communication Skills
Cal Poly Pomona
Essay: Barbara Mellix "From Outside, In"

The thesis in Mellix's essay "from Outside, In" is the co-existence in the African-American community of two distinctly different form of English language and the power each retains. Mellix's thesis statement is "I grew up speaking what I considered two distinctly different languages-black English and standard English (or as I thought of them then, the ordinary everyday speech of "country" coloreds and "proper" English)-and in the process of acquiring these languages, I developed an understanding of when, where, and how to use them. She supports her thesis throughout her essay in a chronological order, she uses personal experiences, demonstrates dialogue, plus her current interpretations.

Mellix starts her essay with dialogue directed towards the reader then switches to dialogue directed towards her daughter. She demonstrates the distinct difference between "standard" English and "black" English. The "black" English is full of expression, character and intimacy verses a formal direct tone of "standard" English. She gives examples of when, where and how each language is used. As a child she referred to "standard" English as the language used by "others". This demonstrates her boundaries that existed between "standard" and "black" English as a child. As a child "standard' English was rarely used, either on school as an English assignment or to prove ones' intelligence. She learned early on that the "standard" form of English retained power in society as a whole, enabling respect from others and represented intelligence. "black" English also retained power but in a family/friend environment, an intimate language, customary and comfortable.

Through her journey of language Mellix, was able to see past her resentment of the "standard" English and became part of it. She resented "standard" English because somehow, somewhere, someone made the decision that it was in correct form of English. She discovered this was untrue, indeed there is distinct differences but also similarities. The great differences between the two forms of English is the environment in which it is used (who, where), the state of mind (she was unable to utilize standard English because she felt unattached). They also retain similarities which is a form of discourse. (reflecting ones opinion, expression, emotion, etc.)

Mellix's attitude toward "standard" English significantly change from her childhood to present adult. She discovered both form of language were correct, but used in different situations. As an adult Mellix is able to grasp the language of "others", in doing so she was able to envision herself as part of that culture. The language gave her wings (liberty) power thus broadening her horizons. Through writing she discovered it contains responsibilities, difficulties, possibilities and its removable power of reincarnation. Mellix is able to combine the two forms of language in her essay, each powerful, unique, and retains meaning , thus forming clear distinction between the two. Mellix is able to utilize both forms of English to express herself, each retains an important existence in her life, neither superior than the other. The coexistence in the African-American community of the two distinctly different forms of the English language are vital in success as well as in intimate bond between one another.

Reader's Journal
Student: Annette
English 095—Basic Communication Skills
Cal Poly Pomona
Essay: Barbara Mellix "From Outside, In"

I like Mellix's opening sentence. "Two years ago, when I started writing this paper, trying to bring order out of chaos, .." This is how I feel when I too have to write a paper. It feels like it takes me forever. When I start it feels like it is pure chaos. It is very hard for me to write papers and essays for some reason. I come across writer block a lot. She also says in the opening paragraph that, "I explained that I was working on something special and needed peace and quiet." This sentence is used at my house quite frequently. When I'm doing my homework it is almost impossible for me to get done with it while watching my son. Even though my son is a typical boy. He is generally very good. He just likes to explore that's all. When my mom is home I try to get her to watch him so I can do my homework. I try to explain to her I need to get it done but she refuses to watch him. Then she throws it back in my face that I'm too young to have had a child.

A lot of what Mellix mentions in her essay is true. If you think about it we all speak two different types of English. One is the slang we use around our friends. The other is what we speak while we are on campus, in our essays and in our papers. I thought it was odd when reading that her teacher encouraged the improper black English.

You don't realize how important English is until you are in college. It is the basis of every subject. You have to write all kind of reports in college. You need to do good in English in order to do good on these papers. I wish I could say that this came easy for me but it didn't.

In her essay she was able to find a job doing what she liked and that was to write letters. These were easy letters to write and she did not realize hoe hard it gets. She realized this once she go to college. I too did not realize this until I got to college.

3

Drafting an Essay

As you begin drafting your essay, you will want to review your annotations of the text and your journal responses. At this point, you will probably need to do some prewriting to help you make sense of your thoughts. Practice with various prewriting strategies: outlining, brainstorming, and/or freewriting to see what works best for you. Don't use an outline just because that is what you have always done. Use your journal entries as springboards for your prewriting. You have already thought about the texts and written about them. Take advantage of the work you have already completed. Be willing to try some new strategies.

Outlining: Creating a sketch of what your essay will look like, including your **controlling idea,** examples, details, and possible excerpts from a text. An outline can help you develop the organization of your project.

Brainstorming: This is a time to write down all your ideas without censoring yourself. List all possible topics and ways to explore these topics. Don't edit as you write—just go with your thoughts.

Freewriting: Freewriting can be focused or unfocused. You might freewrite in an attempt to gather ideas, or you might freewrite to explore the writing assignment to which you are responding. Again, this is not a time to edit yourself, but rather to explore all possible ideas.

The Body of an Essay

It is often beneficial to write the **body** of your paper before writing your "introduction." Sometimes students agonize so much over writing a "perfect" introduction that they never get around to writing the rest of their essay. Once the body of your essay is written, you will have a clearer sense of what you need to say in the beginning of your essay. (More on introductions and conclusions later.)

In order to draft the body of your essay, you need to have a clear understanding of the writing assignment so that you can develop a controlling idea. You may have heard the term *thesis statement* at some point in your education. I prefer the term **controlling idea,** because the controlling idea of an essay is often more than a single sentence or statement. The controlling idea of a text is the main idea or theme that a writer is conveying to the readers; it is the "glue" that allows the pieces of an essay to form a cohesive whole. Your essays need to have clear, direct controlling ideas. Note as you read various essays where you find the writer's controlling idea(s). Why might one writer place the controlling idea early in a text, and another writer place it toward the end? Think about the impact that this placement has on you as a reader. As you write an outline or a first draft of your essay, explore possible controlling ideas. Which idea seems most worthwhile to analyze in an essay? Which controlling idea will allow you to meet the given assignment? A controlling idea needs to be important—something worth writing about—and needs to be an idea you can develop and support.

Write out the controlling idea(s) that you have decided to explore. Review your prewriting and journals to figure out the ways in which you can develop this controlling idea with explicit details and examples. For most of the writing assignments in this text, you will need to return to the text that you read so that you can find ways to support your position. Draft each paragraph with the thought that you are building on your controlling idea.

In order to develop your essay and support your controlling idea, you need carefully developed and organized paragraphs. Each paragraph needs a **topic sentence.** A topic sentence provides a focus for each paragraph and allows a writer to let the readers know what each paragraph is going to be about. Each paragraph in your essay should **develop, support, and expand** your controlling idea.

Sometimes during the early stages of the writing process, the hardest task is putting words on paper. Rather than stare at a blank sheet of paper or a blank computer screen, start writing. You have already done the thinking and planning, and even if you do not feel ready, trust yourself to begin writing. You do not have to know exactly what you are going to write. Write what emerges from your prewriting—your annotations, journal entries, controlling idea(s), and outline. As you write, be willing to explore new ideas that occur to you. Remember that writing is a way of thinking and that your thoughts will change as you write—go with these new ideas and see where they take you.

Once the body of your essay is drafted, leave it alone for a while. If you are on a tight schedule and do not have much time, take half an hour, and go do something that is not related to your project. If you can afford more time, let the project set for a longer period. What you are doing is allowing yourself time for your ideas and thinking to settle. When you come back to your draft, you will have a fresher view of what you have written, and you return to your paper ready to work.

Read your draft. As you read, think about the organization. Are your ideas presented in the order you want? Is your organization consistent? Could a reader follow your ideas as your paper moves from one point to another? Are there sentences and/or paragraphs that need to be moved or changed? Check back and reread your prewriting notes—is there something that you wanted to bring up but that you left out or did not fully develop? If so, consider where and how it would fit into the draft. Or is your draft better without it? You also might find as you read that an idea that seemed good when you were planning is not as good as you thought, or that it really does not fit into the paper. Maybe it is a good idea, but it is just tacked onto your other ideas and does not contribute to the structure of your paper. Cut what does not work, what does not advance your project.

Beginnings and Endings

Once you are satisfied with the overall organization of your essay, go back and write a sketchy outline of the body of your paper. Use this outline to write your introduction. An introduction creates a context or a frame for your audience. You might think of your beginning as a map that will guide your readers through your essay. In the beginning of your essay, you are providing **context** for your audience, a way for your readers to understand where your essay is going to take them. You might try imitating the way certain authors write introductions. If you like how a particular author writes, look closely at the structure of the opening paragraph(s). Studying and imitating beginnings and endings will help you become aware of the many possible ways of approaching various kinds of writing. Review the student essay by Christine on pages 37–45. Read the first paragraph of her rough draft, and then read her revised opening. What does she do in her revision that makes the beginning different? Is the revised introduction stronger? Why, or why not? What might have led her to make these changes? Read the comments from her peers about her beginning. How did this feedback help Christine revise her first paragraph?

With the introduction and body of your essay written, you are ready to write your conclusion or ending. You may have been told that conclusions are a repetition of the introduction: you just restate your controlling ideas or "thesis." Endings can be used to do that, but I'd like to challenge you to move beyond that idea and to think of your conclusion as a place to "hit" your reader with your most powerful argument. You have planned your essay and then guided your readers through your writing. Now pull all your ideas together. Give your reader something to think about. Take the implications of your controlling idea and your examples, and create an explicit conclusion for your readers; show them the bigger picture as you see it. Often the decisions you make about writing will revolve around your specific project, or your controlling idea may lead you to a certain kind of conclusion. There is often a temptation to end an essay with a "moral," such as in the fairy tales you may have read as a child. For example, a writer might end an essay with these statements: "I was once an out-of-control teenager. Now I am a responsible adult. All teenagers should realize the dangers of drinking and stop immediately." This kind of ending is generally weak. Many writers rely on this because it is a quick way to end an essay. Review the endings of one or two of the student essays included here. Which essays have the strongest conclusions? Which essays have the weakest endings? What accounts for the difference?

NOTE: It is usually more effective to understand these ideas by looking at them "in context"; that is, rather than just reading and talking about controlling ideas, topic sentences, beginnings and endings, review the texts you read and the student essays to analyze the way writers create effective texts. Use the essays included here, and, more importantly, the essays you and your peers are writing for this course to review these ideas in real student writing.

Revising and Editing

Student writers often mistake editing for revision. Revision is rethinking your essay and looking at the overall structure and organization once the beginning, body, and ending are in fairly good shape. Editing is the nitty-gritty work you do as a last step in your writing process. For revision, reread your essay, looking specifically for ideas that are not fully developed, unnecessary summary, repetition, and awkward phrases or sentences. Sometimes you will raise an issue or explore an idea that is potentially very significant but is not fully developed. You need to spend time elaborating and refining those ideas; you might consider this type of elaboration as "unpacking" your ideas. Think of unpacking an idea as if you were unpacking a suitcase. If all the clothes and other items stay neatly inside the suitcase, they are not going to be useful. You need to take out the clothes, unfold them, shake out the wrinkles, hang them up, and finally wear them. At first, an idea may be tightly packed together, needing to be unpacked to be useful and understandable to a reader. Take out each aspect of your thought or idea, show it to your reader, give your reader an opportunity to examine all the facets of your point(s), and explain how it all fits together. This process requires you to guide your reader, demonstrating your thinking and point of view. Unpacking your writing is a sophisticated move. Often the ideas that need to be unpacked need unpacking because a writer has not thought the idea through and needs to develop it, or a writer has assumed that the reader is thinking exactly as the writer is. You cannot assume that your reader will follow your thinking exactly. You need to take your reader step by step through your thinking process. You have already had lots of practice unpacking and exploring ideas, questions, and difficult issues in your journals; continue your investigations in your writing, communicating as explicitly as possible with your reader.

Look for unnecessary words or phrases, and then cut them. For example, consider these three sentences: Good writing is always clear. Good writing uses the simplest and most direct language to make the reading smooth and clear. Good writing chooses the exact right words to say, as precisely as possible, what the author wants to say. Now review the three sentences. How would you combine them? What would you cut? How would you arrange the sentences while maintaining the original meaning? What words could be cut or rearranged to sound smoother and clearer? These sentences when combined could become this: "Good writing is clear, uses simple direct language, and chooses words that say precisely what the author intends."

When you are revising your essay, look for places where you have spent a good deal of time summarizing. Most of the time summary does not advance your work. Summary is not bad because it can be a way to move forward in your thinking or to move past a block in thinking, taking you on to more productive writing. But ask yourself if the summary you have provided is necessary to advance your project. If it is unnecessary, cut it. Be careful with repetition, especially because it can make your writing boring. The last thing you want is to put your reader to sleep.

As you revise, you will also be looking for problems in sentence structure and wording. One of the best strategies to use in finding awkward or unclear sentences in your essay is to read it out loud. You should read slowly and carefully, sentence by sentence. When you read silently, you may not read the words that you have written but the words that you intended to write. When you read out loud, you have to look at individual words and pronounce them. If something sounds odd or poorly phrased, you will hear it and so can change it. You will be surprised at the number of mistakes you can catch when you begin reading out loud.

At this point, it's time in the writing process to begin editing. You will edit for errors in spelling, grammar, sentence structure, and punctuation. Being particular now will give your essay a clean, professional look. For editing, work with smaller segments—paragraphs are small, manageable segments that allow you to examine your work for grammar, spelling, and punctuation. Working sentence by sentence is even better. At this stage, you will be working on correcting errors. Once you know you have a particular grammatical problem, this is the time to check your paper carefully line by line. Your instructor may have told you what problems appeared in an essay you wrote early in the term. Review the kinds of errors you've made in the past; if, for example, you sometimes have problems with subject/verb agreement, fragments, and/or comma splices, read each paragraph, checking your sentences to make sure they are correct. You may already have caught many of these errors by reading aloud.

Check spelling: if you use a computer, ALWAYS RUN SPELL CHECK. However, if you spell a word right but use it in the wrong way, spell check will not correct that type of mistake. Always proofread after doing spell check. If you are not sure how a word is spelled, look it up in the dictionary. If you are not satisfied with a word choice, try other words and see whether you can get closer to saying exactly what you want to say. Sometimes students go to a thesaurus to find a word replacement. There is nothing wrong with doing this, but BE CAREFUL. Do not use a word unless you know its meaning. If you are not completely sure what a word means, look it up in the dictionary. When you write, your primary goal is communication. Good writing is not laden with high-priced words that other people do not use. Good writing is clear, uses simple and direct language, and contains words that say precisely what the author intends. That guideline does not mean that you should never use complex or difficult words; however, you do not want your text to sound overpriced and unintelligible. If you misuse a word, you will only confuse your reader.

Finally, you should check your sentences to make sure that they are punctuated correctly. Remember that you are polishing and getting your paper to be as "clean" as possible. Most likely you will be using an English handbook or rhetoric in addition to this textbook. An English handbook will define typical grammatical problems and provide examples of ways to correct these errors.

Beginning on page 37 are student essays done in response to various assignments from *Breaking Boundaries.* As you read these essays, evaluate the effectiveness with which the writer is responding to the assignment. Look for what the writer did well and also for places where the writer might need to "say more." Evaluate the writer's controlling idea, the organization of the paragraphs, the topic sentences, the use of specific examples to develop her or his controlling idea, and whether or not the final draft looks "clean." Included here are early drafts, drafts with peer feedback, and revised final drafts. Examine the ways students gave feedback to one another. You may be doing peer draft workshops, at which time your peers will be reviewing your essay and giving you ideas to make it better. Also included is a Sample Peer Evaluation Form, but there are many other valuable ways to give and receive feedback. Evaluate the ways in which the writers included here incorporated peer feedback into their essays. If you don't do peer workshops, you will probably be getting feedback from your instructor. Use your instructor's comments on one essay to help you as you write your next assignment.

NOTE: The student essays are included in their original form. Any mechanical inconsistencies have been left uncorrected.

Following is an overview of the drafting process for you to use as a reference as you draft your essays:

AN OVERVIEW OF THE DRAFTING PROCESS

First Draft and Organization

1. Mark up the texts you read, keep a reader's journal, develop a controlling idea, and organize your ideas and key points.
2. Write the body of your paper; then
   a. Check the structure, and be flexible and willing to change;
   b. Group similar ideas together; and
   c. Check for logical order.
3. Write your introduction.
4. Write your conclusion.
5. Set the paper aside for a while, and let it rest.

Revision

1. Unpack underdeveloped ideas.
2. Read your essay out loud.
3. Cut unnecessary words and phrases.
4. Cut unnecessary summary.
5. Cut repetition.
6. Change and rewrite awkward phrases and sentences.

Final Editing

1. Check your grammar.
2. Check your spelling.
3. Check your punctuation.

Student Essays

Student: Christine
English 095—Basic Communication Skills
Cal Poly Pomona
Rough Draft with Peer Feedback: Barbara Mellix "From Outside, In"
Option 5-page 298

Include an example of Tagalog

Do not use contractions in essays

Introduce Mellix

Give Examples

As I was growing up in my household, we would speak mainly Tagalog [What is This?] because it's the language my parents grew up to. Sometimes we spoke English for my parents' practice. As for my siblings and I, it is English [Awkward wording] that we use to each other. It's hard for me to compare myself to Mellix because I didn't grow up learning two different types of English however, like Mellix I grew up speaking two different languages- Tagalog and English. It was hard growing up having these two languages in my mind. One day I would think in Tagalog and the other days I would think in English. It's really hard for me to tell what my first language was although I was born here in America. I remember before I started school, my family and I would speak Tagalog eighty percent of the time, the other twenty percent world be English. I also watched a lot of cartoons and learned English that way. When I started kindergarten, I spoke English like any other kid that grew up in a home with only English speakers. I had no accent so I felt like I fit in with the rest of the kids. It was a routine for me everyday to go to school, speaking and thinking in English in the classroom and playground. When I was at home I would then change by speaking and thinking in Tagalog, unless I was doing my homework.

I don't see a controlling idea

Awkward

I know that having that English was important to my parents in different ways . They came to American in the mid seventies to have a better life for themselves and especially for my siblings and I. They knew it was important that their kids were going to need the proper education to succeed in life. They knew the only way was to come to America. Knowing that English is the prime language not only in America but throughout the whole world, it is important that we can speak it properly. My parents know that with well educated, proper English speaking children, it will give their children many opportunities to advance in society. This was a way to let my siblings and I to live the life that they felt they never had when they were our age. I strongly agree with my parents' motives to why English is important to them.

Discuss how you moved from outside in

Relate this to Mellix

The ability to speak Tagalog means a lot to my parents. To my parents, speaking Tagalog was knowing the culture of the Philippines even though I have never been to the place. At family parties when I was younger, I would speak Tagalog like the rest of my family and I felt like I knew the culture just by speaking it. My siblings and I along with my cousins are all first generation Filipino Americans among our families. That is why it means a lot to them, to have children as "Americanized" as we are today and still be able to speak Tagalog. I personally feel obligated to be able to speak in proper English at the same time speak proper Tagalog. I am sure my parents would want me to continue the tradition of the language to my children.

How does this compare to Black English for Mellix's Family?

Over the years, I noticed that the more I went to school and became older, the less I would speak Tagalog at home. I didn't do it on purpose, it just happened. It wasn't only me, but it was my parents also who spoke more English at home when we were all together. I also started speaking English in my mind more than I would Tagalog. Whereas when I was younger it was visa versa. I felt myself changing and it scared me, It scared me because I felt like I was forgetting the culture my parents had taught me.

You have already said some of this—your readers might lose interest.

In family parties now, we all speak English except for my parents, aunts and uncles. It was like two different worlds during the party. All the adults together in one room speaking Tagalog like they were in the Philippines as kids. All the cousins together in another room speaking straight English using slang and profanity not one time speaking in Tagalog as if the language was foreign to us. A majority of my cousins have forgotten the language. It is as if they have forgotten their own culture. Those of us who didn't, would say a phrase very seldom just for the fun of it and together we would smile and laugh being proud that we haven't forgotten Tagalog. It is one thing to be able to understand it through listening but it is more important to be able to speak it. It was the culture we were born into.

Add: different experiences more background—clear controlling idea.

It is not forgetting the culture which make my cousins and I different, it's learning a new culture and becoming a part of it. Sure our parents are experiencing the same thing we are tool However it's different because they grew up in the Philippines and my cousins and I grew up in America. English became an everyday part of my life because it is what I have been learning since the kindergarten. It is the way I have been communicating with other children on the playground when I was young. I have became familiar with English, and as I get older, I speak more proper English because of my education. Today, it is a part of me. It is now a part of my culture as being a Filipina American.

Student: Christine
English 095—Basic Communication Skills
Cal Poly Pomona
Revised Draft: Barbara Mellix "From Outside, In"
Option 5-page 298

"Psssst bata! Wag ka mag takbo sa young' calle!" If my grandmother were to tell me this in English she would have said: "Hay kid, Don't run in the street!" This was something my grandmother would always say to me in Tagalog. Tagalog is the native language of the Philippines. I am a Filipina. As I was growing up in my household, we would speak mainly Tagalog because it is the language my parents grew up with. My grandparents had taught my parents Tagalog and have passed the tradition to my siblings and me. I call it a tradition because my definition of tradition is passing a significant trait or event from generation to generation. The tradition of speaking Tagalog is a way of reassuring myself that I know a part of the Filipino culture.

Barbara Mellix is the author of "From Outside, In" It is an essay about language and the two different types of English she used when growing up. The two types of English the Mellix grew up with where "Black English and standard English (or as I thought of them then, the ordinary everyday speech of 'country' coloreds and 'proper' English)"(page 288). It is hard for me to compare myself to Mellix because I did not grow up learning two different types of English. However, like Mellix I grew up speaking two different languages- Tagalog and English.

It is really hard for me to tell what my first language was although I was born here in America. It was hard growing up having these two languages in my mind. One day I would think in Tagalog and the other days I would think in English. I remember before I started school, my family and I would speak Tagalog eighty percent of the time, the other twenty percent would be English. I also watched a lot of cartoons and learned English that way. When I started kindergarten, I spoke English like any other kid that grew up in a home with only English speakers. I had no accent so I felt like I fit in with the rest of the kids. It was a routine for me everday to go to school, speaking and thinking in English in the classroom and playground. When I was at home I would then change by speaking and thinking in Tagalog, unless I was doing my homework.

When Mellix was in elementary school, there were only black students in the classroom. "My teachers taught standard English but used black English to do it." I think this is ironic in a way. The teacher is telling her students how to use standard English but explains it to them in black English. Why couldn't Mellix's teacher teach them standard English using standard English? I have come to the conclusion that black English is a part of their culture. All of the students including the teacher happened to be black in the classroom. This is why the teacher used black English to explain standard English. It was easier for the teacher to explain it in black English and have her students comprehend standard English. This was easier for her students to understand because black English is what they use in their households.

I know that have proper English was important to my parents in different ways. They came to America in the mid-seventies to have a better life for themselves and especially for my siblings and me. They knew it was important that their kids were going to need the proper education to succeed in life. They knew the only way was to come to America. Knowing that English is the prime language not only in America but througout the whole world, it is important that we can speak it properly. My parents know that with well educated, proper English speaking children, it will give their children many opportunities to advance in society.

Over the years, I noticed that the more I went to school and became older, the less I would speak Tagalog at home. I did not do it on purpose, it just happened. It was not only me, but it was my parents who spoke more English at home when we were all together. I also started speaking English in my mind more than I would Tagalog. Whereas when I was younger it was visa versa. I felt myself changing and it scared me. It scared my because I felt like I was forgetting the culture my parents had taught me.

Mellix talks about how she felt like "being split in two." Mellix wrote "...use the language of the old me, yet I couldn't imagine myself in the language of the 'others'." This made me realize how I also felt the same way. This is where my fear kicked in. I felt the old Christine was no longer in me because I did not speak the way I use to when I was younger. I no longer spoke in Tagalog. I felt like I was losing my culture because I was becoming more exposed to English everyday. I got scared thinking I could never be the same. This new

Christine has become to much like everyone else in society, being a part of society's culture and not the one she was born to.

When I was younger at family parties when, I would speak Tagalog like the rest of my family, and I felt like I knew the culture just by speaking it. Today at family parties we all speak English except for my parents, aunts and uncles. It is like two different worlds during the party: all the adults together in one room speaking Tagalog like they were in the Philippines as kids, all the cousins together in another romm speaking straight English using slang and profanity, not one time speaking in Tagalog as if the language is foreign to us. My cousins are like my friends I hang out with on weekends. A majority of my cousins have forgotten the language. It is as if they have forgotten their own culture. Those of us who didn't would say a phrase very seldom just for the fun of it, and together we would smile and laugh being proud that we have not forgotten Tagalog. It is one thing to be able to understand it through listening, but it is more important to be able to speak it. It is the cuture we were born into.

During Mellix's family gatherings they used standard English although they all grew up with black English. Mellix comments on how her parents carried great pride when they spoke. This was a way to let her parents "show off" their ability to speak proper English to other family members. I learned that standard English to them was something that was used on special occasions. Their ability to speak proper English was llike a special weapon they carried. All though this was the way they felt about standard English, it was not normal for them to were it made them uneasy. "But he (Mellix's father) held his proud head higher, a signal that he, too, was uncomfortable."(page 288).

It is not forgetting the culture which make my cousins and I different, it is learning a new culture and becoming a part of it. Sure our parents are experiencing the same thing we are too. However, it is different because they brew up in the Philippines and my cousins and I grew up in America. I have encountered similar problems Mellix had with language. Mellix said "And to do that, I had to learn to imagine myself a part of the culture of that language, and therefore someone free to manage that language, to take the liberties of it."(page 297). Tagalog is the language I was born with and black English Mellis was born with. Together learning the language became a part of learning the culture yet standard English has changed our lives dramatically. English has become an everyday part of my life because it is what I have been learning since the kindergarten. It is the way I have been communicating with other children on the playground when I was young. I have become familiar with English, and as I get older I speak more proper English because of my education. Today, it is a part of me. It is now a part of my culture as being a Filipina American.

Student: Shannon
English 095—Basic Communication Skills
Cal Poly Pomona
Rough Draft with Peer Feedback: Ernest Hemingway "Hills Like White Elephants" and Susan Glaspell "Trifles"
Option 6—page 195

What kind of communication?

Communication is something we need to pay more attention to in the world today. Without communication it's hard to understand people in what they are trying to say. When we don't understand each other, by miss communications, alot of deception starts to occur with one another. I think if we communicated more with each other, we would be able to express how we felt about things, instead of hiding them. It would give us a more comfortable feeling in having to communicate to help us understand one another better. With communication we could understand what each other is trying to say or do without miss leading one another with deception. I think communicating more could help everyone stop by decieving people.

capitalize

In "Hills like white elephants" by

spelling

Earnest Hemingway, a man and a women are conversing on whether or not to have an abortion. The man thought it was necessary because it was going to get in their way and it is so simple to get rid of. He makes her think that he really cares about her decision and only wants the best for her, but he really just wants to get rid of it so he can stop thinking about it. When the women wants a change in life and thinks the baby could help their relationship for a positive change. The couple is miss communicating with each other and not saying how they really feel. Good observation

Give specific examples—maybe some dialogue

Instead of expressing how they really feel, they both use deception to miss lead one another and make each other thing something different then whay they really believe in. The man really wants to tell the women to forget it, I like my life and I do not want to change it for a baby, but he decieves her by making her think it's the best thing to do for the both of them and that he really cares for their life and her decison. The women really wants to tell the man that their relationship is boring and she wants a change in life to experience new things. She thinks the baby would be the perfect new experience to start a change together in their life, but she decieves him by making him think that she really does not care and she will do anything he wants because she loves him.

True—it does seem like she'll do anything for him

With miss communication the couple decieved one another and never understood what each other wanted or what they were trying to say. If they would of expressed how they felt through communication then they could of talked things over and come to a decision in both of their needs. Instead of only giving one person what they want,they both could have been happy.

More here dig deeper

How could both of them have been happy? Unpack this

The play 'Trifles" written by Susan Glaspell, is a murder mystery play in which the county attorney, sherieff, and with the help of a witness Hale, were investigating the murder. The murder took place in the farm of the Wright's. Where John Wright was murdered in bed by a rope around his neck. His wife Mrs. Wright didn't hear anything and says she didn't know who did it. When Hale came over to see John, Mrs. Wright was just sitting in a chair pleating on her apron. Hale asked her where John was and she laughed and said he was dead and didn't know who did it.

Deception start in this play right from the beginning. It starts with Mrs. Wright telling Hale that she does not know who killed her husband and didn't show any feelings towards him. Hale then calls the authorities and they take Mrs. Wright to jail for custody during the investigation of the house.

During the investigation Hale told the county attorney and the sherieff what happened when he was there and what he saw. They also brought two women with them. Mrs. Hale and Mrs. Peters and Mrs. Peters was married to the sherieff. The women came with the men to pick up some clothes for Mrs. Wright. During the whole investigation the men were making fun of the little trifles the women were picking out. In other words they laughed at the women for caring about the little things that did not have any importance to the men. The reason it had no importance to the men because they didn't see the significance in it, yet the women did.

Awkward wording

Good transition

The women took interest in several things throughout the house. They say Mrs. Wright's jars of fruit, for every women is always worried about their fruit staying fresh. They also found a quilt she was working on and they were curious if she used the knot or quilt in her pattern. The men laughed at the women and thought that they were ridculous for caring about a quilt pattern during an investigation. With the curiosity of the knot or quilt pattern, the women noticed that the pattern went off track, as if she got side tracked or nervous about something. So, Mrs. Hale pulled a few stitches out and fixed the pattern in the quilt. They came to a decision that she used the knot pattern. I think Mrs. Halle fixed the stiching in the quilt to decieve the men, not only because they made fun of them, but to hide the fact that something side tracked or made Mrs. Wright nervous. Yes

The women then discoverd a bird cage with a broken door and no bird. They were trying to figure out what happened to the bird. Mrs. Hale mentions that Mrs. Wright reminded her of a bird. That she dressed nice, was really pretty, and sang wonderfully. Mr. Wright like silence and Mrs. Wright stopped singing because of him. In a beautiful box the women found the dead bird and came to the conclusion that the bird drove Mr. Wright crazy, just as Mrs. Wright singing did, and killed it by wringing the birds neck, This made Mrs. Wright mad, so she killed Mr. Wright by strugling his neck with a rope, the way he killed her bird. With this evidence of the dead bird they could of put Mrs. Wright in jail for good, but the women hid the evidence from the men. I think they hid the evidence because the men made fun of the women for carrying about the little things, yet they found evidence and

Does not make sense here– Doesn't sound right–stick to the "facts"

men did not. You know what they always say, "The little things in life always mean so much". I believe in this quote, for the little things are harder to find and that's what makes them so important.

The women got away with hiding evidence because the men figured what could the women have found with an importance of this investigation for Mrs. Peters is married to the law the they only care about the little things that have no significance to us. Little did the men know that the women do have important evidence and it has a big significance to the investigation. With the mens miss communication with the women, the did not see the importance of the little things the women were picking out. If the men would of took a little more interest in what the women were pointing out, I think the women would have shared the evidence with the men.

Since the men only made fun of the women and made them feel unimportant, they tricked the men by using deception and making them think they found nothing. I think in this play the men deserve what they get for not believing in the women. If they would of taken a little more interest in communication and understaning the women they would have found the evidence with the women.

Good Point– relate to "Hills like White Elephants"

In these two stories it clearly points out that deception was being used through miss communication. We need to take more interest in one another to understand what people are trying to say or do, by expressing ourselves or others through communication. By using communication people will be alot happier not only understanding each other, but maybe getting what we all want or finding out information that could help us. Just as the man and women both could of been happy if they communicated and the men could of found evidence if they took interest in what the women were saying. Communicating will always help us throughout the world. We just need to use it with each other on a regular basis.

Some of your sentences are awkward—too long.
Be sure to support what you claim.

Student: Shannon
English 095—Basic Communication Skills
Cal Poly Pomona
Revised Draft: Ernest Hemingway "Hills Like White Elephants" and Susan Glaspell "Trifles"
Option 6—page 195

Communication is something we need to pay more attention to in the world today. Without communication it's hard to understand people in what they are trying to say. When we don't understand each other, by miss communication, a lot of deception starts to occur with one another. I think if we communicated more with each other, we would be able to express how we felt about things, instead of hiding them. It would give us a more comfortable feeling in having to communicate to help us understand one another better. With communication we can understand what each other is trying to say or do without misleading one another with deception. I think communicating more could help everyone stop by deceiving people.

In "Hills Like White Elephants" by Earnest Hemingway, a man and woman are conversing on whether or not to have an abortion. The man thought it was necessary because it was going to get in their way and that it is so simple to get rid of. He makes her think that he really cares about her decision and only wants the best for her, but he really just wants to get rid of it so he can stop thinking about it. The woman wants a change in life and thinks that the baby could help their relationship build a positive change. The couple is miss communicating with each other and not saying how they really feel.

Instead of expressing how they really feel, they both use deception to mislead one another. They make each other think something different then what they really believe in. The man really wants to tell the woman to forget it. He likes his life and he doesn't want to change it for a baby, but he decieves her by making her think it's the best thing to do for the both of them. He tries to show that he really cares for their life together and her decison. The woman really wants to tell the man that their relationship is boring and she wants a change in life to experience new things. She thinks the baby would be the perfect new experience to start a change together in their life, but she deceives him by making him think that she really does not care and she will do anything he wants because she loves him.

With miss communication the couple deceived one another and never understood what each other wanted or what they were trying to say. If they would of expressed how they felt through communicating, then they could of talked things over and come to a decision involving both of their needs. Instead of giving only one person what they want,they both could have been happy. They both could of been happy by the man taking in considersation that the baby might be good in their life, instead of trying to get rid of it so fast. They also could of been happy together if the man would have promised the woman that their life can still change without the baby. That they could explore different things around the world together. The man and the woman didn't communicate well together and they didn't know what they other wanted, so one of them was gonna have to give up their happiness. The woman gave up her change of life to the man, by deciding not to have the baby.

The play 'Trifles" written by Susan Glaspell, is a murder mystery play in which the county attorney, The Sheriff, and with the help of a witness Hale, were investigating the murder. The murder took place in the farm of the Wrights, where John Wright was murdered in bed by a rope around his neck. His wife Mrs. Wright didn't hear anything and says she didn't know who did it. When Hale came over to see John, Mrs. Wright was sitting in a chair pleating on her apron. Hale asked her where John was and she laughed and said he was dead and didn't know who did it.

Deception starts in this play right from the beginning. It starts with Mrs. Wright telling Hale that she does not know who killed her husband and didn't show any feelings towards him. Then Halle calls the authorities and they take Mrs. Wright to jail as a suspect during the investigation of the house.

During the investigation Hale told the county attorney and the sheriff what happened when he was there and what he saw. They also brought two women with them,Mrs. Hale and Mrs. Peters whom was married to the sheriff. The women came with the men to pick up some clothes for Mrs. Wright. During the whole investigation the men were making fun of the little trifles the women were picking up as evidence. In other words, they laughed at the women for caring about the little things that did not have any importance to the men. The reason it had no importance to the men was because they didn't see the significance in it, yet the women did.

The women took interest in several things throughout the house. They saw Mrs. Wright's jars of fruit. Every women is always worried about their fruit staying fresh. They also found a quilt Mrs. Wright was working on and they were curious if she used the knot or quilted in her pattern. The men laughed at the women and thought that they were ridculous for caring about a quilted pattern during an investigation. With the curiosity of the knot or quilted pattern, the women noticed that the pattern went off track, as if she got side tracked or nervous about something. Mrs. Hale pulled a few stitches out and fixed the pattern in the quilt. They came to a decision that she used the knot pattern. I think Mrs. Hale fixed the stitching in the quilt to deceive the men, not only because they made fun of them, but to hide the fact that something side tracked or made Mrs. Wright nervous.

The women then discoverd a bird cage with a broken door and no bird inside. They were trying to figure out what happened to the bird. Mrs. Hale mentioned that Mrs. Wright reminded her of a bird. She dressed nice, was really pretty, and sang wonderfully. Mr. Wright liked silence and Mrs. Wright stopped singing because of him. In a beautiful box the women found the dead bird and came to the conclusion that the bird drove Mr. Wright crazy, just as Mrs. Wright singing did. He killed it by wringing the birds neck, This made Mrs. Wright mad, so she killed Mr. Wright by strangling his neck with a rope the same way he killed her bird. With this evidence of the dead bird the women could have put Mrs. Wright in jail for good, but the women hid the evidence from the men. I think they hid the evidence because the men made fun of the women for caring about the little things, yet they found evidence and the men did not.

The women got away with hiding evidence because the men figured what could the women have found with any importance of this investigation for Mrs. Peters is married to the law the they only care about the little things that have no significance to us. Little did the men know that the women did have important evidence and it has a big significance to the investigation. With the mens miss communication with the women, they did not see the importance of the little things the women were picking out. If the men would of took a little more interest in what the women were pointing out, I think the women would have shared the evidence with the men.

Since the men only made fun of the women and made them feel unimportant, they tricked the men by using deception and making them think that they didn't find anything. I think in this play the men deserve what they get for not believing in the women. If they would of taken a little more interest in communication and understanding the women, they would have found the evidence with the women.

In these two stories it clearly points out that deception was being used through miss communication. We need to take more interest in one another to understand what people are trying to say or do. By using communication people will be a lot happier not only understanding each other, but maybe getting what we all want and finding out information that could help us. In "Trifles" the men and women both could have been happy if they would have communicated well together. The men could have found evidence with the women, if they would have communicated and taken interest in what the women were saying. Intead the men only made fun of the women for pointing of things that the men thought had little importance to the case, so the women deceived the men for not communicating. Communicating will always help us throughout the world. By communicating we are able to understand were people are coming from and how they feel about things. It helps us get closer to one another in solving things in today's society. As in "Hills Like White Elephants", the couple could have understood one another by communicating. They could have developed a happy life together, but they didn't understand each others feelings. If they would have expressed how they felt to each other they could of came to a decision together to make both of them happy. To understand everyone thought the world we just need to use communication on a regular basis.

Student: Marlene
English 095—Basic Communication Skills
Cal Poly Pomona
Rough Draft with Peer Feedback: Barbara Mellix "From Outside, In"
Option 5—page 298

After reading *From Outside, In* By Barbara Mellix, I noticed the tittle itself contained the controlling idea of her essay. Meix explains her story of the two distinctly different forms of the English language which retains a coexistence in the African-American community. Mellix's thesis statement is the following, "I grew up speaking what I considered two different languages-black English and standard English (or as I thought of them then, the ordinary everyday speech of "country" coloreds and "proper" English)-and in the process of acquiring these languages, I developed an understanding of when, where, and how to use them." Throughout her essay in a chronological order Mellix uses personal experiences, demonstrates dialogue, and includes analysis of past ideologies to present. Mellix's style of writing triggered questions what experiences have I had that are similar to those of Mellix, how can I relate and disagree? As my thoughts regress similarities

Sounds awkward— I don't know what this means

use clear, direct language

controlling idea?

come to mind but they are not as significant as Mellix's.

Do you need this?

[It all started as a child,] I noticed the different languages used within my family. My mother spoke to my grandparents in Spanish and spoke to us in English (intermediate family) in English. Spanish was the "other" language as mellix would put it. Melix considered standard English to be foreign, and resented the language because it was thought of as superior to black English; the intimate customary manner of speaking. Standard English had a certain time, place, and environment for its usage. In my case, I saw Spanish as a foreign language because I could not comprehend the words Mellix under stood standard English but it was consider a barrier which isolated her form "others" proper black and whites.

How did you learn this?

I like this

As fore me, I under stood Spanish was form of discourse between the elders in my family. I felt excluded form conversations because I was enable to understand the quick flowing sound, I was puzzled. I understood the language barrier which existed within our family was unintentional. Yes, I was unable to express my thought and emotions to my elders in a verbal manner, but that did not stop the communication. I improvised with gestures (hand movement, smiles, nods, etc.) and was very successful. As I grew older the barriers grew stronger, the difference in language grew significant and created exclusion. I under stood the formal way of communication was through verbal discourse oppose to the primitive manner of body language. Thus every word in Spanish I questioned, my mother would quickly interpret Spanish phrase, but not word for word. I was enable to pick up the language for one, it was not used in my house hold and I did not know the word for word translation. Spanish became a form of isolation, cousins and other relatives my age were able to speak the language because their parents emphasized its importance. I resented the fact that I was unable to understand the language. Family members spoke Spanish purposely so I wuld not be able to under stand. I grew very frustrated, so I decided to make up my own Spanish sounding words, this was not a success, actually they made fun. The frustration grew stronger, thus creating resentment and a hatred for the language. A first Spanish was an unintentional boundary which evolved in to a purposely formed boundary due to the change in environment and cognition's. This is sort of the reverse

more here?

?? Are words missing?

reaction Mellix encountered with the difference of language, at first standard English was foreign, as time went by the language intrigued her and became significant to her every day life. As for me I became more and more distant form the language.

Were you like Mellix? Were you on the outside, looking in?

Understanding the importance of education I realized Spanish was an important language and would serve as a vital tool in my future, in communication with family members as well as a benefit in the business world. As I grew older I was able to understand Spanish in a choppy manner, in which my mother translated the phrases. I decided to take Spanish as my foreign language in high school hoping for improvement. The Spanish classes at my high school were poor and easy to pass, thus I did not learn anythigh new, I was stuck in the same position. Although, taking Spanish helped me realized I knew more than I thought I knew. Words were familiar and I knew the translations, my greatest problem was speaking the language. Relating to Mellix, she was able to see the significance at an early age, thus she enrolled in the necessary classes to further her understanding and correct usage of the language. Mellix had a much harder task because she had to put her black

Good idea to explore further.

English on reserve while exploring the standard English. She took her education serious and know the outcome would be a positive expansion, enabling power in society. As for me, I did not take my education as serious because the system was weak and I had other priorities at the time (basketball). Till this day I wished my parents would have brought me up in a bilingual household. Today I have many regrets because I am unable to speak the Spanish language.

It's the "system's fault? What system? Who created this "system"?

Someday I plan to right word? future my education in Spanish, it may take a few years because of other priorities in life, but I feel the need to learn the language of my ancestors. Hopefully my success story will be similar to that of Mellix. Throughout her journey Mellix was able to see past her resentment of the "standard" English and became united. She discovered that both languages contained power, importance, and were a necessity, neither superior to the other. Mellix's attitude towards "standard" English significantly changed from her childhood to present day adult. She discovered both forms of language were correct, but used in different situations. As an adult Mellix is able to grasp the language of "others" in doing so she was able to envision herself as part of that culture. The language gave her wings (liberty), power, thus broadening her horizons. Through writing she discovered the responsibilities, difficulties, possibilities and its remarkable power of reincarnation. Mellix is able to utilize both forms of English to express herself, each retains an important existence in her life. The coexistence in the African-American community of the two distinctly different forms of the English language are vital in success as well as an intimate bond. I believe my experience with the Spanish language it similar to that of Mellix, with a few exceptions. I hope the outcome of the futherment of my education will be as successful as Mellix's.

I'm lost here.

Student: Marlene
English 095—Basic Communication Skills
Cal Poly Pomona
Revised Draft: Barbara Mellix "From Outside, In"
Option 5—page 298

After reading *From Outside, In* By Barbara Mellix, I noticed the tittle itself contained the controlling idea of her essay. Mellix explains her story of the two distinctly different forms of the English language which exist in the African-American community. Mellix's controlling idea is the following, "I grew up speaking what I considered two different languages-black English and standard English (or as I thought of them then, the ordinary everyday speech ofd "country" coloreds and "proper" English)-and in the process of acquiring these languages, I developed an understanding of when, where, and how to use them." Throughout her essay Mellix uses personal experiences, dialogue, and an analysis of past ideologies to present in order to demonstrate the acute differences as well as the evolution of her thoughts. Mellix's style of writing triggered questions what experiences have I had that are similar to those of Mellix, how can I relate and disagree? As my thoughts expolred personal experinces with language many similarities as well as differences came to mind.

As child, I noticed the different languages used within my family. My mother spoke to my grandparents in Spanish and spoke to our intermediate family in English. Spanish was the "other" language as Mellix would put it. Melix used the word "other" to demonstrate her resistance to the standard English. She considered standard English to be foreign, and resented the language because it was thought of as superior to black English; the intimate customary manner of speaking. Standard English had a certain time, place, and environment for its usage. In my case, I saw Spanish as a foreign language because I could not comprehend the words. Mellix understood standard English but it was consider a barrier which isolated her form "others" proper blacks and whites.

I understood Spanish was a form of discourse between the elders in my family. I felt excluded, from conversations, I was on the outside looking in; unable to understand the quick flowing sound, I was puzzled. I understood the language barrier which existed within our family was unintentional. Yes, I was unable to express my thought and emotions to my elders in a verbal manner, but that did not stop the communication. I improvised with gestures (hand movement, smiles, nods, etc.) and was very successful. As I grew older, the barriers grew stronger the difference in language grew significant and created exclusion. I understood the formal way of communication was through verbal discourse oppose to the primitive manner of body language. Thus, every word in Spanish I questioned. Mny mother would quickly interpret Spanish phrase, but not a word for word translation. Spanish became a form of isolation, cousins and other relatives my age were able to speak the language because their parents emphasized its importance. I resented the fact that I was unable to understand the language. Family members spoke Spanish purposely so I would not be able to understand thier covversations. I grew very frustrated, so I decided to make up my own Spanish sounding words. This was not a success, actually they made fun of the silly sounds and I recived the nick name "lost case". The frustration grew stronger, thus creating resentment and a hatred for the language. A first Spanish was an unintentional boundary which evolved in to a purposely formed boundary due to the change in environment and cognition.

This is sort of the reverse reaction Mellix encountered with the difference of language, at first standard English was foreign, as time went by the language intrigued her and became significant to her every day life. As for me I became more and more distant. When my parents watched Spanish programs or listened to Spanish music I would get angry, I tell them to turn it off and call them "wet-backs". I could not understand the language and I was not interested in learning it.

Understanding the importance of education I realized Spanish was an important language and would serve as a vital tool in my future, in communication with family members as well as a benefit in the business world. As I grew older I was able to understand Spanish in a choppy manner, in which my mother translated the phrases. I deceded to take Spanish as a foreign language in high school, hoping for improvement. the Spanish classes at my high school were poor and easy to pass, thus I did not learn anything new. I was stuck in the same position. Although, taking Spanish helped me realize I knew more than I thought I knew. Words were familiar and I knew some translations, my greatest problem was speaking the language. Relating to Mellix, she was able to see the significance at an early age, thus she enrolled in the necessary classes to further her understanding and correct usage of the language. Mellix had a much harder task because, she had to put her black English on reserve while exploring the standard English. She took her education serious and knew the outcome would be a positive expanision, enabling power in society. As for me, I did not take my education as serious because the system was weak and I had other priorities at the time (basketball). Till this day I wished my parents would have brought me up in a bilingual household. Today I have many regrets because I am unable to speak the Spanish language.

Not only did I feel isolation from the Spanish language, but I also faced boundaries with English. My parents never emphasized the importance of reading and writing. Actually my father had reading and writing disabilities. Knowing this, I felt awkward reading or asking for help with reading in front of my father; I thought I would insult his intelligence. I also had trouble with spelling, which created many problems with my writing. I would find myself stuck when I could not spell a word. I could not leave miss-spelled words on my paper because I was afraid that peers and teacher would think of me as dumb. I would replace the miss-spelled words with similar word I could spell, sometimes the words did not fit, so I would eliminate sentences. When I would pause to think about spelling, I would loose track of my ideas, thus creating confusion. Realizing my problems I started taking spelling seriously. I found myself studding harder and I would pay close attention to printed words. I came to the conclusion that a few spelling errors did not mean the end of the world, I could always go back and correct them. The main idea of writing is to get thoughts on paper. While grasping a better under standing of reading and writing I found myself searching for complex words. Thinking it would enhance my writing and prove my intelligence. I am not quite sure who or where I got this idea, but it is embedded in my thoughts every time I write. I formed a stilted, formal style of writing, which is impersonal and ineffective. I studied different writing (book, peers, instructors, newspapers, etc.) and sort of regurgitated the language. This is very similar to Mellix's experience in the work place. She discovered herself studding letter form and letters written by co-worker in order to write proper business letters. In my understanding we tried to copy other because we felt this was the only way to survive.

Someday I plan to further my education in Spanish, but my main priority is improving my writing skills. Writing is the most important tool in my success. At the university every class requires a certain level of reading, writing, and comprehending. Taking English 95 has helped me realize the areas in which I need improvement. I am taking this class seriously, knowing how vital the pay off is to my future. I have plenty of work ahead of my but for now I will take it one step at a time. Writing is accumulative and improves through experience, effort and devotion.

Hopefully my successs story will be similar to that of Mellix. Throughout her journey Mellix was able to see past her resentment of the "standard" English and became united. She discovered that both languages contained power, importance, and were a necessity, neither superior to the other. Mellix's attitude towards "standard" English significantly changed from her childhood to present day adult. She discovered both forms of language were correct, but used in different situations. As an adult Mellix is able to grasp the language of "others" in doing so she was able to envision herself as part of that culture. The language gave her wings (liberty), power, thus broadening her horizons. Through writing she discovered the responsibilities, difficulties, possibilities and its remarkable power of reincarnation. Mellix is able to utilize both forms of English to express herself, each retains an important existence in her life. The coexistence in the African-American community of the two distinctly different forms of the English language are vital in success as well as an intimate bond. I believe my experience with the Spanish and English are similar to that of Mellix, with a few exceptions. Knowing hard work pay off I am able to envision a bright future.

Sample Peer Evaluation Form

Author:
Evaluator:

1. What do you like best about this essay? Why? What do you think the writer has done well?

2. What is this writer's controlling idea? How does the writer develop and support her/his controlling idea?

3. Discuss three places where you want to hear more. What points are unclear?

4. Has the writer failed to address certain aspects of the given assignment?

5. List three specific ideas for revision.

Part Two

Writing and Word Processing

4

Reading, Writing, and Word Processing

STEPHEN ELIAS

Introduction

On any given night, you can walk into a Starbuck's coffee shop in Hollywood and see individuals hunched over portable computers. Some of these individuals are writing the next great screenplay, while others are finishing up essays. Regardless of their purpose for writing, they each rely on a computer to assist them in drafting, revising, editing, and saving their written work. Computers are changing the way many things are done. In the world of writing, computers—more specifically, word processing programs—are replacing the notebook and pen as the primary physical tools of a writer, but the actual writing itself is still the sole responsibility of the human writer.

Plus ça change, plus c'est la même chose—the more things change, the more they stay the same. This adage is especially true in the world of writing. The tools a writer uses have changed dramatically over time. Quill pens, ink pots, and parchment gave way to rudimentary mechanical typewriters, which gave way to fancier electronic typewriters, which have given way to the current crop of powerful word processing programs that are run on computer. Today's writers may find themselves dealing with bytes, megabytes, gigabytes, hard drives, floppy drives, and zip drives. Despite amazing technological advances, the work of writing remains the same. Words like thesis, organization, development, flow, coherence, subject, and predicate still represent the central concerns of experienced writers. Writers must still grapple with ideas, words, sentences, and rhetorical choices in an effort to communicate effectively.

Writers who produce text on a computer enjoy two major benefits over writers who use a notebook and pencil. The computer-based writer can ignore minor mistakes when they first appear (misspelled words, weak verbs, faulty pronoun references) and stay focused on writing down thoughts and ideas, because writing done on a computer is easily edited and repaired. As a result, writers who compose on a computer are able to generate more words in a writing session than writers who use the older paper and pencil format.

The second major benefit of computer-based writing is that drafts can quickly and easily be revised and edited. Instead of crossing out words with a pencil, the writer can simply delete unnecessary words from a computer-based draft. Instead of trying to squeeze sentences that need to be added to a text in the margins of a handwritten draft, the writer can simply insert new text into a computer-based draft. Instead of rewriting a handwritten draft in order to fit in paragraphs that should have been included the first time around, the computer-based writer can insert entire sections of new text, copy sections of other texts directly into the text that is currently under construction, and cut paragraphs out of the text and paste them into new, more appropriate locations. Word processors enable you to generate a lot of words and to easily revise and edit the words once you have created them.

It Is Better to Look Good Than to Feel Good . . .

When I was a young child, my mother used to hide foul-tasting medicine in chocolate pudding in order to trick me into taking the medicine. The use of the computer can have much the same effect on a person who does not enjoy the foul-tasting work of writing but does enjoy the sugary sweetness of using computer technology. Writing is still writing (take a moment to enjoy this profundity), but the use of technology can make the writing process easier and more enjoyable. If the use of a computer improves your perception of yourself as a writer, then you have improved as a writer. If a computer helps increase your interest in writing, then you have improved as a writer.

If the ease with which you can edit and revise your work with a computer encourages you to spend more time rewriting, then you have become a better writer. Confidence, attitude, and determination are very important tools for a writer.

Another aspect of writing on a computer that can affect the way you feel about your writing is the simple fact that words, sentences, and paragraphs are presented with a very professional look in a word processing program. Instead of having a draft of an essay in difficult-to-read handwriting, marred by scratched-out mistakes and lines of text that need to be inserted into your essay, the words in the draft you composed on a computer are easy to read, professional looking, convincing, and seemingly, more powerful. As the comedian Billy Crystal put it, "It is better to look good than to feel good." Although this sentiment is not really true for writers (substance is more important than style), looking good can make you feel good and can build your self-confidence as a writer.

The Dark Side of Computer-Assisted Writing

As a writer, you should try to eliminate writing behaviors that cause you to waste time. Writing with a word processing program can certainly save you a substantial amount of time in the editing and revising process. However, you might be seduced by the dark side of computer-based writing. Avoid the dark side by being aware of the following potential traps and mistakes that computer-assisted writing invites.

Saving Regularly: If you do not save your writing at regular intervals, something bad will happen to you. A pack of wild dogs may enter your classroom, knock over your computer, and cause you to lose everything you have written. Don't let yourself become a victim of this kind of tragedy! Save your work every ten minutes or so.

Writing first, editing and revising later: Because it is so easy to correct mistakes in a word processing program, many writers will pause repeatedly while writing to make changes in the word or words they have just written. Do not do this! Premature editing takes your mind off the significant ideas that you are writing about and focuses your attention on minute details that are not worthy of your attention in the early stages of the writing process. Premature editing distracts you from the primary purpose of writing a draft in the first place—getting your ideas onto paper (word processor in this case).

Being buried under an avalanche of words: Another potential danger in writing with a word processing program is that you may lose your self-control and include more words or phrases in a sentence than you really need. You may do this with the idea in mind that you can go back later and decide which words should stay in the sentence and which should go. If you try to cover as many options as possible in a sentence or paragraph by adding additional words, you may have an overwhelming amount of editing and revising to do later. Or you may be tempted to use the easy editing features of the word processor to find homes for all of your extra words. After all, the extra words look professional and useful when seen through a word processor. If you subscribe to this writing habit, be warned that extra words do not necessarily mean extra substance.

Editing from the screen: Editing and revising is often easier if you work from a hard copy of your draft. A computer screen can show you only a small portion of your draft at a time. By printing up a hard copy of your draft, you can see the big picture more easily than if you must continually scroll from one section of your draft to another. When it comes time to edit your draft, edit your work on the computer, but keep a hard copy handy as a reference.

Before You Begin . . .

Before you begin to write using a word processor, there are a few basic computer terms you should be familiar with and a few skills that you should have in order to make the word processor a useful tool.

Cut, Copy, and Paste . . .

The cut, copy, and paste features are perhaps the writer's greatest asset when composing on a computer. When it is time to revise and edit your work, the cut, copy, and paste features allow you quickly and easily to move words, sentences, and paragraphs around in your text. If you find that a sentence that you had originally written into the second paragraph of an essay really belongs in the seventh paragraph, you can quickly highlight the sentence using the mouse, cut it out of the second paragraph, and paste it into the seventh paragraph. *Voilà!* Instant revision without an ugly mess.

Introductory Exercise: How to Cut, Copy, and Paste

Step 1. Type some text into your word processor to use for practicing the cutting, copying, and pasting skills.

Step 2. Using the mouse, place the blinking cursor at the beginning of a word or sentence.

Step 3. Press the mouse button and continue to hold it down.

Step 4. While you continue to press on the mouse button, move the mouse around.

Step 5. You should notice that sections of your text will become highlighted.

Step 6. Once you have highlighted the word or sentence that you wish to cut out, release the mouse button.

Step 7. The next step is to engage the CUT function. This may be done in a variety of ways, depending on the word processing program that you are using. Newer, graphically based programs will have an icon (a button with a picture on it) that engages the CUT function. Usually this icon has a picture of scissors on it, which makes a certain kind of sense. If your word processor does not have a graphical user interface (GUI), you will need to press a combination of keys to engage the CUT function (usually CTRL+X or CTRL+C).

Step 8. Using the mouse, move the blinking cursor to the spot in your text where you wish to insert or PASTE the item that you have just removed or CUT out of the text. Once the blinking cursor is at the spot where you wish to insert the text that you CUT, press the mouse button once so that the cursor is "locked in" to position.

Step 9. Engage the PASTE function. On word processors with GUIs, look for an icon with a pot of glue on it, a clipboard with a small piece of paper attached to it, or some other relatively appropriate picture. Press the icon, and the text you removed earlier will be pasted into the new location you have selected for it. That's all there is to it.

The COPY function works in the same way as the CUT function, except that your computer will make a copy of the text that you highlight instead of removing it from your document. Once you have copied the highlighted text, follow the steps just listed to PASTE the text you have copied into a new location within your document (or in another, separate document).

Save, Save, Save . . .

SAVE YOUR WORK AT REGULAR INTERVALS! There are few things more frustrating than losing one or two hours worth of writing when your computer is hit by lightning or when the power cord is ripped from the wall by your baby brother. Some word processing programs come with an "autosave" feature that allows the computer to save your file at predetermined time intervals. If you set up your computer to save your file every five minutes, you won't have to interrupt your thinking/writing process to save files on your own. If the word processing software program that you are using does not have an autosave feature, then you should take the time to learn the quickest and easiest way to save your document (usually pressing CTRL + S will be the quickest way to save your file) and thereby minimize the time spent saving when you need to be writing.

Save all of your revisions so that you have a step-by-step record of your writing process. Keep all of your prewriting exercises (freewrites, brainstorms, reading journals) together in a single "Prewriting" file. Keep all of your exercises for shaping ideas together in a single "Shaping" file. Save each rough draft in its own file (Draft 1, Draft 2, and so on). When you have finished working on your essay, you should have a collection of documents that represent all of your generating, organizing, writing, and revising work. This paper trail left by an essay is very important in analyzing your development as a writer. Looking back over this "portfolio" can help you to identify personal strengths and weaknesses.

Trust Not the Spell Checker . . .

Trust not the spell checker, least ewe bee betrayed buy it. As the previous sentence demonstrates, you can have words that are spelled correctly but that do not belong in your sentence. The spell checking component of a word processing program is useful as a tool for a preliminary search for misspelled words. However, your task as spelling editor is not complete until you have read through the text and searched for words that are spelled in such a way that their meaning is consistent with your intentions as a writer.

Be Wary of the Grammar Checker . . .

Grammar checkers work in the same way that spell checkers do. The computer will locate potential grammatical transgressions, give you a very brief description of what's wrong, and then make one or more suggestions on how to fix the problem. Resist any urges you may have to treat the grammar checker as the ultimate authority on all things grammatical. It will evaluate your writing on the basis of specific writing conventions that may or may not be appropriate for your writing situation. The writing conventions valued by your grammar checker may be very different from those valued by your instructor, just as the accepted writing conventions in the world of business are different from the conventions of academic writing. Despite the limitations of grammar checkers, they can be quite useful in helping you develop as a writer. As the grammar checker alerts you to potential problems with your writing, you may start to notice certain error patterns in your writing. In addition, some grammar checkers provide you with a summary of your essay after they have finished checking it. These summaries will tell you such things as the percentage of sentences written in the active voice relative to the percentage of sentences written in the passive voice. The summary may also tell you how many words are in your essay, how many run-on sentences you have, and so on. By analyzing your writing in these ways, you can identify problem areas that you need to focus on as you work to develop your writing skills.

You Must Remember This . . .

The computer is merely a tool designed to assist the writer. It does not make decisions for the writer. It does not create sentences for the writer. It is the writer who shapes ideas through words, sentences, and paragraphs in an effort to produce meaning. The writer and the writing are still the heart of any computer-based writing assignment.

Time to Exercise

The exercises in this chapter are meant to serve as working examples of how a word processing program can be used to assist you in the writing process. The variety of ways in which you can effectively utilize the computer's capabilities is limited only by your imagination and the limitations of your computer's hardware and software. Developing your own exercises and methods for using a word processor effectively will help you grow as a writer. Some writers are more successful if they plan extensively before they write their first draft of an essay, whereas other writers prefer to spend most of their time revising and editing a quickly written first draft. Still other writers thrive by maintaining a balance between the prewriting, writing, and revision stages. Decide which kind of writer you are, and develop a core group of computer exercises that you use regularly to enhance your strengths and help compensate for your weaknesses as a writer.

As you read through the following exercises, you will notice certain patterns. For instance, the exercises for generating ideas, shaping ideas, and drafting rely on the fact that the CUT, COPY, and PASTE functions allow easy manipulation of words and ideas. All of the editing exercises make use of the SEARCH or FIND function to locate potential problems. These patterns can easily be modified to serve different purposes.

The exercises in this chapter are organized by their relationship to the writing process. Each exercise includes a very brief introduction that explains why the exercise is valuable from a writing standpoint. Another element to this chapter is the very general computer instruction for completing the exercises. Because these exercises combine the writing process, rhetorical guidance, and computer instruction, they suffer from some severe limitations. Use a grammar handbook or rhetorical guide to provide a complete explanation of why weak verbs should be replaced. Use a computer handbook to learn the characteristics of your particular computer system.

Exercises for Generating Ideas

In most academic writing situations, you will be asked to write in response to a specific question or topic. When a situation arises in which you must select what you are going to write about, it may be difficult to deal with the newfound freedom that allows you to select a topic of your own. What should you write about? What would be the best topic? Where are you going to get ideas to write about? Waiting for some magical answer to these questions can be a very frustrating and time-wasting experience. Instead of waiting for an epiphany, generate a topic through freewriting, brainstorming, or clustering. Each of these traditional "idea generating" exercises may readily be adapted to the word-processor writing environment.

Exercise 1: Freewriting (Generating a Topic)

Freewriting is an exercise that enables you to "take pictures of your mind." By writing down (without stopping to edit or censor) whatever thoughts are in your mind, you are creating a written picture of your mind. The associative power of words will lead your thoughts and your writing from one place to another, from idea to idea. When you have finished your freewriting exercise, you will have generated potential topics and ideas for use in an essay.

Step 1. Type nonstop for 10 minutes. Do not stop to make corrections in your writing.
Step 2. Read what you have just written. Highlight (***BOLDFACE***) any words or phrases that capture your interest as you read.
Step 3. COPY the highlighted words, phrases, and ideas, and then PASTE them so that you have created a list of the highlights from your freewrite.
Step 4. Can you identify a common idea or theme that connects the items on your list? Does one item on your list seem more significant than the others? Use the common idea, theme, or the most significant item from your list as the general topic for an essay. An essay topic selected in this manner may not seem very exciting or useful at this point. However, once you begin to develop the topic further, its appeal will usually increase dramatically.
Step 5. SAVE your work.

Exercise 2: Focused Freewriting (Generating Ideas)

A focused freewrite works the same way as a freewrite, except that the freewrite is "focused" on a specific topic or theme. Instead of generating a topic to write about (freewrite), you are generating ideas that can be used for further exploration of a specific topic (focused freewrite).

Step 1. Type the topic or main idea (your focus) of the freewrite that you are about to do at the top of the page.
Step 2. Write nonstop for 10 minutes. Do not stop to make corrections in your writing. Do not edit or censor your thoughts, except to keep your writing connected to your focus.
Step 3. Read what you have just written. Highlight (***BOLDFACE***) the words, phrases, and ideas that stand out.
Step 4. COPY the highlighted words, phrases, and ideas, and then PASTE them directly below your focused freewrite so that you create a list of ideas that you can use when you write about your topic.
Step 5. SAVE your work.

Multiple freewrites that become increasingly narrow in scope may be used to create an effective rough draft of an essay in a very short amount of time. For example, your first freewrite may be for the purpose of creating a topic for an essay. Your second freewrite may focus on your newfound topic and be used to generate ideas for your essay. Subsequent freewrites would focus on each of these ideas individually.

Exercise 3: Brainstorming

Brainstorming works much like a focused freewrite, but you write down only one or two word representations of ideas. Brainstorming works well as an individual task, but it comes into its own as an idea-generating tool when it is done collaboratively.

Step 1. Collaboratively or individually, create a list of words and phrases that come to mind while you are thinking about a particular subject or topic.

Step 2. Once you have finished the initial brainstorming session, use the CUT and PASTE functions to change your single list of ideas into multiple lists of related ideas.

Step 3. Use the CUT and PASTE functions to arrange the ideas in your list(s) in a logical order. In doing so, not only have you generated ideas for discussion in your essay, but you also have already begun developing a pattern of organization.

Step 4. SAVE your work.

Exercises for Shaping Ideas

The second step in the writing process is to give shape to your ideas. Translating a newly generated collection of thoughts and ideas into a cohesive unit of ideas that can support an essay requires you to identify your focus, audience, and purpose for writing. Another traditional method for organizing and shaping ideas that lends itself readily to computer assistance is the outline. Outlining ideas for a paragraph or essay tests (and develops) your ability to arrange your ideas in a logical and useful order. An outline reduces your draft to its essential ideas. Excess words and sentences are eliminated, and you can clearly see which ideas are well supported (or not), which paragraphs are unified around a central idea (or not), and whether or not your ideas are presented in a sensible order. The following exercises, while simplistic in design, require careful thought. What examples and supporting details would best support your major ideas? What order should your ideas have? Should you save your best idea for last? As you answer questions like these, you will be making decisions that affect the shape of your essay. Fortunately, word processors allow you quickly and easily to rearrange your outline almost as quickly and easily as you can change your mind about where you want to place a particular paragraph.

Exercise 4: Outlining

If you already have a good sense of what you wish to say in an essay, you are probably ready to begin shaping your ideas into logical and useful patterns of organization. The following exercise requires you to build an outline level by level.

Step 1. Create a list of the major ideas you have for your essay. Many writers find it useful to classify the main idea of each paragraph as a "major idea."
Step 2. Once you have completed your list of major ideas, INSERT a list of details and examples under each major idea. The details and examples that you include should clearly connect to the major idea.
Step 3. Indent 5 spaces (TAB) for each detail or example that supports a major idea. This indention will help identify the detail or example as subordinate to the major idea.
Step 4. SAVE your work.

Exercise 5: Outlining Directly from a Freewrite

From a previous focused freewriting session, you should have a series of ideas that are related to the general topic of the essay you are working on. The next step in the writing process is to arrange your ideas in a logical and useful pattern of organization. The following exercise utilizes the CUT, PASTE, and INSERT capabilities of the word processing program to assist you in developing an outline of your ideas.

Step 1. Open the document in which you saved your brainstorming or freewriting exercise (see Exercises 2 and 3).
Step 2. CUT the highlighted words from your freewrite, and then PASTE them in list form below your brainstorm or focused freewrite.
Step 3. Identify the major ideas in your list. Below each major idea, make a list of details and examples that support the major idea.
Step 4. After you have finished making a supporting list for each major idea, use the CUT and PASTE functions to rearrange the major ideas (and their support) in a logical and useful order.
Step 5. Indent all the supporting details or examples 5 spaces to emphasize that they are subordinate to a major idea.
Step 6. SAVE your work.

Exercises for Drafting

One of the easiest ways to eliminate wasted time within the writing process is to assign yourself a series of specific tasks with specific time limits for completion. This writing method is especially well suited for writing a first draft of an essay. If you have a fairly good idea of what you want to say and do in your essay, then the timed writing exercise will help you write a first draft of your essay as quickly as possible. If you feel comfortable only with certain ideas in your essay, then the sectional writing exercise may prove more beneficial. Regardless of which exercise you elect to do, you must be disciplined in your approach. If you have allotted yourself a specific amount of time to write, then write nonstop for exactly that amount of time. If you are writing your essay one section at a time, stay focused on the current topic—try to keep your mind from wandering too far away from the task at hand.

Exercise 6: Timed Writing

A time limit, whether enforced by your instructor or self-imposed, can serve as a strong motivational tool. You have probably spent hours or days creating a rough draft for an essay assignment. If you were given the same essay assignment as a one- or two-hour in-class exam, you would probably produce a draft as good or better than the one you had labored over for days. By applying time limits to yourself, you can pressure yourself into working through mental blocks and other potential delays. The important element of this exercise is that you must be disciplined enough to work diligently throughout the predetermined "writing time."

Step 1. Designate a specific amount of time (one hour, for example) during which you will focus on writing a first draft of your essay.

Step 2. Write nonstop for the entire time. Do not censor new ideas that develop as your write. Do not censor your sentences. Accept awkward sentences and misspelled words as you write, and do not spend time correcting them while you are "drafting."

Step 3. Do not stop writing until your time is up, or until you have come to the natural end of your essay.

Step 4. Save your work.

Exercise 7: Sectional Writing

This exercise works very well when used in conjunction with a previously constructed outline (see Exercises 6 and 7). By writing paragraphs directly from sections of your outline, you should stay focused on the main idea of individual paragraphs; thus it is much less likely that you will go off on a tangent. By focusing on individual sections of your essay, each paragraph and/or section will be more focused, complete, and true to your outlined pattern of organization.

Step 1. COPY your entire outline so that you have a duplicate of your outline that you can freely manipulate and change.

Step 2. Insert a few blank lines between the different sections of your outline. Each "section" should contain the amount of outlined information that would allow you to write a corresponding paragraph.

Step 3. Develop your outline into a complete paragraph by writing your paragraph directly below the outline section.

Step 4. Continue writing your essay paragraph by paragraph, and outline section by outline section, until you have completed a first draft of your essay.

Step 5. Once your draft is complete, go back through your draft and delete the remnants of your outline. (Remember, you should still have the original copy of your outline saved elsewhere).

Step 6. SAVE your work.

Exercise 8: Split Screen

When you are required to write an essay in response to a specific question or problem, it is usually a good idea to keep the question or problem clearly in mind as you write. By doing so, you decrease the chance that you will get off track and fail to answer the question or solve the problem. Most word processors allow the writer to have multiple documents open at one time. When you have two documents open at the same time and one occupies the top half of the computer screen while the other occupies the bottom half, you have achieved a "split screen" setup. This setup can be very useful if you have difficulty staying focused on your thesis because it keeps your assignment directly above your current writing.

Step 1. Open the document that contains the question or problem you must respond to. If the question is not already in a usable computer document, write the assignment into a new file and save it.

Step 2. Engage the SPLIT function of your word processor (if your word processor does not have this function, you can use the mouse manually to adjust the size of the window in which your original document appears) and place your assignment question in the upper window.

Step 3. Open a NEW file in the lower window.

Step 4. Write your draft in the lower window while keeping an eye on the assignment that is displayed in the upper window.

Step 5. SAVE your work.

Exercises For Revision

Once you have completed a rough draft of an essay, you will need to spend time revising its content, organization, and coherence. Revision is the most important part of the writing process. Experienced writers revise their work repeatedly until they feel that their draft is ready for editing. The term *revise* means to see something in a new way, to rethink and reshape. When you revise your writing, you consider how to rearrange your writing better to fit your purpose for writing. When you revise, you consider new and improved ways to present your ideas to your audience. The process of revision commonly requires the writer to consider such things as using alternative patterns of organization; eliminating unnecessary words, sentences, and ideas; and repeating key words or phrases.

Exercise 9: Testing Your Organization

Many writers rely on an outline that is created before the first draft is written to ensure that the essay's organization is effective. However, the first draft of an essay does not always follow the plan of the outline. Writers come up with new ideas that are added as they write, and more than one writer has gone off on a tangent and forgotten all about the outline. The following exercise allows the writer to evaluate the essay's organization after it has been written, thereby avoiding the pitfalls inherent in relying on an outline that was created before the first draft. Every paragraph should be built around one controlling idea, and assembling these controlling ideas in a paragraph of their own will enable the reader to evaluate the organization, the flow of ideas, and the overriding logic of the essay.

Step 1. Read the first paragraph of your essay. Identify the one sentence that best represents the main point of that paragraph.

Step 2. COPY the "main point sentence," and PASTE the single sentence a few lines below the end of the essay.

Step 3. Read the second paragraph of your essay. Identify the one sentence that best represents the main point of that paragraph.

Step 4. COPY the "main point sentence," and PASTE the single sentence a few lines below the end of the essay, just after the copied sentence from the first paragraph.

Step 5. Repeat the process until a single "main point sentence" has been copied from each paragraph in the essay and pasted in order at the end of the essay. Ultimately you will have constructed a new paragraph built with the single representative sentences from each paragraph of the essay.

Step 6. SAVE your work.

Step 7. Analyze the newly created paragraph for organization. Compare the first and last sentences of the paragraph. Since they represent the introduction and conclusion of the essay, they should work together in an obvious manner. In general the entire paragraph should represent a reasonable and logical order of ideas and, perhaps, arguments. If your paragraph is completely illogical, or unreadable, then, in all likelihood, you need to revise your essay.

Exercise 10: Eliminating Unnecessary Sentences

Unnecessary sentences distract the reader from the real meaning and purpose of a paragraph. If a sentence does not clearly support the main idea of your paragraph or if it unnecessarily repeats an idea in an adjacent sentence, it should be eliminated (or moved to a place where it serves a useful purpose).

Step 1. Highlight your thesis statement and topic sentences in **BOLDFACE.**

Step 2. Read each paragraph individually, and underline all sentences that are not clearly related to the topic sentence.

Step 3. Italicize all paragraphs that are not clearly and logically related to your thesis statement.

Step 4. SAVE your revised draft, and each subsequent revision, under a different name so that you will have a copy of your draft before and after you have completed this exercise.

Step 5. DELETE all unnecessary sentences and paragraphs (the italicized and underlined sections) from your draft.

Step 6. SAVE your work.

Exercise 11: Eliminating Unnecessary Words

Unnecessary words contribute nothing to a sentence. Instead, they detract from both substance and style. Sentences with unnecessary words removed are clearer in meaning, more graceful, and more effective in doing what you want them to do.

Step 1. Read your draft sentence by sentence.
Step 2. Italicize all words that can be deleted without changing the meaning or the effectiveness of the sentence.
Step 3. Underline all groups of words that could be replaced with a single word that would say the same thing.
Step 4. Place brackets [ ] around sentences that you suspect could be made more concise (while retaining their meaning and purpose) if they were completely rewritten.
Step 5. SAVE the revised copy of your draft under a new name.
Step 6. Delete all unnecessary words, replace word groups with individual words that convey the same meaning, and rewrite unnecessarily wordy sentences so that they are more concise.
Step 7. SAVE your work.

Exercise 12: Organization

The ideas in an essay may follow many different patterns of development. Development may be chronological, it may build to an effect, or it may follow some other method of organization. The important thing to realize is that the order of development that you, as the writer, choose will make an impact on the reader. The purpose of this exercise is to test your arrangement of paragraphs.

Step 1. Save your original document under a new name ("Organize," for example).
Step 2. Open the backup document that you just created.
Step 3. Using the cut and paste functions of your word processor, rearrange your paragraphs in a random order.
Step 4. Save the newly arranged document to your floppy disk.
Step 5. Give your floppy disk to a classmate, ask her to open your newly rearranged document, and have her use the cut and paste functions to rearrange your document in an order that seems logical to her.
Step 6. Have the classmate save her version of your essay onto your disk (under the same name) and return the disk to you.
Step 7. Open up her version of your essay, and compare it with the arrangement of paragraphs in your original document. Has she organized your document in the same way that you did? If not, what did she do differently? Why do you think your classmate arranged your paragraphs in a different order? If you do not see a logical pattern to her organization of your paragraphs, ask her to explain why she did what she did.

Step 8. Decide what arrangement of paragraphs you like best, and use the CUT and PASTE functions to create a final pattern of organization.

Step 9. Save your work.

Exercise 13: Repetition

Repeating a key word or phrase is an effective way to improve coherence in an essay. Richard Rodriguez uses the key phrase "scholarship boy" repeatedly in his autobiography to emphasize one of the main ideas in his book. If you repeatedly use a key word or phrase that is representative of a central idea in your essay, the reader will have an easier time understanding your message.

Step 1. Use the search function to locate all occurrences of a key word or phrase.

Step 2. **BOLDFACE** each occurrence of the word or phrase.

Step 3. Review your essay (you may wish to print a hard copy for this step). Look for sections of your essay that do not have the key word or phrase. If these barren sections are lengthy, try to find places within sentences where you can effectively insert the key word or phrase.

Step 4. SAVE your work.

Exercise 14: Revisionary Outlines

Outlines have long been a recommended part of the prewriting or organizing step in the writing process. However, outlining can also be used as an effective revision tool. Revisionary outlines are outlines that are created after you finish writing a draft of your essay. A revisionary outline reveals the organization and arrangement of ideas in a manner that allows you to see places where your draft lacks sufficient supporting details, examples, and ideas. Once you have identified gaps in your essay, it is a relatively simple chore to fill in the needed text, using the word processor's INSERT capability.

Step 1. OPEN the file containing your draft.

Step 2. INSERT some blank lines between your first and second paragraphs.

Step 3. In the blank area below your first paragraph, type an outline of the first paragraph.

Step 4. Repeat steps two and three for each subsequent paragraph.

Step 5. When you have outlined each paragraph, use the CUT and PASTE functions to place each paragraph-level outline at the end of your draft (in the same order as they appear within your draft).

Step 6. Once you have a complete revisionary outline of your draft, analyze it. What ideas need more support? What ideas need more development? Where would additional examples be useful? Use your newly created outline to identify gaps in your draft, and then fill the gaps with supporting details, examples, and additional ideas.

Step 7. SAVE your work.

Exercise 15: Connecting your Introduction to Your Conclusion

When your conclusion is clearly connected to your introduction, your reader is more likely to feel that the essay has come to a natural and logical conclusion. A good connection may come from a direct answer to a question posed in the introduction, from speculation about what your thesis implies for the future, or from a brief summary of the main points in your essay. By writing the conclusion as a response to the introduction, you make your essay more unified and coherent.

Step 1. Open the latest draft of your essay.

Step 2. Insert a few blank lines between the end of your introductory paragraph(s) and the rest of your essay.

Step 3. Read your introduction, and then write your conclusion directly below your introductory paragraph. As you write, be sure to make a clear connection between the introduction and your conclusion. Use key words from your introduction in your conclusion, or directly answer (briefly) any questions that you raised in your introduction. Do not repeat information from your introduction word for word in your conclusion.

Step 4. Once you have finished writing the conclusion, CUT it from the text, and PASTE it onto the end of your essay. The completed conclusion should then have a clear connection to the introduction.

Step 5. SAVE your work.

Exercise 16: Peer Review

After spending a great deal of time writing a draft of an essay, a writer often finds it difficult to achieve enough distance from the text to evaluate it effectively. One way to overcome this problem is to set the draft aside for a few days (if you haven't put the writing off until the last minute) and then to review it with a fresh perspective. Another way to evaluate a draft is to have a friend or classmate review it. This method has the advantage of giving you practical feedback on the way the reader responds to your writing.

Step 1. Open the classmate's draft that is to be reviewed.

Step 2. As you read through the draft, you will react to various aspects of the text. Misspelled words, awkward sentences, unsupported statements, or a thought that is expressed exceptionally well are some of the things that will probably catch your attention. Whenever you encounter an attention-grabbing item, comment on it within the text. You can enter your comments unobtrusively in word processors that have an ANNOTATION function. When you engage the ANNOTATION function, you will be able to write notes to the author in such a way that they won't print in the document. If the word processor does not have this ability, you should insert your comments directly into the text but in a different or an italicized font so that the author can easily distinguish his or her writing from your comments.

Step 3. SAVE your work.

Step 4. Return the disk to the author of the draft.

Step 5. The author of the draft should then open the reviewed draft and engage the VIEW ANNOTATIONS function so that the reviewer's comments can be seen. If annotations were not used by the reviewer, the author should simply read the comments, act upon them if possible or necessary, and delete the comments once they are no longer needed. Once all the comments have been read and the necessary corrections made, the author should SAVE the revised draft.

A major advantage of having a peer review done with a word processor is that the comments and constructive criticisms can be acted upon as soon as they are read.

Exercises for Editing

Editing is the final part of the writing process. Editing refers to the process of identifying and correcting errors. Each type of writing, whether it is business, academic, technical, or professional, has its own conventions for the writer to follow. Some conventions are universal, that is, they apply to all types of writing. Awkward pronoun references, weak verbs, and sexist language are universally recognized forms of error. Within an academic setting, readers expect a writing to contain familiar qualities. Because readers have these expectations, a writer's use of unconventional sentence forms (slang, for example) can be very distracting. The closer your sentences are to standard forms of sentence structure, grammar, and spelling, the more adept you will be in communicating your ideas effectively to your reader.

Exercise 17: Eliminating Awkward Pronoun References

There are many ways in which pronouns can be misused. Using the FIND or SEARCH function of the word processor can help you to locate all of the pronouns in your essay and evaluate them for correct usage.

Step 1. Use the SEARCH or FIND function to locate pronouns.
Step 2. Evaluate each pronoun. Is it clear what noun the pronoun is referring to?
Step 3. If it is unclear what the pronoun is referring to, replace the pronoun with a more specific word or words.
Step 4. SAVE your work.

Exercise 18: Eliminating Sexist Language

Sexist language demeans women or men (usually women) and reflects stereotypical thinking. Two popular ways in which writers eliminate sexist language are (1) to substitute a pair of pronouns ("he or she") and (2) to write in the plural form (they, their).

Step 1. Use the SEARCH or FIND function to locate all occurrences of potentially sexist words like he, she, men, women, and so on.
Step 2. Evaluate each occurrence of potentially sexist language.
Step 3. Replace all occurrences of sexist language with a nonsexist replacement (repace "he" with "he or she," replace "chairman" with "chairperson," and so on).
Step 4. SAVE your work.

Exercise 19: Eliminating the Authorial "I"

There are two reasons for removing the first person pronouns such as "I" and "we." (1) These pronouns make the writing sound casual and informal. (2) Extensive use of "I" and "we" focuses too much attention on the author and not enough attention on the ideas in the essay.

Step 1. Use the SEARCH or FIND function to locate all occurrences of the words "I" and "we."
Step 2. If the egocentric reference is unnecessary, eliminate it, and then rewrite the sentence so that the focus is on the most important idea in the sentence.
Step 3. SAVE your work.

Exercise 20: Eliminating Weak Verbs

Weak verbs can severely limit the effectiveness of a sentence. Examples are forms of the verb *to be* (am, are, is, was, were, being, been) or other vague, actionless verbs like *have* or *exist.* When you find a weak verb in a sentence, replace it with a stronger, more vigorous verb.

Step 1. Use the SEARCH or FIND function to locate the various forms of the verb "to be" that occur in your essay.

Step 2. Replace these weak verbs, whenever possible, with stronger verbs.

Step 3. SAVE you work.

Miscellaneous Debris

Word processors have plenty of tools and tricks that can distract you from the more important task of writing. However, since all work and no play makes Jack a dull boy, let's discuss (discuss as in, I write—you read) some of these distractions.

Fonts

A font is a typeface that can come in a variety of sizes. Standard writing conventions dictate that you select a font of normal size (10 or 12 points), in a style that is clean and easy to read. Making your reader battle through an essay that is written with a font that can best be described as "thick gothic calligraphy," can be very annoying. Since your primary reader is often the person giving you a grade for your writing, you should probably choose the most agreeable font that you can find. However, choosing an easy-to-read font that is subtly different from the most standard font (such as Times New Roman font) is one way for you to add some personality to your essay without straying too far from the conventions of standard academic writing. When in doubt over your choice of font, consult your primary reader.

Justification

Most word processors offer you the option of having an unjustified (ragged) right margin or having a right margin that is justified (this text is an example of justified text). When you elect to justify the right margin of your text, you may be forcing the word processor to create additional spaces between letters and words. These additional spaces can be very distracting for your reader. Some word processors will avoid creating these extra spaces by hyphenating words. Unfortunately, the necessity to hyphenate in order to justify the right margin can result in overhyphenated text that distracts the reader. As a general rule, you should format your essays with a ragged (unjustified) right margin.

Graphics

Academic essays traditionally rely on text rather than graphics for presenting ideas to the reader. One of the primary reasons for this reliance on text is that a writer can completely control the way that words are presented, and to a lesser extent, the reader's response to the words. A more utilitarian reason for the reliance on text is that technology has only recently made desktop publishing accessible to the general public. The final and most important reason why writers rely on text is that writers, by definition, produce text (not graphics). Writers use words and sentences to communicate with readers. Photographs, tables, charts, graphs, and other visuals are traditionally the tools of artists. However, it is becoming increasingly common for writers to use graphics to supplement their writing. Adding graphics to an essay can have a dramatic effect on the way information is processed by your reader. A sentence full of statistical data will probably have less impact on your reader than a graph that presents the same statistics. Most word processors now include charting and drawing features that allow you easily to add charts, graphs, and clip art to your essays. If your computer is equipped with a scanner and scanning software, you can scan pictures directly into your essays. When deciding whether or not to include graphics with your essay, consider your purpose for writing, your audience, and the writing conventions by which your essay will be evaluated.

The Internet

Most university computer systems are part of **the Internet**. The Internet is a global collection of computers that are connected via phone lines so that information can be shared easily and conveniently between computer users across the world. Originally developed for use by the government and academic institutions, the Internet has now become accessible by the private home user as well. The result is an information database that is growing and evolving at a rapid rate. Computer users can now purchase shoes in a store in

Italy from the comfort of their home in Needles, California. More importantly, students can use the Internet to send electronic mail to one another, establish contacts with people who share a common interest, and collect information that would normally be unavailable because of physical and financial constraints.

E-mail

The ability to send and receive electronic mail (E-mail) is a very useful tool. Through E-mail you can leave messages for your classmates, ask questions of your instructor, or simply correspond with friends. You can ask a professor a question about your homework assignment on a Saturday morning, receive a response on Saturday night, and be prepared for class on Monday, instead of showing up for class unprepared with your question unanswered. E-mail allows communication at a much faster rate than that of the post office and at a minuscule fraction of the cost of a phone call.

Newsgroups and Mailing Lists

Newsgroups and mailing lists allow you to communicate with groups of people who share your interests. You can subscribe to mailing lists as well as newsgroups, and as a subscriber you receive (electronically) all information that is associated with the mailing list you have subscribed to. As a subscriber to a newsgroup, you will be able to post messages about your group's topic, receive answers, and read the messages that other members of your newsgroups are posting.

Research

One of the primary difficulties in using the Internet to conduct research is the fact that the Internet is chaotic. In the past, an Internet user would have to spend hours searching for desirable pieces of information. These searches could take very long periods of time because there was no "universal directory" to help researchers find the information they needed. Although there is still no universal directory, various groups have begun to organize the information that can be found on the Internet. Text-based search programs such as WAIS, Lynx, Veronica, and Archie can help you find information on a specific subject. Graphical Web Browsers such as Mosaic and Netscape have made it even easier to find information on the World Wide Web. Mosaic and Netscape (the most popular Internet browser at the moment) allow the user to search for information in an environment that is similar to the Windows environment of IBM compatible computers and the Apple Macintosh environment. A variety of search programs can be found within these graphical browsers that allow you to search for information by subject or key words, much as you would at your campus library.

When All Is Said And Done

The next time you walk into the Starbuck's coffee shop in Hollywood or into some other, more local, establishment where writers sit pecking away at their laptop computers, pay close attention to what is taking place. If you look closely enough, you will see that the writers are trying to shape ideas through words, sentences, and paragraphs in an effort to produce meaning. You will see that the computers act only as assistants, simplifying the physical tasks of writing, revising, and editing so that the writer remains free to focus on expressing ideas through written words. No matter how often technology changes the physical tools available to writers, the task of writing will remain a personal exercise in human creativity. Therefore, your goal as a computer-based writer is to develop exercises that ease the task of generating ideas, shaping ideas, drafting, revising, and editing. With the proper use of a computer, you will soon improve your ability to craft effective essays.

Part Three

The Readings

Paula Gunn Allen

WHERE I COME FROM IS LIKE THIS

Paula Gunn Allen, who was raised in New Mexico, is of Laguna Pueblo, Sioux, Scottish, and Lebanese-American descent. She is a prolific writer; her poetry, essays, and fiction have appeared in numerous journals and anthologies. The selection included here is from her book The Woman Who Owned the Shadows. *Allen lives in the Los Angeles area and teaches in the Department of English at UCLA.*

Prereading Journal Questions

1. This essay, in part, discusses the ways in which women "define themselves." How do you think all people come to a definition of themselves, as people, as men, as women?
2. How does your culture define women? What are women's roles, and what can they contribute to your culture or to society?
3. How do you think Native American cultures define women? What has led you to these conclusions?

Reading tip: There may be many unfamiliar words in this essay. Try to figure them out within the context of the text. If there are words or terms you cannot understand, jot them down in your journal, and look them up after you have read the entire essay. Once you have an understanding of the words, reread the text, and note how your understanding of the work as a whole changes.

I

Modern American Indian women, like their non-Indian sisters, are deeply engaged in the struggle to redefine themselves. In their struggle they must reconcile traditional tribal definitions of women with industrial and postindustrial non-Indian definitions. Yet while these definitions seem to be more or less mutually exclusive, Indian women must somehow harmonize and integrate both in their own lives.

An American Indian woman is primarily defined by her tribal identity. In her eyes, her destiny is necessarily that of her people, and her sense of herself as a woman is first and foremost prescribed by her tribe. The definitions of woman's roles are as diverse as tribal cultures in the

Americas. In some she is devalued, in others she wields considerable power. In some she is a familial/clan adjunct, in some she is as close to autonomous as her economic circumstances and psychological traits permit. But in no tribal definitions is she perceived in the same way as are women in western industrial and postindustrial cultures.

In the west, few images of women form part of the cultural mythos, and these are largely sexually charged. Among Christians, the madonna is the female prototype, and she is portrayed as essentially passive: her contribution is simply that of birthing. Little else is attributed to her and she certainly possesses few of the characteristics that are attributed to mythic figures among Indian tribes. This image is countered (rather than balanced) by the witch-goddess/whore characteristics designed to reinforce cultural beliefs about women, as well as western adversarial and dualistic perceptions of reality.

The tribes see women variously, but they do not question the power of femininity. Sometimes they see women as fearful, sometimes peaceful, sometimes omnipotent and omniscient, but they never portray women as mindless, helpless, simple, or oppressed. And while the women in a given tribe, clan, or band may be all these things, the individual woman is provided with a variety of images of women from the interconnected supernatural, natural, and social worlds she lives in.

As a half-breed American Indian woman, I cast about in my mind for negative images of Indian women, and I find none that are directed to Indian women alone. The negative images I do have are of Indians in general and in fact are more often of males than of females. All these images come to me from non-Indian sources, and they are always balanced by a positive image. My ideas of womanhood, passed on largely by my mother and grandmothers, Laguna Pueblo women, are about practicality, strength, reasonableness, intelligence, wit, and competence. I also remember vividly the women who came to my father's store, the women who held me and sang to me, the women at Feast Day, at Grab Days,[1] the women in the kitchen of my Cubero home, the women I grew up with; none of them appeared weak or helpless, none of them presented herself tentatively. I remember a certain reserve on those lovely brown faces; I remember the direct gaze of eyes framed by bright-colored shawls draped over their heads and cascading down their backs. I remember the clean cotton dresses and carefully pressed hand-

[1]*Grab Days:* Laguna ritual in which women throw food and small items (like pieces of cloth) to those attending.

embroidered aprons they always wore; I remember laughter and good food, especially the sweet bread and the oven bread they gave us. Nowhere in my mind is there a foolish woman, a dumb woman, a vain woman, or a plastic woman, though the Indian women I have known have shown a wide range of personal style and demeanor.

My memory includes the Navajo woman who was badly beaten by her Sioux husband; but I also remember that my grandmother abandoned her Sioux husband long ago. I recall the stories about the Laguna woman beaten regularly by her husband in the presence of her children so that the children would not believe in the strength and power of femininity. And I remember the women who drank, who got into fights with other women and with the men, and who often won those battles. I have memories of tired women, partying women, stubborn women, sullen women, amicable women, selfish women, shy women, and aggressive women. Most of all I remember the women who laugh and scold and sit uncomplaining in the long sun on feast days and who cook wonderful food on wood stoves, in beehive mud ovens, and over open fires outdoors.

Among the images of women that come to me from various tribes as well as my own are White Buffalo Woman, who came to the Lakota long ago and brought them the religion of the Sacred Pipe which they still practice; Tinotzin the goddess who came to Juan Diego to remind him that she still walked the hills of her people and sent him with her message, her demand and her proof to the Catholic bishop in the city nearby. And from Laguna I take the images of Yellow Woman, Coyote Woman, Grandmother Spider (Spider Old Woman), who brought the light, who gave us weaving and medicine, who gave us life. Among the Keres she is known as Thought Woman who created us all and who keeps us in creation even now. I remember Iyatiku, Earth Woman, Corn Woman, who guides and counsels the people to peace and who welcomes us home when we cast off this coil of flesh as huskers cast off the leaves that wrap the corn. I remember Iyatiku's sister, Sun Woman, who held metals and cattle, pigs and sheep, highways and engines and so many things in her bundle, who went away to the east saying that one day she would return.

II

Since the coming of the Anglo-Europeans beginning in the fifteenth century, the fragile web of identity that long held tribal people secure has gradually been weakened and torn. But the oral tradition has prevented the complete destruction of the web, the ultimate disruption of tribal ways. The oral tradition is vital; it heals itself and the tribal web by adapting to the flow of the present while never relinquishing its connection to the past. Its adaptability has always been required, as many generations have experienced. Certainly the modern American Indian woman bears slight resemblance to her forebears—at least on superficial examination—but she is still a tribal woman in her deepest being. Her tribal sense of relationship to all that is continues to flourish. And though she is at times beset by her knowledge of the enormous gap between the life she lives and the life she was raised to live, and while she adapts her mind and being to the circumstances of her present life, she does so in tribal ways, mending the tears in the web of being from which she takes her existence as she goes.

My mother told me stories all the time, though I often did not recognize them as that. My mother told me stories about cooking and childbearing; she told me stories about menstruation and pregnancy; she told me stories about gods and heroes, about fairies and elves, about goddesses and spirits; she told me stories about the land and the sky, about cats and dogs, about snakes and spiders; she told me stories about climbing trees and exploring the mesas; she told me stories about going to dances and getting married; she told me stories about dressing and undressing, about sleeping and waking; she told me stories about herself, about her mother, about her grandmother. She told me stories about grieving and laughing, about thinking and doing; she told me stories about school and about people; about darning and mending; she told me stories about turquoise and about gold; she told me European stories and Laguna stories; she told me Catholic stories and Presbyterian stories; she told me city stories and country stories; she told me political stories and religious stories. She told me stories about living and stories about dying. And in all of those stories she told me who I was, who I was supposed to be, whom I came from, and who would follow me. In this way she taught me the meaning of the words she said, that all life is a circle and everything has a place within it. That's what she said and what she showed me in the things she did and the way she lives.

Of course, through my formal, white, Christian education, I discovered that other people had stories of their own—about women, about Indians, about fact, about reality—and I was amazed by a number of startling suppositions that others made about tribal customs and beliefs. According to the un-Indian, non-Indian view, for instance, Indians barred menstruating women from ceremonies and indeed segregated them from the rest of the people, consigning them to some space specially designed for them. This showed that Indians considered menstruating women unclean and not fit to enjoy the company of decent (nonmenstruating) people, that is, men. I was surprised and confused to hear this because my mother had taught me that white people had strange attitudes toward menstruation: they thought something was bad about it, that it meant you were sick, cursed, sinful, and weak and that you had to be very careful during that time. She taught me that menstruation was a normal occurrence, that I could go swimming or hiking or whatever else I wanted to do during my period. She actively scorned women who took to their beds, who were incapacitated by cramps, who "got the blues."

As I struggled to reconcile these very contradictory interpretations of American Indians' traditional beliefs concerning menstruation, I realized that the menstrual taboos were about power, not about sin or filth. My conclusion was later borne out by some tribes' own explanations, which, as you may well imagine, came as quite a relief to me.

The truth of the matter as many Indians see it is that women who are at the peak of their fecundity are believed to possess power that throws male power totally out of kilter. They emit such force that, in their presence, any male-owned or -dominated ritual or sacred object cannot do its usual task. For instance, the Lakota say that a menstruating woman anywhere near a yuwipi man, who is a special sort of psychic, spirit-empowered healer, for a day or so before he is to do his ceremony will effectively disempower him. Conversely, among many if not most tribes, important ceremonies cannot be held without the presence of women. Sometimes the ritual woman who empowers the ceremony must be unmarried and virginal so that the power she channels is unalloyed, unweakened by sexual arousal and penetration by a male. Other ceremonies require tumescent women, others the presence of mature women who have borne children, and still others depend for empowerment on postmenopausal women. Women may be segregated from the company of the whole band or village on certain occasions, but on certain occasions men are also segregated. In short, each ritual depends on a certain balance of power, and the positions of women within the phases of womanhood are used by tribal people to empower certain rites. This does not derive from a male-dominant view; it is not a ritual observance imposed on women by men. It derives from a tribal view of reality that distinguishes tribal people from feudal and industrial people.

Among the tribes, the occult power of women, inextricably bound to our hormonal life, is thought to be very great; many hold that we possess innately the blood-given power to kill—with a glance, with a step, or with a judicious mixing of menstrual blood into somebody's soup. Medicine women among the Pomo of California cannot practice until they are sufficiently mature; when they are immature, their power is diffuse and is likely to interfere with their practice until time and experience have it under control. So women of the tribes are not especially inclined to see themselves as poor helpless victims of male domination. Even in those tribes where something akin to male domination was present, women are perceived as powerful, socially, physically, and metaphysically. In times past, as in times present, women carried enormous burdens with aplomb. We were far indeed from the "weaker sex," the designation that white aristocratic sisters unhappily earned for us all.

I remember my mother moving furniture all over the house when she wanted it changed. She didn't wait for my father to come home and help—she just went ahead and moved the piano, a huge upright from the old days, the couch, the refrigerator. Nobody had told her she was too weak to do such things. In imitation of her, I would delight in loading trucks at my father's store with cases of pop or fifty-pound sacks of flour. Even when I was quite small I could do it, and it gave me a belief in my own physical strength that advancing middle age can't quite erase. My mother used to tell me about the Acoma Pueblo women she had seen as a child carrying huge ollas (water pots) on their heads as they wound their way up the tortuous stairwell carved into the face of the "Sky City" mesa, a feat I tried to imitate with books and tin buckets. ("Sky City" is the term used by the Chamber of Commerce for the mother village of Acoma, which is situated atop a high sandstone table mountain.) I was never very successful, but even the attempt reminded me that I was supposed to be strong and balanced to be a proper girl.

Of course, my mother's Laguna people are Keres Indian, reputed to be the last extreme mother-right people on earth. So it is no wonder that I got notably nonwhite notions about the natural strength and prowess of women. Indeed, it is only when I am trying to get non-Indian approval, recognition, or acknowledgement that my "weak sister" emotional and intellectual ploys get the better of my tribal woman's good sense. At such times I forget that I just moved the piano or just wrote a competent paper or just completed a financial transaction satisfactorily or have supported myself and my children for most of my adult life.

Nor is my contradictory behavior atypical. Most Indian women I know are in the same bicultural bind: we vacillate between being dependent and strong, self-reliant and powerless, strongly motivated and hopelessly insecure. We resolve the dilemma in various ways:

some of us party all the time; some of us drink to excess; some of us travel and move around a lot; some of us land good jobs and then quit them; some of us engage in violent exchanges; some of us blow our brains out. We act in these destructive ways because we suffer from the societal conflicts caused by having to identify with two hopelessly opposed cultural definitions of women. Through this destructive dissonance we are unhappy prey to the self-disparagement common to, indeed demanded of, Indians living in the United States today. Our situation is caused by the exigencies of a history of invasion, conquest, and colonization whose searing marks are probably ineradicable. A popular bumper sticker on many Indian cars proclaims: "If You're Indian You're In," to which I always find myself adding under my breath, "Trouble."

III

No Indian can grow to any age without being informed that her people were "savages" who interfered with the march of progress pursued by respectable, loving, civilized white people. We are the villains of the scenario when we are mentioned at all. We are absent from much of white history except when we are calmly, rationally, succinctly, and systematically dehumanized. On the few occasions we are noticed in any way other than as howling, bloodthirsty beings, we are acclaimed for our noble quaintness. In this definition, we are exotic curios. Our ancient arts and customs are used to draw tourist money to state coffers, into the pocketbooks and bank accounts of scholars, and into support of the American-in-Disneyland promoters' dream.

As a Roman Catholic child I was treated to bloody tales of how the savage Indians martyred the hapless priests and missionaries who went among them in an attempt to lead them to the one true path. By the time I was through high school I had the idea that Indians were people who had benefitted mightily from the advanced knowledge and superior morality of the Anglo-Europeans. At least I had, perforce, that idea to lay beside the other one that derived from my daily experience of Indian life, an idea less dehumanizing and more accurate because it came from my mother and the other Indian people who raised me. That idea was that Indians are a people who don't tell lies, who care for their children and their old people. You never see an Indian orphan, they said. You always know when you're old that someone will take care of you—one of your children will. Then they'd list the old folks who were being taken care of by this child or that. No child is ever considered illegitimate among the Indians, they said. If a girl gets pregnant, the baby is still part of the family, and the mother is too. That's what they said, and they showed me real people who lived according to those principles.

Of course the ravages of colonization have taken their toll; there are orphans in Indian country now, and abandoned, brutalized old folks; there are even illegitimate children, though the very concept still strikes me as absurd. There are battered children and neglected children, and there are battered wives and women who have been raped by Indian men. Proximity to the "civilizing" effects of white Christians has not improved the moral quality of life in Indian country, though each group, Indian and white, explains the situation differently. Nor is there much yet in the oral tradition that can enable us to adapt to these inhuman changes. But a force is growing in that direction, and it is helping Indian women reclaim their lives. Their power, their sense of direction and of self will soon be visible. It is the force of the women who speak and work and write, and it is formidable.

Through all the centuries of war and death and cultural and psychic destruction have endured the women who raise the children and tend the fires, who pass along the tales and the traditions, who weep and bury the dead, who are the dead, and who never forget. There are always the women, who make pots and weave baskets, who fashion clothes and cheer their children on at powwow, who make fry bread and piki bread, and corn soup and chili stew, who dance and sing and remember and hold within their hearts the dream of their ancient peoples—that one day the woman who thinks will speak to us again, and everywhere there will be peace. Meanwhile we tell the stories and write the books and trade tales of anger and woe and stories of fun and scandal and laugh over all manner of things that happen every day. We watch and we wait.

My great-grandmother told my mother: never forget you are Indian. And my mother told me the same thing. This, then, is how I have gone about remembering, so that my children will remember too.

Postreading Writing Assignments

Option 1: How do Allen's definitions of Native American* women differ from definitions of women (both Native American and nonnative

*The term "Native American" does not distinguish between the hundreds of different tribes and cultures. It is used in these assignments to differentiate between indigenous and nonindigenous peoples.

women) by nonnative Americans? Use specific sections of text to support your assertions.

Option 2: In what ways is Allen's essay about racism? Use specific examples from her text to demonstrate where and how Allen discusses "racist" views about American Indians.

Extended Writing Assignments

Option 3: Do some outside reading. Find one or two Laguna Pueblo stories. How do these stories add to your understanding of Allen's essay? You might try to find stories that discuss the significance of the "spider web" to Laguna Pueblo culture and identity. How does Allen use the metaphor of the web throughout her text?

Option 4: Is this a "feminist" essay? To respond to this question, you will first need to define feminism: What does it mean to be a "feminist"? What are feminist values? Respond to specific sections of text that you see as particularly feminist. If you don't see this as a feminist essay, find another way to classify or categorize this work.

Option 5: Review your response to prereading question number two. For this assignment, address the following issue: If you are male, how does your culture define males? How are you attempting to define yourself within this definition? If you are female, how does your culture define females, and how are you defining yourself? Use Allen's text as a model. Compare your way of defining yourself with Allen's exploration of "self."

Forging Connections

Option 6: Read or reread Michael Dorris's text "The Broken Cord." Both Dorris and Allen are Native American writers exploring issues that involve Native American women. What are the differences between the two essays? What are the similarities? What do you imagine these two writers might have to say to one another? Write an essay discussing these two texts and the implications that both have for Native American women. It would also be interesting to discuss the role of Native American men and nonnative peoples. What roles do Allen and Dorris see such groups playing? What roles do you see for these groups?

Maya Angelou

GRADUATION

Maya Angelou has written a number of autobiographical works, including I Know Why the Caged Bird Sings, *which "Graduation" is taken from. She has also written poetry and television screenplays. Angelou explores the many facets of growing up black in the American south of the 1930s.*

Prereading Journal Questions

1. Angelou discusses her eighth-grade graduation. Think back to one of your own graduations. What do you remember most clearly? What were your expectations for the day? Did the event turn out as you expected?
2. Has your education been affected by others' expectations of you? In other words, have you set your own standards, or have others influenced you?
3. What happens if or when society or individuals expect an entire group of people, because of race, culture, income level, and so on, to fail? Have you ever been part of a group that led others to form certain expectations of you—positive or negative?

Reading tip: This excerpt from Angelou's autobiography is rich with visual detail. As you read, try to create visual images of the pictures that Angelou's words evoke. Watch the looks on the faces of the graduates, see the changes that occur as Donleavy speaks, see Henry Reed as he gives his valedictory address. After reading "Graduation," write down a description of your visual images.

The children in Stamps trembled visibly with anticipation. Some adults were excited too, but to be certain the whole young population had come down with graduation epidemic. Large classes were graduating from both the grammar school and the high school. Even those who were years removed from their own day of glorious release were anxious to help with preparations as a kind of dry run. The junior students who were moving into the vacating classes' chairs were tradition-bound to show their talents for leadership and management. They strutted through the school and around the campus exerting pressure on the lower grades. Their authority was so new that occasionally if they pressed a little too hard it had to be overlooked. After all, next term was coming, and it never hurt a sixth grader to have a play sister in the eighth grade, or a tenth-year student to be able to call a twelfth grader Bubba. So all was endured in a spirit of shared understanding. But the graduating classes themselves were the nobility. Like travelers with exotic destinations on their minds, the graduates were remarkably forgetful. They came to school without their books, or tablets or even pencils. Volunteers fell over themselves to secure replacements for the missing equipment. When accepted, the willing workers might or might not be thanked, and it was of no importance to the pregraduation rites. Even teachers were respectful of the now quiet and aging seniors, and tended to speak to them, if not as equals, as beings only slightly lower than themselves. After tests were returned and grades given, the student body, which acted like an extended family, knew who did well, who excelled, and what piteous ones had failed.

Unlike the white high school, Lafayette County Training School distinguished itself by having neither lawn, nor hedges, nor tennis court, nor climbing ivy. Its two buildings (main classrooms, the grade school and home economics) were set on a dirt hill with no fence to limit either its boundaries or those of bordering farms. There was a large expanse to the left of the school which was used alternately as a baseball diamond or a basketball court. Rusty hoops on the swaying poles represented the permanent recreational equipment, although bats and balls could be borrowed from the P. E. teacher if the borrower was qualified and if the diamond wasn't occupied.

Over this rocky area relieved by a few shady tall persimmon trees the graduating class walked. The girls often held hands and no longer bothered to speak to the lower students. There was a sadness about them, as if this old world was not their home and they were bound for higher ground. The boys, on the other hand, had become more friendly, more outgoing. A decided change from the closed attitude they projected while studying for finals. Now they seemed not ready to give up the old school, the familiar paths and classrooms. Only a small percentage would be continuing on to college—one of the South's A & M (agricultural and mechanical) schools, which trained Negro youths to be carpenters, farmers, handymen, masons, maids, cooks and baby nurses. Their future rode heavily on their shoulders, and blinded them to the collective joy that had pervaded the lives of the boys and girls in the grammar school graduating class.

Parents who could afford it had ordered new shoes and ready-made clothes for themselves from Sears and Roebuck or Montgomery Ward. They also engaged the best seamstresses to make the floating graduating dresses and to cut down secondhand pants which would be pressed to a military slickness for the important event.

Oh, it was important, all right. Whitefolks would attend the ceremony, and two or three would speak of God and home, and the Southern way of life, and Mrs. Parsons, the principal's wife, would play the graduation march while the lower-grade graduates paraded down the aisles and took their seats below the platform. The high school seniors would wait in empty classrooms to make their dramatic entrance.

In the Store I was the person of the moment. The birthday girl. The center. Bailey had graduated the year before, although to do so he had had to forfeit all pleasures to make up for his time lost in Baton Rouge.

My class was wearing butter-yellow piqué dresses, and Momma launched out on mine. She smocked the yoke into tiny crisscrossing puckers, then shirred the rest of the bodice. Her dark fingers ducked in and out of the lemony cloth as she embroidered raised daisies around the hem. Before she considered herself finished she had added a crocheted cuff on the puff sleeves, and a pointy crocheted collar.

I was going to be lovely. A walking model of all the various styles of fine hand sewing and it didn't worry me that I was only twelve years old and merely graduating from the eighth grade. Besides, many teachers in Arkansas Negro schools had only that diploma and were licensed to impart wisdom.

The days had become longer and more noticeable. The faded beige of former times had been replaced with strong and sure colors. I began to see my classmates' clothes, their skin tones, and the dust that waved off pussy willows. Clouds that lazed across the sky were objects of great concern to me. Their shiftier shapes might have held a message that in my new happiness and with a little bit of time I'd soon decipher. During that period I looked at the arch of heaven so religiously my neck kept a steady ache. I had taken to smiling more often, and my jaws hurt from the unaccustomed activity. Between the two physical sore spots, I suppose I could have been uncomfortable, but that was not the case. As a member of the winning team (the graduating class of 1940) I had outdistanced unpleasant sensations by miles. I was headed for the freedom of open fields.

Youth and social approval allied themselves with me and we trammeled memories of slights and insults. The wind of our swift passage remodeled my features. Lost tears were pounded to mud and then to dust. Years of withdrawal were brushed aside and left behind, as hanging ropes of parasitic moss.

My work alone had awarded me a top place and I was going to be one of the first called in the graduating ceremonies. On the classroom blackboard, as well as on the bulletin board in the auditorium, there were blue stars and white stars and red stars. No absences, no tardinesses, and my academic work was among the best of the year. I could say the preamble to the Constitution even faster than Bailey. We timed ourselves often: "WethepeopleoftheUnitedStatesinordertoformamoreperfectunion . . ." I had memorized the Presidents of the United States from Washington to Roosevelt in chronological as well as alphabetical order.

My hair pleased me too. Gradually the black mass had lengthened and thickened, so that it kept at last to its braided pattern, and I didn't have to yank my scalp off when I tried to comb it.

Louise and I had rehearsed the exercises until we tired out ourselves. Henry Reed was class valedictorian. He was a small, very black boy with hooded eyes, a long, broad nose and an oddly shaped head. I had admired him for years because each term he and I vied for the best grades in our class. Most often he bested me, but instead of being disappointed I was pleased that we shared top places between us. Like many Southern Black children, he lived with his grandmother, who was as strict as Momma and as kind as she knew how to be. He was courteous, respectful and soft-spoken to elders, but on the playground he chose to play the roughest games. I admired him. Anyone, I reckoned, sufficiently afraid or sufficiently dull could be polite. But to be able to operate at a top level with both adults and children was admirable.

His valedictory speech was entitled "To Be or Not to Be." The rigid tenth-grade teacher had helped him write it. He'd been working on the dramatic stresses for months.

The weeks until graduation were filled with heady activities. A group of small children were to be presented in a play about buttercups and daisies and bunny rabbits. They could be heard throughout the building practicing their hops and their little songs that sounded like silver bells. The older girls (non-graduates, of course) were assigned the task of making refreshments for the night's festivities. A tangy scent of ginger, cinnamon, nutmeg and chocolate wafted around the home economics building as the budding cooks made samples for themselves and their teachers.

In every corner of the workshop, axes and saws split fresh timber as the woodshop boys made sets and stage scenery. Only the graduates were left out of the general bustle. We were free to sit in the library at the back of the building or look in quite detachedly, naturally, on the measures being taken for our event.

Even the minister preached on graduation the Sunday before. His subject was, "Let your light so shine that men will see your good works and praise your Father, Who is in Heaven." Although the sermon was purported to be addressed to us, he used the occasion to speak to backsliders, gamblers and general ne'er-do-wells. But since he had called our names at the beginning of the service we were mollified.

Among Negroes the tradition was to give presents to children going only from one grade to another. How much more important this was when the person was graduating at the top of the class. Uncle Willie and Momma had sent away for a Mickey Mouse watch like Bailey's. Louise gave me four embroidered handkerchiefs. (I gave her three crocheted doilies.) Mrs. Sneed, the minister's wife, made me an underskirt to wear for graduation, and nearly every customer gave me a nickel or maybe even a dime with the instruction "Keep on moving to higher ground," or some such encouragement.

Amazingly the great day finally dawned and I was out of bed before I knew it. I threw open the back door to see it more clearly, but Momma said, "Sister, come away from that door and put your robe on."

I hoped the memory of that morning would never leave me. Sunlight was itself still young, and the day had none of the insistence maturity would bring it in a few hours. In my robe and barefoot in the backyard, under cover of going to see about my new beans, I gave myself up to the gentle warmth and thanked God that no matter what evil I had done in my life He had allowed me to live to see this day. Somewhere in my fatalism I had expected to die, accidentally, and never have the chance to walk up the stairs in the auditorium and gracefully receive my hard-earned diploma. Out of God's merciful bosom I had won reprieve.

Bailey came out in his robe and gave me a box wrapped in Christmas paper. He said he had saved his money for months to pay for it. It felt like a box of chocolates, but I knew Bailey wouldn't save money to buy candy when we had all we could want under our noses.

He was as proud of the gift as I. It was a soft-leather-bound copy of a collection of poems by Edgar Allan Poe, or, as Bailey and I called him, "Eap." I turned to "Annabel Lee" and we walked up and down the garden rows, the cool dirt between our toes, reciting the beautifully sad lines.

Momma made a Sunday breakfast although it was only Friday. After we finished the blessing, I opened my eyes to find the watch on my plate. It was a dream of a day. Everything went smoothly and to my credit I didn't have to be reminded or scolded for anything. Near evening I was too jittery to attend to chores, so Bailey volunteered to do all before his bath.

Days before, we had made a sign for the Store, and as we turned out the lights Momma hung the cardboard over the doorknob. It read clearly: CLOSED. GRADUATION.

My dress fitted perfectly and everyone said that I looked like a sunbeam in it. On the hill, going toward the school, Bailey walked behind with Uncle Willie, who muttered, "Go on, Ju." He wanted him to walk ahead with us because it embarrassed him to have to walk so slowly. Bailey said he'd let the ladies walk together, and the men would bring up the rear. We all laughed, nicely.

Little children dashed by out of the dark like fireflies. Their crepe-paper dresses and butterfly wings were not made for running and we heard more than one rip, dryly, and the regretful "uh uh" that followed.

The school blazed without gaiety. The windows seemed cold and unfriendly from the lower hill. A sense of ill-fated timing crept over me, and if Momma hadn't reached for my hand I would have drifted back to Bailey and Uncle Willie, and possibly beyond. She made a few slow jokes about my feet getting cold, and tugged me along to the now-strange building.

Around the front steps, assurance came back. There were my fellow "greats," the graduating class. Hair brushed back, legs oiled, new dresses and pressed pleats, fresh pocket handkerchiefs and little handbags, all homesewn. Oh, we were up to snuff, all right. I joined my comrades and didn't even see my family go in to find seats in the crowded auditorium.

The school band struck up a march and all classes filed in as had been rehearsed. We stood in front of our seats, as assigned, and on a signal from the choir director, we sat. No sooner had this been accomplished than the band started to play the national anthem. We rose again and sang the song, after which we recited the pledge of allegiance. We remained standing for a brief minute before the choir director and the principal signaled to us, rather desperately I thought, to take our seats. The command was so unusual that our carefully rehearsed and smooth-running machine was thrown off. For a full minute we fumbled for our chairs and bumped into each other awkwardly. Habits change or solidify under pressure, so in our state of nervous tension we had been ready to follow our usual assembly pattern: the American national anthem, then the pledge of allegiance, then the song every Black person I knew called the Negro National Anthem. All done in the same key, with the same passion and most often standing on the same foot.

Finding my seat at last, I was overcome with a presentiment of worse things to come. Something unrehearsed, unplanned, was going to happen, and we were going to be made to look bad. I distinctly remember being explicit in the choice of pronoun. It was "we," the graduating class, the unit, that concerned me then.

The principal welcomed "parents and friends" and asked the Baptist minister to lead us in prayer. His invocation was brief and punchy, and for a second I thought we were getting back on the high road to right action. When the principal came back to the dais, however, his voice had changed. Sounds always affected me profoundly and the principal's voice was one of my favorites. During assembly it melted and lowed weakly into the audience. It had not been in my plan to listen to him, but my curiosity was piqued and I straightened up to give him my attention.

He was talking about Booker T. Washington, our "late great leader," who said we can be as close as the fingers on the hand, etc. . . . Then he said a few vague things about friendship and the friendship of kindly people to those less fortunate than themselves. With that his voice nearly faded, thin, away. Like a river diminishing to a stream and then to a trickle. But he cleared his throat and said, "Our speaker tonight, who is also our friend, came from Texarkana to deliver the commencement address, but due to the irregularity of the train schedule, he's going to, as they say, 'speak and run.'" He said that we understood and wanted the man to know that we were most grateful for the time he was able to give us and then something about how we were willing always to adjust to another's program, and without more ado—"I give you Mr. Edward Donleavy."

Not one but two white men came through the door offstage. The shorter one walked to the speaker's platform, and the tall one moved over to the center seat and sat down. But that was our principal's seat, and already occupied. The dislodged gentleman bounced around for a long breath or two before the Baptist minister gave him his chair, then with more dignity than the situation deserved, the minister walked off the stage.

Donleavy looked at the audience once (on reflection, I'm sure that he wanted only to reassure himself that we were really there), adjusted his glasses and began to read from a sheaf of papers.

He was glad "to be here and to see the work going on just as it was in the other schools."

At the first "Amen" from the audience I willed the offender to immediate death by choking on the word. But Amens and Yes, sir's began to fall around the room like rain through a ragged umbrella.

He told us of the wonderful changes we children in Stamps had in store. The Central School (naturally, the white school was Central) had already been granted improvements that would be in use in the fall. A well-known artist was coming from Little Rock to teach art to them. They were going to have the newest microscopes and chemistry equipment for their laboratory. Mr. Donleavy didn't leave us long in the dark over who made these improvements available to Central High. Nor were we to be ignored in the general betterment scheme he had in mind.

He said that he had pointed out to people at a very high level that one of the first-line football tacklers at Arkansas Agricultural and Mechanical College had graduated from good old Lafayette County Training School. Here fewer Amen's were heard. Those few that did break through lay dully in the air with the heaviness of habit.

He went on to praise us. He went on to say how he had bragged that "one of the best basketball players at Fisk sank his first ball right here at Lafayette County Training School."

The white kids were going to have a chance to become Galileos and Madame Curies and Edisons and Gauguins, and our boys (the girls weren't even in on it) would try to be Jesse Owenses and Joe Louises.

Owens and the Brown Bomber were great heroes in our world, but what school official in the white-goddom of Little Rock had the right to decide that those two men must be our only heroes? Who decided that for Henry Reed to become a scientist he had to work like George Washington Carver, as a bootblack, to buy a lousy microscope? Bailey was obviously always going to be too small to be an athlete, so which concrete angel glued to what country seat had decided that if my brother wanted to become a lawyer he had to first pay penance for his skin by picking cotton and hoeing corn and studying correspondence books at night for twenty years?

The man's dead words fell like bricks around the auditorium and too many settled in my belly. Constrained by hard-learned manners I couldn't look behind me, but to my left and right the proud graduating class of 1940 had dropped their heads. Every girl in my row had found something new to do with her handkerchief. Some folded the tiny squares into love knots, some into triangles, but most were wadding them, then pressing them flat on their yellow laps.

On the dais, the ancient tragedy was being replayed. Professor Parsons sat, a sculptor's reject, rigid. His large, heavy body seemed devoid of will or willingness, and his eyes said he was no longer with us. The other teachers examined the flag (which was draped stage right) or their notes, or the windows which opened on our now-famous playing diamond.

Graduation, the hush-hush magic time of frills and gifts and congratulations and diplomas, was finished for me before my name was called. The accomplishment was nothing. The meticulous maps, drawn in three colors of ink, learning and spelling decasyllabic words, memorizing the whole of *The Rape of Lucrece*—it was for nothing. Donleavy had exposed us.

We were maids and farmers, handymen and washerwomen, and anything higher that we aspired to was farcical and presumptuous.

Then I wished that Gabriel Prosser and Nat Turner had killed all whitefolks in their beds and that Abraham Lincoln had been assassinated before the signing of the Emancipation Proclamation, and that Harriet Tubman had been killed by that blow on her head and Christopher Columbus had drowned in the *Santa María.*

It was awful to be Negro and have no control over my life. It was brutal to be young and already trained to sit quietly and listen to charges brought against my color with no chance of defense. We should all be dead. I thought I should like to see us all dead, one on top of the other. A pyramid of flesh with the whitefolks on the bottom, as the broad base, then the Indians with their silly tomahawks and teepees and wigwams and treaties, the Negroes with their mops and recipes and cotton sacks and spirituals sticking out of their mouths. The Dutch children should all stumble in their wooden shoes and break their necks. The French should choke to death on the Louisiana Purchase (1803) while silkworms ate all the Chinese with their stupid pigtails. As a species, we were an abomination. All of us.

Donleavy was running for election, and assured our parents that if he won we could count on having the only colored paved playing field in that part of Arkansas. Also—he never looked up to acknowledge the grunts of acceptance—also, we were bound to get some new equipment for the home economics building and the workshop.

He finished, and since there was no need to give any more than the most perfunctory thank-you's, he nodded to the men on the stage, and the tall white man who was never introduced joined him at the door. They left with the attitude that now they were off to something really important. (The graduation ceremonies at Lafayette County Training School had been a mere preliminary.)

The ugliness they left was palpable. An uninvited guest who wouldn't leave. The choir was summoned and sang a modern arrangement of "Onward, Christian Soldiers," with new words pertaining to graduates seeking their place in the world. But it didn't work. Elouise, the daughter of the Baptist minister, recited "Invictus," and I could have cried at the impertinence of "I am the master of my fate, I am the captain of my soul."

My name had lost its ring of familiarity and I had to be nudged to go and receive my diploma. All my preparations had fled. I neither marched up to the stage like a conquering Amazon, nor did I look in the audience for Bailey's nod of approval. Marguerite Johnson, I heard the name again, my honors were read, there were noises in the audience of appreciation, and I took my place on the stage as rehearsed.

I thought about colors I hated: ecru, puce, lavender, beige and black.

There was shuffling and rustling around me, then Henry Reed was giving his valedictory address, "To Be or Not to Be." Hadn't he heard the whitefolks? We couldn't *be*, so the question was a waste of time. Henry's voice came out clear and strong. I feared to look at him. Hadn't he got the message? There was no "nobler in the mind" for Negroes because the world didn't think we had minds, and they let us know it. "Outrageous fortune"? Now, that was a joke. When the ceremony was over I had to tell Henry Reed some things. That is, if I still cared. Not "rub," Henry, "erase." "Ah, there's the erase." Us.

Henry had been a good student in elocution. His voice rose on tides of promise and fell on waves of warnings. The English teacher had helped him to create a sermon winging through Hamlet's soliloquy. To be a man, a doer, a builder, a leader, or to be a tool, an unfunny joke, a crusher of funky toadstools. I marveled that Henry could go through with the speech as if we had a choice.

I had been listening and silently rebutting each sentence with my eyes closed; then there was a hush, which in an audience warns that something unplanned is happening. I looked up and saw Henry Reed, the conservative, the proper, the A student, turn his back to the audience and turn to us (the proud graduating class of 1940) and sing, nearly speaking,

> "Lift ev'ry voice and sing
> Till earth and heaven ring
> Ring with the harmonies of Liberty . . ."

It was the poem written by James Weldon Johnson. It was the music composed by J. Rosamond Johnson. It was the Negro national anthem. Out of habit we were singing it.

Our mothers and fathers stood in the dark hall and joined the hymn of encouragement. A kindergarten teacher led the small children onto the stage and the buttercups and daisies and bunny rabbits marked time and tried to follow:

"Stony the road we trod
Bitter the chastening rod
Felt in the days when hope, unborn, had died.
Yet with a steady beat
Have not our weary feet
Come to the place for which our fathers sighed?"

Every child I knew had learned that song with his ABC's and along with "Jesus Loves Me This I Know." But I personally had never heard it before. Never heard the words, despite the thousands of times I had sung them. Never thought they had anything to do with me.

On the other hand, the words of Patrick Henry had made such an impression on me that I had been able to stretch myself tall and trembling and say, "I know not what course others may take, but as for me, give me liberty or give me death."

And now I heard, really for the first time:

"We have come over a way that with tears has been watered,
We have come, treading our path through the blood of the slaughtered."

While echoes of the song shivered in the air, Henry Reed bowed his head, said "Thank you," and returned to his place in the line. The tears that slipped down many faces were not wiped away in shame.

We were on top again. As always, again. We survived. The depths had been icy and dark, but now a bright sun spoke to our souls. I was no longer simply a member of the proud graduating class of 1940; I was a proud member of the wonderful, beautiful Negro race.

Oh, Black known and unknown poets, how often have your auctioned pains sustained us? Who will compute the lonely nights made less lonely by your songs, or by the empty pots made less tragic by your tales?

If we were a people much given to revealing secrets, we might raise monuments and sacrifice to the memories of our poets, but slavery cured us of that weakness. It may be enough, however, to have it said that we survive in exact relationship to the dedication of our poets (include preachers, musicians and blues singers).

Postreading Writing Assignments

Option 1: Discuss the changes you observe in Angelou's attitude as Donleavy begins speaking. What is his prophecy for her future? Does she believe this prophecy? Write a response in which you explore Donleavy's predictions for the future of the Lafayette graduates and the ways in which his speech affects Angelou and the others at the ceremony.

Option 2: Valedictorian Henry Reed is able to restore some sense of self-worth to the graduates and their families. Write a response in which you explore and analyze Reed's speech. What is Reed predicting for the graduates of Lafayette County Training School, and why do they and the audience react the way that they do?

Option 3: Discuss the differences between Lafayette County Training School and the "white" schools. Are the differences significant? Explore what these differences are and what they reflect about society's attitudes toward students and communities that are not part of the dominant culture. Do you think these attitudes still exist in our communities?

Option 4: Compare your own graduation from middle school or high school with Angelou's graduation. Do you remember events as clearly as she does? Was there someone from your school or family who played a role similar to that of either Donleavy or Henry Reed?

Extended Writing Assignments

Option 5:

> Unlike the white high school, Lafayette County Training School distinguished itself by having neither lawn, nor hedges, nor tennis court, nor climbing ivy. Its two buildings (main classrooms, the grade school and home economics) were set on a dirt hill with no fence to limit either its boundaries or those of bordering farms.
>
> (page 107)

The expectations of others can be powerful. Most of us, at one time or another, have been faced with the low expectations of others. Write an essay in which you examine the role of others' expectations in your own academic life. Who has or has had preconceived notions of what you can or cannot achieve: parents, teachers, community members, society, yourself? Use Angelou's essay as a way to frame the discussion of your experiences. How did reading Angelou's story give you a new way to talk about your experiences?

Option 6: Explore Angelou's essay in light of the title of her autobiography: *I Know Why the Caged Bird Sings*. In what ways is Angelou (and the other graduates) like a caged bird? What is Henry Reed's role, and what might you say about him? Here, you are examining the metaphor of a "caged bird." Which individuals do you see as being caged birds in this essay? Write an essay in which you explore the meaning of Angelou's title, the role of the caged bird metaphor, and its significance in "Graduation."

Forging Connections

Option 7: Read or reread Lynn Smith's "Minorities: Alienation and Failure in Academia" in light of Angelou's text. What is each writer saying here about the role of society and society's expectations? From the two readings, what problems do you see occurring when a society imposes limits on certain groups of students, telling them what they can and cannot achieve? Write an essay in which you examine the different kinds of "tracking," placement, and imposed limitations Angelou and Smith discuss: it would be beneficial to your project to include a discussion of one specific moment from your own education, a moment when you have been tracked or limited in some way.

Gloria Anzaldúa

HOW TO TAME A WILD TONGUE

Gloria Anzaldúa defines herself as a "Chicano tejana patlache poet and dyke-feminist" from the Rio Grande Valley of south Texas. Her book Borderlands/La Frontera: The New Mestiza *(Aunt Lute Books, 1987), which combines Spanish and English, poetry, memoir, and historical analysis, was chosen as one of the best books of 1987 by* Literary Journal. *She received the Lesbian Rights Award in 1991 and the Sappho Award of Distinction in 1992.*

Prereading Journal Questions

1. Respond to Anzaldúa's headnote. What are you expecting from her essay?
2. Consider the title of Anzaldúa's essay. What do you think a "wild tongue" is, and how might one go about taming it?

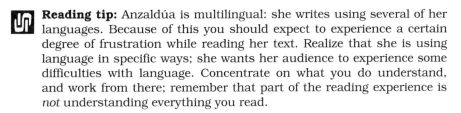

Reading tip: Anzaldúa is multilingual: she writes using several of her languages. Because of this you should expect to experience a certain degree of frustration while reading her text. Realize that she is using language in specific ways; she wants her audience to experience some difficulties with language. Concentrate on what you do understand, and work from there; remember that part of the reading experience is *not* understanding everything you read.

"We're going to have to control your tongue," the dentist says, pulling out all the metal from my mouth. Silver bits plop and tinkle into the basin. My mouth is a motherlode.

The dentist is cleaning out my roots. I get a whiff of the stench when I gasp. "I can't cap that tooth yet, you're still draining," he says.

"We're going to have to do something about your tongue," I hear the anger rising in his voice. My tongue keeps pushing out the wads of cotton, pushing back the drills, the long thin needles. "I've never seen anything as strong or as stubborn," he says. And I think, how do you tame a wild tongue, train it to be quiet, how do you bridle and saddle it? How do you make it lie down?

> *Who is to say that robbing a people of its language is less violent than war?*
>
> —Ray Gwyn Smith[1]

[1]Ray Gwyn Smith, *Moorland Is Cold Country,* unpublished book.

I remember being caught speaking Spanish at recess—that was good for three licks on the knuckles with a sharp ruler. I remember being sent to the corner of the classroom for "talking back" to the Anglo teacher when all I was trying to do was tell her how to pronounce my name. "If you want to be American, speak 'American.' If you don't like it, go back to Mexico where you belong."

"I want you to speak English. *Pa' hallar buen trabajo tienes que saber hablar el inglés bien. Qué vale toda tu educación si todavía hablas inglés con un* 'accent,'" my mother would say, mortified that I spoke English like a Mexican. At Pan American University, I, and all Chicano students were required to take two speech classes. Their purpose: to get rid of our accents.

Attacks on one's form of expression with the intent to censor are a violation of the First Amendment. *El Anglo con cara de inocente nos arrancó la lengua.* Wild tongues can't be tamed, they can only be cut out.

Overcoming the Tradition of Silence

Ahogadas, escupimos el oscuro.
Peleando con nuestra propia sombra
el silencio nos sepulta.

En boca cerrada no entran moscas. "Flies don't enter a closed mouth" is a saying I kept hearing when I was a child. *Ser habladora* was to be a gossip and a liar, to talk too much. *Muchachitas bien criadas,* well-bred girls don't answer back. *Es una falta de respeto* to talk back to one's mother or father. I remember one of the sins I'd recite to the priest in the confession box the few times I went to confession: talking back to my mother, *hablar pa' 'tras, repelar. Hocicona, repelona, chismosa,* having a big mouth, questioning, carrying tales are all signs of being *mal criada.* In my culture they are all words that are derogatory if applied to women—I've never heard them applied to men.

The first time I heard two women, a Puerto Rican and a Cuban, say the word *"nosotras,"* I was shocked. I had not known the word existed. Chicanas use *nosotros* whether we're male or female. We are robbed of our female being by the masculine plural. Language is a male discourse.

And our tongues have become
dry the wilderness has
dried out our tongues and
we have forgotten speech.

—Irena Klepfisz[2]

Even our own people, other Spanish speakers *nos quieren poner candados en la boca.* They would hold us back with their bag of *reglas de academia.*

Oyé como ladra: el lenguaje de la frontera

Quien tiene boca se equivoça.

—Mexican saying

"*Pocho,* cultural traitor, you're speaking the oppressor's language by speaking English, you're ruining the Spanish language," I have been accused by various Latinos and Latinas. Chicano Spanish is considered by the purist and by most Latinos deficient, a mutilation of Spanish.

But Chicano Spanish is a border tongue which developed naturally. Change, *evolución, enriquecimiento de palabras nuevas por invención o adopción* have created variants of Chicano Spanish, *un nuevo lenguaje. Un lenguaje que corresponde a un modo de vivir.* Chicano Spanish is not incorrect, it is a living language.

For a people who are neither Spanish nor live in a country in which Spanish is the first language; for a people who live in a country in which English is the reigning tongue but who are not Anglo; for a people who cannot entirely identify with either standard (formal, Castillian) Spanish nor standard English, what recourse is left to them but to create their own language? A language which they can connect their identity to, one capable of communicating the realities and values true to themselves—a language with terms that

[2]Irena Klepfisz, "*Di rayze aheym*/The Journey Home," in *The Tribe of Dina: A Jewish Women's Anthology,* eds. Melanie Kaye/Kantrowitz, and Irena Klepfisz (Montpelier, VT: Sinister Wisdom Books, 1986), p. 49.

are neither *español ni inglés,* but both. We speak a patois, a forked tongue, a variation of two languages.

Chicano Spanish sprang out of the Chicanos' need to identify ourselves as a distinct people. We needed a language with which we could communicate with ourselves, a secret language. For some of us, language is a homeland closer than the Southwest—for many Chicanos today live in the Midwest and the East. And because we are a complex, heterogeneous people, we speak many languages. Some of the languages we speak are:

1. Standard English
2. Working class and slang English
3. Standard Spanish
4. Standard Mexican Spanish
5. North Mexican Spanish dialect
6. Chicano Spanish (Texas, New Mexico, Arizona and California have regional variations)
7. Tex-Mex
8. *Pachuco* (called caló)

My "home" tongues are the languages I speak with my sister and brothers, with my friends. They are the last five listed, with 6 and 7 being closest to my heart. From school, the media and job situations, I've picked up standard and working class English. From Mamagrande Locha and from reading Spanish and Mexican literature, I've picked up Standard Spanish and Standard-Mexican Spanish. From *los recién llegados,* Mexican immigrants, and *braceros,* I learned the North Mexican dialect. With Mexicans I'll try to speak either Standard Mexican Spanish or the North Mexican dialect. From my parents and Chicanos living in the Valley, I picked up Chicano Texas Spanish, and I speak it with my mom, younger brother (who married a Mexican and who rarely mixes Spanish with English), aunts and older relatives.

With Chicanas from *Nuevo México* or *Arizona* I will speak Chicano Spanish a little, but often they don't understand what I'm saying. With most California Chicanas I speak entirely in English (unless I forget). When I first moved to San Francisco, I'd rattle off something in Spanish, unintentionally embarrassing them. Often it is only with another Chicana *tejana* that I can talk freely.

Words distorted by English are known as anglicisms or *pochismos.* The *pocho* is an anglicized Mexican or American of Mexican origin who speaks Spanish with an accent characteristic of North Americans and who distorts and reconstructs the language according to the influence of English.[3] Tex-Mex, or Spanglish, comes most naturally to me. I may switch back and forth from English to Spanish in the same sentence or in the same word. With my sister and my brother Nune and with Chicano *tejano* contemporaries I speak Tex-Mex.

From kids and people my own age I picked up *Pachuco. Pachuco* (the language of the zoot suiters) is a language of rebellion, both against Standard Spanish and Standard English. It is a secret language. Adults of the culture and outsiders cannot understand it. It is made up of slang words from both English and Spanish. *Ruca* means girl or woman, *vato* means guy or dude, *chale* means no, *simón* means yes, *churro* is sure, talk is *periquiar, pigionear* means petting, *que gacho* means how nerdy, *ponte águila* means watch out, death is called *la pelona.* Through lack of practice and not having others who can speak it, I've lost most of the *Pachuco* tongue.

Chicanos, after 250 years of Spanish/Anglo colonization, have developed significant differences in the Spanish we speak. We collapse two adjacent vowels into a single syllable and sometimes shift the stress in certain words such as *maíz/maiz, cohete/cuete.* We leave out certain consonants when they appear between vowels: *lado/lao, mojado/mojao.* Chicanos from South Texas pronounce *f* as *j* as in *jue (fue).* Chicanos use "archaisms," words that are no longer in the Spanish language, words that have been evolved out. We say *semos, truje, haiga, ansina,* and *naiden.* We retain the "archaic" *j,* as in *jalar,* that derives from an earlier *h* (the French *halar* or the Germanic *halon* which was lost to standard Spanish in the 16th century), but which is still found in several regional dialects such as the one spoken in South Texas. (Due to geography, Chicanos from the Valley of South Texas were cut off linguistically from other Spanish speakers. We tend to use words that the Spaniards brought over from Medieval Spain. The majority of the Spanish colonizers in Mexico and the Southwest came from Extremadura—Hernán Cortés was one of them—and Andalucía. Andalucians pronounce *ll* like a *y,* and their *d's* tend to be absorbed by adjacent vowels: *tirado* becomes *tirao.* They brought *el lenguaje popular, dialectos y regionalismos.*)[4]

[3]R. C. Ortega, *Dialectologia Del Barrio,* trans. Hortencia S. Alwan (Los Angeles: R. C. Ortega Publisher & Bookseller, 1977), p. 132.

[4]Eduardo Hernandéz-Chávez, Anderew D. Cohen, and Anthony F. Beltramo, *El Lenguaje de los Chicanos: Regional and Social Characteristics of Language Used by Mexican Americanas* (Arlington, VA: Center for Applied Linguistics, 1975), p. 39.

Chicanos and other Spanish speakers also shift *ll* to *y* and *z* to *s*.[5] We leave out initial syllables, saying *tar* for *estar*, *toy* for *estoy*, *hora* for *ahora* (*cubanos* and *puertorriqueños* also leave out initial letters of some words). We also leave out the final syllable such as *pa* for *para*. The intervocalic *y*, the *ll* as in *tortilla*, *ella*, *botella* gets replaced by *tortia* or *tortiya*, *ea*, *botea*. We add an additional syllable at the beginning of certain words: *atocar* for *tocar*, *agastar* for *gastar*. Sometimes we'll say *lavaste las vacijas*, other times *lavates* (substituting the *ates* verb endings for the *aste*).

We use anglicisms, words borrowed from English: *bola* from ball, *carpeta* from carpet, *máchina de lavar* (instead of *lavadora*) from washing machine. Tex-Mex argot, created by adding a Spanish sound at the beginning or end of an English word such as *cookiar* for cook, *watchar* for watch, *parkiar* for park, and *rapiar* for rape, is the result of the pressures on Spanish speakers to adapt to English.

We don't use the word *vosotros/as* or its accompanying verb form. We don't say *claro* (to mean yes), *imagínate*, or *me emociona*, unless we picked up Spanish from Latinas, out of a book, or in a classroom. Other Spanish-speaking groups are going through the same, or similar, development in their Spanish.

Linguistic Terrorism

> Deslenguadas. Somos los del español deficiente. *We are your linguistic nightmare, your linguistic aberration, your linguistic* mestisaje, *the subject of your* burla. *Because we speak with tongues of fire we are culturally crucified. Racially, culturally and linguistically* somos huérfanos—*we speak an orphan tongue.*

Chicanas who grew up speaking Chicano Spanish have internalized the belief that we speak poor Spanish. It is illegitimate, a bastard language. And because we internalize how our language has been used against us by the dominant culture, we use our language differences against each other.

Chicana feminists often skirt around each other with suspicion and hesitation. For the longest time I couldn't figure it out. Then it dawned on me. To be close to another Chicana is like looking into the mirror. We are afraid of what we'll see there. *Pena.* Shame. Low estimation of self. In childhood we are told that our language is

[5]Ibid., p. xvii.

wrong. Repeated attacks on our native tongue diminish our sense of self. The attacks continue throughout our lives.

Chicanas feel uncomfortable talking in Spanish to Latinas, afraid of their censure. Their language was not outlawed in their countries. They had a whole lifetime of being immersed in their native tongue; generations, centuries in which Spanish was a first language, taught in school, heard on radio and TV, and read in the newspaper.

If a person, Chicana or Latina, has a low estimation of my native tongue, she also has a low estimation of me. Often with *mexicanas y latinas* we'll speak English as a neutral language. Even among Chicanas we tend to speak English at parties or conferences. Yet, at the same time, we're afraid the other will think we're *agringadas* because we don't speak Chicano Spanish. We oppress each other trying to out-Chicano each other, vying to be the "real" Chicanas, to speak like Chicanos. There is no one Chicano language just as there is no one Chicano experience. A monolingual Chicana whose first language is English or Spanish is just as much a Chicana as one who speaks several variants of Spanish. A Chicana from Michigan or Chicago or Detroit is just as much a Chicana as one from the Southwest. Chicano Spanish is as diverse linguistically as it is regionally.

By the end of this century, Spanish speakers will comprise the biggest minority group in the U.S., a country where students in high schools and colleges are encouraged to take French classes because French is considered more "cultured." But for a language to remain alive it must be used.[6] By the end of this century English, and not Spanish, will be the mother tongue of most Chicanos and Latinos.

So, if you want to really hurt me, talk badly about my language. Ethnic identity is twin skin to linguistic identity—I am my language. Until I can take pride in my language, I cannot take pride in myself. Until I can accept as legitimate Chicano Texas Spanish, Tex-Mex and all the other languages I speak, I cannot accept the legitimacy of myself. Until I am free to write bilingually and to switch codes without having always to translate, while I still have to speak English or Spanish when I would rather speak Spanglish, and as long as I have to accommodate the English speakers rather than having them accommodate me, my tongue will be illegitimate.

I will no longer be made to feel ashamed of existing. I will have my voice: Indian, Spanish, white. I will have my serpent's tongue—my woman's voice, my sexual voice, my poet's voice. I will overcome the tradition of silence.

[6]Irena Klepfisz, "Secular Jewish Identity: Yidishkayt in America," in *The Tribe of Dina*, eds. Kaye/Kantrowitz and Klepfisz, p. 43.

My fingers
move sly against your palm
Like women everywhere, we speak in code . . .

—Melanie Kaye/Kantrowitz[7]

"Vistas," corridos, y comida: *My Native Tongue*

In the 1960s, I read my first Chicano novel. It was *City of Night* by John Rechy, a gay Texan, son of a Scottish father and a Mexican mother. For days I walked around in stunned amazement that a Chicano could write and could get published. When I read *I Am Joaquín*[8] I was surprised to see a bilingual book by a Chicano in print. When I saw poetry written in Tex-Mex for the first time, a feeling of pure joy flashed through me. I felt like we really existed as a people. In 1971, when I started teaching High School English to Chicano students, I tried to supplement the required texts with works by Chicanos, only to be reprimanded and forbidden to do so by the principal. He claimed that I was supposed to teach "American" and English literature. At the risk of being fired, I swore my students to secrecy and slipped in Chicano short stories, poems, a play. In graduate school, while working toward a Ph.D., I had to "argue" with one advisor after the other, semester after semester, before I was allowed to make Chicano literature an area of focus.

Even before I read books by Chicanos or Mexicans, it was the Mexican movies I saw at the drive-in—the Thursday night special of $1.00 a carload—that gave me a sense of belonging. *"Vámonos a las vistas,"* my mother would call out and we'd all—grandmother, brothers, sister and cousins—squeeze into the car. We'd wolf down cheese and bologna white bread sandwiches while watching Pedro Infante in melodramatic tearjerkers like *Nosotros los pobres*, the first "real" Mexican movie (that was not an imitation of European movies). I remember seeing *Cuando los hijos se van* and surmising that all Mexican movies played up the love a mother has for her children and what ungrateful sons and daughters suffer when they are not devoted to their mothers. I remember the singing-type "westerns" of

[7]Melanie Kay/Kantrowitz, "Sign," in *We Speak in Code: Poems and Other Writings* (Pittsburgh: Motheroot Publications, 1980), p. 85.

[8]Rodolfo Gonzales, *I Am Joaquín/Yo Soy Joaquín* (New York: Bantam Books, 1972). It was first published in 1967.

Jorge Negrete and Miquel Aceves Mejía. When watching Mexican movies, I felt a sense of homecoming as well as alienation. People who were to amount to something didn't go to Mexican movies, or *bailes,* or tune their radios to *bolero, rancherita,* and *corrido* music.

The whole time I was growing up, there was *norteño* music, sometimes called North Mexican border music, or Tex-Mex music, or Chicano music, or *cantina* (bar) music. I grew up listening to *conjuntos,* three- or four-piece bands made up of folk musicians playing guitar, *bajo sexto,* drums and button accordion, which Chicanos had borrowed from the German immigrants who had come to Central Texas and Mexico to farm and build breweries. In the Rio Grande Valley, Steve Jordan and Little Joe Hernández were popular, and Flaco Jiménez was the accordion king. The rhythms of Tex-Mex music are those of the polka, also adapted from the Germans, who in turn had borrowed the polka from the Czechs and Bohemians.

I remember the hot, sultry evenings when *corridos*—songs of love and death on the Texas-Mexican borderlands—reverberated out of cheap amplifiers from the local *cantinas* and wafted in through my bedroom window.

Corridos first became widely used along the South Texas/Mexican border during the early conflict between Chicanos and Anglos. The *corridos* are usually about Mexican heroes who do valiant deeds against the Anglo oppressors. Pancho Villa's song, *"La cucaracha,"* is the most famous one. *Corridos* of John F. Kennedy and his death are still very popular in the Valley. Older Chicanos remember Lydia Mendoza, one of the great border *corrido* singers who was called *la Gloria de Tejas.* Her "*El tango negro,*" sung during the Great Depression, made her a singer of the people. The everpresent *corridos* narrated one hundred years of border history, bringing news of events as well as entertaining. These folk musicians and folk songs are our chief cultural mythmakers, and they made our hard lives seem bearable.

I grew up feeling ambivalent about our music. Country-western and rock-and-roll had more status. In the 50s and 60s, for the slightly educated and *agringado* Chicanos, there existed a sense of shame at being caught listening to our music. Yet I couldn't stop my feet from thumping to the music, could not stop humming the words, nor hide from myself the exhilaration I felt when I heard it.

There are more subtle ways that we internalize identification, especially in the forms of images and emotions. For me food and certain smells are tied to my identity, to my homeland. Woodsmoke curling up to an immense blue sky; woodsmoke perfuming my grandmother's clothes, her skin. The stench of cow manure and the yellow patches on the ground; the crack of a .22 rifle and the reek of cordite. Homemade white cheese sizzling in a pan, melting inside a folded *tortilla.* My sister Hilda's hot, spicy *menudo, chile colorado* making it deep red, pieces of *panza* and hominy floating on top. My brother Carito barbecuing *fajitas* in the backyard. Even now and 3,000 miles away, I can see my mother spicing the ground beef, pork and venison with *chile.* My mouth salivates at the thought of the hot steaming *tamales* I would be eating if I were home.

Si le preguntas a mi mamá, "¿Qué eres?"

"Identity is the essential core of who we are as individuals, the conscious experience of the self inside."

—KAUFMAN[9]

Nosotros los Chicanos straddle the borderlands. On one side of us, we are constantly exposed to the Spanish of the Mexicans, on the other side we hear the Anglos' incessant clamoring so that we forget our language. Among ourselves we don't say *nosotros los americanos, o nosotros los españoles, o nosotros los hispanos.* We say *nosotros los mexicanos* (by *mexicanos* we do not mean citizens of Mexico; we do not mean a national identity, but a racial one). We distinguish between *mexicanos del otro lado* and *mexicanos de este lado.* Deep in our hearts we believe that being Mexican has nothing to do with which country one lives in. Being Mexican is a state of soul—not one of mind, not one of citizenship. Neither eagle nor serpent, but both. And like the ocean, neither animal respects borders.

Dime con quien andas y te diré quien eres.

(Tell me who your friends are and I'll tell you who you are.)

—MEXICAN SAYING

Si le preguntas a mi mamá, "¿Qué eres?" te dirá, "Soy mexicana." My brothers and sister say the same. I sometimes will answer *"soy mexicana"* and at others will say *"soy Chicana" o "soy tejana."* But I identified as *"Raza"* before I ever identified as *"mexicana"* or "Chicana."

[9]Gershen Kaufman, *Shame: the Power of Caring* (Cambridge: Schenkman Books, 1980), p. 68.

As a culture, we call ourselves Spanish when referring to ourselves as a linguistic group and when copping out. It is then that we forget our predominant Indian genes. We are 70–80% Indian.[10] We call ourselves Hispanic[11] or Spanish-American or Latin American or Latin when linking ourselves to other Spanish-speaking peoples of the Western hemisphere and when copping out. We call ourselves Mexican-American[12] to signify we are neither Mexican nor American, but more the noun "American" than the adjective "Mexican" (and when copping out).

Chicanos and other people of color suffer economically for not acculturating. This voluntary (yet forced) alienation makes for psychological conflict, a kind of dual identity—we don't identify with the Anglo-American cultural values and we don't totally identify with the Mexican cultural values. We are a synergy of two cultures with various degrees of Mexicanness or Angloness. I have so internalized the borderland conflict that sometimes I feel like one cancels out the other and we are zero, nothing, no one. *A veces no soy nada ni nadie. Pero hasta cuando no lo soy, lo soy.*

When not copping out, when we know we are more than nothing, we call ourselves Mexican, referring to race and ancestry; *mestizo* when affirming both our Indian and Spanish (but we hardly ever own our Black) ancestry; Chicano when referring to a politically aware people born and/or raised in the U.S.; *Raza* when referring to Chicanos; *tejanos* when we are Chicanos from Texas.

Chicanos did not know we were a people until 1965 when Cesar Chavez and the farmworkers united and *I Am Joaquín* was published and *La Raza Unida* party was formed in Texas. With that recognition, we became a distinct people. Something momentous happened to the Chicano soul—we became aware of our reality and acquired a name and a language (Chicano Spanish) that reflected that reality. Now that we had a name, some of the fragmented pieces began to fall together—who we were, what we were, how we had evolved. We began to get glimpses of what we might eventually become.

Yet the struggle of identities continues, the struggle of borders is our reality still. One day the inner struggle will cease and a true integration take place. In the meantime, *tenémos que hacer la lucha. ¿Quién está protegiendo los ranchos de mi gente? ¿Quién está*

[10]Hernandéz-Chávez, *El Lenguaje de los Chicanos*, pp. 88–90.

[11]"Hispanic" is derived from *Hispanis* (*España*, a name given to the Iberian Peninsula in ancient times when it was a part of the Roman Empire) and is a term designated by the U.S. government to make it easier to handle us on paper.

[12]The Treaty of Guadalupe Hidalgo created the Mexican-American in 1848.

tratando de cerrar la fisura entre la india y el blanco en nuestra sangre? El Chicano, sí, el Chicano que anda como un ladrón en su propia casa.

Los Chicanos, how patient we seem, how very patient. There is the quiet of the Indian about us. We know how to survive. When other races have given up their tongue, we've kept ours. We know what it is to live under the hammer blow of the dominant *norteamericano* culture. But more than we count the blows, we count the days the weeks the years the centuries the eons until the white laws and commerce and customs will rot in the deserts they've created, lie bleached. *Humildes* yet proud, *quietos* yet wild, *nosotros los mexicanos-Chicanos* will walk by the crumbling ashes as we go about our business. Stubborn, persevering impenetrable as stone, yet possessing a malleability that renders us unbreakable, we, the *mestizas* and *mestizos*, will remain.

Postreading Writing Assignments

Option 1: Do you agree or disagree with Anzaldúa's perspective regarding violence and language? Is the taking away of a person's language a "violent" act? Does Anzaldúa provide concrete examples of violence?

Option 2: Review your response to prereading question number one. In what ways was this essay different from what you expected? How were your predictions accurate? What biases shaped your response to the prereading question, and how did you work through your own biases? Were there sections of the text that were impossible for you to read with the grain?

Option 3: Explore the implications of the term "wild tongue." What does it mean to have a "wild tongue," and why would someone want to "tame" that? Use Anzaldúa's perspective, but use your experiences to support or challenge her assertions.

Extended Writing Assignments

Option 4: Write an essay in which you explore the issues of language that Anzaldúa addresses. First, summarize Anzaldúa's arguments. Read with and against the grain of her conclusions. Then use your own experiences to point out where you can support Anzaldúa's arguments and where you can challenge them.

Option 5: This essay often provokes a deep emotional response from readers. Discuss your reading of this text. Where did you feel yourself "reacting" to Anzaldúa's words. What do you want to say back to her? Write this essay in the form of a letter to Ms. Anzaldúa. Respond directly to certain aspects of her text. Use as many of your own "languages" or dialects as possible. Then assume Anzaldúa's persona, and write a response to your letter. How do you imagine she would respond to you?

Option 6: Students (and others) often find Anzaldúa's text difficult to understand. Even people who understand both English and Spanish have a hard time with pieces of her essay. Write a response in which you examine the way Anzaldúa uses language in this text. Why does she write using different languages or dialects? What does she hope to accomplish by doing this? Once you have evaluated why Anzaldúa writes in this way, evaluate the effectiveness of her approach.

Forging Connections

Option 7: Read or reread Richard Rodriguez's essay "Aria." Rodriguez presents a different view of learning English. For this assignment, write a dialogue between Rodriguez and Anzaldúa. What do you imagine these two writers would say to one another? You will be the writer/interviewer here. Set up a situation (a talk show or newspaper interview) in which you ask questions of both writers, and then develop their responses. You will guide the conversation. As each author responds, you need to imagine their ways of thinking and ways of speaking; explore how these two people would interact with each other and with you. As the writer, you should include your evaluations and conclusions.

Margaret Atwood

RAPE FANTASIES

Margaret Atwood was born in Ottawa, Ontario, Canada. She is a poet, a novelist, and an essayist, and her work has received critical acclaim in Canada, the United States, and Europe. Atwood's female characters are strong, and her writing demonstrates a sense of feminism. "Rape Fantasies" is one of her short stories.

Prereading Journal Questions

1. From the title "Rape Fantasies," what can you predict about the story?
2. What function do fantasies serve? Why do people have them? Do you think people spend time discussing their fantasies with others?

Reading tip: The narrator of this story does not state to whom she is talking. As you read, pay attention to the clues in the text that will help you figure out who is listening to the narrator, where the narrator is, and why she is talking about rape fantasies. Watch the little details, even as you get caught up in the story. The details, words, and phrases can lead you to a better understanding of the story.

The way they're going on about it in the magazines you'd think it was just invented, and not only that but it's something terrific, like a vaccine for cancer. They put it in capital letters on the front cover, and inside they have these questionnaires like the ones they used to have about whether you were a good enough wife or an endomorph or an ectomorph, remember that? with the scoring upside down on page 73, and then these numbered do-it-yourself dealies, you know? RAPE, TEN THINGS TO DO ABOUT IT, like it was ten new hairdos or something. I mean, what's so new about it?

So at work they all have to talk about it because no matter what magazine you open, there it is, staring you right between the eyes, and they're beginning to have it on the television, too. Personally I'd prefer a June Allyson movie anytime but they don't make them any more and they don't even have them that much on the Late Show. For instance, day before yesterday, that would be Wednesday, thank God it's Friday as they say, we were sitting around in the women's lunch room—the *lunch* room, I mean you'd think you could get some peace and quiet in there—and Chrissy closes up the magazine she's been reading and says, "How about it, girls, do you have rape fantasies?"

The four of us were having our game of bridge the way we always do, and I had a bare twelve points counting the singleton with not that much of a bid in anything. So I said one club, hoping Sondra would remember about the one club convention, because the time before when I used that she thought I really meant clubs and she bid us up to three, and all I had was four little ones with nothing higher than a six, and we went down two and on top of that we were vulnerable. She is not the world's best bridge player. I mean, neither am I but there's a limit.

Darlene passed but the damage was done, Sondra's head went round like it was on ball bearings and she said, "*What* fantasies?"

"Rape fantasies," Chrissy said. She's a receptionist and she looks like one; she's pretty but cool as a cucumber, like she's been painted all over with nail polish, if you know what I mean. Varnished. "It says here all women have rape fantasies."

"For Chrissake, I'm eating an egg sandwich," I said, "and I bid one club and Darlene passed."

"You mean, like some guy jumping you in an alley or something," Sondra said. She was eating her lunch, we all eat our lunches during the game, and she bit into a piece of that celery she always brings and started to chew away on it with this thoughtful expression in her eyes and I knew we might as well pack it in as far as the game was concerned.

"Yeah, sort of like that," Chrissy said. She was blushing a little, you could see it even under her makeup.

"I don't think you should go out alone at night," Darlene said, "you put yourself in a position," and I may have been mistaken but she was looking at me. She's the oldest, she's forty-one though you wouldn't know it and neither does she, but I looked it up in the employees' file. I like to guess a person's age and then look it up to see if I'm right. I let myself have an extra pack of cigarettes if I am, though I'm trying to cut down. I figure it's harmless as long as you don't tell. I mean, not everyone has access to that file, it's more or less confidential. But it's all right if I tell you, I don't expect you'll ever meet her, though you never know, it's a small world. Anyway.

"For *heaven's* sake, it's only *Toronto,*" Greta said. She worked in Detroit for three years and she never lets you forget it, it's like she thinks she's a war hero or something, we should all admire her just for the fact that she's still walking this earth, though she was really living in Windsor the whole time, she just worked in Detroit. Which for me doesn't really count. It's where you sleep, right?

"Well, do you?" Chrissy said. She was obviously trying to tell us about hers but she wasn't about to go first, she's cautious, that one.

"I certainly don't," Darlene said, and she wrinkled up her nose, like this, and I had to laugh. "I think it's disgusting." She's divorced, I read that in the file too, she never talks about it. It must've been years ago anyway. She got up and went over to the coffee machine and turned her back on us as though she wasn't going to have anything more to do with it.

"Well," Greta said. I could see it was going to be between her and Chrissy. They're both blondes, I don't mean that in a bitchy way but they do try to outdress each other. Greta would like to get out of Filing, she'd like to be a receptionist too so she could meet more people. You don't meet much of anyone in Filing except other people in Filing. Me, I don't mind it so much, I have outside interests.

"Well," Greta said, "I sometimes think about, you know my apartment? It's got this little balcony, I like to sit out there in the summer and I have a few plants out there. I never bother that much about locking the door to the balcony, it's one of those sliding glass ones, I'm on the eighteenth floor for heaven's sake, I've got a good view of the lake and the CN Tower and all. But I'm sitting around one night in my housecoat, watching TV with my shoes off, you know how you do, and I see this guy's feet, coming down past the window, and the next thing you know he's standing on the balcony, he's let himself down by a rope with a hook on the end of it from the floor above, that's the nineteenth, and before I can even get up off the chesterfield he's inside the apartment. He's all dressed in black with black gloves on"—I knew right away what show she got the black gloves off because I saw the same one—"and then he, well, you know."

"You know what?" Chrissy said, but Greta said, "And afterwards he tells me that he goes all over the outside of the apartment building like that, from one floor to another, with his rope and his hook . . . and then he goes out to the balcony and tosses his rope, and climbs up it and disappears."

"Just like Tarzan," I said, but nobody laughed.

"Is that all?" Chrissy said. "Don't you ever think about, well, I think about being in the bathtub, with no clothes on . . ."

"So who takes a bath in their clothes?" I said, you have to admit it's stupid when you come to think of it, but she just went on, ". . . with lots of bubbles, what I use is Vitabath, it's more expensive but it's so relaxing, and my hair pinned up, and the door opens and this fellow's standing there. . . ."

"How'd he get in?" Greta said.

"Oh, I don't know, through a window or something. Well, I can't very well get out of the bathtub, the bathroom's too small and besides he's blocking the doorway, so I just *lie* there, and he starts to very slowly take his own clothes off, and then he gets into the bathtub with me."

"Don't you scream or anything?" said Darlene. She'd come back with her cup of coffee, she was getting really interested. "I'd scream like bloody murder."

"Who'd hear me?" Chrissy said. "Besides, all the articles say it's better not to resist, that way you don't get hurt."

"Anyway you might get bubbles up your nose," I said, "from the deep breathing," and I swear all four of them looked at me like I was in bad taste, like I'd insulted the Virgin Mary or something. I mean, I don't see what's wrong with a little joke now and then. Life's too short, right?

"Listen," I said, "those aren't *rape* fantasies. I mean, you aren't getting *raped*, it's just some guy you haven't met formally who happens to be more attractive than Derek Cummins"—he's the Assistant Manager, he wears elevator shoes or at any rate they have these thick soles and he has this funny way of talking, we call him Derek Duck—"and you have a good time. Rape is when they've got a knife or something and you don't want to."

"So what about you, Estelle," Chrissy said, she was miffed because I laughed at her fantasy, she thought I was putting her down. Sondra was miffed too, by this time she'd finished her celery and she wanted to tell about hers, but she hadn't got in fast enough.

"All right, let me tell you one," I said. "I'm walking down this dark street at night and this fellow comes up and grabs my arm. Now it so happens that I have a plastic lemon in my purse, you know how it always says you should carry a plastic lemon in your purse? I don't really do it, I tried it once but the darn thing leaked all over my chequebook, but in this fantasy I have one, and I say to him, 'You're intending to rape me, right?' and he nods, so I open my purse to get the plastic lemon, and I can't find it! My purse is full of all this junk, Kleenex and cigarettes and my change purse and my lipstick and my driver's licence, you know the kind of stuff; so I ask him to hold out his hands, like this, and I pile all this junk into them and down at the bottom there's the plastic lemon, and I can't get the top off. So I hand it to him and he's very obliging, he twists the top off and hands it back to me, and I squirt him in the eye."

I hope you don't think that's too vicious. Come to think of it, it is a bit mean, especially when he was so polite and all.

"*That's* your rape fantasy?" Chrissy says. "I don't believe it."

"She's a card," Darlene says, she and I are the ones that've been here the longest and she never will forget the time I got drunk at the office party and insisted I was going to dance under the table instead of on top of it, I did a sort of Cossack number but then I hit my head on the bottom of the table—actually it was a desk—when I went to get up, and I knocked myself out cold. She's decided that's the mark of an original mind and she tells everyone new about it and I'm not sure that's fair. Though I did do it.

"I'm being totally honest," I say. I always am and they know it. There's no point in being anything else, is the way I look at it, and sooner or later the truth will out so you might as well not waste the time, right? "You should hear the one about the Easy-Off Oven Cleaner."

But that was the end of the lunch hour, with one bridge game shot to hell, and the next day we spent most of the time arguing over whether to start a new game or play out the hands we had left over from the day before, so Sondra never did get a chance to tell about her rape fantasy.

It started me thinking though, about my own rape fantasies. Maybe I'm abnormal or something, I mean I have fantasies about handsome strangers coming in through the window too, like Mr. Clean, I wish one would, please god somebody without flat feet and big sweat marks on his shirt, and over five feet five, believe me being tall is a handicap though it's getting better, tall guys are starting to like someone whose nose reaches higher than their belly button. But if you're being totally honest you can't count those as rape fantasies. In a real rape fantasy, what you should feel is this anxiety, like when you think about your apartment building catching on fire and whether you should use the elevator or the stairs or maybe just stick you head under a wet towel, and you try to remember everything you've read about what to do but you can't decide.

For instance, I'm walking along this dark street at night and this short, ugly fellow comes up and grabs my arm and not only is he ugly, you know, with a sort of puffy nothing face, like those fellows you have to talk to in the bank when your account's overdrawn—of course I don't mean they're all like that—but he's absolutely covered in pimples. So he gets me pinned against the wall, he's short but he's heavy, and he starts to undo himself and the zipper gets stuck. I mean, one of the most significant moments in a girl's life, it's almost like getting married or having a baby or something, and he sticks the zipper.

So I say, kind of disgusted, "Oh for Chrissake," and he starts to cry. He tells me he's never been able to get anything right in his entire life, and this is the last straw, he's going to go jump off a bridge.

"Look," I say, I feel so sorry for him, in my rape fantasies I always end up feeling sorry for the guy, I mean there has to be something *wrong* with them, if it was Clint Eastwood it'd be different but worse luck it never is. I was the kind of little girl who buried dead robins, know what I mean? It used to drive my mother nuts, she didn't like me touching them, because of the germs I guess. So I say, "Listen, I know how you feel. You really should do something about those pimples, if you got rid of them you'd be quite good looking, honest; then you wouldn't have to go around doing stuff like this. I had them myself once," I say, to comfort him, but in fact I did, and it ends up I give him the name of my old dermatologist, the one I had in high school, that was back in Leamington, except I used to go to St. Catharines for the dermatologist. I'm telling you, I was really lonely when I first came here; I thought it was going to be such a big adventure and all, but it's a lot harder to meet people in a city. But I guess it's different for a guy.

Or I'm lying in bed with this terrible cold, my face is all swollen up, my eyes are red and my nose is dripping like a leaky tap, and this fellow comes in through the window and *he* has a terrible cold too, it's a new kind of flu that's been going around. So he says, "I'b goig do rabe you"—I hope you don't mind me holding my nose like this but that's the way I imagine it—and he lets out this terrific sneeze, which slows him down a bit, also I'm no object of beauty myself, you'd have to be some kind of pervert to want to rape someone with a cold like mine, it'd be like raping a bottle of LePages mucilage the way my nose is running. He's looking wildly around the room, and I realize it's because he doesn't have a piece of Kleenex! "I'ds ride here," I say, and I pass him the Kleenex, god knows why he even bothered to get out of bed, you'd think if you were going to go around climbing in windows you'd wait till you were healthier, right? I mean, that takes a certain amount of energy. So I ask him why doesn't he let me fix him a NeoCitran and scotch, that's what I always take, you still have the cold but you don't feel it, so I do and we end up watching the Late Show together. I mean, they aren't all sex maniacs, the rest of the time they must lead a normal life. I figure they enjoy watching the Late Show just like anybody else.

I do have a scarier one though . . . where the fellow says he's hearing angel voices that're telling him he's got to kill me, you know, you read about things like that all the time in the papers. In this one I'm not in the apartment where I live now, I'm back in my mother's house in Leamington and the fellow's been hiding in the cellar, he grabs my arm when I go downstairs to get a jar of jam and he's got hold of the axe too, out of the garage, that one is really scary. I mean, what do you say to a nut like that?

So I start to shake but after a minute I get control of myself and I say, is he sure the angel voices have got the right person, because I hear the same angel voices and they've been telling me for some time that I'm going to give birth to the reincarnation of St. Anne who in turn has the Virgin Mary and right after that comes Jesus Christ and the end of the world, and he wouldn't want to interfere with that, would he? So he gets confused and listens some more, and then he asks for a sign, and I show him my vaccination mark, you can see it's sort of an odd-shaped one, it got infected because I scratched the top off, and that does it, he apologizes and climbs out the coal chute again, which is how he got in in the first place, and I say to myself there's some advantage in having been brought up a Catholic even though I haven't been to church since they changed the service into English, it just isn't the same, you might as well be a Protestant. I must write to Mother and tell her to nail up that coal chute, it always has bothered me. Funny, I couldn't tell you at all what this man looks like but I know exactly what kind of shoes he's wearing, because that's the last I see of him, his shoes going up the coal chute, and they're the old-fashioned kind that lace up the ankles, even though he's a young fellow. That's strange, isn't it?

Let me tell you though I really sweat until I see him safely out of there and I go upstairs right away and make myself a cup of tea. I don't think about that one much. My mother always said you shouldn't dwell on unpleasant things and I generally agree with that, I mean, dwelling on them doesn't make them go away. Though not dwelling on them doesn't make them go away either, when you come to think of it.

Sometimes I have these short ones where the fellow grabs my arm but I'm really a Kung-Fu expert, can you believe it, in real life I'm sure it would just be a conk on the head and that's that, like getting your tonsils out, you'd wake up and it would be all over except for the sore places, and you'd be lucky if your neck wasn't broken or something, I could never even hit the volleyball in gym and a volleyball is fairly large, you know?—and I just go *zap* with my fingers into his eyes and that's it, he falls over, or I flip him against a wall or something. But I could never really stick my fingers in anyone's eyes, could you? It would feel like hot jello and I don't even like cold jello, just thinking about it gives me the creeps. I feel a bit guilty about that one, I mean how would you like walking around knowing someone's been blinded for life because of you?

But maybe it's different for a guy.

The most touching one I have is when the fellow grabs my arm and I say, sad and kind of dignified, "You'd be raping a corpse." That pulls him up short and I explain that I've just found out I have leukaemia and the doctors have only given me a few months to live. That's why I'm out pacing the streets alone at night, I need to think, you know, come to terms with myself. I don't really have leukaemia but in the fantasy I do, I guess I chose that particular disease because a girl in my grade four class died of it, the whole class sent her flowers when she was in the hospital. I didn't understand then that she was going to die and I wanted to have leukaemia too so I could get flowers. Kids are funny, aren't they? Well, it turns out that he has leukaemia himself, and *he* only has a few months to live, that's why he's going around raping people, he's very bitter because he's so young and his life is being taken from him before he's really lived it. So we walk along gently under the street lights, it's spring and sort of misty, and we end up going for coffee, we're happy we've found the only other person in the world who can understand what we're going through, it's almost like fate, and after a while we just sort of look at each other and our hands touch, and he comes back with me and moves into my apartment and we spend our last months together before we die, we just sort of don't wake up in the morning, though I've never decided which one of us gets to die first. If it's him I have to go on and fantasize about the funeral, if it's me I don't have to worry about that, so it just about depends on how tired I am at the time. You may not believe this but sometimes I even start crying. I cry at the ends of movies, even the ones that aren't all that sad, so I guess it's the same thing. My mother's like that too.

The funny thing about these fantasies is that the man is always someone I don't know, and the statistics in the magazines, well, most of them anyway, they say it's often someone you do know, at least a little bit, like your boss or something—I mean, it wouldn't be *my* boss, he's over sixty and I'm sure he couldn't rape his way out of a paper bag, poor old thing, but it might be someone like Derek Duck, in his elevator shoes, perish the thought—or someone you just met, who invites you up for a drink, it's getting so you can hardly be sociable any more, and how are you supposed to meet people if you can't trust them even that basic amount? You can't spend your whole life in the Filing Department or cooped up in your own apartment with all the doors and windows locked and the shades down. I'm not what you would call a drinker but I like to go out now and then for a drink or two in a nice place, even if I am by myself, I'm with Women's Lib on that even though I can't agree with a lot of the other things they say. Like here for instance, the waiters all know me and if anyone, you know, bothers me. . . . I don't know why I'm telling you all this, except I think it helps you get to know a person, especially at first, hearing some of the things they think about. At work they call me the office worry wart, but it isn't so much like worrying, it's more like figuring out what you should do in an emergency, like I said before.

Anyway, another thing about it is that there's a lot of conversation, in fact I spend most of my time, in the fantasy that is, wondering what I'm going to say and what he's going to say, I think it would be better if you could get a conversation going. Like, how could a fellow do that to person he's just had a long conversation with, once you let them know you're human, you have a life too, I don't see how they could go ahead with it, right? I mean, I know it happens but I just don't understand it, that's the part I really don't understand.

Postreading Writing Assignments

Option 1: Where does this story take place? How do you know the location? What part of the text did you use to figure this out? To whom is the narrator talking? Why is she telling these stories? Use clues from the text to develop an understanding of the narrator's perspective.

Option 2: Are the narrator's stories really "rape fantasies"? Why, or why not? Use evidence from the text to support your conclusions.

Extended Writing Assignments

Option 3: The title "Rape Fantasies" is ambiguous. Fantasies can be realistic, frightening, or outrageous. Rape is a violent, destructive, terrifying, and dehumanizing crime; yet, Atwood's story takes an almost amusing approach to this subject. Write an essay that explores the underlying subject of "Rape Fantasies"; is it really about rape or about something else? This assignment asks you to do a "close reading" of Atwood's story. Explore all the possibilities; ask yourself, Is this a story about rape fantasies or other kinds of fantasies? What do each of the stories the narrator tells reveal? How are the stories similar? How are they different? What ties the stories together? Provide support from the story for your conclusions.

Option 4: We can read this story as an exploration into a person's mind. Fiction often explores human issues and does the following: tells us what it means to be human, explores the world around us, and gives us insight into ourselves. Write an essay in which you present this story as a text that reveals something about being human. What does this text expose about being human and about storytelling? Look closely at the stories the narrator tells, and explore the stories she repeats about her friends' fantasies. Consider what the stories, collectively, reveal about the human condition.

Forging Connections

Option 5: Read or reread Gabriel García Márquez's short story "The Handsomest Drowned Man in the World." What do both the Atwood and the Màrquez stories tell us about being "human"? Do the stories reflect certain needs or wants of humans? Use specific examples from each text to explore what each story reveals about the nature of humans.

Black Elk (as told through John G. Neihardt)

GRANDMOTHER'S LAND

Black Elk, a holy man of the Oglala Sioux, tells his story in Black Elk Speaks, *from which this selection is taken. Black Elk "was born in the Moon of the Popping Trees (December) on the Little Powder River in the Winter When the Four Crows Were Killed (1863)." In* Black Elk Speaks, *we hear Black Elk's words as they were told to John G. Neihardt (Flaming Rainbow). Neihardt first met Black Elk on the Pine Ridge Reservation in South Dakota, where he had gone in search of a medicine man. Black Elk's son acted as interpreter between the two men.*

Prereading Journal Questions

1. What do you know or believe to be true about Native Americans? Do you know anything about Sioux Indians—if so, what? How have you developed these beliefs, and what has influenced you?
2. Why might someone feel a need to tell his or her life story? What might that person want to accomplish by doing so?
3. What do you remember about being fifteen years old—what were your interests, hobbies, concerns? What was your family's situation? If you were going to write about your fifteenth year, what would you want people to know about you, and why?

Reading tip: There may be some allusions and/or references in this text with which you are unfamiliar: Crazy Horse, visions, the hoop and the holy tree, and so on. Look for ways to understand these references within the context of the text. Use what surrounds each term or reference to find meaning and comprehension. If there are references you would like to know more about, look them up after you read the entire text. (There are a number of texts written by Native Americans that would be helpful as you explore and interpret Black Elk's text. You might ask a reference librarian to assist you in locating specific information.) How does your understanding of the essay change as you understand more fully Black Elk's allusions?

At the end of the Moon of Falling Leaves (October), after they had killed Crazy Horse, the Wasichus told us we must move from where we were over to the Missouri River and live there at different agencies they had made for us. One big band started with Red Cloud, and we started with another big band under Spotted Tail. These two bands were about a day's travel apart.

Our people were all sad because Crazy Horse was dead, and now they were going to pen us up in little islands and make us be like Wasichus. So before we had gone very far, some of us broke away and started for the country where we used to be happy. We traveled fast, and the soldiers did not follow us. But when our little band came to the Powder River country, it was not like it used to be, and we were not ready for the winter. So we kept on traveling north, and we went fast, because we wanted to be with our relatives under Sitting Bull and Gall in Grandmother's Land.[1]

It was very cold before we reached Clay Creek where our relatives were; but they were glad to see us and took care of us. They had made plenty of meat, for there were many bison in that country; and it was a good winter. The soldiers could not come to kill us there.

I was fifteen years old that winter, and I thought much of my vision and wondered when my duty was to come; for the Grandfathers had shown me my people walking on the black road and how the nation's hoop would be broken and the flowering tree be withered, before I should bring the hoop together with the power that was given me, and make the holy tree to flower in the center and find the red road again. Part of this had happened already, and I wondered when my power would grow, so that the rest might be as I had seen it in my vision. But I could say nothing about this to anyone, because I was only a boy and people would think I was foolish and say: "What can you do if even Sitting Bull can do nothing?"

When the grasses appeared again we went bison hunting, and I was big enough now to hunt with the men. My uncle, Running Horse, and I were out together alone one day. I was riding a bay and leading my roan, which was very fast. My uncle was riding a roan and leading a brown horse. We came to Little River Creek and crossed it, and just then I began feeling queer and I knew something was going to happen. So I said to my uncle: "I have a queer feeling and I think something is going to happen soon. I will watch while you kill a bison and we will make quick work of it and go." He looked at me in a strange way awhile. Then he said "How" and started after a bison. There were several grazing in the valley. I held my horses and watched. When he had killed a fat cow, I went to help him butcher, but I held my horses while I was doing this, for I still had the queer feeling. Then I heard a voice that said: "Go at once and look!" I told Running Horse I would go to the top of the hill and see

[1] Canada.

what was there. So I rode up and I saw two Lakota hunters galloping after a bison across a valley toward some bluffs. Just after they went out of sight behind a bluff, my horse began to prick up his ears and look around and sniff the air. Then I heard some fast shooting over there, then many horses' hoofs. Then I saw a band of about fifty horsebacks coming out from behind the bluff where the two hunters had disappeared. They were Crows, and afterwards we learned that they had killed the two hunters.

So my uncle and I took as much meat as we could and rode fast back to our village and told the others.

This showed that my power was growing, and I was glad.

In the Moon of Making Fat (June), Sitting Bull and Gall had a sun dance at Forest Butte, and afterwards we went hunting again. A man by the name of Iron Tail was with me this time, and we were out alone. I killed a big fat bison cow and we were butchering, when a thunder storm was coming up. Then it began to pour rain, and I heard a voice in the clouds that said: "Make haste! Before the day is out something will happen!"

Of course when I heard this I was excited and told Iron Tail I had heard a voice in the clouds and that we must hurry up and go. We left everything but the fat of the cow, and fled. When we got to the camp of our little band, we were excited and told the people we must flee. So they broke camp and started. We came to Muddy Creek. It was still raining hard and we had trouble getting across because the horses sank in the mud. A part of us got across, but there was an old man with an old woman and a beautiful daughter whose pony-drag got stuck in the middle of the creek. Just then a big band of Crows came charging, and there were so many of them that we could not hold them off and we had to flee, shooting back at them as they came after us.

There was a man called Brave Wolf who did a very great deed there by the ford that day. He was close to the pony-drag of the two old people and the beautiful girl when it got stuck in the mud, so he jumped off his horse, which was a very fast bison-runner, and made the beautiful girl get on. Then he stood there by the two old people and fought until all three were killed. The girl got away on his fast horse. My cousin, Hard-to-Hit, did a brave deed too, and died. He charged back alone at a Crow who was shooting at a Lakota in a bush, and he was killed.

The voice in the clouds had told the truth, and it seemed that my power was growing stronger all the time.

When my cousin, Hard-to-Hit, was killed, it was my duty to protect his wife, so I did; and we got lost from our little party in the dark. It rained all night, and my cousin's wife cried so hard that I had to make her quit for fear some enemy might hear her and find us.

When we reached the big camp in the morning my relatives began mourning for my cousin, Hard-To-Hit. They would put their arms across each other's shoulders and wail. They did this all day long, and I had to do it too. I went around crying, "hownh, hownh," and saying over and over: "My cousin—he thought so much of me and I thought so much of him, and now he is dead. Hownh, hownh." I liked my cousin well enough, but I did not feel like crying all day. This was what I had to do, and it was hard work.

We stayed on Clay Creek in Grandmother's Land all that summer and the next winter when I was sixteen years old. That was a very cold winter. There were many blizzards, game was hard to find, and afterwhile the papa (dried meat) that we had made in the summer was all eaten. It looked as though we might starve to death if we did not find some game soon, and everybody was downhearted. Little hunting parties went out in different directions, but it is bad hunting in blizzard weather. My father and I started out alone leading our horses in the deep snow. When we got to Little River Creek we made a shelter with our bison robes against a bank of the stream and started a fire. That evening I saw a rabbit in a hollow tree, and when I chopped the tree down there were four rabbits in there. I killed them all, because the snow was so deep they could not get away. My father and I roasted them and we ate all four of them before we went to sleep, because it was hard walking in the snow and we had been empty a good while.

The wind went down that night and it was still and very cold. While I was lying there in a bison robe, a coyote began to howl not far off, and suddenly I knew it was saying something. It was not making words, but it said something plainer than words, and this was it: "Two-legged one, on the big ridge west of you there are bison; but first you shall see two more two-leggeds over there."

My father had dozed off, so I wakened him and said: "Father, I have heard a coyote say that there are bison on the big ridge west of us, and that we shall first see two people there. Let us get up early."

By this time my father had noticed that I had some kind of queer power, and he believed me. The wind came up again with the daylight, and we could see only a little way ahead when we started west in the morning. Before we came to the ridge, we saw two horses, dim in the blowing snow beside some bushes. They were huddled up with their tails to the wind and their heads hanging low. When we came closer, there was a bison robe shelter in the brush, and in it were an old man and a boy, very cold and hungry and discouraged. They were Lakotas and were glad to see us, but they were feeling weak, because they had been out two days and had seen nothing but snow. We camped there with them in the brush, and then we went up on the ridge afoot. There was much timber up there. We got behind the hill in a sheltered place and waited, but we could see nothing. While we were waiting, we talked about the people starving at home, and we were all sad. Now and then the snow haze would open up for a little bit and you could see quite a distance, then it would close again. While we were talking about our hungry people, suddenly the snow haze opened a little, and we saw a shaggy bull's head coming out of the blowing snow up the draw that led past us below. Then seven more appeared, and the snow haze came back and shut us in there. They could not see us, and they were drifting with the wind so that they could not smell us.

We four stood up and made vows to the four quarters of the world, saying, "Haho! haho!" Then we got our horses from the brush on the other side of the ridge and came around to the mouth of the draw where the bison would pass as they drifted with the wind.

The two old men were to shoot first and then we two boys would follow the others horseback. Soon we saw the bison coming. The old people crept up and shot, but they were so cold, and maybe excited, that they got only one bison. They cried "Hoka!" and we boys charged after the other bison. The snow was blowing hard in the wind that sucked down the draw, and when we came near them the bison were so excited that they backtracked and charged right past us bellowing. This broke the deep snow for our horses and it was easier to catch them. Suddenly I saw the bison I was chasing go out in a big flurry of snow, and I knew they had plunged into a snow-filled gulch, but it was too late to stop, and my horse plunged right in after them. There we were all together—four bison, my horse and I all floundering and kicking, but I managed to crawl out a little way. I had a repeating rifle that they gave me back at the camp, and I killed the four bison right there, but I had thrown my mittens away and the gun froze to my hands while I was shooting, so that I had to tear the skin to get it loose.

When I went back to the others, the other boy had killed three, so we had eight bison scattered around there in the snow. It was still morning, but it took till nearly dark for my father and the other old man to do the butchering. I could not help, because my hands were frozen. We finally got the meat all piled up in one place, and then we made a camp in a fine shelter behind a big rock with brush all around it and plenty of wood. We had a big fire, and we tied our tanned robes on our horses and fed them plenty of cottonwood bark from the woods by the stream. The raw robes we used for the shelter. Then we had a big feast and we sang and were very happy.

The wind went down and it grew very cold, so we had to keep the fire going all night. During the night I heard a whimpering outside the shelter, and when I looked, there was a party of porcupines huddled up as close as they thought they dared to be, and they were crying because they were so cold. We did not chase them away, because we felt sorry for them.

We started afoot for camp next day with as much meat loaded on the horses as they could carry. The rest of it we cached by a big tree where it would be easy to find. We traveled all that day very slowly because the snow was deep, and all the while it seemed to be growing colder. At about sundown of the second day we reached camp, and the people were glad to see us with all that meat. Some other men went back later to bring in the meat we had cached.

The morning after we reached home I went out to look for our horses that were in a draw where there was cottonwood, and five of them had frozen to death. The cold was very bad after the wind stopped blowing.

We began to feel homesick for our own country where we used to be happy. The old people talked much about it and the good days before the trouble came. Sometimes I felt like crying when they did that.

Postreading Writing Assignments

Option 1: How are you reading the idea of Black Elk's "power"? He mentions that his power is growing—what is the source and meaning of this power?

Option 2: In what historical context are you reading "Grandmother's Land"? What do you know about the history surrounding this text? Which references did you investigate? Which references were difficult for you to understand in context?

Option 3: Black Elk is talking here through an interpreter. What happens when we read material that has been filtered through many voices? Whose voices are we hearing here: that of Black Elk; of his son, who acted as interpreter; of John Neihardt; or of Neihardt's daughter, who kept a written record of all conversations? Is it important to know that Black Elk is speaking through his son? Why, or why not?

Extended Writing Assignments

Option 4: Black Elk told John Neihardt during one of his visits, "There is so much to teach you. What I know was given to me for men and it is true and it is beautiful. Soon I shall be under the grass and it will be lost. You were sent to save it, and you must come back so that I can teach you." In telling one's story, choosing which stories to include or exclude is crucial. As you read "Grandmother's Land," one chapter in Black Elk's life, what is it that Black Elk wanted "men" [people] to know? In your essay, examine the significance of the incidents he chooses to tell and of the moments he picked to tell about. What is here that Black Elk did not want to see buried with him? What did he believe his audience/readers needed to hear?

Option 5: Choose a moment from your life that you feel is true and beautiful—a piece of your life that you do not want to be lost when you are "under the grass." Choose your moment carefully; use Black Elk's text as a frame for your own story. Look to his references, what he helps his readers to understand and what we must try to understand on our own. Consider what you want your audience to know about you, your family, the moment in history you are describing, and why your story is one worth reading.

Forging Connections

Option 6: Read or reread one of the other autobiographies included in this text (for example, Angelou, Douglass, hooks, Anzaldúa, Mairs, Rodriguez) Read each text carefully, looking at the different ways in which these two writers tell stories about themselves. Does the other writer whom you choose to discuss tell about a moment in her or his life that is "true and beautiful," or does that author write about a moment that we might not see as "beautiful"? Why, then, did the author choose to tell us this story? In writing your essay, analyze the moments each writer chooses to share, interpret the significance of these moments, and explore the different ways in which each writer communicates with us—the audience.

Michael Dorris

THE BROKEN CORD

Michael Dorris, in his book The Broken Cord, *from which this selection is taken, explores his personal and professional interest in Fetal Alcohol Syndrome (FAS). Dorris, who is of Modoc descent, is particularly interested in the effects of FAS among American Indians.* The Broken Cord, *which was made into a television movie, portrayed the struggles of Dorris's adopted son Adam, who suffered from FAS. The author's death in 1997 at age fifty-two was a shock to those who knew and respected him.*

Prereading Journal Questions

1. Is there any reason why pregnant women should not drink alcohol? Why, or why not? How did you come to your conclusion?
2. If pregnant women engage in activity that is harmful to their unborn child, does society have the right or the moral obligation to prevent those women from engaging in such activity, perhaps by supervising or even jailing the women?
3. Why might FAS be a significant issue among Native Americans?

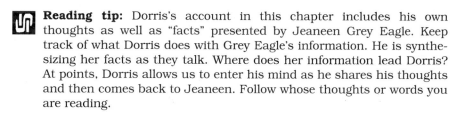

Reading tip: Dorris's account in this chapter includes his own thoughts as well as "facts" presented by Jeaneen Grey Eagle. Keep track of what Dorris does with Grey Eagle's information. He is synthesizing her facts as they talk. Where does her information lead Dorris? At points, Dorris allows us to enter his mind as he shares his thoughts and then comes back to Jeaneen. Follow whose thoughts or words you are reading.

Early on a September morning in 1985, I left the Rapid City airport in a rented tan Citation. It was chilly, drizzling, foggy. The recent rains had made the sagebrush grow tall along the side of the road. Here and there were glistening catches of light where water had collected in potholes. There was an unfinished ambience to the landscape—like a construction site without the construction. Crops of sunflowers were rolled in huge bales to dry in the wind. Two flocks of wild turkeys, each an even dozen, wandered by the side of a gully, and a small herd of antelope, tails white and erect, watched from a swell. I followed the procession of telephone poles that linked the Pine Ridge Reservation to the outside world and tuned in KILI-FM, All-Indian radio, to hear traditional honor songs, intermixed with Elvis Presley tunes, for a twenty-year-old boy, yesterday's suicide.

There was no marker to indicate the reservation boundary, but the road changed from the smooth surface maintained within the Badlands National Monument. The ground on either side was a neutral color like snow, like sand. I had an eleven o'clock appointment with Jeaneen Grey Eagle, director of Project Recovery, the drug and alcohol rehabilitation effort officially sanctioned by the tribal council. I located the office in the Pine Ridge village, on the government buildings' street angling north from the four-way stop at the center of town.

Jeaneen was young, attractive, harried, angry. The eyes behind her glasses were intelligent, measuring, deciding whether or not she would have patience with my questions. Her long black hair was pulled back from her forehead with a beaded clip. She wore a Navajo turquoise necklace, and was dressed in sandals and an electric blue karate suit. She had grown up on the reservation, and after a time away for higher education, she returned to marry Robert Grey Eagle, a University of New Mexico–trained lawyer, now the head judge of the tribal court. As a couple they practiced a curious amalgam of the traditional and the modern: they took sweat baths for spiritual renewal, and Robert had participated in the sun dance, but on another occasion, while attending a South Dakota State convention, Jeaneen found herself snowed in for several days at the Rapid City Holiday Inn with the rock group Quiet Riot and had thoroughly enjoyed the experience.

Jeaneen was praised by everyone to whom I had spoken about fetal alcohol syndrome. "She's the person who knows the realities," I had heard often from sociologists, psychologists, public health service doctors. "She's on the front lines, the person in the thick of the problem. She's smart, she's tough-minded, and she tells the truth." Now I could see what the people I had contacted had meant. Jeaneen was a woman at the center of a crisis. I turned on my tape recorder, tossed out an opening question, and she took over the conversation for three hours.

In Jeaneen's description, fetal alcohol syndrome lost all vestige of academic jargon, all cool distance. It was lethal, on the increase, the more dangerous because it was both commonplace and preventable. Jeaneen's was not an analysis composed of fine distinctions, of cautious calibration, but rather a pastiche of broad strokes, the kind of identification made at the scene of an accident when a quick take is the only hope of saving lives. She was a different kind of expert than I had previously met in FAS readings and lectures; on the subject of maternal drinking she was a zealot, battle-fatigued, impatient with ambiguity; she was not without compassion for chemically dependent women, but she reserved her sympathy for their victims.

I listened to her with the relief that arises from lifted isolation, with the attitude Cassandra might have had if just one other seer had concurred when she foretold the destruction of Troy. Jeaneen's perspective on FAS was no more gentle, no less dire, than my own—on the contrary, in that it was more informed, hers was much worse, confirming and reflecting my most hyperbolic fears—but in her I quickly sensed a strong ally who wore no blinders. Jeaneen must have felt a hint of the same thing. The interview gradually evolved into a conversation, and the conversation into the first foundation of a comradeship.

"People think that I'm Chicken Little saying the sky is falling," she said. "They don't seem to understand the far-reaching consequences of this. They are conditioned to live day to day. I don't know if that comes from having a hard time financially or what the reasons are. I wish there was some way to try to talk to people about long-term effects that this is going to have. How we're breeding a society of people who are not capable of living even in *this* world, let alone the other world, leaving the reservation."

"I don't think you're Chicken Little," I said. "FAS is the most destructive thing to hit Indians since the European diseases five hundred years ago."

Jeaneen agreed and regretted that she lacked the funds to implement a more constructive program.

"I would open up a women's center," she said energetically. "Take in some pregnant women and provide treatment for them. And also have a special care center for FAS children. I think we need a clinic just for those children alone, where experts would work with them at a medical level and at an emotional level as well as at an educational level. FAS children do not have the capability of living within this society. The ones I have seen are so hyperactive—we have them bouncing off the walls down here, tearing the walls apart. Those children end up abused an awful lot. My husband, being a judge, has to issue so many temporary custody orders. Last week there was a ten-month-old baby that came before him, and I wanted to take that baby so badly. I had to force myself not to do it."

While we talked, Jeaneen's eight-month-old son, Jesse, slept in a small crib behind her desk. She often looked at him, smoothed his hair, as if to remind herself of the real issues.

"The problem is in epidemic proportions. You go down the block, and out of ten children you see five, six of them with FAS or FAE. I keep banging my head and thinking, 'How can they do this?

How can they do this?' There's an attitude of 'Oh, that's not going to happen to me.' You see these women who are drunk every single day, and—you ask the doctors and nurses up at the hospital—there have been babies born whose skin, the whole baby, smells like wine. It's like they're pickled and the amniotic fluid is saturated with alcohol. But a lot of times when a baby is born, the [FAE] is not diagnosable from the child's facial features, and difficulties like epilepsy don't show until much later. You know how that goes."

I knew how that went.

". . . Of course, the babies that are born are usually smaller . . ."

According to the health records I had recently received from the South Dakota Department of Child Welfare after years of petitioning, and had since reread so often that I knew them by heart, Adam had weighed three pounds, twelve ounces at his premature birth. "He is not developing at normal rate," his health profile had stated in 1969. "Medical care necessary, feet not normal. Development has been below average, in that at the age of seventeen months he did not walk. He would pull himself up by the furniture and could stand with the aid of a chair. He crept and made cooing noises, but he did not talk, nor did he have any words in his vocabulary. He experienced convulsions—one was in the course of recovery from a severe dehydration with 'enteritis' [inflammation of the intestine] at about six months, and the other occurred approximately two months prior. Pneumonia during the first year of life. Frequent ear infections. *The cause of his physical and mental retardation*" that anonymous Public Health physician had written in the dark ages before anyone in America had ever heard of fetal alcohol syndrome, when the medical textbooks still confidently stated that ethanol had no intrauterine effect, "*is that the cause is undeterminable* [italics mine]."

I brought my attention back to Jeaneen, who continued, unaware of the impact her words had upon me the parent as opposed to me the dutiful researcher.

". . . the growth slows down and the physical stuff starts, but these women don't realize it even then. Why can't they see what's happening? Why don't they care? People say, 'How many FAS kids are born up here?' and I say, 'I don't know because Indian Health can't diagnose it unless it's real obvious.' We had a client come in with a baby in nineteen seventy-seven, and the baby had convulsions, it had DTs [*delerium tremens*] after it was born. I couldn't believe a baby having DTs—it was real hard for me to comprehend. We all have a magic barrier that prevents bad things from going through. But that baby still has convulsions and is real hyperactive. She can't talk.

"The *New York Times* called us a colony—our average income is like three thousand dollars. Our infant mortality rate is almost triple that of the state of South Dakota, for white, okay. So here we are, and people have children to increase their welfare checks. That's basic economics. I don't think President Reagan's ever heard of that branch of economics, but I know people who've gotten pregnant to get a bigger check without stopping to think, 'Okay, this child is going to cost x amount of hundreds of dollars to feed, clothe, and shelter, and welfare is probably not going to cover that amount.' Okay? But in dollars and cents it means a raise. We get a four-percent cost-of-living increase. Well, they go for nine months, have another child, and do the same thing. And then use up all the money in the first week of the month. We have a terribly high birth rate here, and we have a high infant mortality, and we have a high incidence of children born with physical defects. And that's probably it: people are reproducing to get an increase in food stamps and welfare benefits."

I was momentarily taken aback by Jeaneen's candor. She spoke without internal editing, as if too weary of the problem to seek euphemism. I glanced at the tape recorder, its wheels sealing up our thoughts like the filling in jellyroll, and her eyes followed mine. I moved my finger toward the stop button, raised by eyebrows in question. Was this off-the-record? She shook her head. From somewhere a trust had grown between us, and now it was my turn to risk an unpopular opinion.

I wondered aloud whether some of the mothers Jeaneen talked about might not be merely products of economic deprivation and historical exploitation, but might themselves be victims of fetal alcohol effect. They would therefore find it hard, if not impossible, to cope with money and preplanning. Adam had received ten dollars from his grandmother for his seventeenth birthday, and I let him take the cash to school.

"Where's the money?" I asked him when he got home. He had purchased a doughnut: he gave somebody ten dollars, took a doughnut, and asked for no change. End of transaction. It had occurred to me that many adults and young people with undiagnosed FAS or FAE were perhaps in jail for small crimes like shoplifting—offenses that seemed to them like a good idea at the time because they couldn't project the consequences if they were apprehended. And they *would* tend to be caught, over and over. They were not clever thieves.

Jeaneen immediately understood my point. "We had an arrest record within one given year equivalent to like sixty-five percent of this reservation's population," she said. "And that statistic means a lot of repeaters, not that sixty-five percent of the people here committed crimes."

Jeaneen looked out the window, took a phone call, indicating that I need not leave the office. I busied myself with the papers in the file I had brought along—newspaper clippings, demographic studies of reservation versus urban Indian drinking patterns. The theoretical goal of anthropology is an "etic," or outsider's, perspective, combined with an "emic" (group member's) insight, and it's a juggler's balance rarely attained. The participant/observer I learned about in graduate fieldwork classes walks the top of a dam between a stranger's constraint and an insider's abandon, and a misstep in either direction is dangerous. My training resisted the intimacy of shared experience offered by Jeaneen's honesty, and when she was finished, I cleared my throat and moved on to the next subhead on my prepared list of questions.

Was there a particular chronological age when a mother was more at risk for having an FAS child?

"It depends on her *drinking age,*" Jeaneen answered. "I've seen FAS/FAE children born to really young women, but these were girls who started drinking early. I guess another factor is nutrition. If a woman doesn't eat what she needs while she's pregnant, she compounds the effects of alcohol."

I asked Jeaneen whether, having lived on this reservation all her life, she thought that local women were now drinking more or less than previously.

"I was a data coordinator back in the seventies," she answered. "At that time the average age for the women in the alcohol program was like forty-nine, and we had roughly sixty-five to eight-five percent males. We've got more women clients now—probably sixty to sixty-five percent. Their average age is about twenty-five, right smack in the middle of childbearing years, and they're drinking heavily."

"What kind of stuff?" I asked. In Alaska I had known people who made home brew from potatoes, yeast, and sugar, then aged it in a plastic garbage can for a week. The most potent shots came from the bottom.

"A lot of beer, a lot of wine. Not so much the hard liquors because there isn't immediate access to them. We're a 'dry' reservation, but we have our bootleggers, and then two miles over the line here we have five or six little beer joints that do a record business, like they're second to Omaha in alcohol sales for the state of Nebraska. Millions of dollars cross that line. And so many die annually on the road to that place it's got the name 'Killer Highway.' Seven people killed at one time, three people killed at another. They just recently had a poster contest for a sign, and this guy drew a skull, real graphic—it scared the heck out of me. It said, SLOW DOWN, DEATH AHEAD. And the skull has a war bonnet on."

"What's the beer of choice?"

"I believe Budweiser is. Anheuser-Busch, I think, should be more than happy to commit funds to an FAS project."

This sounded to me like a practical idea, and I asked if she had approached the management of the company in St. Louis.

"Somebody did back in the seventies," Jeaneen recalled. "They tried to get backing for some prevention materials, but nothing ever came of it. The wine here is called muscatel. It's in a green bottle, which is why you see all the green glass around on the ground. It's real cheap. It costs like seventy-five cents a bottle, and the bootleggers sell it for like two and a quarter. The scary thing is, the people now are starting to drink Lysol. They call it Montana gin. I asked a doctor a few months ago if he had any research on what Lysol would do because we have women who are pregnant, street people, who are drinking Lysol. I need to know what it is going to do to the children."

I mentioned a recent fad that a former student of mine who lived on Rosebud had told me about: kids would puncture an aerosol can of Lysol, spread the fluid on bread, and call it a Lysol sandwich. It didn't take many bites to fry their brains.

Jeaneen shook her head. "I know of a man who was perfectly sane, had perfect eyesight, could see a bug crawling across the street coming toward his house, and now he's almost blind, his mind is practically gone. It's almost like he has Alzheimer's disease, just real pathetic. He drinks Lysol."

But why, I asked? Why poison when the wine was so cheap?

"To get high. Plus, it can be stolen from the store, and it stretches a lot further than muscatel."

I had no idea what the kick of Lysol might be like.

"They say it's between a gas high and an alcohol high," Jeaneen reported. "You get a ringing in your ears, you feel drunk, you feel like you huffed gas."

Years ago, when I lived on a reservation in eastern Montana, I had known people who sipped perfume they bought in tiny beveled bottles at Woolworth's. Was that still a beverage of choice?

"Yes, every now and then."

But the modern age had arrived in Indian Country. "We have a lot of young people here who are using cocaine, marijuana, acid." Jeaneen ticked off the list on her fingers. "They wanted me to teach a high school class on teenage pregnancy. I had my first baby at seventeen, so that's one subject I'm qualified to talk about. So what I did was use a game. I gave each student a hard-boiled egg, and they had to take care of it like it was a baby for exactly a week's period. They had to document when they had their eggs in their possession, when they neglected them."

I had heard of this technique before, but Jeaneen had given it an extra twist, adapting it to the specific conditions of Pine Ridge. Each girl had drawn a slip of paper to give her a temporary, fictional identity. She could be thirty-one years old and a housewife, or a person who started her day with a bottle of beer, or an alcoholic. Then the students drew again and some of them were pregnant with a second child. Some of them kept drinking or swallowed an aspirin or took acid. Some of them had FAS or FAE babies, and Jeaneen would have them write down how they felt about their guilt.

"I think I ruined a whole generation," she laughed. "These girls no longer wanted to get pregnant!"

What happened to a child with FAS or FAE on this reservation, I wanted to know. What would have happened to Adam?

"Up at Oglala Community School there's a cooperative for children with learning disabilities. When the kids get into high school, though, they don't have that safety net underneath them, and very often they drop out. You go to any mentally handicapped program on the reservation, and you look—most of the kids are FAS children."

Jeaneen had mentioned a subject close to home for me. Adam's eventual life after high school was a territory I could barely imagine. Would he live away from home? Have a girlfriend, a wife? His future was an island I could just make out, but it was a mirage separated from the present by deep water. How was the transit accomplished?

"What happens to them when they drop out?" I asked.

"They usually marry or have children. Then they divorce, and the woman gets on ADC [Aid for Dependent Children] and stays there and continues to have children, and we're back into the cycle. You get a second generation. You know how often FAS people need glasses, braces, wheelchairs, crutches; but here they're like a whole segment of society that's forgotten about or shoved under the table. We don't have a way to document how many there really are—that's the biggest problem."

Jeaneen herself was reluctant to give a rough estimate. She was aware of the relatively low incidence of FAS reported in some published studies—five or six impaired children out of every thousand born in particular communities, but I could tell she didn't give these figures much credence. Neither did I—though I understood where they came from. Firm diagnosis was made only in ironclad instances where every known symptom was manifest. Scientists recorded the bare minimum number of cases, a practice ultimately as unrealistic in terms of generating an accurate account as would be the assignment of an FAS label to *every* infant who gave evidence of only one or two symptoms. The truth necessarily lay somewhere in between.

Jeaneen protested that she had no proof, no absolute documentation to support her subjective impression of the percentage of fetal alcohol victims on this reservation, but I pressed her for an intuitive response. She was, by virtue of the length of time she had worked in her job, in a better position than almost anyone to hazard a guess. She might lack a backup statistical sample, but she had the virtue of being known and trusted in her community; a social scientist who passed through the reservation for only a few days and attempted to survey a population at once reticent to share its secrets and taught by experience to be hostile toward nosey non-Indians might emerge with some very suspect data. What's more, Jeaneen impressed me as having good instincts and a bias against gratuitous exaggeration. She had nothing to gain from me by inflating or deflating her figures. Again I put the question: of those Sioux children born on Pine Ridge, how many did she *think* might be impaired by prenatal drinking?

"I would say right now we probably have about twenty-five percent of our children here on this reservation, and that's conservative. It's probably higher, but twenty-five percent would be a solid base."

One-fourth of the population! I thought out loud, combining that incredible figure with the patterns of FAS behavior my written sources associated with adult activity. If it was true, as logic would suggest, that FAS kids grew up to have more kids, to have them earlier, to drink during their pregnancies because they were harder to counsel, then that meant that more and more impaired infants would be born in a given community.

What percentage of pregnant women did Jeaneen guess currently drank at a level that might be dangerous?

She stared at me, almost defiant, as if to see whether I would believe what she was about to say or whether I would join the ranks of those who called her Chicken Little. She bit her lower lip, decided.

"About fifty percent," she said in a flat voice. "Fifty percent are drinking on a weekly basis, on weekends. That's probably conservative again. When I went to prenatal clinic, I used to look at my peers, and then I was thinking it was like eighty percent who were still drinking while they were pregnant, though they had all heard of the FAS stuff."

We exchanged a look. Even if she was off the mark, even if she overstated the case by as much as half—and I didn't think she did—the figures were horrendous.

"What can be done?" I finally asked.

"Our real problem is finding a way to reach the entire community, those people who are more prone to abuse alcohol. We have to get the laws *here* enacted. It doesn't matter what anybody else says outside, we need to get some of those women in jail. That's what it takes—really severe and harsh methods, but to ruin a small child's life, then that's . . ."

Adam was once that small child. If his mother had been locked up, prevented from even one night of drinking, how much more awareness, how many more possibilities might he now have? If she had come after him with a baseball bat after he was born, if she had smashed his skull and caused brain damage, wouldn't she have been constrained from doing it again and again? Was it her prerogative, moral or legal, to deprive him of the means to live a full life? I had no doubt that there were compelling reasons for her weaknesses, for her mistakes, but reason didn't equal right.

Was it likely that such laws would be passed? What civil liberty overrode the torment of a child?

"We've talked about what the best approach would be," Jeaneen said. "It would have to come from grass-roots people, and what it would take is education first."

"And the law," I insisted. "What would the law entail?" I thought of the judgment of Solomon: to appease two rival parents the king proposed to sacrifice the disputed baby. Should a parental entitlement, in the case of FAS, be abridged by the state to save the child?

"If a woman is pregnant, and if she is going to drink alcohol, then, in very simple language, she should be jailed. We cannot . . ." Jeaneen chose her words carefully, regretfully, relating both sides of the argument. "There is no treatment center here that will take a pregnant woman. There's no place to send them. How do you monitor besides checking on them on a daily basis? The women say that it's their choice to drink or not. But if they want to have children, they're going to have to take care of them—and they don't wind up doing that. Most children end up with foster families, very often are abused on top of being FAS or FAE."

She unconsciously made a fist with her hand, then spoke her mind.

"They just need to put in jail those women who drink when they're pregnant. That's probably what it's going to take, because if a woman's hard core, then she's going to drink."

Adam's mother had been hard core. In the report I received, her cause of death was listed simply as "ingestion of denatured alcohol"—*antifreeze.* Incarceration might have led to treatment. It might have saved her life.

Was there even room in the jails?

"Each solution that comes up is a problem within itself," Jeaneen sighed. "Jail is no place for them, but it's the best alternative for someone who would otherwise drink while she was pregnant. I know of one case in particular in which they have jailed a pregnant woman; they kept her in for like a week, and then her family came and started to get angry about it. She was told that—*the family* was told that—they had to keep her sober, and they were told what could happen to the child if she kept drinking. They were told that if they did not keep her sober, she would be jailed again. And it worked. The family did start keeping her home and watching her so that she didn't drink. Once they were told that she was being kept in jail not for her sake, but for the child's sake, then it was understood."

"Do you ever yourself get really angry when you see a pregnant woman who's drinking?" This was an instinctive, unpremeditated question, intrusive and personal, none of my business. I was ready to call it back, when Jeaneen nodded.

"I know of one case in particular of a woman who has five FAS girls," she said. "One after the other, each of them in foster care, and every time I see her pregnant, I wonder why she can continue to have children. I've even asked—it's probably morally wrong for me as a person to question God's will—why is she continuing to have children when she doesn't want them and they are FAS? There should be some way to make her stop. She's not taking care of them. I've talked to my husband about it, and I think he feels sorry for me because I've gone so far in my thinking about forced sterilization for some of these people. I don't think that's out of the question—I think in the future that's going to be a reality. But I'm not going to be the one to sit and say, 'You can't have any more.' It would take a council of people from various agencies to determine who can and who can't, and that almost sounds like *1984.*"

Her words were shocking, antithetical to every self-evident liberal belief I cherished, yet through my automatic silent denial I felt some current of unexpected assent. It was because we were talking about *babies*—babies who were going to be carried to term. Jeaneen and almost everyone I had spoken to had stated categorically that abortion was a choice almost never made by reservation residents, either because of religious beliefs pertaining to the sanctity of life or because medical facilities were too expensive or inaccessible.

I thought of my son and of all the things he'd never experience or even realize he was missing. What would happen to him when Louise and I died? By all evidence, he had been deprived of the miracle of transcendent imagination, a complex grace that was the quintessence of being human.

Grief can drive you places you never expected to go.

After a pause, Jeaneen continued, echoing my confusing thoughts. "You go back to the moral question, that a person does not have the right to ruin somebody else's life from the beginning. A child is innocent and has not asked to be born, nor is it asking to be abused—and I *do* look at it as child abuse. If a woman is willing to abuse her child before it even has been given a start on this earth, then she probably isn't deserving of another child, but who's going to make the determination?"

"I know," I said. "Even talk about the prohibition of alcohol raises the ethical issue of who can make a choice of what's good or bad for somebody else."

"This one lady comes down here—I can't even force myself to look at her any longer. And it's not in my daily agenda to hate. I try to assess rather than hate, because hate seems to use a lot more energy. *But I hate her.* I hate her for what she's done to her children. And I feel for those children. They'll never be . . . they'll never be *humans,* I guess, as we know humans, because they've never been given that chance. They can never love because they're not going to know the concept. One little girl was so severely affected that she'll never be accepted into society. In fact she'll be stared at, she'll be gawked at. What would we do to somebody who was doing this to our children? We would probably hang them at the street corner. But because alcohol is so accepted, we've become passive to the subject of FAS children."

In her anger, Jeaneen's voice rose, awakening Jesse, who began to cry. Jeaneen lifted him from the crib, let him dip his hand into her cup and stir the cooled coffee at the bottom with his fingers. It splashed on her karate suit, but she paid no attention. "He's eight months old and kind of realizes—like he spent all this time and probably just figured out you're a stranger," she explained. "Plus he's getting teeth. He was born on Jesse James's birthday. Somebody got confused one time and called him Billy Jack."

What would Billy Jack do about FAS, I wonder? It's not a dilemma that gloomy-faced movie stereotype of the macho Indian could solve with a blunt chop to an opponent's neck or even with a hokey snake ceremony. Who would Billy perceive as the enemy? The answer was not long in coming: the bootleggers, of course. They would be sleazy, white, operating out of a messy, smoke-filled shack, and Billy would smash through the door with a few well-placed kicks. He would be furious, vengeful, ready to fight against guns, knives, fists wrapped in chains.

But what if, when the splinters settled, he found inside only a group of pregnant teenagers, gentle voiced, some beautiful, smiling, buzzed on muscatel? What if he were confronted by a thirty-year-old nursing mother, a half-gone can of Bud in her free hand?

We took a break for lunch—Jeaneen went to pick up a bucket of broasted chicken and fries ordered from the village all-purpose grocery store. I stood and stretched. Through the open window came the sounds of a small town at midday: the calls of children at recess, the occasional dull drone of overflying planes on their high passage from one coast to another, the slam of car doors as people parked in front of the government buildings. Far down the road the country stretched flat and empty. The sky hung so low, seemed to dip below the edge of the horizon, to curve under the distant perimeter, that I had the impression I was looking out from on the top of a mesa, from on top of the world. The wind was blowing, and there was caramel color to the fields, mixed with the green from the previous night's rain. It was not so bright a day that the clouds, highlighted in violet, made obvious shadows on the land, but rather they cast subtle shades. The white hills to the north were so smooth and close-cropped that they appeared to be padded in felt, the beacons of other islands across the moving tides of grass. It was a landscape that defined the word *open*, the opposite of the enclosed, blurred myopia that was Adam's legacy. He came from a country that encouraged the farthest sight, but he forever stood in a well shaped by a bottle.

Two figures approached, walking on the bank of the highway. Even from this distance it was clear that they staggered, were propped against each other for support. They were women dressed in dark clothing, scarves about their heads. The younger of them wore quilted lavender snow boots, and the older woman, unlaced men's shoes and thin white anklets, little girl socks. Her bare shins and the hem of her dress were caked with dried mud, and I watched while she stepped without notice through a large puddle. They got nearer, and I could hear snatches of their conversation as they argued loudly in a language I didn't understand.

The one in shoes berated the woman in boots, then alternately pleaded and cooed in the singsong voice of a lullaby. The one in boots shook her head. She absolutely refused whatever was being asked. The old lady began to cry, to shrill high-pitched words ragged with fury. She batted away the other's arms, stopped where she stood, and sank to her knees, keening, until her younger companion helped her up, calmed her, said something so funny that both women laughed and had to grip each other for balance. Cars raced by them without slowing down, and finally they passed within a few feet of my window. Their features were similar. They had the look of a mother and daughter.

I checked my watch when we finished eating. It was nearly three o'clock, and I had a long drive to Rapid City. I proposed that we spend another half hour in conversation today and that I return in a month or so to continue the interview.

"Okay." Jeaneen rocked Jesse in her arms, rolling her desk chair rhythmically back and forth to lull him into sleep.

I turned on my machine, adjusted the sound level, and Jeaneen picked up where she had left off.

"I talked with my husband while I was waiting for the order at the store," she said. "I've given him a lot of FAS education on how to identify people as I've done the research, and he's finding that he's dealing with a lot of FAS adults in the courts. You can tell from the physical characteristics that they're FAS—from the hands, the lines in the hands, different things give them away. And he says these are the people who cannot deal with the bigger realm of things. What we were talking about. He said they almost deal moment to moment. They don't stop to think they can't spend their paychecks now because what are they going to eat next week. So then they go into people's homes and they steal. He gets so frustrated. He used to believe that everybody could think like he thinks, that they could project a week from now, a year from now. But now he says he's got to back off. If he sees somebody with the obvious characteristics of FAS, he tries to take things a little slower with them because they do not understand the way he understands. Their comprehension is much different. I say, 'You see a lot of this?' and he says, 'Yes, more than I ever expected was out there. People in their forties and fifties.'"

The light was fading as I gathered up the papers Jeaneen had given me, packed away my recorder, and said good-bye. I broke the speed limit going north through the Badlands, past Scenic, past the sites of abandoned forts. At first I replayed the tape, listened to Jeaneen's soft voice, modulated so as not to disturb her baby's slumber. I made mental notes to myself of the points to follow up, the statistics to compare, the theories to bounce off other experts. I concentrated on details in order not to think of wider implications and tried to regard today's conversation as a productive collection of material, nothing more. But it didn't work. I was driving through the western remains of the Great Sioux Nation, through Adam's birthright, and before the sun disappeared altogether, I allowed the stillness of helpless reflection to descend. In every direction I went, I trailed those two women, weaving the road into Pine Ridge, my oldest son—all of us—in their erratic wake.

Postreading Writing Assignments

Option 1: Review your response to prereading journal question number one. Is there any reason why pregnant women should not drink alcohol? Did your response change after reading Dorris's text? If so, how did it change?

Option 2: How do Dorris's memories and thoughts of his son Adam add to this passage? Do his recollections make this problem more real than if he provided only "facts" and statistics? How so? What was the impact of these thoughts on you as a reader?

Extended Writing Assignments

Option 3: Dorris and Grey Eagle discuss FAS and the ways in which FAS is manifested in Native American* communities. Explore this line of thought. What are the costs (fiscal, emotional, physical) to the Native American community as a result of FAS? If, as Jeaneen Grey Eagle hypothesizes, twenty-five percent of children on her reservation have FAS, what kind of impact is that going to have on the community as a whole? Use both Dorris's reflections and Grey Eagle's "facts" to explore this issue.

Option 4: How far should society go to ensure that pregnant women do not drink or engage in behavior that can harm their unborn child; for example, smoking or using other kinds of drugs? What role, if any, does society play in determining what a woman can or cannot do while she is pregnant? For this essay, first do some outside reading to determine whether there are any laws in place regarding civil liberties for unborn children and/or for pregnant women; then form your own position. Use Dorris's text to support your position, if appropriate, or use your position to read Dorris against the grain.

*The term "Native American" does not distinguish between the hundreds of different tribes and cultures. It is used in these assignments to differentiate between indigenous and nonindigenous peoples.

Option 5: Who is the "enemy" here? Is it women who drink? Is it an economic structure that leaves many individuals poor and hopeless? What if, as Dorris suggests, the "enemy" once you find it, turns out to be, "a group of pregnant teenagers, gentle voiced, some beautiful, smiling, buzzed on muscatel"?

For this assignment, summarize Dorris's argument; then, on the basis of Dorris's text and your own reading of it, propose a solution for the problem of FAS. Imagine you are writing a proposal to a government agency; what kinds of programs might help both pregnant women and their unborn babies? Although this essay primarily explores the role of women in FAS, don't exclude the role of men. Where are the fathers of these babies while the mothers are out drinking or neglecting the children? Propose a comprehensive plan for this complex issue.

Forging Connections

Option 6: Read or reread Paula Gunn Allen's text "Where I Come From Is Like This". Both Dorris and Allen are Native American writers exploring issues that involve Native American women. What are the differences between the two essays? What are the similarities? What do you imagine these two writers might have to say to one another? Write an essay discussing these two texts and the implications both have for Native American women. It would also be interesting to discuss the role of Native American men and nonnative peoples. What role do Allen and Dorris see such groups playing? What role do you see for these groups?

Frederick Douglass

THE PATHWAY FROM SLAVERY TO FREEDOM

Frederick Douglass lived a long, productive life as an abolitionist, orator, writer, newspaper publisher, politician, and high government official. The selection here is from his book Frederick Douglass: The Narrative and Selected Writings. *Douglass was born into slavery on a plantation on the Eastern Shore of Maryland; he escaped in 1838 and headed north. Within three years, he was lecturing as an agent for the Massachusetts Anti-Slavery Society, proclaiming himself to be "a thief and a robber," because "this head, these limbs, this body," as he put it, "were stolen from my master." Early in his life, Douglass learned a valuable lesson: if reading and writing were dangerous—if knowing more than just what the master wanted him to know was antithetical to being a slave—then education would be an essential means for Douglass to find a path from slavery to freedom.*

Prereading Journal Questions

1. After reading the headnote, what assumptions are you making about reading these two chapters from Douglass's autobiography? What expectations do you have about the material?
2. How might someone "born into slavery" see education as a "path from slavery to freedom"?
3. Have you read slave narratives in the past? In what ways might slave narratives/autobiographies differ from accounts of slavery in a history text?

Reading tip: After reading the headnote and answering the prereading journal questions, you have begun to make assumptions about what you are going to read. Read your responses to the prereading journal questions; what do these responses tell you about your "preconceived notions"? How might having preconceived notions about a text limit your reading; how might it help you read more effectively? Be willing to change your assumptions as a result of the reading that you create.

My new mistress proved to be all she appeared when I first met her at the door—a woman of the kindest heart and finest feelings. She had never had a slave under her control previously to myself, and prior to her marriage she had been dependent upon her own industry for a living. She was by trade a weaver; and by constant application to her business, she had been in a good degree preserved from the blighting and dehumanizing effects of slavery. I was utterly astonished at her goodness. I scarcely knew how to behave towards her. She was entirely unlike any other white woman I had ever seen. I could not approach her as I was accustomed to approach other white ladies. My early instruction was all out of place. The crouching servility, usually so acceptable a quality in a slave, did not answer when manifested toward her. Her favor was not gained by it; she seemed to be disturbed by it. She did not deem it impudent or unmannerly for a slave to look her in the face. The meanest slave was put fully at ease in her presence, and none left without feeling better for having seen her. Her face was made of heavenly smiles, and her voice of tranquil music.

But, alas! this kind heart had but a short time to remain such. The fatal poison of irresponsible power was already in her hands, and soon commenced its infernal work. That cheerful eye, under the influence of slavery, soon became red with rage; that voice, made all of sweet accord, changed to one of harsh and horrid discord; and that angelic face gave place to that of a demon.

Very soon after I went to live with Mr. and Mrs. Auld, she very kindly commenced to teach me the A, B, C. After I had learned this, she assisted me in learning to spell words of three or four letters. Just at this point of my progress, Mr. Auld found out what was going on, and at once forbade Mrs. Auld to instruct me further, telling her, among other things, that it was unlawful, as well as unsafe, to teach a slave to read. To use his own words, further, he said, "If you give a nigger an inch, he will take an ell. A nigger should know nothing but to obey his master—to do as he is told to do. Learning would *spoil* the best nigger in the world. Now," said he, "if you teach that nigger (speaking of myself) how to read, there would be no keeping him. It would forever unfit him to be a slave. He would at once become unmanageable, and of no value to his master. As to himself, it could do him no good, but a great deal of harm. It would make him discontented and unhappy." These words sank deep into my heart, stirred up sentiments within that lay slumbering, and called into existence an entirely new train of thought. It was a new and special revelation, explaining dark and mysterious things, with which my youthful understanding had struggled, but struggled in vain. I now understood what had been to me a most perplexing difficulty—to wit, the white man's power to enslave the black man. It was a grand achievement, and I prized it highly. From that moment, I understood the pathway from slavery to freedom. It was just what I wanted, and I got it at a time when I the least expected it. Whilst I was saddened by the thought of losing the aid of my kind mistress, I was gladdened by the invaluable instruction which, by the merest accident, I had gained from my master. Though conscious of the difficulty of learning without a teacher, I set out with high hope, and a fixed purpose, at whatever cost of trouble, to learn how to read. The very decided manner with which he spoke, and strove to impress his wife with the evil consequences of giving me instruction, served to convince me that he was deeply sensible of the truths he was uttering. It gave me the best assurance that I might rely with the utmost confidence on the results which, he said, would flow from teaching me to read. What he most dreaded, that I most desired. What he most loved, that I most hated. That which to him was a great evil, to be carefully shunned, was to me a great good, to be diligently sought; and the argument which he so warmly urged, against my learning to read, only served to inspire me with a desire and determination to learn. In learning to read, I owe almost as much to the bitter opposition of my master, as to the kindly aid of my mistress. I acknowledge the benefit of both.

I had resided but a short time in Baltimore before I observed a marked difference, in the treatment of slaves, from that which I had witnessed in the country. A city slave is almost a freeman, compared with a slave on the plantation. He is much better fed and clothed, and enjoys privileges altogether unknown to the slave on the plantation. There is a vestige of decency, a sense of shame, that does much to curb and check those outbreaks of atrocious cruelty so commonly enacted upon the plantation. He is a desperate slaveholder, who will shock the humanity of his nonslaveholding neighbors with the cries of his lacerated slave. Few are willing to incur the odium attaching to the reputation of being a cruel master; and above all things, they would not be known as not giving a slave enough to eat. Every city slaveholder is anxious to have it known of him, that he feeds his slaves well; and it is due to them to say, that most of them do give their slaves enough to eat. There are, however, some painful exceptions to this rule. Directly opposite to us, on Philpot Street, lived Mr. Thomas Hamilton. He owned two slaves. Their names were Henrietta and Mary. Henrietta was about twenty-two years of age, Mary was about fourteen; and of all the mangled and emaciated creatures I ever looked upon, these two were the most so. His heart must be harder than stone, that could look upon these unmoved. The head, neck, and shoulders of Mary were literally cut to pieces. I have frequently felt her head, and found it nearly covered with festering sores, caused by the lash of her cruel mistress. I do not know that her master ever whipped her, but I have been an eye-witness to the cruelty of Mrs. Hamilton. I use to be in Mr. Hamilton's house nearly every day. Mrs. Hamilton used to sit in a large chair in the middle of the room, with a heavy cowskin always by her side, and scarce an hour passed during the day but was marked by the blood of one of these slaves. The girls seldom passed her without her saying, "Move faster, you *black gip!*" at the same time giving them a blow with the cowskin over the head or shoulders, often drawing the blood. She would then say, "Take that, you *black gip!*"—continuing, "If you don't move faster, I'll move you!" Added to the cruel lashings to which these salves were subjected, they were kept nearly half-starved. They seldom knew what it was to eat a full meal. I have seen Mary contending with the pigs for the offal thrown into the street. So much was Mary kicked and cut to pieces, that she was oftener called *"pecked"* than by her name.

I lived in Master Hugh's family about seven years. During this time, I succeeded in learning to read and write. In accomplishing this, I was compelled to resort to various stratagems. I had no regular teacher. My mistress, who had kindly commenced to instruct me, had, in compliance with the advice and direction of her husband, not only ceased to instruct, but had set her face against my being instructed by any one else. It is due, however, to my mistress to say of her, that she did not adopt this course of treatment immediately. She at first lacked the depravity indispensable to shutting me up in mental darkness. It was at least necessary for her to have some training in the exercise of irresponsible power, to make her equal to the task of treating me as though I were a brute.

My mistress was, as I have said, a kind and tender-hearted woman; and in the simplicity of her soul she commenced, when I first went to live with her, to treat me as she supposed one human being ought to treat another. In entering upon the duties of a slaveholder, she did not seem to perceive that I sustained to her the relation of a mere chattel, and that for her to treat me as a human being was not only wrong, but dangerously so. Slavery proved as injurious to her as it did to me. When I went there, she was a pious, warm, and tender-hearted woman. There was no sorrow or suffering for which she had not a tear. She had bread for the hungry, clothes for the naked, and comfort for every mourner that came within her reach. Slavery soon proved its ability to divest her of these heavenly qualities. Under its influence, the tender heart became stone, and the lamblike disposition gave way to one of tiger-like fierceness. The step in her downward course was in her ceasing to instruct me. She now commenced to practise her husband's precepts. She finally became even more violent in her opposition than her husband himself. She was not satisfied with simply doing as well as he had commanded; she seemed anxious to do better. Nothing seemed to make her more angry than to see me with a newspaper. She seemed to think that here lay the danger. I have had her rush at me with a face made all up of fury, and snatch from me a newspaper, in a manner that fully revealed her apprehension. She was an apt woman; and a little experience soon demonstrated, to her satisfaction, that education and slavery were incompatible with each other.

From this time I was most narrowly watched. If I was in a separate room any considerable length of time, I was sure to be suspected of having a book, and was at once called to give an account of myself. All this, however, was too late. The first step had been taken. Mistress, in teaching me the alphabet, had given me the *inch,* and no precaution could prevent me from taking the *ell.*

The plan which I adopted, and the one by which I was most successful, was that of making friends of all the little white boys whom I met in the street. As many of these as I could, I converted into teachers. With their kindly aid, obtained at different times and in different places, I finally succeeded in learning to read. When I was sent of errands, I always took my book with me, and by going one part of my errand quickly, I found time to get a lesson before my return. I used also to carry bread with me, enough of which was always in the house, and to which I was always welcome; for I was much better off in this regard than many of the poor white children in our neighborhood. This bread I used to bestow upon the hungry little urchins, who, in return, would give me that more valuable bread of knowledge. I am strongly tempted to give the names of two or three of those little boys, as a testimonial of the gratitude and affection I bear them; but prudence forbids;—not that it would injure me, but it might embarrass them; for it is almost an unpardonable offence to teach slaves to read in this Christian country. It is enough to say of the dear little fellows, that they lived on Philpot Street, very near Durgin and Bailey's ship-yard. I used to talk this matter of slavery over with them. I would sometimes say to them, I wished I could be as free as they would be when they got to be men. "You will be free as soon as you are twenty-one, *but I am a slave for life!* Have not I as good a right to be free as you have?" These words used to trouble them; they would express for me the liveliest sympathy, and console me with the hope that something would occur by which I might be free.

I was now about twelve years old, and the thought of being *a slave for life* began to bear heavily upon my heart. Just about this time, I got hold of a book entitled "The Columbian Orator." Every opportunity I got, I used to read this book. Among much of other interesting matter, I found in it a dialogue between a master and his slave. The slave was represented as having run away from his master three times. The dialogue represented the conversation which took place between them, when the slave was retaken the third time. In this dialogue, the whole argument in behalf of slavery was brought forward by the master, all of which was disposed of by the slave. The slave was made to say some very smart as well as impressive things in reply to his master—things which had the desired though unexpected effect; for the conversation resulted in the voluntary emancipation of the slave on the part of the master.

In the same book, I met with one of Sheridan's mighty speeches on and in behalf of Catholic emancipation. These were choice documents to me. I read them over and over again with unabated interest. They gave tongue to interesting thoughts of my own soul, which had frequently flashed through my mind, and died away for want of utterance. The moral which I gained from the dialogue was the power of truth over the conscience of even a slaveholder. What I got from Sheridan was a bold denunciation of slavery, and a powerful vindication of human rights. The reading of these documents enabled me to utter my thoughts, and to meet the arguments brought forward to sustain slavery; but while they relieved me of one difficulty, they brought on another even more painful than the one of which I was relieved. The more I read, the more I was led to abhor and detest my enslavers. I could regard them in no other light than a band of successful robbers, who had left their homes, and gone to Africa, and stolen us from our homes, and in a strange land reduced us to slavery. I loathed them as being the meanest as well as the most wicked of men. As I read and contemplated the subject, behold! that very discontentment which Master Hugh had predicted would follow my learning to read had already come, to torment and sting my soul to unutterable anguish. As I writhed under it, I would at times feel that learning to read had been a curse rather than a blessing. It had given me a view of my wretched condition, without the remedy. It opened my eyes to the horrible pit, but to no ladder upon which to get out. In moments of agony, I envied my fellow-slaves for their stupidity. I have often wished myself a beast. I preferred the condition of the meanest reptile to my own. Any thing, no matter what, to get rid of thinking! It was this everlasting thinking of my condition that tormented me. There was no getting rid of it. It was pressed upon me by every object within sight or hearing, animate or inanimate. The silver trump of freedom had roused my soul to eternal wakefulness. Freedom now appeared, to disappear no more forever. It was heard in every sound, and seen in every thing. It was ever present to torment me with a sense of my wretched condition. I saw nothing without seeing it, I heard nothing without hearing it, and felt nothing without feeling it. It looked from every star, it smiled in every calm, breathed in every wind, and moved in every storm.

I often found myself regretting my own existence, and wishing myself dead; and but for the hope of being free, I have no doubt but that I should have killed myself, or done something for which I should have been killed. While in this state of mind, I was eager to hear any one speak of slavery. I was a ready listener. Every little while, I could hear something about the abolitionists. It was some time before I found what the word meant. It was always used in such connections as to make it an interesting word to me. If a slave ran away and succeeded in getting clear, or if a slave killed his master, set fire to a barn, or did any thing very wrong in the mind of a slaveholder, it was spoken of as the fruit of *abolition.* Hearing the word in this connection very often, I set about learning what it meant. The dictionary afforded me little or no help. I found it was "the act of abolishing;" but then I did not know what was to be abolished. Here I was perplexed. I did not dare to ask any one about its meaning, for I was satisfied that it was something they wanted me to know very little about. After a patient waiting, I got one of our city papers, containing an account of the number of petitions from the north, praying for the abolition of slavery in the District of Columbia, and of the slave trade between the States. From this time I understood the words *abolition* and *abolitionist,* and always drew near when that word was spoken, expecting to hear something of importance to myself and fellow-slaves. The light broke in upon me by degrees. I went one day down on the wharf of Mr. Waters; and seeing two Irishmen unloading a scow of stone, I went, unasked, and helped them. When we had finished, one of them came to me and asked me if I were a slave. I told him I was. He asked, "Are ye a slave for life?" I told him that I was. The good Irishman seemed to be deeply affected by the statement. He said to the other that it was a pity so fine a little fellow as myself should be a slave for life. He said it was a shame to hold me. They both advised me to run away to the north; that I should find friends there, and that I should be free. I pretended not to be interested in what they said, and treated them as if I did not understand them; for I feared they might be treacherous. White men have been known to encourage slaves to escape, and then, to get the reward, catch them and return them to their masters. I was afraid that these seemingly good men might use me so; but I nevertheless remembered their advice, and from that time I resolved to run away. I looked forward to a time at which it would be safe for me to escape. I was too young to think of doing so immediately; besides, I wished to learn how to write, as I might have occasion to write my own pass. I consoled myself with the hope that I should one day find a good chance. Meanwhile, I would learn to write.

The idea as to how I might learn to write was suggested to me by being in Durgin and Bailey's ship-yard, and frequently seeing the ship carpenters, after hewing, and getting a piece of timber ready for use, write on the timber the name of that part of the ship for which it was intended. When a piece of timber was intended for the larboard side, it would be marked thus—"L." When a piece was for the starboard side, it would be marked thus—"S." A piece for the larboard side forward, would be marked thus—"L.F." When a piece was for starboard side forward, it would be marked thus—"S.F." For larboard aft, it would be marked thus—"L.A." For starboard aft, it would be marked thus—"S.A." I soon learned the names of these letters, and for what they were intended when placed upon a piece of timber in the ship-yard. I immediately commenced copying them, and in a short time was able to make the four letters named. After that, when I met with any boy who I knew could write, I would tell him I could write as well as he. The next word would be, "I don't believe you. Let me see you try it." I would then make the letters which I had been so fortunate as to learn, and ask him to beat that. In this way I got a good many lessons in writing, which it is quite possible I should never have gotten in any other way. During this time, my copy-book was the board fence, brick wall, and pavement; my pen and ink was a lump of chalk. With these, I learned mainly how to write. I then commenced and continued copying the Italics in Webster's Spelling Book, until I could make them all without looking on the book. By this time, my little Master Thomas had gone to school, and learned how to write, and had written over a number of copybooks. These had been brought home, and shown to some of our near neighbors, and then laid aside. My mistress used to go to class meeting at the Wilk Street meeting-house every Monday afternoon, and leave me to take care of the house. When left thus, I used to spend the time in writing in the spaces left in Master Thomas's copybook, copying what he had written. I continued to do this until I could write a hand very similar to that of Master Thomas. Thus, after a long, tedious effort for years, I finally succeeded in learning how to write.

Postreading Writing Assignments

Option 1: Look back at how you answered prereading journal question number three; after reading Douglass, what can you add to your response? Is Douglass's account significantly different from accounts of slavery told by a nonslave? How so?

Option 2: Respond to Douglass's realization that he would be a "slave for life." What does this realization impel him to do?

Option 3: What does Mary's story add to Douglass's narrative? How might he expect Mary's story to affect readers? Do you think Douglass, as a writer, achieved the effect he hoped for with his readers?

Extended Writing Assignments

Option 4: At one point Douglass says, "I would at times feel that learning to read had been a curse rather than a blessing. . . . I envied my fellow slaves for their stupidity." Look closely at the ways in which Douglass learns to read and write—the prices he is willing to pay to become literate. Why is literacy—reading and writing—so powerful here? Mr. Auld (upon discovering that Mrs. Auld is teaching Douglass to read) tells his wife, "Learning would *spoil* the best nigger in the world. . . . If you teach [Douglass] . . . how to read, there would be no keeping him. It would forever unfit him to be a slave."

Write an essay exploring the power of literacy as it is presented in this text. Include Douglass's perspective, Mr. Auld's ideas, and your own reading of Douglass's experience. Your essay might focus on any one of the following issues: Douglass's reasons for wanting to be literate, the slave-owners' reasons for wanting slaves to remain illiterate, and/or the ways in which Douglass came to see his literacy as both a blessing and a curse.

Option 5: Explore the ways in which Douglass finds people to teach him how to read and write. In many instances, he subverts the power of those who hold him enslaved. Trace Douglass's journey into education. In your essay, interpret the ways he interacts with those who have something he wants—literacy. Analyze what Douglass does to circumvent not being allowed legally to pursue an education and how he is able to subvert the power of those who can teach him. You might consider the following questions as well as others that you find significant: What is it that literacy offers Douglass? What consequences is he willing to face in order to become educated?

Forging Connections

Option 6: Read or reread Harriet Jacobs's "Flight and a Safe Retreat." Douglass and Jacobs are both writing "slave narratives." After reading these two texts, what differences do you notice in the way that Jacobs and Douglass tell their stories—what aspects of slavery does each one emphasize? Other than the fact that these are both narratives about slavery, are there any other similarities? Read Jacobs's text from Douglass's perspective and vice versa. Write an essay in which you define and interpret the differences between the story that each writer chooses to tell and the different ways in which each tells it.

Gabriel García Márquez

THE HANDSOMEST DROWNED MAN IN THE WORLD: A TALE FOR CHILDREN

Gabriel García Márquez was born in Aracataca, Colombia. He is a journalist and novelist who has been compared with Hemingway and Faulkner. In 1982, he was awarded the Nobel Prize for Literature for his novel One Hundred Years of Solitude. *García Márquez blends fact and fable throughout his texts.*

Prereading Journal Questions

1. The subtitle of this story is "A Tale for Children". What do you know of fairy tales? What is their purpose? What do they tell children about the world?
2. How do people use folk or fairy tales to discuss the origin of the world or stories about their particular culture and beliefs?
3. What is a story you remember being told as a child that led you to develop certain beliefs about the world?

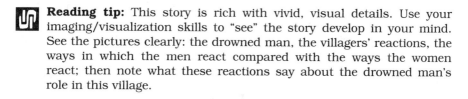

Reading tip: This story is rich with vivid, visual details. Use your imaging/visualization skills to "see" the story develop in your mind. See the pictures clearly: the drowned man, the villagers' reactions, the ways in which the men react compared with the ways the women react; then note what these reactions say about the drowned man's role in this village.

The first children who saw the dark and slinky bulge approaching through the sea let themselves think it was an enemy ship. Then they saw it had no flags or masts and they thought it was a whale. But when it was washed up on the beach, they removed the clumps of seaweed, the jellyfish tentacles, and the remains of fish and flotsam, and only then did they see that it was a drowned man.

They had been playing with him all afternoon, burying him in the sand and digging him up again, when someone chanced to see them and spread the alarm in the village. The men who carried him to the nearest house noticed that he weighed more than any dead man they had ever known, almost as much as a horse, and they said to each other that maybe he'd been floating too long and the water had got into his bones. When they laid him on the floor they said he'd been taller than all other men because there was barely enough room for him in the house, but they thought that maybe the ability to keep on growing after death was part of the nature of certain drowned men. He had the small of the sea about him and only his shape gave one to suppose that it was the corpse of a human being, because the skin was covered with a crust of mud and scales.

They did not even have to clean off his face to know that the dead man was a stranger. The village was made up of only twenty-odd wooden houses that had stone courtyards with no flowers and which were spread about on the end of a desertlike cape. There was so little land that mothers always went about with the fear that the wind would carry off their children and the few dead that the years had caused among them had to be thrown off the cliffs. But the sea was calm and bountiful and all the men fit into seven boats. So when they found the drowned man they simply had to look at one another to see that they were all there.

That night they did not go out to work at sea. While the men went to find out if anyone was missing in neighboring villages, the women stayed behind to care for the drowned man. They took the mud off with grass swabs, they removed the underwater stones entangled in his hair, and they scraped the crust off with tools used for scaling fish. As they were doing that they noticed that the vegetation on him came from faraway oceans and deep water and that his clothes were in tatters, as if he had sailed through labyrinths of coral. They noticed too that he bore his death with pride, for he did not have the lonely look of other drowned men who came out of the sea or that haggard, needy look of men who drowned in rivers. But only when they finished cleaning him off did they become aware of the kind of man he was and it left them breathless. Not only was he the tallest, strongest, most virile, and best built man they had ever seen, but even though they were looking at him there was no room for him in their imagination.

They could not find a bed in the village large enough to lay him on nor was there a table solid enough to use for his wake. The tallest men's holiday pants would not fit him, not the fattest ones' Sunday shirts, nor the shoes of the one with the biggest feet. Fascinated by his huge size and his beauty, the women then decided to make him some pants from a large piece of sail and a shirt from some bridal brabant linen so that he could continue through his death with dignity. As they sewed, sitting in a circle and gazing at the corpse between stitches, it seemed to them that the wind had never been so steady nor the sea so restless as on that night and they supposed that the change had something to do with the dead man. They thought that if that magnificent man had lived in the village, his house would have had the widest doors, the highest ceiling, and the strongest floor, his bedstead would have been made from a midship frame held together by iron bolts, and his wife would have been the happiest woman. They thought that he would have had so much authority that he could have drawn fish out of the sea simply by calling their names and that he would have put so much work into his land that springs would have burst forth from among the rocks so that he would have been able to plant flowers on the cliffs. They secretly compared him to their own men, thinking that for all their lives theirs were incapable of doing what he could do in one night, and they ended up dismissing them deep in their hearts as the weakest, meanest, and most useless creatures on earth. They were wandering through that maze of fantasy when the oldest woman, who as the oldest had looked upon the drowned man with more compassion than passion, sighed:

"He has the face of someone called Esteban."

It was true. Most of them had only to take another look at him to see that he could not have any other name. The more stubborn among them, who were the youngest, still lived for a few hours with the illusion that when they put his clothes on and he lay among the flowers in patent leather shoes his name might be Lautaro. But it was a vain illusion. There had not been enough canvas, the poorly cut and worse sewn pants were too tight, and the hidden strength of his heart popped the buttons on his shirt. After midnight the whistling of the wind died down and the sea fell into its Wednesday drowsiness. The silence put an end to any last doubts: he was Esteban. The women who had dressed him, who had combed his hair, had cut his nails and shaved him were unable to hold back a shudder of pity when they had to resign themselves to his being dragged along the ground. It was then that they understood how unhappy he must have been with that huge body since it bothered him even after death. They could see him in life, condemned to going through doors sideways, cracking his head on crossbeams, remaining on his feet during visits, not knowing what to do with his soft, pink, sea lion hands while the lady of the house looked for her most resistant chair and begged him, frightened to death, sit here, Esteban, please, and he, leaning against the wall, smiling, don't bother, ma'am, I'm fine where I am, his heels raw and his back roasted from having done the same thing so many times whenever he paid a visit, don't bother, ma'am, I'm fine where I am, just to avoid the embarrassment of breaking up the chair, and never knowing perhaps that the ones who said don't go, Esteban, at least wait till the coffee's ready, were the ones who later on would whisper the big boob finally left, how nice, the handsome fool has gone. That was what the women were thinking beside the body a little before dawn. Later, when they covered his face with a handkerchief so that the light would not bother him, he looked so forever dead, so defenseless, so much like their men that the furrows of tears opened in their hearts. It was one of the younger ones who began the weeping. The others, coming to, went from sighs to wails, and the more they sobbed the more they felt like weeping, because the drowned man was becoming all the more Esteban for them, and so they wept so much, for he was the most destitute, most peaceful, and most obliging man on earth, poor Esteban. So when the men returned with the news that the drowned man was not from the neighboring villages either, the women felt an opening of jubilation in the midst of their tears.

"Praise the Lord," they sighed, "he's ours!"

The men thought the fuss was only womanish frivolity. Fatigued because of the difficult nighttime inquiries, all they wanted was to get rid of the bother of the newcomer once and for all before the sun grew strong on that arid, windless day. They improvised a litter with the remains of foremasts and gaffs, tying it together with rigging so that it would bear the weight of the body until they reached the cliffs. They wanted to tie the anchor from a cargo ship to him so that he would sink easily into the deepest waves, where fish are blind and divers die of nostalgia, and bad currents would not bring him back to shore, as had happened with other bodies. But the more they hurried, the more the women thought of ways to waste time. They walked about like startled hens, pecking with the sea charms on their breasts, some interfering on one side to put a scapular of the good wind on the drowned man, some on the other side to put a wrist compass on him, and after a great deal of *get away from there, woman, stay out of the way, look, you almost made me fall on top of the dead man,* the men began to feel mistrust in their livers and started grumbling about why so many main-altar decorations for a stranger, because no matter how many nails and holy-water jars he had on him, the sharks would chew him all the same, but the women kept piling on their junk relics, running back and forth, stumbling, while they released in sighs what they did not in tears, so that the men finally exploded with *since when has there ever been such a fuss over a drifting corpse, a drowned nobody, a piece of cold Wednesday meat.* One of the women, mortified by so much lack of care, then removed the handkerchief from the dead man's face and the men were left breathless too.

He was Esteban. It was not necessary to repeat it for them to recognize him. If they had been told Sir Walter Raleigh, even they might have been impressed with his gringo accent, the macaw on his shoulder, his cannibal-killing blunderbuss, but there could be only one Esteban in the world and there he was, stretched out like a sperm whale, shoeless, wearing the pants of an undersized child, and with those stony nails that had to be cut with a knife. They only had to take the handkerchief off his face to see that he was ashamed, that it was not his fault that he was so big or so heavy or so handsome, and if he had known that this was going to happen, he would have looked for a more discreet place to drown in, seriously, I even would have tied the anchor off a galleon around my neck and staggered off a cliff like someone who doesn't like things in order not to be upsetting people now with this Wednesday dead body, as you people say, in order not to be bothering anyone with this filthy piece of cold meat that doesn't have anything to do with me. There was so much truth in his manner that even the most mistrustful men, the ones who felt the bitterness of endless nights at sea fearing that their women would tire of dreaming about them and begin to dream of drowned men, even they and others who were harder still shuddered in the marrow of their bones at Esteban's sincerity.

That was how they came to hold the most splendid funeral they could conceive of for an abandoned drowned man. Some women who had gone to get flowers in the neighboring villages returned with other women who could not believe what they had been told, and those women went back for more flowers when they saw the dead man, and they brought more and more until there were so many flowers and so many people that it was hard to walk about. At the final moment it pained them to return him to the waters as an orphan and they chose a father and mother from among the best people, and aunts and uncles and cousins, so that through him all the inhabitants of the village became kinsmen. Some sailors who heard the weeping from a distance went off course and people heard of one who had himself tied to the mainmast, remembering ancient fables about sirens. While they fought for the privilege of carrying him on their shoulders along the steep escarpment by the cliffs, men and women became aware for the first time of the desolation of their streets, the dryness of their courtyards, the narrowness of their dreams as they faced the splendor and beauty of their drowned man. They let him go without an anchor so that he could come back if he wished and whenever he wished, and they all held their breath for the fraction of centuries the body took to fall into the abyss. They did not need to look at one another to realize that they were no longer all present, that they would never be. But they also knew that everything would be different from then on, that their houses would have wider doors, higher ceilings, and stronger floors so that Esteban's memory could go everywhere without bumping into beams and so that no one in the future would dare whisper the big boob finally died, too bad, the handsome fool has finally died, because they were going to paint their house fronts gay colors to make Esteban's memory eternal and they were going to break their backs digging for springs among the stones and planting flowers on the cliffs so that in future years at dawn the passengers on great liners would awaken, suffocated by the smell of gardens on the high seas, and the captain would have to come down from the bridge in his dress uniform, with his astrolabe, his pole star, and his row of war medals and, pointing to the promontory of roses on the horizon, he would say in fourteen languages, look there, where the wind is so peaceful now that it's gone to sleep beneath the beds, over there, where the sun's so bright that the sunflowers don't know which way to turn, yes, over there, that's Esteban's village.

Postreading Writing Assignments

Option 1: The term "magical realism" is sometimes used to describe a certain kind of fiction. How would you define this term? Discuss specific sections of the story that you see as examples of magical realism.

Option 2: In what ways is this a "tale for children"? How does this story compare with other "tales for children" that you have read or been told?

Option 3: Is Estaban a "Christ-figure"? How so? Do the villagers see him as a savior? What happens in the village after Estaban's arrival?

Extended Writing Assignments

Option 4: Discuss the importance of myth and storytelling in your own family or culture. Does your family or culture share a story similar to "The Handsomest Drowned Man in the World"? Write an essay in which you explore and interpret a "myth" or story that played a vital role in your family or culture. You will need to "tell" the story, discuss the context in which you learned the story (who usually told it), analyze what the storyteller hoped you might gain from hearing or learning this story, and discuss ways in which this particular story influenced your beliefs and understanding about the world.

Option 5: Examine this story in relation to other stories of salvation and rebirth. Where is García Márquez drawing from the beliefs of particular religions? How does he redefine these beliefs? One way to read this story is to see it as a "revisionist" account of traditional "Christian" beliefs, a different way to present or believe such stories. If you read the story in this way, what can you say about the author's "likely intention"? Frame your response to this story with what you know of other religions and beliefs, and explore what García Márquez is doing with the beliefs of a number of religions—how does Estaban compare with other "Christ" figures, and how can the reactions of the villagers be compared with those of followers of these other religions?

Forging Connections

Option 6: Read "The Handsomest Drowned Man in the World" in light of two or three other fairy tales you have read or been told. Look closely at what each one is saying about a people's beliefs, values, and the like. Where do you see fairy tales as being used to teach children certain things about their world? Where do they seem to be directed toward adults and "adult issues"? You might also include a discussion of tales that are important to you and that have enabled you to see your world in a particular way.

Susan Glaspell

TRIFLES

Susan Glaspell, born in Iowa, was a journalist, playwright, and novelist who is remembered primarily for her plays. In 1931, she won the Pulitzer Prize for drama for Alison's House, *a play she wrote in 1930.* Trifles *is one of her best-known plays and addresses issues that are perhaps as relevant to today's society as they were in the 1930s.*

Prereading Journal Questions

1. Although the title *Trifles* does not provide a lot of information, it does give you some insight into the play. You will understand the significance of the title more completely after reading the play. For now, though, explore the meaning of the word *trifles*. What is the definition of the word? What kinds of things do you see as "trifles"?
2. This play was written in the 1930s. What changes in the roles of men and women have taken place since this was written?
3. The setting of this play is a country farm. What kinds of predictions can you make about the play? About the characters?

Reading tip: Reading a play requires you to read differently from the way you read other kinds of texts. As you read, imagine that you are "watching" the play being performed. You might even want to "act out" certain scenes to develop a more complete reading. It is crucial to pay attention to details in this play that seem insignificant. Details that appear to be meaningless may be the clues needed to unravel the murder that this play explores.

Scene: The kitchen in the now abandoned farmhouse of John Wright, a gloomy kitchen, and left without having been put in order—unwashed pans under the sink, a loaf of bread outside the breadbox, a dish towel on the table—other signs of incompleted work. At the rear the outer door opens, and the Sheriff comes in, followed by the County Attorney and Hale. The Sheriff and Hale are men in middle life, the County Attorney is a young man; all are much bundled up and go at once to the stove. They are followed by the two women—the Sheriff's wife first; she is a slightly wiry woman, a thin nervous face. Mrs. Hale is larger and would ordinarily be called more comfortable looking, but she is disturbed now and looks fearfully about as she enters. The women have come in slowly and stand close together near the door.

County Attorney (*rubbing his hands*). This feels good. Come up to the fire, ladies.

Mrs. Peters (*after taking a step forward*). I'm not—cold.

Sheriff (*unbuttoning his overcoat and stepping away from the stove as if to the beginning of official business*). Now, Mr. Hale, before we move things about, you explain to Mr. Henderson just what you saw when you came here yesterday morning.

County Attorney. By the way, has anything been moved? Are things just as you left them yesterday?

Sheriff (*looking about*). It's just the same. When it dropped below zero last night, I thought I'd better send Frank out this morning to make a fire for us—no use getting pneumonia with a big case on; but I told him not to touch anything except the stove—and you know Frank.

County Attorney. Somebody should have been left here yesterday.

Sheriff. Oh—yesterday. When I had to send Frank to Morris Center for that man who went crazy—I want you to know I had my hands full yesterday. I knew you could get back from Omaha by today, and as long as I went over everything here myself—

County Attorney. Well, Mr. Hale, tell just what happened when you came here yesterday morning.

Hale. Harry and I had started to town with a load of potatoes. We came along the road from my place; and as I got here, I said, "I'm going to see if I can't get John Wright to go in with me on a party telephone!" I spoke to Wright about it once before, and he put me off, saying folks talked too much anyway, and all he asked was peace and quiet—I guess you know about how much he talked himself; but I thought maybe if I went to the house and talked about it before his wife, though I said to Harry that I didn't know as what his wife wanted made much difference to John—

County Attorney. Let's talk about that later, Mr. Hale. I do want to talk about that, but tell now just what happened when you got to the house.

Hale. I didn't hear or see anything; I knocked at the door, and still it was all quiet inside. I knew they must be up, it was past eight o'clock. So I knocked again, and I thought I heard somebody say, "Come in." I wasn't sure, I'm not sure yet, but I opened the door—this door (*indicating the door by which the two women are still standing*), and there in that rocker—(*pointing to it*) sat Mrs. Wright. (*They all look at the rocker.*)

County Attorney. What was she doing?

Hale. She was rockin' back and forth. She had her apron in her hand and was kind of—pleating it.

COUNTY ATTORNEY. And how did she—look?

HALE. Well, she looked queer.

COUNTY ATTORNEY. How do you mean—queer?

HALE. Well, as if she didn't know what she was going to do next. And kind of done up.

COUNTY ATTORNEY. How did she seem to feel about your coming?

HALE. Why, I don't think she minded—one way or other. She didn't pay much attention. I said, "How do, Mrs. Wright, it's cold, ain't it?" And she said, "Is it?" —and went on kind of pleating at her apron. Well, I was surprised; she didn't ask me to come up to the stove, or to set down, but just sat there, not even looking at me, so I said, "I want to see John." And then she—laughed. I guess you would call it a laugh. I thought of Harry and the team outside, so I said a little sharp: "Can't I see John?" "No," she says, kind o' dull like. "Ain't he home?" says I. "Yes," says she, "he's home." "Then why can't I see him?" I asked her, out of patience. "'Cause he's dead," says she. *"Dead?"* says I. She just nodded her head, not getting a bit excited, but rockin' back and forth. "Why—where is he?" says I, not knowing what to say. She just pointed upstairs—like that (*himself pointing to the room above*). I got up, with the idea of going up there. I walked from there to here—then I says, "Why, what did he die of?" "He died of a rope around his neck," says she, and just went on pleatin' at her apron. Well, I went out and called Harry. I thought I might—need help. We went upstairs, and there he was lyin'—

COUNTY ATTORNEY. I think I'd rather have you go into that upstairs, where you can point it all out. Just go on now with the rest of the story.

HALE. Well, my first thought was to get that rope off. I looked . . . (*Stops, his face twitches.*) . . . but Harry, he went up to him, and he said, "No, he's dead all right, and we'd better not touch anything." So we went back downstairs. She was still sitting that same way. "Has anybody been notified?" I asked. "No," says she, unconcerned. "Who did this, Mrs. Wright?" said Harry. He said it businesslike—and she stopped pleatin' of her apron. "I don't know," she says. "You don't *know?*" says Harry. "No," says she, "Weren't you sleepin' in the bed with him?" says Harry. "Yes," says she, "but I was on the inside." "Somebody slipped a rope round his neck and strangled him, and you didn't wake up?" says Harry. "I didn't wake up," she said after him. We must 'a looked as if we didn't see how that could be, for after a minute she said, "I sleep sound." Harry was going to ask her more questions, but I said maybe we ought to let her tell her story first to the coroner, or the sheriff, so Harry went fast as he could to Rivers' place, where there's a telephone.

COUNTY ATTORNEY. And what did Mrs. Wright do when she knew that you had gone for the coroner?

HALE. She moved from that chair to this over here . . . (*Pointing to a small chair in the corner*) . . . and just sat there with her hands held together and looking down. I got a feeling that I ought to make some conversation, so I said I had come in to see if John wanted to put in a telephone, and at that she started to laugh, and then she stopped and looked at me—scared. (*The County Attorney, who has had his notebook out, makes a note.*) I dunno, maybe it wasn't scared. I wouldn't like to say it was. Soon Harry got back, and then Dr. Lloyd came, and you, Mr. Peters, and so I guess that's all I know that you don't.

COUNTY ATTORNEY (*looking around*). I guess we'll go upstairs first—and then out to the barn and around there. (*To the Sheriff.*) You're convinced that there was nothing important here—nothing that would point to any motive?

SHERIFF. Nothing here but kitchen things.

(The County Attorney, after again looking around the kitchen, opens the door of a cupboard closet. He gets up on a chair and looks on a shelf. Pulls his hand away, sticky.)

COUNTY ATTORNEY. Here's a nice mess.

(The women draw nearer.)

MRS. PETERS (*to the other woman*). Oh, her fruit; it did freeze. (*To the Lawyer.*) She worried about that when it turned so cold. She said the fir'd go out and her jars would break.

SHERIFF. Well, can you beat the women! Held for murder and worryin' about her preserves.

COUNTY ATTORNEY. I guess before we're through she may have something more serious than preserves to worry about.

HALE. Well, women are used to worrying over trifles.

(*The two women move a little closer together.*)

COUNTY ATTORNEY (*with the gallantry of a young politician*). And yet, for all their worries, what would we do without the ladies? (*The women do not unbend. He goes to the sink, takes a dipperful of water from the pail and, pouring it into a basin, washes his hands. Starts to wipe them on the roller towel, turns it for a cleaner place.*) Dirty towels! (*Kicks his foot against the pans under the sink.*) Not much of a housekeeper, would you say, lades?

MRS. HALE (*stiffly*). There's a great deal of work to be done on a farm.

COUNTY ATTORNEY. To be sure. And yet . . . (*With a little bow to her*) . . . I know there are some Dickson county farmhouses which do not have such roller towels. (*He gives it a pull to expose its full length again.*)

MRS. HALE. Those towels get dirty awful quick. Men's hand's aren't always as clean as they might be.

COUNTY ATTORNEY. Ah, loyal to your sex I see. But you and Mrs. Wright were neighbors. I suppose you were friends, too.

MRS. HALE (*shaking her head*). I've not seen much of her of late years. I've not been in this house—it's more than a year.

COUNTY ATTORNEY. And why was that? You didn't like her?

MRS. HALE. I liked her well enough. Farmers' wives have their hands full, Mr. Henderson. And then—

COUNTY ATTORNEY. Yes—?

MRS. HALE (*looking about*). It never seemed a very cheerful place.

COUNTY ATTORNEY. No—it's not cheerful. I shouldn't say she had the homemaking instinct.

MRS. HALE. Well, I don't know as Wright had, either.

COUNTY ATTORNEY. You mean that they didn't get on very well?

MRS. HALE. No, I don't mean anything. But I don't think a place'd be any cheerfuler for John Wright's being in it.

COUNTY ATTORNEY. I'd like to talk more of that a little later. I want to get the lay of things upstairs now. (*He goes to the left, where three steps lead to a stair door*).

SHERIFF. I suppose anything Mrs. Peters does'll be all right. She was to take in some clothes for her, you know, and a few little things. We left in such a hurry yesterday.

COUNTY ATTORNEY. Yes, but I would like to see what you take, Mrs. Peters, and keep an eye out for anything that might be of use to us.

MRS. PETERS. Yes, Mr. Henderson.

(*The women listen to the men's steps on the stairs, then look about the kitchen.*)

MRS. HALE. I'd hate to have men coming into my kitchen, snooping around and criticizing. (*She arranges the pans under sink which the Lawyer had shoved out of place.*)

MRS. PETERS. Of course it's no more than their duty.

MRS. HALE. Duty's all right, but I guess that deputy sheriff that came out to make the fire might have got a little of this on. (*Gives the roller towel a pull.*) Wish I'd thought of that sooner. Seems mean to talk about her for not having things slicked up when she had to come away in such a hurry.

MRS. PETERS (*who has gone to a small table in the left rear corner of the room, and lifted one end of a towel that covers a pan*). She had bread set. (*Stands still.*)

MRS. HALE (*eyes fixed on a loaf of bread beside the breadbox, which is on a low shelf at the other side of the room. Moves slowly toward it*). She was going to put this in there. (*Picks up loaf, then abruptly drops it. In a manner of returning to familiar things.*) It's a shame about her fruit. I wonder if it's all gone. (*Gets up on the chair and looks.*) I think there's some here that's all right, Mrs. Peters. Yes—here; (*Holding it toward the window.*) this is cherries, too. (*Looking again.*) I declare I believe that's the only one. (*Gets down, bottle in her hand. Goes to the sink and wipes it off on the outside.*) She'll feel awful bad after all her hard work in the hot weather. I remember the afternoon I put up my cherries last summer. (*She puts the bottle on the big kitchen table, center of the room, front table. With a sigh, is about to sit down in the rocking chair. Before she is seated realizes what chair it is; with a slow look at it, steps back. The chair, which she has touched, rocks back and forth.*)

MRS. PETERS. Well, I must get those things from the front room closet. (*She goes to the door at the right, but after looking into the other room steps back.*) You coming with me, Mrs. Hale? You could help me carry them. (*They go into the other room; reappear, Mrs. Peters carrying a dress and skirt, Mrs. Hale following with a pair of shoes.*)

MRS. PETERS. My, it's cold in there. (*She puts the cloth on the big table, and hurries to the stove.*)

MRS. HALE (*examining the skirt*). Wright was close. I think maybe that's why she kept so much to herself. She didn't even belong to the Ladies' Aid. I suppose she felt she couldn't do her part, and then you don't enjoy things when you feel shabby. She used to wear pretty clothes and be lively, when she was Minnie Foster, one of the town girls singing in the choir. But that—oh, that was thirty years ago. This all you was to take in?

MRS. PETERS. She said she wanted an apron. Funny thing to want, for there isn't much to get you dirty in jail, goodness knows. But I suppose just to make her feel more natural. She said they was in the top drawer in this cupboard. Yes, here. And then her little shawl that always hung behind the door. (*Opens stair door and looks*). Yes, here it is. (*Quickly shuts door leading upstairs.*)

MRS. HALE (*abruptly moving toward her*). Mrs. Peters?

MRS. PETERS. Yes, Mrs. Hale?

MRS. HALE. Do you think she did it?

MRS. PETERS (*in a frightened voice*). Oh, I don't know.

MRS. HALE. Well, I don't think she did. Asking for an apron and her little shawl. Worrying about her fruit.

MRS. PETERS (*starts to speak, glances up, where footsteps are heard in the room above. In a low voice*). Mr. Peters says it looks bad for her. Mr. Henderson is awful sarcastic in speech, and he'll make fun of her sayin' she didn't wake up.

MRS. HALE. Well, I guess John Wright didn't wake when they was slipping that rope under his neck.

MRS. PETERS. No, it's strange. It must have been done awful crafty and still. They say it was such a—funny way to kill a man, rigging it all up like that.

MRS. HALE. That's just what Mr. Hale said. There was a gun in the house. He says that's what he can't understand.

MRS. PETERS. Mr. Henderson said coming out that what was needed for the case was a motive; something to show anger, or—sudden feeling.

MRS. HALE (*who is standing by the table*). Well, I don't see any signs of anger around here. (*She puts her hand on the dish towel which lies on the table, stands looking down at the table, one half of which is clean, the other half messy.*) It's wiped here. (*Makes a move as if to finish work, then turns and looks at loaf of bread outside the breadbox. Drops towel. In that voice of coming back to familiar things.*) Wonder how they are finding things upstairs? I hope she had it a little more red-up there. You know, it seems kind of *sneaking*. Locking her up in town and then coming out here and trying to get her own house to turn against her!

MRS. PETERS. But, Mrs. Hale, the law is the law.

MRS. HALE. I s'pose 'tis. (*Unbuttoning her coat.*) Better loosen up your things, Mrs. Peters. You won't feel them when you go out.

(*Mrs. Peters takes off her fur tippet, goes to hang it on hook at the back of room, stands looking at the under part of the small corner table.*)

MRS. PETERS. She was piecing a quilt. (*She brings the large sewing basket, and they look at the bright pieces.*)

MRS. HALE. It's log cabin pattern. Pretty, isn't it? I wonder if she was goin' to quilt or just knot it?

(*Footsteps have been heard coming down the stairs. The Sheriff enters, followed by Hale and the County Attorney.*)

SHERIFF. They wonder if she was going to quilt it or just knot it. (*The men laugh, the women look abashed.*)

COUNTY ATTORNEY (*rubbing his hands over the stove*). Frank's fire didn't do much up there, did it? Well, let's go out to the barn and get that cleared up. (*The men go outside.*)

MRS. HALE (*resentfully*). I don't know as there's anything so strange, our takin' up our time with little things while we're waiting for them to get the evidence. (*She sits down at the big table, smoothing out a block with decision.*) I don't see as it's anything to laugh about.

MRS. PETERS (*apologetically*). Of course they've got awful important things on their minds. (*Pulls up a chair and joins Mrs. Hale at the table.*)

MRS. HALE (*examining another block*). Mrs. Peters, look at this one. Here, this is the one she was working on, and look at the sewing! All the rest of it has been so nice and even. And look at this! It's all over the place! Why, it looks as if she didn't know what she was about! (*After she has said this, they look at each other, then started to glance back at the door. After an instant Mrs. Hale has pulled at a knot and ripped the sewing.*)

MRS. PETERS. Oh, what are you doing, Mrs. Hale?

MRS. HALE (*mildly*). Just pulling out a stitch or two that's not sewed very good. (*Threading a needle.*) Bad sewing always made me fidgety.

MRS. PETERS (*nervously*). I don't think we ought to touch things.

MRS. HALE. I'll just finish up this end. (*Suddenly stopping and leaning forward.*) Mrs. Peters?

MRS. PETERS. Yes, Mrs. Hale?

MRS. HALE. What do you suppose she was so nervous about?

MRS. PETERS. Oh—I don't know. I don't know as she was nervous. I sometimes sew awful queer when I'm just tired. (*Mrs. Hale starts to say something, looks at Mrs. Peters, then goes on sewing.*) Well, I must get these things wrapped up. They may be through sooner than we think. (*Putting apron and other things together.*) I wonder where I can find a piece of paper, and string.

MRS. HALE. In that cupboard, maybe.

MRS. PETERS (*looking in cupboard*). Why, here's a birdcage. (*Holds it up.*) Did she have a bird, Mrs. Hale?

MRS. HALE. Why, I don't know whether she did or not—I've not been here for so long. There was a man around last year selling canaries cheap, but I don't know as she took one; maybe she did. She used to sing real pretty herself.

MRS. PETERS (*glancing around*). Seems funny to think of a bird here. But she must have had one, or why should she have a cage? I wonder what happened to it?

MRS. HALE. I s'pose maybe the cat got it.

MRS. PETERS. No, she didn't have a cat. She's got that feeling some people have about cats—being afraid of them. My cat got in her room, and she was real upset and asked me to take it out.

MRS. HALE. My sister Bessie was like that. Queer, ain't it?

MRS. PETERS (*examining the cage*). Why, look at this door. It's broke. One hinge is pulled apart.

MRS. HALE (*looking, too*). Looks as if someone must have been rough with it.

MRS. PETERS. Why, yes. (*She brings the cage forward and puts it on the table.*)

MRS. HALE. I wish if they're going to find any evidence they'd be about it. I don't like this place.

MRS. PETERS. But I'm awful glad you came with me, Mrs. Hale. It would be lonesome for me sitting here alone.

MRS. HALE. It would, wouldn't it? (*Dropping her sewing.*) But I tell you what I do wish, Mrs. Peters. I wish I had come over sometimes when *she* was here. I—(*looking around the room.*)—wish I had.

MRS. PETERS. But of course you were awful busy, Mrs. Hale—your house and your children.

MRS. HALE. I could've come. I stayed away because it weren't cheerful—and that's why I ought to have come. I—I've never liked this place. Maybe because it's down in a hollow, and you don't see the road. I dunno what it is, but it's a lonesome place and always was. I wish I had come over to see Minnie Foster sometimes. I can see now—(*Shakes her head.*)

MRS. PETERS. Well, you mustn't reproach yourself, Mrs. Hale. Somehow we just don't see how it is with other folks until—something comes up.

MRS. HALE. Not having children makes less work—but it makes a quiet house, and Wright out to work all day, and no company when he did come in. Did you know John Wright, Mrs. Peters?

MRS. PETERS. Not to know him; I've seen him in town. They say he was a good man.

MRS. HALE. Yes—good; he didn't drink, and kept his word as well as most, I guess, and paid his debts. But he was a hard man, Mrs. Peters. Just to pass the time of day with him. (*Shivers.*) Like a raw wind that gets to the bone. (*Pauses, her eye falling on the cage.*) I should think she would 'a wanted a bird. But what do you suppose went with it?

MRS. PETERS. I don't know, unless it got sick and died. (*She reaches over and swings the broken door, swings it again; both women watch it.*)

MRS. HALE. You weren't raised round here, were you? (*Mrs. Peters shakes her head.*) You didn't know—her?

MRS. PETERS. Not till they brought her yesterday.

MRS. HALE. She—come to think of it, she was kind of like a bird herself—real sweet and pretty, but kind of timid and—fluttery. How—she—did—change. (*Silence; then as if struck by a happy thought and relieved to get back to everyday things.*) Tell you what, Mrs. Peters, why don't you take the quilt in with you? It might take up her mind.

MRS. PETERS. Why, I think that's a real nice idea, Mrs. Hale. There couldn't possibly be any objection to it, could there? Now, just what would I take? I wonder if her patches are in here—and her things. (*They look in the sewing basket.*)

MRS. HALE. Here's some red. I expect this has got sewing things in it. (*Brings out a fancy box.*) What a pretty box. Looks like something somebody would give you. Maybe her scissors are in here. (*Opens box. Suddenly puts her hand to her nose.*) Why—(*Mrs. Peters bends nearer; then turns her face away.*) There's something wrapped up in this piece of silk.

MRS. PETERS. Why, this isn't her scissors.

MRS. HALE (*lifting the silk*). Oh, Mrs. Peters—it's—(*Mrs. Peters bends closer*)

MRS. PETERS. It's the bird.

MRS. HALE (*jumping up*). But, Mrs. Peters—look at it. Its neck! Look at its neck! It's all—other side *to*.

MRS. PETERS. Somebody—wrung—its neck.

(Their eyes meet. A look of growing comprehension of horror. Steps are heard outside. Mrs. Hale slips box under quilt pieces, and sinks into her chair. Enter Sheriff and County Attorney. Mrs. Peters rises.)

COUNTY ATTORNEY (*as one turning from serious things to little pleasantries*). Well, ladies, have you decided whether she was going to quilt it or knot it?

MRS. PETERS. We think she was going to—knot it.

COUNTY ATTORNEY. Well, that's interesting, I'm sure. (*Seeing the birdcage.*) Has the bird flown?

MRS. HALE (*putting more quilt pieces over the box*). We think the—cat got it.

COUNTY ATTORNEY (*preoccupied*). Is there a cat?

(*Mrs. Hale glances in a quick covert way at Mrs. Peters.*)

MRS. PETERS. Well, not now. They're superstitious, you know. They, leave.

COUNTY ATTORNEY (*to Sheriff Peters, continuing an interrupted conversation*). No sign at all of anyone having come from the outside. Their own rope. Now let's go up again and go over it piece by piece. (*They start upstairs.*) It would have to have been someone who knew just the—

(*Mrs. Peters sits down. The two women sit there not looking at one another, but as if peering into something and at the same time holding back. When they talk now, it is the manner of feeling their way over strange ground, as if afraid of what they are saying, but as if they cannot help saying it.*)

MRS. HALE. She liked the bird. She was going to bury it in that pretty box.

MRS. PETERS (*in a whisper*). When I was a girl—my kitten—there was a boy took a hatchet, and before my eyes—and before I could get there—(*Covers her face an instant.*) If they hadn't held me back, I would have—(*Catches herself, looks upstairs where steps are heard, falters weakly.*)—hurt him.

MRS. HALE (*with a slow look around her*). I wonder how it would seem never to have had any children around. (*Pause.*) No, Wright wouldn't like the bird—a thing that sang. She used to sing. He killed that, too.

MRS. PETERS (*moving uneasily*). We don't know who killed the bird.

MRS. HALE. I knew John Wright.

MRS. PETERS. It was an awful thing was done in this house that night, Mrs. Hale. Killing a man while he slept, slipping a rope around his neck that choked the life out of him.

MRS. HALE. His neck. Choked the life out of him.

(*Her hand goes out and rests on the birdcage.*)

MRS. PETERS (*with a rising voice*). We don't know who killed him. We don't know.

MRS. HALE (*her own feeling not interrupted*). If there'd been years and years of nothing, then a bird to sing to you, it would be awful—still, after the bird was still.

MRS. PETERS (*something within her speaking*). I know what stillness is. When we homesteaded in Dakota, and my first baby died—after he was two years old, and me with no other then—

MRS. HALE (*moving*). How soon do you suppose they'll be through, looking for evidence?

MRS. PETERS. I know what stillness is. (*Pulling herself back.*) The law has got to punish crime, Mrs. Hale.

MRS. HALE (*not as if answering that*). I wish you'd seen Minnie Foster when she wore a white dress with blue ribbons and stood up there in the choir and sang. (*A look around the room.*) Oh I *wish* I'd come over here once in a while! That was a crime! That was a crime! Who's going to punish that?

MRS. PETERS (*looking upstairs*). We mustn't—take on.

MRS. HALE. I might have known she needed help! I know how things can be—for women. I tell you, it's queer, Mrs. Peters. We live close together and we live far apart. We all go through the same things—it's all just a different kind of the same thing. (*Brushes her eyes, noticing the bottle of fruit, reaches out for it.*) If I was you, I wouldn't tell her her fruit was gone. To her it *ain't.* Tell her it's all right. Take this in to prove it to her. She—she may never know whether it was broke or not.

MRS. PETERS (*takes the bottle, looks about for something to wrap it in; takes petticoat from the clothes brought from the other room, very nervously begins winding this around the bottle. In a false voice*). My, it's a good thing the men couldn't hear us. Wouldn't they just laugh! Getting all stirred up over a little thing like a—dead canary. As if that could have anything to do with—with—wouldn't they *laugh!*

(*The men are heard coming downstairs.*)

MRS. HALE (*under her breath*). Maybe they would—maybe they wouldn't.

COUNTY ATTORNEY. No, Peters, it's all perfectly clear except a reason for doing it. But you know juries when it comes to women. If there was something definite. Something to show—something to make a story about—a thing that would connect up with this strange way of doing it.

(*The women's eyes meet for an instant. Enter Hale from outer door.*)

HALE. Well, I've got the team around. Pretty cold out there.

COUNTY ATTORNEY. I'm going to stay here awhile by myself. (*To the Sheriff.*) You can send Frank out for me, can't you? I want to go over everything, I'm not satisfied that we can't do better.

SHERIFF. Do you want to see what Mrs. Peters is going to take in? (*The Lawyer goes to the table, picks up the apron, laughs.*)

COUNTY ATTORNEY. Oh I guess they're not very dangerous things the ladies have picked up. (*Moves a few things about, disturbing the quilt pieces which cover the box. Steps back.*) No, Mrs. Peters doesn't need supervising. For that matter, a sheriff's wife is married to the law. Ever think of it that way, Mrs. Peters?

MRS. PETERS. Not—just that way.

SHERIFF (*chuckling*). Married to the law. (*Moves toward the other room.*) I just want you to come in here a minute, George. We ought to take a look at these windows.

COUNTY ATTORNEY (*scoffingly*). Oh, windows!

SHERIFF. We'll be right out, Mr. Hale.

(*Hale goes outside. The Sheriff follows the County Attorney into the other room. Then Mrs. Hale rises, hands tight together, looking intensely at Mrs. Peters, whose eyes take a slow turn, finally meeting Mrs. Hale's. A moment Mrs. Hale holds her, then her own eyes point the way to where the box in the bag she is wearing. It is too big. She opens box, starts to take the bird out, cannot touch it, goes to pieces, stands there helpless. Sound of a knob turning in the other room. Mrs. Hale snatches the box and puts it in the pocket of her big coat. Enter County Attorney and Sheriff.*)

COUNTY ATTORNEY (*facetiously*). Well, Henry, at least we found out that she was not going to quilt it. She was going to—what is it you call it, ladies?

MRS. HALE (*her hand against her pocket*). We call it—knot it, Mr. Henderson.

CURTAIN

Postreading Writing Assignments

Option 1: Rewrite this play setting it in the 1990s or early 2000s. What needs to change about the characters, the setting, and the dialogue between the men and the women?

Option 2: Write a response exploring the "clues" (to solve the murder) uncovered in this play. Which clues do the men discover? Which clues do the women discover? Who has gained your sympathy by the end? Why?

Extended Writing Assignments

Option 3: The gender issues in this play surface early and become key to the entire plot. Notice the ways in which the men and the women treat one another in this play. Write an essay exploring the gender issues apparent in this play that most interest you; for example, you might explore the following questions: How do the men respond to the women? Is this response important in the play? Do the men underestimate the women? Do the women take advantage of the men's attitude toward them? Do we still hold any of these attitudes toward women today, or have we "come a long way"?

Option 4: Part of the power that the women characters have over the men involves language. The men stereotype and dismiss the women's ways of thinking, analyzing, and voicing their thoughts. The men seem to create an undercurrent of hostility. Write an essay in which you examine issues of language and stereotyping. Analyze the dialogue between the male and the female characters. What do the men do with language? What do the women do? How did you, as a reader, respond to the way the women were treated?

Forging Connections

Option 5: Read or reread Ernest Hemingway's short story "Hills Like White Elephants." Both texts present men and women talking around and past each other. Write an essay analyzing the ways that each story presents men and women talking and interacting. Consider the following questions: Are the men and the women in both stories misunderstanding one another? How so? Do you think that the men and the women are "choosing" to misunderstand one another? Explore specific sections of dialogue from both texts to come to your own understanding of gender issues presented in *Trifles* and "Hills Like White Elephants."

Ernest Hemingway

HILLS LIKE WHITE ELEPHANTS

Ernest Hemingway, born in Oak Park, Illinois, lead a colorful and diverse life, working as a reporter, ambulance driver, European correspondent in the Spanish Civil War, and as a war correspondent in China; he was also an avid sportsman and game hunter. Noted for his simple writing style, he uses short sentences and dialogue to explore the issues of his generation, which is sometimes called the "Lost Generation." "Hills Like White Elephants" first appeared in Men Without Women, *a collection of short stories published in 1927.*

Prereading Journal Questions

1. What are white elephants? Propose various possible meanings of this phrase.
2. Explore the simile that hills are like white elephants.

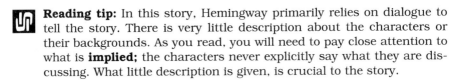

Reading tip: In this story, Hemingway primarily relies on dialogue to tell the story. There is very little description about the characters or their backgrounds. As you read, you will need to pay close attention to what is **implied;** the characters never explicitly say what they are discussing. What little description is given, is crucial to the story.

The hills across the valley of the Ebro were long and white. On this side there was no shade and no trees and the station was between two lines of rails in the sun. Close against the side of the station there was the warm shadow of the building and a curtain, made of strings of bamboo beads, hung across the open door into the bar, to keep out flies. The American and the girl with him sat at a table in the shade, outside the building. It was very hot and the express from Barcelona would come in forty minutes. It stopped at this junction for two minutes and went on to Madrid.

"What should we drink?" the girl asked. She had taken off her hat and put it on the table.

"It's pretty hot," the man said.

"Let's drink beer."

"Dos cervezas," the man said into the curtain.

"Big ones?" a woman asked from the doorway.

"Yes. Two big ones."

The woman brought two glasses of beer and two felt pads. She put the felt pads and the beer glasses on the table and looked at the man and the girl. The girl was looking off at the line of hills. They were white in the sun and the country was brown and dry.

"They look like white elephants," she said.

"I've never seen one," the man drank his beer.

"No, you wouldn't have."

"I might have," the man said. "Just because you say I wouldn't have doesn't prove anything."

The girl looked at the bead curtain. "They're painted something on it," she said. "What does it say?"

"Anis del Toro. It's a drink."

"Could we try it?"

The man called "Listen" through the curtain. The woman came out from the bar.

"Four reales."

"We want two Anis del Toro."

"With water?"

"Do you want it with water?"

"I don't know," the girl said. "Is it good with water?"

"It's all right."

"You want them with water?" asked the woman.

"Yes, with water."

"It tastes like licorice," the girl said and put the glass down.

"That's the way with everything."

"Yes," said the girl. "Everything tastes of licorice. Especially all the things you've waited so long for, like absinthe."

"Oh, cut it out."

"You started it," the girl said. "I was being amused. I was having a fine time."

"Well, let's try and have a fine time."

"All right. I was trying. I said the mountains looked like white elephants. Wasn't that bright?"

"That was bright."

"I wanted to try this new drink. That's all we do, isn't it—look at things and try new drinks?"

"I guess so."

The girl looked across at the hills.

"They're lovely hills," she said. "They don't really look like white elephants. I just meant the coloring of their skin through the trees."

"Should we have another drink?"

"All right."

The warm wind blew the bead curtain against the table.

"The beer's nice and cool," the man said.

"It's lovely," the girl said.

"It's really an awfully simple operation, Jig," the man said. "It's not really an operation at all."

The girl looked at the ground the table legs rested on.

"I know you wouldn't mind it, Jig. It's really not anything. It's just to let the air in."

The girl did not say anything.

"I'll go with you and I'll stay with you all the time. They just let the air in and then it's all perfectly natural."

"Then what will we do afterward?"

"We'll be fine afterward. Just like we were before."

"What makes you think so?"

"That's the only thing that bothers us. It's the only thing that's made us unhappy."

The girl looked at the bead curtain, put her hand out and took hold of two of the strings of bead.

"And you think then we'll be all right and be happy."

"I know we will. You don't have to be afraid. I've known lots of people that have done it."

"So have I," said the girl. "And afterward they were all so happy."

"Well," the man said, "if you don't want to you don't have to. I wouldn't have you do it if you didn't want to. But I know it's perfectly simple."

"And you really want to?"

"I think it's the best thing to do. But I don't want you to do it if you don't really want to."

"And if I do it you'll be happy and things will be like they were and you'll love me?"

"I love you now. You know I love you."

"I know. But if I do it, then it will be nice again if I say things are like white elephants, and you'll like it?"

"I'll love it. I love it now but I just can't think about it. You know how I get when I worry."

"If I do it you won't ever worry?"

"I won't worry about that because it's perfectly simple."

"Then I'll do it. Because I don't care about me."

"What do you mean?"

"I don't care about me."

"Well, I care about you."

"Oh, yes. But I don't care about me. And I'll do it and then everything will be fine."

"I don't want you to do it if you feel that way."

The girl stood up and walked to the end of the station. Across, on the other side, were fields of grain and trees along the banks of the Ebro. Far away, beyond the river, were mountains. The shadow of a cloud moved across the field of grain and she saw the river through the trees.

"And we could have all this," she said. "And we could have everything and every day we make it more impossible."

"What did you say?"

"I said we could have everything."

"We can have everything."

"No, we can't."

"We can have the whole world."

"No, we can't."

"We can go everywhere."

"No, we can't. It isn't ours any more."

"It's ours."

"No, it isn't. And once they take it away, you never get it back."

"But they haven't taken it away."

"We'll wait and see."

"Come on back in the shade," he said. "You mustn't feel that way."

"I don't feel any way," the girl said. "I just know things."

"I don't want you to do anything that you don't want to do——"

"Nor that isn't good for me," she said. "I know. Could we have another beer?"

"All right. But you've got to realize——"

"I realize," the girl said. "Can't we maybe stop talking?"

They sat down at the table and the girl looked across at the hills on the dry side of the valley and the man looked at her and at the table.

"You've got to realize," he said, "that I don't want you to do it if you don't want to. I'm perfectly willing to go through with it if it means anything to you."

"Doesn't it mean anything to you? We could get along."

"Of course it does. But I don't want anybody but you. I don't want any one else. And I know it's perfectly simple."

"Yes, you know it's perfectly simple."

"It's all right for you to say that, but I do know it."

"Would you do something for me now?"

"I'd do anything for you."

"Would you please please please please please please please stop talking?"

He did not say anything but looked at the bags against the wall of the station. There were labels on them from all the hotels where they had spent nights.

"But I don't want you to," he said, "I don't care anything about it."

"I'll scream," the girl said.

The woman came out through the curtains with two glasses of beer and put them down on the damp felt pads. "The train comes in five minutes," she said.

"What did she say?" asked the girl.

"That the train is coming in five minutes."

The girl smiled brightly at the woman, to thank her.

"I'd better take the bags over to the other side of the station," the man said. She smiled at him.

"All right. Then come back and we'll finish the beer."

He picked up the two heavy bags and carried them around the station to the other tracks. He looked up the tracks but could not see the train. Coming back, he walked through the barroom, where people waiting for the train were drinking. He drank an Anis at the bar and looked at the people. They were all waiting reasonably for the train. He went out through the bead curtain. She was sitting at the table and smiled at him.

"Do you feel better?" he asked.

"I feel fine," she said. "There's nothing wrong with me. I feel fine."

Postreading Writing Assignments

Option 1: Hemingway never explicitly states what the man and the woman are discussing. Write a response exploring what you believe their discussion to be about. What led you to your conclusion? Use specific evidence from the text to support your assertions.

Option 2: Analyze the significance of the title. Use the responses from your prereading journal questions as a springboard. Explore several possible meanings, but use the text to support your position.

Option 3: Discuss a time when you were at a crossroads in your life and were required to make a significant decision. Compare or contrast your experience to that of the man or the woman in Hemingway's story.

Extended Writing Assignments

Option 4: Write an essay analyzing the relationship between the man and the woman. They are dealing with a serious issue and have made a decision that affects both their lives. How do you understand their relationship, the decision they have reached, and their future together? Where do you think this relationship will go? Will the couple stay together? Why, or why not?

Option 5: Consider the symbolism of the landscape in this story. There are two contrasting landscapes: one white hills and barren, the other a rich fertile valley. What does the landscape add to the story? How does the symbolism of the landscape add to your understanding of the story?

Forging Connections

Option 6: Read or reread Susan Glaspell's play *Trifles*. Both texts present men and women talking around and past each other. Write an essay analyzing the ways each story presents men and women talking and interacting. Consider the following questions: Are the men and the women in both stories misunderstanding one another? How so? Do you think the men and the women are "choosing" to misunderstand one another? Explore specific sections of dialogue from both texts to come to your own understanding of gender issues presented in *Trifles* and "Hills Like White Elephants."

E. D. Hirsch, Jr.

THE DECLINE OF TEACHING CULTURAL LITERACY

E. D. Hirsch, Jr., from 1989–1994, was the Lincoln Kent Professor of English at the University of Virginia, Charlottesville. In addition to writing a number of texts and articles on education and curriculum, Hirsch is the founder and president of the Core Knowledge Foundation. The selection here is from his book Cultural Literacy.

Prereading Journal Questions

1. Define the term "cultural literacy." You might want to look up both words in a dictionary, define them separately, and draw inferences as to how Hirsch might use this particular term. After doing this, think about the title of the text you are about to read: "The Decline of Teaching Cultural Literacy." What are you expecting from this text?
2. What kinds of things do you think "culturally literate" people should know? What has lead you to include some things and not others? What are your criteria?

Reading tip: This is an academic text. Hirsch refers to various educational theories, political groups, and so on. There may be some terms that are unfamiliar to you; try defining or understanding these terms in the context of the essay. Rather than skipping them, hoping they are not important, note any references that puzzle you, respond to them in your journal, bring them up during class discussion, and/or look them up if possible. Do whatever you can to create, as much as possible, an understanding of the whole of this essay.

Why have our schools failed to fulfill their fundamental acculturative responsibility? In view of the immense importance of cultural literacy for speaking, listening, reading, and writing, why has the need for a definite, shared body of information been so rarely mentioned in discussions of education? In the educational writings of the past decade, I find almost nothing on this topic, which is not arcane. People who are introduced to the subject quickly understand why oral or written communication requires a lot of shared background knowledge. It's not the difficulty or novelty of the idea that has caused it to receive so little attention.

Let me hazard a guess about one reason for our neglect of the subject. We have ignored cultural literacy in thinking about education—certainly I as a researcher also ignored it until recently—precisely because it was something we have been able to take for granted. We ignore the air we breathe until it is thin or foul. Cultural literacy is the oxygen of social intercourse. Only when we run into cultural illiteracy are we shocked into recognizing the importance of the information that we had unconsciously assumed.

To be sure, a minimal level of information is possessed by any normal person who lives in the United States and speaks elementary English. Almost everybody knows what is meant by *dollar* and that cars must travel on the right-hand side of the road. But this elementary level of information is not sufficient for a modern democracy. It isn't sufficient to read newspapers (a sin against Jeffersonian democracy), and it isn't sufficient to achieve economic fairness and high productivity. Cultural literacy lies *above* the everyday levels of knowledge that everyone possesses and *below* the expert level known only to specialists. It is that middle ground of cultural knowledge possessed by the "common reader." It includes information that we have traditionally expected our children to receive in school, but which they no longer do.

During recent decades Americans have hesitated to make a decision about the specific knowledge that children need to learn in school. Our elementary schools are not only dominated by the content-neutral ideas of Rousseau and Dewey, they are also governed by approximately sixteen thousand independent school districts. We have viewed this dispersion of educational authority as an insurmountable obstacle to altering the fragmentation of the school curriculum even when we have questioned that fragmentation. We have permitted school policies that have shrunk the body of information that Americans share, and these policies have caused our national literacy to decline.

At the same time we have searched with some eagerness for causes such as television that lie outside the schools. But we should direct our attention undeviatingly toward what the schools teach rather than toward family structure, social class, or TV programming. No doubt, reforms outside the schools are important, but they are harder to accomplish. Moreover, we have accumulated a great deal of evidence that faulty policy in the schools is the chief cause of deficient literacy. Researchers who have studied the factors influencing educational outcomes have found that the school curriculum is the most important controllable influence on what our children know and don't know about our literate culture.

It will not do to blame television for the state of our literacy. Television watching does reduce reading and often encroaches on homework. Much of it is admittedly the intellectual equivalent of junk food. But in some respects, such as its use of standard written English, television watching is acculturative. Moreover, as Herbert Walberg points out, the schools themselves must be held partly responsible for excessive television watching, because they have not firmly insisted that students complete significant amounts of homework, an obvious way to increase time spent on reading and writing. Nor should our schools be excused by an appeal to the effects of the decline of the family or the vicious circle of poverty, important as these factors are. Schools have, or should have, children for six or seven hours a day, five days a week, nine months a year, for thirteen years or more. To assert that they are powerless to make a significant impact on what their students learn would be to make a claim about American education that few parents, teachers, or students would find it easy to accept.

Just how fragmented the American public school curriculum has become is described in *The Shopping Mall High School,* a report on five years of firsthand study inside public and private secondary schools. The authors report that our high schools offer courses of so many kinds that "the word 'curriculum' does not do justice to this astonishing variety." The offerings include not only academic courses of great diversity, but also courses in sports and hobbies and a "services curriculum" addressing emotional or social problems. All these courses are deemed "educationally valid" and carry course credit. Moreover, among academic offerings are numerous versions of each subject, corresponding to different levels of student interest and ability. Needless to say, the material covered in these "content area" courses is highly varied.

Cafeteria-style education, combined with the unwillingness of our schools to place demands on students, has resulted in a steady diminishment of commonly shared information between generations and between young people themselves. Those who graduate from the same school have often studied different subjects, and those who graduate from different schools have often studied different material even when their courses have carried the same titles. The inevitable consequence of the shopping mall high school is a lack of shared knowledge across and within schools. It would be hard to invent a more effective recipe for cultural fragmentation.

The formalistic educational theory behind the shopping mall school (the theory that any suitable content will inculcate reading, writing, and thinking skills) has had certain political advantages for school administrators. It has allowed them to stay scrupulously neutral with regard to content. Educational formalism enables them to regard the indiscriminate variety of school offerings as a positive virtue, on the grounds that such variety can accommodate the different interests and abilities of different students. Educational formalism has also conveniently allowed school administrators to meet objections to the traditional literate materials that used to be taught in the schools. Objectors have said that traditional materials are class-bound, white, Anglo-Saxon, and Protestant, not to mention racist, sexist, and excessively Western. Our schools have tried to offer enough diversity to meet these objections from liberals and enough Shakespeare to satisfy conservatives. Caught between ideological parties, the schools have been attracted irresistibly to a quantitative and formal approach to curriculum making rather than one based on sound judgments about what should be taught.

Some have objected that teaching the traditional literate culture means teaching conservative material. Orlando Patterson answered that objection when he pointed out that mainstream culture is not the province of any single social group and is constantly changing by assimilating new elements and expelling old ones. Although mainstream culture is tied to the written word and may therefore seem more formal and elitist than other elements of culture, that is an illusion. Literate culture is the most democratic culture in our land: it excludes nobody; it cuts across generations and social groups and classes; it is not usually one's first culture, but it should be everyone's second, existing as it does beyond the narrow spheres of family, neighborhood, and region.

As the universal second culture, literate culture has become the common currency for social and economic exchange in our democracy, and the only available ticket to full citizenship. Getting one's membership card is not tied to class or race. Membership is automatic if one learns the background information and the linguistic conventions that are needed to read, write, and speak effectively. Although everyone is literate in some local, regional, or ethnic culture, the connection between mainstream culture and the national written language justifies calling mainstream culture *the* basic culture of the nation.

The claim that universal cultural literacy would have the effect of preserving the political and social status quo is paradoxical because in fact the traditional forms of literate culture are precisely the most effective instruments for political and social change. All political discourse at the national level must use the stable forms of the national language and its associated culture. Take the example of

The Black Panther, a radical and revolutionary newspaper if ever this country had one. Yet the *Panther* was highly conservative in its language and cultural assumptions, as it had to be in order to communicate effectively. What could be more radical in sentiment but more conservative in language and assumed knowledge than the following passages from that paper?

> The present period reveals the criminal growth of bourgeois democracy since the betrayal of those who died that this nation might live "free and indivisible." It exposes through the trial of the Chicago Seven, and its law and order edicts, its desperate turn toward the establishment of a police state. (January 17, 1970)
>
> In this land of "milk and honey," the "almighty dollar" rules supreme and is being upheld by the faithful troops who move without question in the name of "law and order." Only in this garden of hypocrisy and inequality can a murderer not be considered a murderer—only here can innocent people be charged with a crime and be taken to court with the confessed criminal testifying against them. Incredible? (March 28, 1970)
>
> In the United States, the world's most technologically advanced country, one million youths from 12 to 17 years of age are illiterate—unable to read as well as the average fourth grader, says a new government report. Why so much illiteracy in a land of so much knowledge? The answer is because there is racism. Blacks and other Nonwhites receive the worst education. (May 18, 1974)

The last item of the Black Panther Party platform, issued March 29, 1972, begins

> 10. WE WANT LAND, BREAD, HOUSING, EDUCATION, CLOTHING, JUSTICE, PEACE AND PEOPLE'S CONTROL OF MODERN TECHNOLOGY.
>
> When in the course of human events it becomes necessary for one people to dissolve the political bands which have connected them with another, and to assume among the powers of the earth the separate and equal station to which the laws of nature and nature's God entitle them, a decent respect to the opinions of mankind requires that they should declare the causes which impel them to the separation.

And so on for the first five hundred of Jefferson's words without the least hint, or need of one, that this is a verbatim repetition of an earlier revolutionary declaration. The writers for *The Black Panther* had clearly received a rigorous traditional education in American history, in the Declaration of Independence, the Pledge of Allegiance to the Flag, the Gettysburg Address, and the Bible, to mention only some of the direct quotations and allusions in these passages. They also received rigorous traditional instruction in reading, writing, and spelling. I have not found a single misspelled word in the many pages of radical sentiment I have examined in that newspaper. Radicalism in politics, but conservatism in literate knowledge and spelling: to be a conservative in the *means* of communication is the road to effectiveness in modern life, in whatever direction one wishes to be effective.

To withhold traditional culture from the school curriculum, and therefore from students, in the name of progressive ideas is in fact an unprogressive action that helps preserve the political and economic status quo. Middle-class children acquire mainstream literate culture by daily encounters with other literate persons. But less privileged children are denied consistent interchanges with literate persons and fail to receive this information in school. The most straightforward antidote to their deprivation is to make the essential information more readily available inside the schools.

Providing our children with traditional information by no means indoctrinates them in a conservative point of view. Conservatives who wish to preserve traditional values will find that these are not necessarily inculcated by a traditional education, which can in fact be subversive of the status quo. As a child of eleven, I turned against the conservative views of my family and the Southern community in which I grew up, precisely because I had been given a traditional education and was therefore literate enough to read Gunnar Myrdal's *An American Dilemma*, an epoch-making book in my life.

Although teaching children national mainstream culture doesn't mean forcing them to accept its values uncritically, it does enable them to understand those values in order to predict the typical attitudes of other Americans. The writers for *The Black Panther* clearly understood this when they quoted the Declaration of Independence. George Washington, for instance, is a name in our received culture that we associate with the truthfulness of the hero of the story of the cherry tree. Americans should be taught that value association, whether or not they believe the story. Far from accepting the cherry-tree tale or its implications, Oscar Wilde in "The Decay of Lying" used it ironically, in a way that is probably funnier to Americans than to the British audience he was addressing.

> [Truth telling is] vulgarizing mankind. The crude commercialism of America, its materializing spirit, its indifference to the poetical side of things, and its lack of imagination and of high unattainable ideals, are entirely due to that country having adopted for its national hero a man who, according to his own confession, was incapable of telling a lie, and it is not too much to say that the story of George Washington and the cherry tree has done more harm, and in a shorter space of time, than any other moral tale in the whole of literature. . . . And the amusing part of the whole thing is that the story of the cherry tree is an absolute myth.

For us no less than for Wilde, the values affirmed in traditional literate culture can serve a whole spectrum of value attitudes. Unquestionably, decisions about techniques of conveying traditions to our children are among the most sensitive and important decisions of a pluralistic nation. But the complex problem of how to teach values in American schools mustn't distract attention from our fundamental duty to teach shared content.

The failure of our schools to create a literate society is sometimes excused on the grounds that the schools have been asked to do too much. They are asked, for example, to pay due regard to the demands of both local and national acculturation. They are asked to teach not only American history but also state and city history, driving, cardiopulmonary resuscitation, consumerism, carpentry, cooking, and other special subjects. They are given the task of teaching information that is sometimes too rudimentary and sometimes too specialized. If the schools did not undertake this instruction, much of the information so provided would no doubt go unlearned. In some of our national moods we would like the schools to teach everything, but they cannot. There is a pressing need for clarity about our educational priorities.

As an example of the priorities we need to set, consider the teaching of local history in the Commonwealth of Virginia. Suppose Virginians had to choose between learning about its native son Jeb Stuart and Abraham Lincoln. The example is arbitrary, but since choices have to be made in education, we might consider the two names emblematic of the kind of priority decision that has to be made. Educational policy always involves choices between degrees of worthiness.

The concept of cultural literacy helps us to make such decisions because it places a higher value on national than on local information. We want to make our children competent to communicate with Americans throughout the land. Therefore, if Virginians did have to decide between Stuart and Lincoln they ought to favor the man from Illinois over the one from Virginia. All literate Americans know traditional information about Abraham Lincoln but relatively few know about Jeb Stuart. To become literate it's therefore more important to know about Lincoln than about Stuart. The priority has nothing to do with inherent merit, only with the accidents of culture. Stuart certainly had more merit than Benedict Arnold did, but Arnold also should be given educational priority over Stuart. Why? Because Benedict Arnold is as much a part of our national language as is, say, Judas.

To describe Benedict Arnold and Abraham Lincoln as belonging to the national language discloses another way of conceiving cultural literacy—as a vocabulary that we are able to use throughout the land because we share associations with others in our society. A universally shared national vocabulary is analogous to a universal currency like the dollar. Of course the vocabulary consists of more than just words. *Benedict Arnold* is part of national cultural literacy; *eggs Benedict* isn't.

The Critical Importance of Early Schooling

Once we become aware of the inherent connection between literacy and cultural literacy, we have a duty to those who lack cultural literacy to determine and disclose its contents. To someone who is unaware of the things a literate person is expected to know, a writer's assumption that readers possess cultural literacy could appear to be a conspiracy of the literate against the illiterate, for the purpose of keeping them out of the club. But there is no conspiracy. Writers *must* make assumptions about the body of information their readers know. Unfortunately for the disadvantaged, no one ever spells out what that information is. But, as the Appendix illustrates, the total quantity of commonly shared information that the schools need to impart is less daunting than one might think, for the crucial background knowledge possessed by literate people is, as I have pointed out, telegraphic, vague, and limited in extent.

Preschool is not too early for starting earnest instruction in literate national culture. Fifth grade is almost too late. Tenth grade usually *is* too late. Anyone who is skeptical of this assertion should take a look at a heterogeneous class of fifth-graders engaged in summarizing a piece they have read. There are predictable differences between the summaries given by children with culturally adequate backgrounds and those given by children without. Although disadvantaged children often show an acceptable ability to decode and pronounce individual words, they are frequently unable to gain an integrated sense of a piece as a whole. They miss central implications and associations because they don't possess the background knowledge necessary to put the text in context. Hearing they hear not, and seeing they do not understand.

Yet if you observe a kindergarten or first-grade class in which pupils have the same diversity of family background, you will *not* find a similar spread in the reading performances of pupils from different social classes. Disadvantaged first-graders do as well as middle class ones in sounding out letters and simple words. What happens between first grade and fifth grade to change the equality of performance? The impression that something significant has occurred or has failed to occur in these early grades is confirmed by international comparisons of reading attainment at early ages in different countries. Before grade three, when reading skills are more mechanical than interpretive, the United States stands in the top group of countries. Later, when reading requires an understanding of more complex content, our comparative ranking drops. Although our schools do comparatively well in teaching elementary decoding skills, they do less well than schools of some other countries in teaching the background knowledge that pupils must possess to succeed at mature reading tasks.

The importance of this evidence for improving our national literacy can scarcely be overemphasized. If in the early grades our children were taught texts with cultural content rather than "developmental" texts that develop abstract skills, much of the specific knowledge deficit of disadvantaged children could be overcome. For it is clear that one critical difference in the reading performances of disadvantaged fifth-graders as compared with advantaged pupils is the difference in their cultural knowledge. Background knowledge does not take care of itself. Reading and writing are cumulative skills; the more we read the more necessary knowledge we gain for further reading.

Around grade four, those who lack the initial knowledge required for significant reading begin to be left behind permanently. Having all too slowly built up their cultural knowledge, they find reading and learning increasingly toilsome, unproductive, and humiliating. It follows that teaching cultural information in the early grades would do more than just improve the reading performance of all our children. By removing one of the causes of failure, it would especially enhance the motivation, self-esteem, and performance of disadvantaged children.

Really effective reforms in the teaching of cultural literacy must therefore begin with the earliest grades. Every improvement made in teaching very young children literate background information will have a multiplier effect on later learning, not just by virtue of the information they will gain but also by virtue of the greater motivation for reading and learning they will feel when they actually understand what they have read.

Young children enjoy absorbing formulaic knowledge. Even if they did not, our society would still find it essential to teach them all sorts of traditions and facts. Critical thinking and basic skills, two areas of current focus in education, do not enable children to create out of their own imaginations the essential names and concepts that have arisen by historical accident. The Rio Grande, the Mason-Dixon line, "The Night Before Christmas," and *Star Wars* are not products of basic skills or critical thought. Many items of literate culture are arbitrary, but that does not make them dispensable. Facts are essential components of the basic skills that a child entering a culture must have.

I'm not suggesting that we teach our children exactly what our grandparents learned. We should teach children current mainstream culture. It's obvious that the content of cultural literacy changes over the years. Today the term "Brown decision" belongs to cultural literacy, but in 1945 there hadn't been any Brown decision. The name Harold Ickes was current in 1945 but no long is. Such mutability is the fate of most names and events of recent history. Other changes come through the contributions of various subnational cultures. Ethnic words (like *pizza*) and art forms (like *jazz*) are constantly entering and departing from mainstream culture. Other subnational cultures, including those of science and technology, also cause changes in the mainstream culture. DNA and quarks, now part of cultural literacy, were unknown in 1945. In short, terms that literate people know in the 1980s are different from those they knew in 1945, and forty years hence the literate culture will again be different.

The flux in mainstream culture is obvious to all. But stability, not change, is the chief characteristic of cultural literacy. Although historical and technical terms may follow the ebb and flow of events, the more stable elements of our national vocabulary, like George Washington, the tooth fairy, the Gettysburg Address, Hamlet, and the Declaration of Independence, have persisted for a long time. These stable elements of the national vocabulary are at the core of cultural literacy, and for that reason are the most important contents of schooling. Although the terms that ebb and flow are tremendously important at a given time, they belong, from an educational standpoint, at the periphery of literate culture. The persistent, stable elements belong at the educational core.

Let me give some concrete examples of the kinds of core information I mean. American readers are assumed to have a general knowledge of the following people (I give just the beginning of a list): John Adams, Susan B. Anthony, Benedict Arnold, Daniel Boone, John Brown, Aaron Burr, John C. Calhoun, Henry Clay, James Fenimore Cooper, Lord Cornwallis, Davy Crockett, Emily Dickinson, Stephen A. Douglas, Frederick Douglass, Jonathan Edwards, Ralph Waldo Emerson, Benjamin Franklin, Robert Fulton, Ulysses S. Grant, Alexander Hamilton, and Nathaniel Hawthorne. Most of us know rather little about these people, but that little is of crucial importance, because it enables writers and speakers to assume a starting point from which they can treat in detail what they wish to focus on.

Here is another alphabetical list that no course in critical thinking skills, however masterful, could ever generate: Antarctic Ocean, Arctic Ocean, Atlantic Ocean, Baltic Sea, Black Sea, Caribbean Sea, Gulf of Mexico, North Sea, Pacific Ocean, Red Sea. It has a companion list: Alps, Appalachians, Himalayas, Matterhorn, Mount Everest, Mount Vesuvius, Rocky Mountains. Because literate people mention such names in passing, usually without explanation, children should acquire them as part of their intellectual equipment.

Children also need to understand elements of our literary and mythic heritage that are often alluded to without explanation, for example, Adam and Eve, Cain and Abel, Noah and the Flood, David and Goliath, the Twenty-third Psalm, Humpty Dumpty, Jack Sprat, Jack and Jill, Little Jack Horner, Cinderella, Jack and the Beanstalk, Mary had a little lamb, Peter Pan, and Pinocchio. Also Achilles, Adonis, Aeneas, Agamemnon, Antigone, and Apollo, as well as Robin Hood, Paul Bunyan, Satan, Sleeping Beauty, Sodom and Gomorrah, the Ten Commandments, and Tweedledum and Tweedledee.

Our current distaste for memorization is more pious than realistic. At an early age when their memories are most retentive, children have an almost instinctive urge to learn specific tribal traditions. At that age they seem to be fascinated by catalogues of information and are eager to master the materials that authenticate their membership in adult society. Observe for example how they memorize the rather complex materials of football, baseball, and basketball, even without benefit of formal avenues by which that information is inculcated.

The weight of human tradition across many cultures supports the view that basic acculturation should largely be completed by age thirteen. At that age Catholics are confirmed, Jews bar or bat mitzvahed, and tribal boys and girls undergo the rites of passage into the tribe. According to the anthropological record, all cultures whose educational methods have been reported in the *Human Relations Area Files* (a standard source for anthropological data) have used early memorization to carry on their traditions.

In Korea, "numerous books must be memorized, including the five *Kyung*, and the four *Su*." In Tibet, "from eight to ten years of age, the boy spends most of his time reading aloud and memorizing the scriptures." In Chile, the Araucanian Indians use the memorization of songs as a educational technique to teach "the subtleties of the native tongue, and an insight into the customs and traditions of their tribe." In southern Africa, the children of the Kung bushmen listen for hours to discussions of which they understand very little until they "know the history of every object, every exchange between their families, before they are ten or twelve years old." In Indonesia, "memorization is the method commonly used." In Thailand, children "repeat their lessons until they know them by heart." In Arizona, the Papago Indians take children through the lengthy rituals "as many times as needed for the learner to say it all through, which may take a year."

The new kind of teaching espoused by Rousseau and Dewey, which avoids rote learning and encourages the natural development of the child on analogy with the development of an acorn into an oak, has one virtue certainly: it encourages independence of mind. But the theory also has its drawbacks, one of which is that a child is not in fact like an acorn. Left to itself, a child will not grow into a thriving creature; Tarzan is pure fantasy. To thrive, a child needs to learn the traditions of the particular human society and culture it is born into. Like children everywhere, American children need traditional information at a very early age.

A great deal is at stake in understanding and acting on this essential perception as soon as possible. The opportunity of acquiring cultural literacy, once lost in the early grades is usually lost for good. That is most likely to be true for children of parents who were not themselves taught the literate national culture.

In the technological age, Washington and the cherry tree, Scrooge and Christmas, the fights historical, the oceans geographical, the "beings animalculus," and all the other shared materials of literate culture have become more, not less, important. The more computers we have, the more we need shared fairy tales, Greek myths, historical images, and so on. That is not really the paradox it seems to be. The more specialized and technical our civilization becomes, the harder it is for nonspecialists to participate in the decisions that deeply affect their lives. If we do not achieve a literate society, the technicians, with their arcane specialties, will not be able to communicate with us nor we with them. That would contradict the basic principles of democracy and must not be allowed to happen.

The antidote to growing specialization is to reinvigorate the unspecialized domain of literate discourse, where all can meet on common ground. That this ideal *can* be achieved is proved by such admirable writers as Theodore H. White, John Kenneth Galbraith, Lewis Thomas, Peter Medawar, and Richard Feynman, who are able to communicate their complex expertise to a wide audience of educated people. We will be able to achieve a just and prosperous society only when our schools ensure that everyone commands enough shared background knowledge to be able to communicate effectively with everyone else.

Postreading Writing Assignments

Option 1: Review your response to prereading question number one. Is your definition of "cultural literacy" close to Hirsch's definition? How is his definition different from yours?

Option 2: Who are the "disadvantaged" people to whom Hirsch refers? Do you agree with him that these people are disadvantaged? Why, or why not? What has led you to agree or disagree with Hirsch's definitions?

Option 3: Hirsch provides a sampling of people, places, and ideas that *he believes* culturally literate Americans should know. Do you agree with this listing? What might you add or remove from his list? Why? What are Hirsch's criteria for determining what people should know; what are yours? According to Hirsch's criteria and excerpts from his lists, how culturally literate are you? According to your criteria, how culturally literate is Hirsch?

Extended Writing Assignments

Option 4: What do you see as Hirsch's most compelling argument? Write an essay in which you carefully trace the path that Hirsch takes in this essay. You will want to summarize, in part, what you think he is saying, contemplate his intended audience, and analyze the effectiveness of his argument. In doing this, you will be reading with the grain of Hirsch's text; then, though, play the *devil's advocate* and read "against" the grain. Where do you see gaps between Hirsch's *intentions* and his *execution* of these intentions? What arguments can you pose in response to Hirsch's assertion that possessing shared knowledge is crucial to being a "literate" person? Whether you agree or disagree with Hirsch's agenda, this assignment requires you to see his point of view before interpreting and exploring your response to Hirsch's agenda.

Option 5: In response to Hirsch's essay, write an essay establishing your own criteria for a culturally literate America. Imagine that you have been asked to propose a curriculum for your local school district or college. Through convincing analysis, persuade a school board or university curriculum committee that your agenda is worthwhile. Which people, places, events, historical moments, and so on would be emphasized under your curriculum? What would be excluded? As you examine Hirsch's criteria, look closely at the reasoning behind his proposals. As you create your own criteria, notice that what you include says something about you; in the same way, what you exclude from your curriculum also reveals something about you and your values and beliefs. You can use Hirsch as a way to support your position or as someone to argue against.

Option 6: Hirsch uses the terms "acculturation" and "assimilation". How are these terms integral to his arguments for "shared knowledge"? If someone does not believe total assimilation is necessary for being literate, what arguments might they pose as they read against Hirsch? In your essay, define the ways in which Hirsch uses the terms "acculturation" and "assimilation"; then redefine the terms in your own way. Explore and analyze how Hirsch uses these terms to create an argument; go on to explore what happens if the words are used differently or if people do not "buy into" Hirsch's argument. In this assignment, you are using the specific terms "acculturation" and "assimilation" to gauge the validity of Hirsch's argument.

Forging Connections

Option 7: In his essay Hirsch argues for teaching children about the "information that Americans share." After reading Hirsch's essay, read or reread Frederick Douglass's narrative "The Pathway from Slavery to Freedom". Where might Douglass's slave narrative fit into

Hirsch's idea of "shared literacy"? Hirsch mentions Douglass as a person whom all culturally literate Americans should know; why would Hirsch feel this way? What is Douglass doing in his narrative that Hirsch sees as contributing to "cultural literacy"? Define Douglass's account through the lens of E. D. Hirsch, Jr. What might Hirsch do with this text—what might Hirsch's critics say about his inclusion of Douglass? Write an essay in which you explore Douglass from Hirsch's point of view; then examine what you have to say about Hirsch, Douglass, and cultural literacy.

bell hooks

KEEPING CLOSE TO HOME: CLASS AND EDUCATION

hooks grew up as Gloria Watkins in a traditional Southern black world where children were meant to be seen and not heard. "Talking back" (to one's elders or to any authority) was punished with silence. Watkins writes under her great-grandmother's name, bell hooks. In the text Talking Back, *hooks explores, among other things, the point where public and private meet. hooks was educated at Stanford University; she is currently a Professor of English and Women's Studies at Oberlin College. She lectures and writes on issues surrounding race, class, and gender. The selection you are reading is Chapter 11 from* Talking Back: thinking feminist, thinking black. *hooks's other works include:* Yearning: race, gender, and cultural politics *and* Ain't I a Woman: black women and feminism.

Prereading Journal Questions

1. In what ways, if any, does the language you use at home or with friends differ from the language you use at school or in any number of contexts?
2. After reading the headnote, what do you think that hooks might have to say about language and also about silence?
3. The headnote indicates that the essay you will be reading is excerpted from *Talking Back: thinking feminist, thinking black.* What kinds of assumptions are you making on the basis of this information? How might you work through any preconceived notions you might have in order to do a "with the grain" reading of hooks?

Reading tip: Effective reading is largely dependent on "prediction," imagining or predicting what might happen next in a reading. Before reading hooks's essay, predict what this work might be exploring—look at the title and the biographical sketch of the author for clues. After completing the essay, check your predictions. How accurate were you?

We are both awake in the almost dark of 5 a.m. Everyone else is sound asleep. Mama asks the usual questions. Telling me to look around, make sure I have everything, scolding me because I am uncertain about the actual time the bus arrives. By 5:30 we are waiting outside the closed station. Alone together, we have a chance to really talk. Mama begins. Angry with her children, especially the ones who whisper behind her back, she says bitterly, "Your childhood could not have been that bad. You were fed and clothed. You did not have to do without—that's more than a lot of folks have and I just can't stand the way y'all go on." The hurt in her voice saddens me. I have always wanted to protect mama from hurt, to ease her burdens. Now I am part of what troubles. Confronting me, she says accusingly, "It's not just the other children. You talk too much about the past. You don't just listen." And I do talk. Worse, I write about it.

Mama has always come to each of her children seeking different responses. With me she expresses the disappointment, hurt, and anger of betrayal: anger that her children are so critical, that we can't even have the sense to like the presents she sends. She says, "From now on there will be no presents. I'll just stick some money in a little envelope the way the rest of you do. Nobody wants criticism. Everybody can criticize me but I am supposed to say nothing." When I try to talk, my voice sounds like a twelve year old. When I try to talk, she speaks louder, interrupting me, even though she has said repeatedly, "Explain it to me, this talk about the past." I struggle to return to my thirty-five year old self so that she will know by the sound of my voice that we are two women talking together. It is only when I state firmly in my very adult voice, "Mama, you are not listening," that she becomes quiet. She waits. Now that I have her attention, I fear that my explanations will be lame, inadequate. "Mama," I begin, "people usually go to therapy because they feel hurt inside, because they have pain that will not stop, like a wound that continually breaks open, that does not heal. And often these hurts, that pain has to do with things that have happened in the past, sometimes in childhood, often in childhood, or things that we believe happened." She wants to know, "What hurts, what hurts are you talking about?" "Mom, I can't answer that. I can't speak for all of us, the hurts are different for everybody. But the point is you try to make the hurt better, to heal it, by understanding how it came to be. And I know you feel mad when we say something happened or hurt that you don't remember being that way, but the past isn't like that, we don't have the same memory of it. We remember things differently. You know that. And sometimes folk feel hurt about stuff and you just don't know or didn't realize it, and they need to talk about it. Surely you understand the need to talk about it."

Our conversation is interrupted by the sight of my uncle walking across the park toward us. We stop to watch him. He is on his way to work dressed in a familiar blue suit. They look alike, these two who rarely discuss the past. This interruption makes me think about life in a small town. You always see someone you know. Interruptions, intrusions are part of daily life. Privacy is difficult to maintain. We leave our private space in the car to greet him. After the hug and kiss he has given me every year since I was born, they talk about the day's funerals. In the distance the bus approaches. He walks away knowing that they will see each other later. Just before I board the bus I turn, staring into my mother's face. I am momentarily back in time, seeing myself eighteen years ago, at this same bus stop, staring into my mother's face, continually turning back, waving farewell as I returned to college—that experience which first took me away from our town, from family. Departing was as painful then as it is now. Each movement away makes return harder. Each separation intensifies distance, both physical and emotional.

To a southern black girl from a working-class background who had never been on a city bus, who had never stepped on an escalator, who had never travelled by plane, leaving the comfortable confines of a small town Kentucky life to attend Stanford University was not just frightening; it was utterly painful. My parents had not been delighted that I had been accepted and adamantly opposed my going so far from home. At the time, I did not see their opposition as an expression of their fear that they would lose me forever. Like many working-class folks, they feared what college education might do to their children's minds even as they unenthusiastically acknowledged its importance. They did not understand why I could not attend a college nearby, an all-black college. To them, any college would do. I would graduate, become a school teacher, make a decent living and a good marriage. And even though they reluctantly and skeptically supported my educational endeavors, they also subjected them to constant harsh and bitter critique. It is difficult for me to talk about my parents and their impact on me because they have always felt wary, ambivalent, mistrusting of my intellectual aspirations even as they have been caring and supportive. I want to speak about these contradictions because sorting through them, seeking resolution and reconciliation has been important to me both as it affects my development as a writer, my effort to be fully self-realized, and my longing to remain close to the family and community that provided the groundwork for much of my thinking, writing, and being.

Studying at Stanford, I began to think seriously about class differences. To be materially underprivileged at a university where most folks (with the exception of workers) are materially privileged provokes such thought. Class differences were boundaries no one wanted to face or talk about. It was easier to downplay them, to act as though we were all from privileged backgrounds, to work around them, to confront them privately in the solitude of one's room, or to pretend that just being chosen to study at such an institution meant that those of us who did not come from privilege were already in transition toward privilege. To not long for such transition marked one as rebellious, as unlikely to succeed. It was a kind of treason not to believe that it was better to be identified with the world of material privilege than with the world of the working class, the poor. No wonder our working-class parents from poor backgrounds feared our entry into such a world, intuiting perhaps that we might learn to be ashamed of where we had come from, that we might never return home, or come back only to lord it over them.

Though I hung with students who were supposedly radical and chic, we did not discuss class. I talked to no one about the sources of my shame, how it hurt me to witness the contempt shown the brown-skinned Filipina maids who cleaned our rooms, or later my concern about the $100 a month I paid for a room off-campus which was more than half of what my parents paid for rent. I talked to no one about my efforts to save money, to send a little something home. Yet these class realities separated me from fellow students. We were moving in different directions. I did not intend to forget my class background or alter my class allegiance. And even though I received an education designed to provide me with a bourgeois sensibility, passive acquiescence was not my only option. I knew that I could resist. I could rebel. I could shape the direction and focus of the various forms of knowledge available to me. Even though I sometimes envied and longed for greater material advantages (particularly at vacation times when I would be one of few if any students remaining in the dormitory because there was no money for travel), I did not share the sensibility and values of my peers. That was important—class was not just about money; it was about values which showed and determined behavior. While I often needed more money, I never needed a new set of beliefs and values. For example, I was profoundly shocked and disturbed when peers would talk about their parents without respect, or would even say that they hated their parents. This was especially troubling to me when it seemed that these parents were caring and concerned. It was often explained to me that such hatred was "healthy and normal." To my white, middle-class California roommate, I explained the way we were taught to value our parents and their care, to understand that they were not obligated to give us care. She would always shake her head, laughing all the while, and say, "Missy, you will learn that it's different here, that we think differently." She was right. Soon, I lived alone, like the one Mormon student who kept to himself as he made a concentrated effort to remain true to his religious beliefs and values. Later in graduate school I found that classmates believed "lower class" people had no beliefs and values. I was silent in such discussions, disgusted by their ignorance.

Carol Stack's anthropological study, *All Our Kin*, was one of the first books I read which confirmed my experiential understanding that within black culture (especially among the working class and poor, particularly in southern states), a value system emerged that was counter-hegemonic, that challenged notions of individualism and private property so important to the maintenance of white-supremacist, capitalist patriarchy. Black folk created in marginal spaces a world of community and collectivity where resources were shared. In the preface to *Feminist Theory: from margin to center,* I talked about how the point of difference, this marginality can be the space for the formation of an oppositional world view. That world view must be articulated, named if it is to provide a sustained blueprint for change. Unfortunately, there has existed no consistent framework for such naming. Consequently both the experience of this difference and documentation of it (when it occurs) gradually loses presence and meaning.

Much of what Stack documented about the "culture of poverty," for example, would not describe interactions among most black poor today irrespective of geographical setting. Since the black people she described did not acknowledge (if they recognized it in theoretical terms) the oppositional value of their world view, apparently seeing it more as a survival strategy determined less by conscious efforts to oppose oppressive race and class biases than by circumstance, they did not attempt to establish a framework to transmit their beliefs and values from generation to generation. When circumstances changed, values altered. Efforts to assimilate the values and beliefs of privileged white people, presented through media like television, undermine and destroy potential structures of opposition.

Increasingly, young black people are encouraged by the dominant culture (and by those black people who internalize the values of this hegemony) to believe that assimilation is the only possible way to survive, to succeed. Without the framework of an organized civil rights or black resistance struggle, individual and collective efforts at black liberation that focus on the primacy of self-definition and self-determination often go unrecognized. It is crucial that those among us who resist and rebel, who survive and succeed, speak openly and honestly about our lives and the nature of our personal struggles, the means by which we resolve and reconcile contradictions. This is no easy task. Within the educational institutions where we learn to develop and strengthen our writing and analytical skills, we also learn to think, write, and talk in a manner that shifts attention away from personal experience. Yet if we are to reach our people and all people, if we are to remain connected (especially those of us whose familial backgrounds are poor and working-class), we must understand that the telling of one's personal story provides a meaningful example, a way for folks to identify and connect.

Combining personal with critical analysis and theoretical perspectives can engage listeners who might other wise feel estranged, alienated. To speak simply with language that is accessible to as many folks as possible is also important. Speaking about one's personal experience or speaking with simple language is often considered by academics and/or intellectuals (irrespective of their political inclinations) to be a sign of intellectual weakness or even anti-intellectualism. Lately, when I speak, I do not stand in place—reading my paper, making little or no eye contact with audiences—but instead make eye contact, talk extemporaneously, digress, and address the audience directly. I have been told that people assume I am not prepared, that I am anti-intellectual, unprofessional (a concept that has everything to do with class as it determines actions and behavior), or that I am reinforcing the stereotype of black people as non-theoretical and gutsy.

Such criticism was raised recently by fellow feminist scholars after a talk I gave at Northwestern University at a conference on "Gender, Culture, Politics" to an audience that was mainly students and academics. I deliberately chose to speak in a very basic way, thinking especially about the few community folks who had come to hear me. Weeks later, Kum-Kum Sangari, a fellow participant who shared with me what was said when I was no longer present, and I engaged in quite rigorous critical dialogue about the way my presentation had been perceived primarily by privileged white female academics. She was concerned that I not mask my knowledge of theory, that I not appear anti-intellectual. Her critique compelled me to articulate concerns that I am often silent about with colleagues. I spoke about class allegiance and revolutionary commitments, explaining that it was disturbing to me that intellectual radicals who speak about transforming society, ending the domination of race, sex, class, cannot break with behavior patterns that reinforce and perpetuate domination, or continue to use as their sole reference point how we might be or are perceived by those who dominate, whether or not we gain their acceptance and approval.

This is a primary contradiction which raises the issue of whether or not the academic setting is a place where one can be truly radical or subversive. Concurrently, the use of a language and style of presentation that alienates most folks who are not also academically trained reinforces the notion that the academic world is separate from real life, that everyday world where we constantly adjust our language and behavior to meet diverse needs. The academic setting is separate only when we work to make it so. It is a false dichotomy which suggests that academics and/or intellectuals can only speak to one another, that we cannot hope to speak with the masses. What is true is that we make choices, that we choose our audiences, that we choose voices to hear and voices to silence. If I do not speak in a language that can be understood, then there is little chance for dialogue. This issue of language and behavior is a central contradiction all radical intellectuals, particularly those who are members of oppressed groups, must continually confront and work to resolve. One of the clear and present dangers that exists when we move outside our class of origin, our collective ethnic experience, and enter hierarchical institutions which daily reinforce domination by race, sex, and class, is that we gradually assume a mindset similar to those who dominate and oppress, that we lose critical consciousness because it is not reinforced or affirmed by the environment. We must be ever vigilant. It is important that we know who we are speaking to, who we most want to hear us, who we most long to move, motivate, and touch with our words.

When I first came to New Haven to teach at Yale, I was truly surprised by the marked class divisions between black folks—students and professors—who identify with Yale and those black folks who work at Yale or in surrounding communities. Style of dress and self-presentation are most often the central markers of one's position. I soon learned that the black folks who spoke on the street were likely to be part of the black community and those who carefully shifted their glance were likely to be associated with Yale. Walking with a black female colleague one day, I spoke to practically every black person in sight (a gesture which reflects my upbringing), an action which disturbed my companion. Since I addressed black folk who were clearly not associated with Yale, she wanted to know whether or not I knew them. That was funny to me. "Of course not," I answered. Yet when I thought about it seriously, I realized that in a deep way, I knew them for they, and not my companion or most of my colleagues at Yale, resemble my family. Later that year, in a black women's support group I started for undergraduates, students from poor backgrounds spoke about the shame they sometimes feel when faced with the reality of their connection to working-class and poor black people. One student confessed that her father is a street person, addicted to drugs, someone who begs from passersby. She, like other Yale students, turns away from street people often, sometimes showing anger or contempt; she hasn't wanted anyone to know that she was related to this kind of person. She struggles with this, wanting to find a way to acknowledge and affirm this reality, to claim this connection. The group asked me and one another what we do to remain connected, to honor the bonds we have with working-class and poor people even as our class experience alters.

Maintaining connections with family and community across class boundaries demands more than just summary recall of where one's roots are, where one comes from. It requires knowing, naming, and being ever-mindful of those aspects of one's past that have enabled and do enable one's self-development in the present, that sustain and support, that enrich. One must also honestly confront barriers that do exist, aspects of that past that do diminish. My parent's ambivalence about my love for reading led to intense conflict. They (especially my mother) would work to ensure that I had access to books, but would threaten to burn the books or throw them away if I did not conform to other expectations. Or they would insist that reading too much would drive me insane. Their ambivalence nurtured in me a like uncertainty about the value and significance of intellectual endeavor which took years for me to unlearn. While this aspect of our class reality was one that wounded and diminished, their vigilant insistence that being smart did not make me a "better" or "superior" person (which often got on my nerves because I think I wanted to have that sense that it did indeed set me apart, make me better) made a profound impression. From them I learned to value and respect various skills and talents folk might have, not just to value people who read books and talk about ideas. They and my grandparents might say about somebody, "Now he don't read nor write a lick, but he can tell a story," or as my grandmother would say, "call out the hell in words."

Empty romanticization of poor or working-class backgrounds undermines the possibility of true connection. Such connection is based on understanding difference in experience and perspective and working to mediate and negotiate these terrains. Language is a crucial issue for folk whose movement outside the boundaries of poor and working-class backgrounds changes the nature and direction of their speech. Coming to Stanford with my own version of a Kentucky accent, which I think of always as a strong sound quite different from Tennessee or Georgia speech, I learned to speak differently while maintaining the speech of my region, the sound of my family and community. This was of course much easier to keep up when I returned home to stay often. In recent years, I have endeavored to use various speaking styles in the classroom as a teacher and find it disconcerts those who feel that the use of a particular patois excludes them as listeners, even if there is translation into the usual, acceptable mode of speech. Learning to listen to different voices, hearing different speech challenges the notion that we must all assimilate—share a single, similar talk—in educational institutions. Language reflects the culture from which we emerge. To deny ourselves daily use of speech patterns that are common and familiar, that embody the unique and distinctive aspect of our self is one of the ways we become estranged and alienated from our past. It is important for us to have as many languages on hand as we can know or learn. It is important for those of us who are black, who speak in particular patois as well as standard English to express ourselves in both ways.

Often I tell students from poor and working-class backgrounds that if you believe what you have learned and are learning in schools and universities separates you from your past, this is precisely what will happen. It is important to stand firm in the conviction that nothing can truly separate us from our pasts when we nurture and cherish that connection. An important strategy for maintaining contact is ongoing acknowledgment of the primacy of one's past, of one's background, affirming the reality that such bonds are not severed automatically solely because one enters a new environment or moves toward a different class experience.

Again, I do not wish to romanticize this effort, to dismiss the reality of conflict and contradiction. During my time at Stanford, I did go through a period of more than a year when I did not return home. That period was one where I felt that it was simply too difficult to mesh my profoundly disparate realities. Critical reflection about the choice I was making, particularly about why I felt a choice had to be made, pulled me through this difficult time. Luckily I recognized that the insistence on choosing between the world of family and community and the new world of privileged white people and privileged ways of knowing was imposed upon me by the outside. It is as though a mythical contract had been signed somewhere which demanded of us black folks that once we entered these spheres we would immediately give up all vestiges of our underprivileged past. It was my responsibility to formulate a way of being that would allow me to participate fully in my new environment while integrating and maintaining aspects of the old.

One of the most tragic manifestations of the pressure black people feel to assimilate is expressed in the internalization of racist perspectives. I was shocked and saddened when I first heard black professors at Stanford downgrade and express contempt for black students, expecting us to do poorly, refusing to establish nurturing bonds. At every university I have attended as a student or worked at as a teacher, I have heard similar attitudes expressed with little or no understanding of factors that might prevent brilliant black students from performing to their full capability. Within universities, there are few educational and social spaces where students who wish to affirm positive ties to ethnicity—to blackness, to working-class backgrounds—can receive affirmation and support. Ideologically, the message is clear—assimilation is the way to gain acceptance and approval from those in power.

Many white people enthusiastically supported Richard Rodriguez's vehement contention in his autobiography, *Hunger of Memory*, that attempts to maintain ties with his Chicano background impeded his progress, that he had to sever ties with community and kin to succeed at Stanford and in the larger world, that family language, in his case Spanish, had to be made secondary or discarded. If the terms of success as defined by the standards of ruling groups within white-supremacist, capitalist patriarchy are the only standards that exist, then assimilation is indeed necessary. But they are not. Even in the face of powerful structures of domination, it remains possible for each of us, especially those of us who are members of oppressed and/or exploited groups as well as those radical visionaries who may have race, class, and sex privilege, to define and determine alternative standards, to decide on the nature and extent of compromise. Standards by which one's success is measured, whether student or professor, are quite different for those of us who wish to resist reinforcing the domination of race, sex, and class, who work to maintain and strengthen our ties with the oppressed, with those who lack material privilege, with our families who are poor and working-class.

When I wrote my first book, *Ain't I A Woman: black women and feminism*, the issue of class and its relationship to who one's reading audience might be came up for me around my decision not to use footnotes, for which I have been sharply criticized. I told people that my concern was that footnotes set class boundaries for readers, determining who a book is for. I was shocked that many academic folks scoffed at this idea. I shared that I went into working-class black communities as well as talked with family and friends to survey whether or not they ever read books with footnotes and found that they did not. A few did not know what they were, but most folks saw them as indicating that a book was for college-educated people.

These responses influenced my decision. When some of my more radical, college-educated friends freaked out about the absence of footnotes, I seriously questioned how we could ever imagine revolutionary transformation of society if such a small shift in direction could be viewed as threatening. Of course, many folks warned that the absence of footnotes would make the work less credible in academic circles. This information also highlighted the way in which class informs our choices. Certainly I did feel that choosing to use simple language, absence of footnotes, etc. would mean I was jeopardizing the possibility of being taken seriously in academic circles but then this was a political matter and a political decision. It utterly delights me that this has proven not to be the case and that the book is read by many academics as well as by people who are not college-educated.

Always our first response when we are motivated to conform or compromise within structures that reinforce domination must be to engage in critical reflection. Only by challenging ourselves to push against oppressive boundaries do we make the radical alternative possible, expanding the realm and scope of critical inquiry. Unless we share radical strategies, ways of rethinking and revisioning with students, with kin and community, with a larger audience, we risk perpetuating the stereotype that we succeed because we are the exception, different from the rest of our people. Since I left home and entered college, I am often asked, usually by white people, if my sisters and brothers are also high achievers. At the root of this question is the longing for reinforcement of the belief in "the exception" which enables race, sex, and class biases to remain intact. I am careful to separate what it means to be exceptional from a notion of "the exception."

Frequently I hear smart black folks, from poor and working-class backgrounds, stressing their frustration that at times family and community do not recognize that they are exceptional. Absence of positive affirmation clearly diminishes the longing to excel in academic endeavors. Yet it is important to distinguish between the absence of basic positive affirmation and the longing for continued reinforcement that we are special. Usually liberal white folks will willingly offer continual reinforcement of us as exceptions—as special. This can be both patronizing and very seductive. Since we often work in situations where we are isolated from other black folks, we can easily begin to feel that encouragement from white people is the primary or only source of support and recognition. Given the internalization of racism, it is easy to view this support as more validating and legitimizing than similar support from black people. Still, nothing takes the place of being valued and appreciated by one's own, by one's family and community. We share a mutual and reciprocal responsibility for affirming one another's successes. Sometimes we have to talk to our folks about the fact that we need their ongoing support and affirmation, that it is unique and special to us. In some cases we may never receive desired recognition and acknowledgment of specific achievements from kin. Rather than seeing this as a basis for estrangement, for severing connection, it is useful to explore other sources of nourishment and support.

I do not know that my mother's mother ever acknowledged my college education except to ask me once, "How can you live so far away from your people?" Yet she gave me sources of affirmation and nourishment, sharing the legacy of her quilt-making, of family history, of her incredible way with words. Recently, when our father retired after more than thirty years of work as a janitor, I wanted to pay tribute to this experience, to identify links between his work and my own as writer and teacher. Reflecting on our family past, I recalled ways he had been an impressive example of diligence and hard work, approaching tasks with a seriousness of concentration I work to mirror and develop, with a discipline I struggle to maintain. Sharing these thoughts with him keeps us connected, nurtures our respect for each other, maintaining a space, however large or small, where we can talk.

Open, honest communication is the most important way we maintain relationships with kin and community as our class experience and backgrounds change. It is as vital as the sharing of resources. Often financial assistance is given in circumstances where there is no meaningful contact. However helpful, this can also be an expression of estrangement and alienation. Communication between black folks from various experiences of material privilege was much easier when we were all in segregated communities sharing common experiences in relation to social institutions. Without this grounding, we must work to maintain ties, connection. We must assume greater responsibility for making and maintaining contact, connections that can shape our intellectual visions and inform our radical commitments.

The most powerful resource any of us can have as we study and teach in university settings is full understanding and appreciation of the richness, beauty, and primacy of our familial and community backgrounds. Maintaining awareness of class differences, nurturing ties with the poor and working-class people who are our most intimate kin, our comrades in struggle, transforms and enriches our intellectual experience. Education as the practice of freedom becomes not a force which fragments or separates, but one that brings us closer, expanding our definitions of home and community.

Postreading Writing Assignments

Option 1: hooks begins this essay with a conversation between herself and her mother. What does this add to her essay; what does it do to help shape it? Explore the function of this conversation within the essay.

Option 2: What does it take, according to hooks, to maintain "connections with family and community across class boundaries"? First define this idea, and then discuss whether or not maintaining such connections is a realistic goal. Explain your perspective.

Extended Writing Assignments

Option 3:

> . . . the use of a language and style of presentation that alienates most folks who are not also academically trained reinforces the notion that the academic world is separate from real life, that everyday world where we constantly adjust our language and behavior to meet diverse needs. The academic setting is separate only when we work to make it so. It is a false dichotomy which suggests that academics and/or intellectuals can only speak to one another, that we cannot hope to speak with the masses.
>
> (page 223)

Everyone engages in various kinds of discourse—we communicate in various ways with families, friends, coworkers, and peers and instructors in the academy, among others. Look closely at your primary "private language," and, in light of hooks's essay and perspective, analyze your experience using hooks's lens. First you should interpret hooks's essay and assertions. Then you can use your life as a way of testing hooks's essay; explore your experiences with and against the grain of hooks's text. In other words, where do your experiences support or undermine hooks's assertions?

Option 4: Use hooks's essay as a way to examine the connections between social class, language, and education. Can one maintain ties to a particular social class (one that is not part of the dominant culture) and still succeed in mainstream "American" life? As you prepare to write your essay, you might consider and explore some of these questions: Are there problems and difficulties in handling a balancing act as described by hooks? What are the benefits, drawbacks, and sacrifices in maintaining such a lifestyle? Is there one right answer or solution to this dilemma? Is this a personal issue, or does society have a moral obligation to value social, racial, and cultural diversity?

Forging Connections

Option 5:

> Many white people enthusiastically supported Richard Rodriguez's vehement contention in his autobiography, *Hunger of Memory*, that attempts to maintain ties with his Chicano background impeded his progress, that he had to sever ties with community and kin to succeed at Stanford and in the larger world, that family language, in his case Spanish, had to be made secondary or discarded.
>
> (page 226)

Read or reread Richard Rodriguez's essay "Aria" from hooks's perspective. Create a dialogue between hooks, Rodriguez, and yourself in which you define and explore both writers' ideologies. This should be more than a comparison/contrast essay; you should go beyond simply agreeing with one writer while disagreeing with the other. Rather, you should explore each writer's ideas from a number of perspectives—present a with/against the grain reading of each piece. One way to approach this assignment is to create a believable setting in which the three of you meet and discuss issues of race, class, and language (perhaps on a talk show where you are the host and hooks and Rodriguez are your guests; you write the transcript). Your perspective should be important to both hooks and Rodriguez as they are both, at times, writing about students who are in some ways like you. Be sure to allow equal time and space to hooks, Rodriguez, and yourself, as all three of you have powerful views that deserve to be heard and explored.

Harriet Jacobs

FLIGHT AND A SAFE RETREAT

Harriet Jacobs was born in North Carolina. In her autobiography Incidents in the Life of a Slave Girl, *from which this selection is taken, Jacobs details her life as a slave, someone else's property. Jacobs remained in a "slave state" for twenty-seven years before fleeing to New York. Jacobs published* Incidents *in 1861 under the pseudonym Linda Brent.*

Prereading Journal Questions

1. Read the headnote and the title of Jacob's autobiography. What kinds of "incidents" might you expect in a narrative written by a "slave girl"?
2. What kinds of people do you imagine as being "slave owners" or "slave traders"? What has led you to form these ideas?

Reading tip: After reading the headnote and answering the prereading journal questions, you have begun to make assumptions about what you are going to read. Read your responses to the prereading journal questions; what do these responses tell you about your "preconceived notions"? How might having preconceived notions about a text limit your reading, and how might it help you read more effectively? Be willing to change your assumptions as a result of the reading you create and your interpretation of a writer's likely intention.

XVII. The Flight

Mr. Flint was hard pushed for house servants, and rather than lose me he had restrained his malice. I did my work faithfully, though not, of course, with a willing mind. They were evidently afraid I should leave them. Mr. Flint wished that I should sleep in the great house instead of the servants' quarters. His wife agreed to the proposition, but said I mustn't bring my bed into the house, because it would scatter feathers on her carpet. I knew when I went there that they would never think of such a thing as furnishing a bed of any kind for me and my little one. I therefore carried my own bed, and now I was forbidden to use it. I did as I was ordered. But now that I was certain my children were to be put in their power, in order to give them a stronger hold on me, I resolved to leave them that night. I remembered the grief this step would bring upon my dear old grandmother; and nothing less than the freedom of my children would have induced me to disregard her advice. I went about my evening work with trembling steps. Mr. Flint twice called from his chamber door to inquire why the house was not locked up. I replied that I had not done my work. "You have had time enough to do it," said he. "Take care how you answer me!"

I shut all the windows, locked all the doors, and went up to the third story, to wait till midnight. How long those hours seemed, and how fervently I prayed that God would not forsake me in this hour of utmost need! I was about to risk every thing on the throw of a die; and if I failed, O what would become of me and my poor children? They would be made to suffer for my fault.

At half past twelve I stole softly down stairs. I stopped on the second floor, thinking I heard a noise. I felt my way down into the parlor, and looked out the window. The night was so intensely dark that I could see nothing. I raised the window very softly and jumped out. Large drops of rain were falling, and the darkness bewildered me. I dropped on my knees, and breathed a short prayer to God for guidance and protection. I groped my way to the road, and rushed towards the town with almost lightning speed. I arrived at my grandmother's house, but dared not see her. She would say, "Linda, you are killing me;" and I knew that would unnerve me. I tapped softly at the window of a room, occupied by a woman, who had lived in the house several years. I knew she was a faithful friend, and could be trusted with my secret. I tapped several times before she heard me. At last she raised the window, and I whispered, "Sally, I have run away. Let me in, quick." She opened the door softly, and said in low tones, "For God's sake, don't. Your grandmother is trying to buy you and de chillern. Mrs. Sands was here last week. He tole her he was going away on business, but he wanted her to go ahead about buying you and de chillern, and he would help her all he could. Don't run away, Linda. Your grandmother is all bowed down wid trouble now."

I replied, "Sally, they are going to carry my children to the plantation to-morrow; and they will never sell them to any body so long as they have me in their power. Now, would you advise me to go back?"

"'No, chile, no," answered she. "When dey finds you is gone, dey won't want de plague ob de chillern; but where is you going to hide? Dey knows ebery inch ob dis house."

I told her I had a hiding-place, and that was all it was best for her to know. I asked her to go into my room as soon as it was light, and take all my clothes out of my trunk, and pack them in hers; for I knew Mr. Flint and the constable would be there early to search my room. I feared the sight of my children would be too much for my full heart; but I could not go out into the uncertain future without one last look. I bent over the bed where lay my little Benny and baby Ellen. Poor little ones! fatherless and motherless! Memories of their father came over me. He wanted to be kind to them; but they were not all to him, as they were to my womanly heart. I knelt and prayed for the innocent little sleepers. I kissed them lightly, and turned away.

As I was about to open the street door, Sally laid her hand on my shoulder, and said, "Linda, is you gwine all alone? Let me call your uncle."

"No, Sally," I replied, "I want no one to be brought into trouble on my account."

I went forth into the darkness and rain. I ran on till I came to the house of the friend who was to conceal me.

Early the next morning Mr. Flint was at my grandmother's inquiring for me. She told him she had not seen me, and supposed I was at the plantation. He watched her face narrowly, and said, "Don't you know any thing about her running off?" She assured him that she did not. He went on to say, "Last night she ran off without the least provocation. We had treated her very kindly. My wife liked her. She will soon be found and brought back. Are her children with you?" When told that they were, he said, "I am very glad to hear that. If they are here, she cannot be far off. If I find out that any of my niggers have had any thing to do with this damned business, I'll give 'em five hundred lashes." As he started to go to his father's, he turned round and added, persuasively, "Let her be brought back, and she shall have her children to live with her."

The tidings made the old doctor rave and storm at a furious rate. It was a busy day for them. My grandmother's house was searched from top to bottom. As my trunk was empty, they concluded I had taken my clothes with me. Before ten o'clock every vessel northward bound was thoroughly examined, and the law against harboring fugitives was read to all on board. At night a watch was set over the town. Knowing how distressed my grandmother would be, I wanted to send her a message; but it could not be done. Every one who went in or out of her house was closely watched. The doctor said he would take my children, unless she became responsible for them; which of course she willingly did. The next day was spent in searching. Before night, the following advertisement was posted at every corner, and in every public place for miles round:—

> $300 Reward! Ran away from the subscriber, an intelligent, bright, mulatto girl, named Linda, 21 years of age. Five feet four inches

high. Dark eyes, and black hair inclined to curl; but it can be made straight. Has a decayed spot on a front tooth. She can read and write, and in all probability will try to get to the Free States. All persons are forbidden, under penalty of law, to harbor or employ said slave. $150 will be given to whoever takes her in the state, and $300 if taken out of state and delivered to me, or lodged in jail.

DR. FLINT.

XVIII. Months of Peril

The search for me was kept up with more perseverence than I had anticipated. I began to think that escape was impossible. I was in great anxiety lest I should implicate the friend who harbored me. I knew the consequences would be frightful; and much as I dreaded being caught, even that seemed better than causing an innocent person to suffer for kindness to me. A week had passed in terrible suspense, when my pursuers came into such close vicinity that I concluded they had tracked me to my hiding-place. I flew out of the house, and concealed myself in a thicket of bushes. There I remained in an agony of fear for two hours. Suddenly, a reptile of some kind seized my leg. In my fright, I struck a blow which loosened its hold, but I could not tell whether I had killed it; it was so dark, I could not see what it was; I only knew it was something cold and slimy. The pain I felt soon indicated that the bite was poisonous. I was compelled to leave my place of concealment, and I groped my way back into the house. The pain had become intense, and my friend was startled by my look of anguish. I asked her to prepare a poultice of warm ashes and vinegar, and I applied it to my leg, which was already much swollen. The application gave me some relief, but the swelling did not abate. The dread of being disabled was greater than the physical pain I endured. My friend asked an old woman, who doctored among the slaves, what was good for the bite of a snake or a lizard. She told her to steep a dozen coppers in vinegar, over night, and apply the cankered vinegar to the inflamed part.

I had succeeded in cautiously conveying some messages to my relatives. They were harshly threatened, and despairing of my having a chance to escape, they advised me to return to my master, ask his forgiveness, and let him make an example of me. But such counsel had no influence with me. When I started upon this hazardous undertaking, I had resolved that, come what would, there should be no turning back. "Give me liberty, or give me death," was my motto. When my friend contrived to make known to my relatives the painful situation I had been in for twenty-four hours, they said no more about my going back to my master. Something must be done, and that speedily; but where to return for help, they knew not. God in his mercy raised up "a friend in need."

Among the ladies who were acquainted with my grandmother, was one who had known her from childhood, and always been very friendly to her. She had also known my mother and her children, and felt interested for them. At this crisis of affairs she called to see my grandmother, as she not unfrequently did. She observed the sad and troubled expression of her face, and asked if she knew where Linda was, and whether she was safe. My grandmother shook her head, without answering. "Come, Aunt Martha," said the kind lady, "tell me all about it. Perhaps I can do something to help you." The husband of this lady held many slaves, and bought and sold slaves. She also held a number in her own name; but she treated them kindly, and would never allow any of them to be sold. She was unlike the majority of slaveholders' wives. My grandmother looked earnestly at her. Something in the expression of her face said "Trust me!" and she did trust her. She listened attentively to the details of my story, and sat thinking for a while. At last she said, "Aunt Martha, I pity you both. If you think there is any chance of Linda's getting to the Free States, I will conceal her for a time. But first you must solemnly promise that my name shall never be mentioned. If such a thing should become known, it would ruin me and my family. No one in my house must know of it, except the cook. She is so faithful that I would trust my own life with her; and I know she likes Linda. It is a great risk; but I trust no harm will come of it. Get word to Linda to be ready as soon as it is dark, before the patrols are out. I will send the housemaids on errands, and Betty shall go to meet Linda." The place where we were to meet was designated and agreed upon. My grandmother was unable to thank the lady for this noble deed; overcome by her emotions, she sank on her knees and sobbed like a child.

I received a message to leave my friend's house at such an hour, and go to a certain place where a friend would be waiting for me. As a matter of prudence no names were mentioned. I had no means of conjecturing who I was to meet, or where I was going. I did not like to move thus blindfolded, but I had no choice. It would not do for me to remain where I was. I disguised myself, summoned up courage to meet the worst, and went to the appointed place. My friend Betty was there; she was the last person I expected to see. We hurried along in silence. The pain in my leg was so intense that it seemed as if I should drop; but fear gave me strength. We reached the house and entered unobserved. Her first words were: "Honey, now you is safe. Dem devils ain't coming to search *dis* house. When I get you into missis' safe place, I will bring some nice hot supper. I specs you need it after all dis skeering." Betty's vocation led her to think eating the most important thing in life. She did not realize that my heart was too full for me to care much about supper.

The mistress came to meet us, and led me up stairs to a small room over her own sleeping apartment. "You will be safe here, Linda," said she; "I keep this room to store away things that are out of use. The girls are not accustomed to be sent to it, and they will not suspect any thing unless they hear some noise. I always keep it locked, and Betty shall take care of the key. But you must be very careful, for my sake as well as your own; and you must never tell my secret; for it would ruin me and my family. I will keep the girls busy in the morning, that Betty may have a chance to bring your breakfast; but it will not do for her to come to you again till night. I will come to see you sometimes. Keep up your courage. I hope this state of things will not last long." Betty came with the "nice hot supper," and the mistress hastened down stairs to keep things straight till she returned. How my heart overflowed with gratitude! Words choked in my throat; but I could have kissed the feet of my benefactress. For that deed of Christian womanhood, may God forever bless her!

I went to sleep that night with the feeling that I was for the present the most fortunate slave in town. Morning came and filled my little cell with light. I thanked the heavenly Father for this safe retreat. Opposite my window was a pile of feather beds. On the top of these I could lie perfectly concealed, and command a view of the street through which Dr. Flint passed to his office. Anxious as I was, I felt a gleam of satisfaction when I saw him. Thus far I had outwitted him, and I triumphed over it. Who can blame slaves for being cunning? They are constantly compelled to resort to it. It is the only weapon of the weak and oppressed against the strength of their tyrants.

I was daily hoping to hear that my master had sold my children; for I knew who was on the watch to buy them. But Dr. Flint cared even more for revenge than he did for money. My brother William and the good aunt who had served in his family twenty years, and my little Benny, and Ellen, who was a little over two years old, were thrust into jail, as a means of compelling my relatives to give some information about me. He swore my grandmother should never see one of them again till I was brought back. They kept these facts from me for several days. When I heard that my little ones were in a loathsome jail, my first impulse was to go to them. I was encountering dangers for the sake of freeing them, and must I be the cause of their death? The thought was agonizing. My benefactress tried to soothe me by telling me that my aunt would take good care of the children while they remained in jail. But it added to my pain to think that the good old aunt, who had always been so kind to her sister's orphan children, should be shut up in prison for no other crime than loving them. I suppose my friends feared a reckless movement on my part, knowing, as they did, that my life was bound up in my children. I received a note from my brother William. It was scarcely legible, and ran thus: "Wherever you are, dear sister, I beg of you not to come here. We are all much better off than you are. If you come, you will ruin us all. They would force you to tell where you had been, or they would kill you. Take the advice of your friends; if not for the sake of me and your children, at least for the sake of those you would ruin."

Poor William! He also must suffer for being my brother. I took his advice and kept quiet. My aunt was taken out of jail at the end of a month, because Mrs. Flint could not spare her any longer. She was tired of being her own housekeeper. It was quite too fatiguing to order her dinner and eat it too. My children remained in jail, where brother William did all he could for their comfort. Betty went to see them sometimes, and brought me tidings. She was not permitted to enter the jail; but William would hold them up to the grated window while she chatted with them. When she repeated their prattle, and told me how they wanted to see their ma, my tears would flow. Old Betty would exclaim, "Lors, chile! what's you crying 'bout? Dem young uns vil kill you dead. Don't be so chick'n hearted! If you does, you vil nebber git thro' dis world."

Good old soul! She had gone through the world childless. She had never had little ones to clasp their arms round her neck; she had never seen their soft eyes looking into hers; no sweet little voices had called her mother; she had never pressed her own infants to her heart, with the feeling that even in fetters there was something to live for. How could she realize my feelings? Betty's husband loved children dearly, and wondered why God had denied them to him. He expressed great sorrow when he came to Betty with the tidings that Ellen had been taken out of jail and carried to Dr. Flint's. She had the measles a short time before they carried her to jail, and the disease had left her eyes affected. The doctor had taken her home to attend to them. My children had always been afraid of the doctor and his wife. They had never been inside of their house. Poor little Ellen cried all day to be carried back to prison. The instincts of childhood are true. She knew she was loved in the jail. Her screams and sobs annoyed Mrs. Flint. Before night she called one of the slaves, and said, "Here, Bill, carry this brat back to the jail. I can't stand her noise. If she would be quiet I should like to keep the little minx. She would make a handy waiting-maid for my daughter by and by. But if she staid here, with her white face, I suppose I should either kill her or spoil her. I hope the doctor will sell them as far as wind and water can carry them. As for their mother, her ladyship will find out yet what she gets by running away. She hasn't so much feeling for her children as a cow has for its calf. If she had, she would have come back long ago, to get them out of jail, and save all this expense and trouble. The good-for-nothing hussy! When she is caught, she shall stay in jail, in irons, for one six months, and then be sold to a sugar plantation. I shall see her broke in yet. What do you stand there for, Bill? Why don't you go off with the brat? Mind, now, that you don't let any of the niggers speak to her in the street!"

When these remarks were reported to me, I smiled at Mrs. Flint's saying that she should either kill my child or spoil her. I thought to myself there was very little danger of the latter. I have always considered it as one of God's special providences that Ellen screamed till she was carried back to jail.

That same night Dr. Flint was called to a patient, and did not return till near morning. Passing my grandmother's, he saw a light in the house, and thought to himself, "Perhaps this has something to do with Linda." He knocked, and the door was opened. "What calls you up so early?" said he. "I saw your light, and I thought I would just stop and tell you that I have found out where Linda is. I know where to put my hands on her, and I shall have her before twelve o'clock." When he had turned away, my grandmother and my uncle looked anxiously at each other. They did not know whether or not it was merely one of the doctor's tricks to frighten them. In their uncertainty, though, they thought it was best to have a message conveyed to my friend Betty. Unwilling to alarm her mistress, Betty resolved to dispose of me herself. She came to me, and told me to rise and dress quickly. We hurried down stairs, and across the yard, into the kitchen. She locked the door, and lifted up a plank in the floor. A buffalo skin and a bit of carpet were spread for me to lie on, and a quilt thrown over me. "Stay dar," said she, "till I sees if dey know 'bout you. Dey say dey vil put thar hans on you afore twelve o'clock. If dey *did* know whar you are, dey won't know *now*. Dey'll be disapinted dis time. Dat's all I got to say. If dey comes rummagin 'mong *my* tings, de'll get one bressed sarssin from dis 'ere nigger." In my shallow bed I had but just room enough to bring my hands to my face to keep the dust out of my eyes; for Betty walked over me twenty times in an hour, passing from the dresser to the fireplace. When she was alone, I could hear her pronouncing anathemas over Dr. Flint and all his tribe, every now and then saying, with a chuckling laugh, "Dis nigger's too cute for 'em dis time." When the housemaids were about, she had sly ways of drawing them out, that I might hear what they would say. She would repeat stories she had heard about my being in this, or that, or the other place. To which they would answer, that I was not fool enough to be staying round there; that I was in Philadelphia or New York before this time. When all were abed and asleep, Betty raised the plank, and said, "Come out, chile; come out. Dey don't know nottin 'bout you. 'Twas only white folks' lies, to skeer de niggers."

Some days after this adventure I had a much worse fright. As I sat very still in my retreat above stairs, cheerful visions floated through my mind. I thought Dr. Flint would soon get discouraged, and would be willing to sell my children, when he lost all hopes of making them the means of my discovery. I knew who was ready to buy them. Suddenly I heard a voice that chilled my blood. The sound was too familiar to me, it had been too dreadful, for me not to recognize at once my old master. He was in the house, and I at once concluded he had come to seize me. I looked round in terror. There was no way of escape. The voice receded. I supposed the constable was with him, and they were searching the house. In my alarm I did not forget the trouble I was bringing on my generous benefactress. It seemed as if I were born to bring sorrow on all who befriended me, and that was the bitterest drop in the bitter cup of my life. After a while I heard approaching footsteps; the key was turned in my door. I braced myself against the wall to keep from falling. I ventured to look up, and there stood my kind benefactress alone. I was too much overcome to speak, and sunk down upon the floor.

"I thought you would hear your master's voice," she said; "and knowing you would be terrified, I came to tell you there is nothing to fear. You may even indulge in a laugh at the old gentleman's expense. He is so sure you are in New York, that he came to borrow five hundred dollars to go in pursuit of you. My sister had some money to loan on interest. He has obtained it, and proposes to start for New York to-night. So, for the present, you see you are safe. The doctor will merely lighten his pocket hunting after the bird he has left behind."

XIX. The Children Sold

The doctor came back from New York, of course without accomplishing his purpose. He had expended considerable money, and was rather disheartened. My brother and the children had now been in jail two months, and that also was some expense. My friends thought it was a favorable time to work on his discouraged feelings. Mr. Sands sent a speculator to offer him nine hundred dollars for my brother William, and eight hundred for the two children. These were high prices, as slaves were then selling; but the offer was rejected. If it had been merely a question of money, the doctor would have sold any boy of Benny's age for two hundred dollars; but he could not bear to give up the power of revenge. But he was hard pressed for money, and he revolved the matter in his mind. He knew that if he could keep Ellen till she was fifteen, he could sell her for a high price; but I presume he reflected that she might die, or might be stolen away. At all events, he came to the conclusion that he had better accept the slave-trader's offer. Meeting him in the street, he inquired when he would leave town. "To-day, at ten o'clock," he replied. "Ah, do you go so soon?" said the doctor; "I have been reflecting upon your proposition, and I have concluded to let you have the three negroes if you will say nineteen hundred dollars." After some parley, the trader agreed to his terms. He wanted the bill of sale drawn up and signed immediately, as he had a great deal to attend to during the short time he remained in town. The doctor went to the jail and told William he would take him back into his service if he would promise to behave himself; but he replied that he would rather be sold. "And you *shall* be sold, you ungrateful rascal!" exclaimed the doctor. In less than an hour the money was paid, the paper were signed, sealed, and delivered, and my brother and children were in the hands of the trader.

It was a hurried transaction; and after it was over, the doctor's characteristic caution returned. He went back to the speculator, and said, "Sir, I have come to lay you under obligations of a thousand dollars not to sell any of those negroes in this state." "You come too late," replied the trader; "our bargain is closed." He had, in fact, already sold them to Mr. Sands, but he did not mention it. The doctor required him to put irons on "that rascal, Bill," and to pass through the back streets when he took his gang out of town. The trader was privately instructed to concede to his wishes. My good old aunt went to the jail to bid the children good by, supposing them to be the speculator's property, and that she should never see them again. As she held Benny in her lap, he said, "Aunt Nancy, I want to show you something." He led her to the door and showed her a long row of marks, saying, "Uncle Will taught me to count. I have made a mark for every day I have been here, and it is sixty days. It is a long time; and the speculator is going to take me and Ellen away. He's a bad man. It's wrong for him to take grandmother's children. I want to go to my mother."

My grandmother was told that the children would be restored to her, but she was requested to act as if they were really to be sent away. Accordingly, she made up a bundle of clothes and went to the jail. When she arrived, she found William hand-cuffed among the gang, and the children in the trader's cart. The scene seemed too much like reality. She was afraid there might have been some deception or mistake. She fainted, and was carried home.

When the wagon stopped at the hotel, several gentlemen came out and proposed to purchase William, but the trader refused their offers, without stating that he was already sold. And now came the trying hour for that drove of human beings, driven away like cattle, to be sold they knew not where. Husbands were torn from wives, parents from children, never to look upon each other again this side the grave. There was wringing of hands and cries of despair.

Dr. Flint had the supreme satisfaction of seeing the wagon leave town, and Mrs. Flint had the gratification of supposing that my children were going "as far as wind and water would carry them." According to agreement, my uncle followed the wagon some miles, until they came to an old farm house. There the trader took the irons from William, and as he did so, he said, "You are a damned clever fellow. I should like to own you myself. Them gentlemen that wanted to buy you said you was a bright, honest chap, and I must git you a good home. I guess your old master will swear to-morrow, and call himself an old fool for selling the children. I reckon he'll never git their mammy back agin. I expect she's made tracks for the north. Good by, old boy. Remember, I have done you a good turn. You must thank me by coaxing all the pretty gals to go with me next fall. That's going to be my last trip. This trading in niggers is a bad business for a fellow that's got any heart. Move on, you fellows!" And the gang went on, God alone knows where.

Much as I despise and detest the class of slave-traders, whom I regard as the vilest wretches on earth, I must do this man the justice to say that he seemed to have some feeling. He took a fancy to William in the jail, and wanted to buy him. When he heard the story of my children, he was willing to aid them in getting out of Dr. Flint's power, even without charging the customary fee.

My uncle procured a wagon and carried William and the children back to town. Great was the joy in my grandmother's house! The curtains were closed, and the candles lighted. The happy grandmother cuddled the little ones to her bosom. They hugged her, and kissed her, and clapped their hands, and shouted. She knelt down and poured forth one of her heartfelt prayers of thanksgiving to god. The father was present for a while; and though such a "parental relation" as existed between him and my children takes slight hold on the hearts or consciences of slaveholders, it must be that he experienced some moments of pure joy in witnessing the happiness he had imparted.

I had no share in the rejoicings of that evening. The events of the day had not come to my knowledge. And now I will tell you something that happened to me; though you will, perhaps, think it illustrates the superstition of slaves. I sat in my usual place on the floor near the window, where I could hear much that was said in the street without being seen. The family had retired for the night, and all was still. I sat there thinking of my children, when I heard a low strain of music. A band of serenaders were under the window, playing "Home, sweet home." I listened till the sounds did not seem like music, but like the moaning of children. It seemed as if my heart would burst. I rose from my sitting posture, and knelt. A streak of moonlight was on the floor before me, and in the midst of it appeared the forms of my two children. They vanished; but I had seen them distinctly. Some will call it a dream, others a vision. I know not how to account for it, but it made a strong impression on my mind, and I felt certain something had happened to my little ones.

I had not seen Betty since morning. Now I heard her softly turning the key. As soon as she entered, I clung to her, and begged her to let me know whether my children were dead, or whether they were sold; for I had seen their spirits in my room, and I was sure something had happened to them. "Lor, chile," said she, putting her arms round me, "you's got de high-sterics. I'll sleep wid you to-night, 'cause you'll make a noise, and ruin missis. Something has stirred you up mightily. When you is done cryin, I'll talk wid you. De chillern is well, and mighty happy. I seed 'em myself. Does dat satisfy you? Dar, chile, be still! Somebody vill hear you." I tried to obey her. She lay down, and was soon sound asleep; but no sleep would come to my eyelids.

At dawn, Betty was up and off to the kitchen. The hours passed on, and the vision of the night kept constantly recurring to my thoughts. After a while I heard the voices of two women in the entry. In one of them I recognized the housemaid. The other said to her, "Did you know Linda Brent's children was sold to the speculator yesterday. They say ole massa Flint was might glad to see 'em drove out of town; but they say they've come back agin. I 'spect it's all their daddy's doings. They say he's bought William too. Lor! how it will take hold of ole massa Flint! I'm going roun' to aunt Marthy's to see 'bout it."

I bit my lips till the blood came to keep from crying out. Were my children with their grandmother, or had the speculator carried them off? The suspense was dreadful. Would Betty *never* come, and tell me the truth about it? At last she came, and I eagerly repeated what I had overheard. Her face was one broad, bright smile. "Lor, you foolish ting!" said she. "I'se gwine to tell you all 'bout it. De gals is eating thar breakfast, and missus tole me to let her tell you; but, poor creeter! t'aint right to keep you waitin', and I'se gwine to tell you. Brudder, chillern, all is bought by de daddy! I'se laugh more dan nuff, tinking 'bout ole massa Flint. Lor, how he *vill* swar! He's got ketched dis time, any how; but I must be getting out o' dis, or dem gals vill come and ketch *me*."

Betty went off laughing; and I said to myself, "Can it be true that my children are free? I have not suffered for them in vain. Thank God!"

Great surprise was expressed when it was known that my children had returned to their grandmother's. The news spread through the town, and many a kind word was bestowed on the little ones.

Dr. Flint went to my grandmother's to ascertain who was the owner of my children, and she informed him. "I expected as much," said he. "I am glad to hear it. I have had news from Linda lately, and I shall soon have her. You need never expect to see *her* free. She shall be my slave as long as I live, and when I am dead she shall be the slave of my children. If I ever find out that you or Phillip had anything to do with her running off I'll kill him. And if I meet William in the street, and he presumes to look at me, I'll flog him within an inch of his life. Keep those brats out of my sight!"

As he turned to leave, my grandmother said something to remind him of his own doings. He looked back upon her, as if he would have been glad to strike her to the ground.

I had my season of joy and thanksgiving. It was the first time since my childhood that I had experienced any real happiness. I heard of the old doctor's threats, but they no longer had the same power to trouble me. The darkest cloud that hung over my life had rolled away. Whatever slavery might do to me, it could not shackle my children. If I fell a sacrifice, my little ones were saved. It was well for me that my simple heart believed all that had been promised for their welfare. It is always better to trust than to doubt.

Postreading Writing Assignments

Option 1: What issues does Jacobs raise regarding "ownership", for example, ownership of one's body and/or one's children? Discuss the significance of the examples she provides.

Option 2: Jacobs discusses certain slave-owners and traders as being "kind" or as having "some feelings." What is paradoxical about these statements? Is it possible to be a good slave-owner? Examine Jacobs's criteria for determining who is a good slave-owner; how do her criteria compare with yours?

Option 3: In what ways are you responding to this essay on an emotional level? What do you bring from your past, your beliefs, and your values, that leads you to respond in this way?

Extended Writing Assignments

Option 4: Write an essay in which you analyze one specific moment in Jacobs's text that you found particularly significant, intriguing, or troubling. Do a close reading of this section: What do you see as Jacobs's likely intention here; what is she conveying to her readers; what kinds of social or moral questions does this section raise? What do you want to say back to Jacobs after reading this? After interpreting the specific section that you chose, discuss what this section reveals about the rest of the text; how is this moment integral to the whole of the essay?

Option 5: This assignment requires you to do some outside reading. Find one or two standard history textbooks that address some aspect of slavery. What issues do these texts introduce? Whose point of view is emphasized? Do the accounts provide personal stories or generic information? After reading these texts, reread Jacobs's narrative. Is her account different? How do you explain the differences? If you had read only the textbook accounts of slavery, what does Jacobs's story add to your understanding of slavery? You are looking here specifically at how Jacobs's story adds a new or different dimension to your understanding of slavery.

Forging Connections

Option 6:

> Who can blame slaves for being cunning? They are constantly compelled to resort to it. It is the only weapon of the weak and oppressed against the strength of their tyrants.
>
> (page 236)

Read or reread Frederick Douglass's essay "The Pathway from Salvery to Freedom" and Susan Glaspell's play *Trifles*. Write an essay in which you look into the ways that Douglass, Jacobs, and the women in *Trifles* subvert the power of those dominant over them. Douglass learns to read and write by manipulating those in power; Jacobs arranges to have her children freed; and the women in *Trifles* solve a murder mystery, all by subverting the power that is supposed to control and silence them. How do Jacobs, Douglass, and the women in *Trifles*, people who are silenced and dismissed, use that silencing and submission to get something they want? What do these stories tell us about power and subversion? Explore specific moments in each text. How does one text complement or challenge another?

Maxine Hong Kingston

NO NAME WOMAN

Maxine Hong Kingston lives in California with her husband. The Woman Warrior *was the winner of the National Book Critics award for the best work of nonfiction in 1976. This text, which is taken from* The Woman Warrior *is her account of growing up female and Chinese-American in California.*

Prereading Journal Questions

1. "No Name Woman" is one chapter from Kingston's autobiographical text *The Woman Warrior*. After thinking about these two titles, what expectations do you have for this text? Why? What leads you to develop these assumptions?
2. "No Name Woman" is an exploration of a family story. How have family stories helped shape your perception of the world? When does your family tell stories—and for what purpose?

Reading tip: Watch for a number of voices in this text: those of the storyteller, the listener, and the narrator. The narrator uses the story of her aunt to lead to other stories. Note who is speaking at various moments throughout this text. Pay close attention to the way Kingston interprets and reinterprets the story her mother tells her.

"You must not tell anyone," my mother said, "what I am about to tell you. In China your father had a sister who killed herself. She jumped into the family well. We say that your father has all brothers because it is as if she had never been born.

"In 1924 just a few days after our village celebrated seventeen hurry-up weddings—to make sure that every young man who went 'out on the road' would responsibly come home—your father and his brothers and your grandfather and his brothers and your aunt's new husband sailed for America, the Gold Mountain. It was your grandfather's last trip. Those lucky enough to get contracts waved good-bye from the decks. They fed and guarded the stowaways and helped them off in Cuba, New York, Bali, Hawaii. 'We'll meet in California next year,' they said. All of them sent money home.

"I remember looking at your aunt one day when she and I were dressing; I had not noticed before that she had such a protruding melon of a stomach. But I did not think, 'She's pregnant,' until she began to look like other pregnant women, her shirt pulling and the white tops of her black pants showing. She could not have been pregnant, you see, because her husband had been gone for years. No one said anything. We did not discuss it. In early summer she was ready to have the child, long after the time when it could have been possible.

"The village had also been counting. On the night the baby was to be born the villagers raided our house. Some were crying. Like a great saw, teeth strung with lights, files of people walked zigzag across our land, tearing the rice. Their lanterns doubled in the disturbed black water, which drained away through the broken bunds. As the villagers closed in, we could see that some of them, probably men and women we knew well, wore white masks. The people with long hair hung it over their faces. Women with short hair made it stand up on end. Some had tied white bands around their foreheads, arms, and legs.

"At first they threw mud and rocks at the house. Then they threw eggs and began slaughtering our stock. We could hear the animals scream their deaths—the roosters, the pigs, a last great roar from the ox. Familiar wild heads flared in our night windows; the villagers encircled us. Some of the faces stopped to peer at us, their eyes rushing like searchlights. The hands flattened against the panes, framed heads, and left red prints.

"The villagers broke in the front and the back doors at the same time, even though we had not locked the doors against them. Their knives dripped with the blood of our animals. They smeared blood on the doors and walls. One woman swung a chicken, whose throat she had slit, splattering blood in red arcs about her. We stood together in the middle of our house, in the family hall with the pictures and tables of the ancestors around us, and looked straight ahead.

"At that time the house had only two wings. When the men came back, we would build two more to enclose our courtyard and a third one to begin a second courtyard. The villagers pushed through both wings, even your grandparents' rooms, to find your aunt's, which was also mine until the men returned. From this room a new wing for one of the younger families would grow. They ripped up her clothes and shoes and broke her combs, grinding them underfoot. They tore her work from the loom. They scattered the cooking fire and rolled the new weaving in it. We could hear them in the kitchen breaking our bowls and banging the pots. They overturned the great waist-high earthenware jugs; duck eggs, pickled fruits, vegetables burst out and mixed in acrid torrents. The old woman from the next field swept a broom through the air and loosed the spirits-of-the-broom over our heads. 'Pig.' 'Ghost.' 'Pig,' they sobbed and scolded while they ruined our house.

"When they left, they took sugar and oranges to bless themselves. They cut pieces from the dead animals. Some of them took bowls that were not broken and clothes that were not torn. Afterward we swept up the rice and sewed it back up into sacks. But the smells from the spilled preserves lasted. Your aunt gave birth in the pigsty that night. The next morning when I went for the water, I found her and the baby plugging up the family well.

"Don't let your father know that I told you. He denies her. Now that you have started to menstruate, what happened to her could happen to you. Don't humiliate us. You wouldn't like to be forgotten as if you had never been born. The villagers are watchful."

Whenever she had to warn us about life, my mother told stories that ran like this one, a story to grow up on. She tested our strength to establish realities. Those in the emigrant generations who could not reassert brute survival died young and far from home. Those of us in the first American generations have had to figure out how the invisible world the emigrants built around our childhoods fits in solid America.

The emigrants confused the gods by diverting their curses, misleading them with crooked streets and false names. They must try to confuse their offspring as well, who, I suppose, threaten them in similar ways—always trying to get things straight, always trying to name the unspeakable. The Chinese I know hide their names; sojourners take new names when their lives change and guard their real names with silence.

Chinese-Americans, when you try to understand what things in you are Chinese, how do you separate what is peculiar to childhood, to poverty, insanities, one family, your mother who marked your growing with stories, from what is Chinese? What is Chinese tradition and what is the movies?

If I want to learn what clothes my aunt wore, whether flashy or ordinary, I would have to begin, "Remember Father's drowned-in-the-well sister?" I cannot ask that. My mother has told me once and for all the useful parts. She will add nothing unless powered by Necessity, a riverbank that guides her life. She plants vegetable gardens rather than lawns; she carries the odd-shaped tomatoes home from the fields and eats food left for the gods.

Whenever we did frivolous things, we used up energy; we flew high kites. We children came up off the ground over the melting cones our parents brought home from work and the American movie on New Year's Day—*Oh, You Beautiful Doll* with Betty Grable one year, and *She Wore a Yellow Ribbon* with John Wayne another year. After the one carnival ride each, we paid in guilt; our tired father counted his change on the dark walk home.

Adultery is extravagance. Could people who hatch their own chicks and eat the embryos and the heads for delicacies and boil the feet in vinegar for party food, leaving only the gravel, eating even the gizzard lining—could such people engender a prodigal aunt? To be a woman, to have a daughter in starvation time was a waste enough. My aunt could not have been the lone romantic who gave up everything for sex. Women in the old China did not choose. Some man had commanded her to lie with him and be his secret evil. I wonder whether he masked himself when he joined the raid on her family.

Perhaps she had encountered him in the fields or on the mountain where the daughters-in-law collected fuel. Or perhaps he first noticed her in the marketplace. He was not a stranger because the village housed no strangers. She had to have dealings with him other than sex. Perhaps he worked an adjoining field, or he sold her the cloth for the dress she sewed and wore. His demand must have surprised, then terrified her. She obeyed him; she always did as she was told.

When the family found a young man in the next village to be her husband, she had stood tractably beside the best rooster, his proxy, and promised before they met that she would be his forever. She was lucky that he was her age and she would be the first wife, an advantage secure now. The night she first saw him, he had sex with her. Then he left for America. She had almost forgotten what he looked like. When she tried to envision him, she only saw the black and white face in the group photograph the men had had taken before leaving.

The other man was not, after all, much different from her husband. They both gave orders: she followed. "If you tell your family, I'll beat you. I'll kill you. Be here again next week." No one talked sex, ever. And she might have separated the rapes from the rest of living if only she did not have to buy her oil from him or gather wood in the same forest. I want her fear to have lasted just as long as rape lasted so that the fear could have been contained. No drawn-out fear. But women at sex hazarded birth and hence lifetimes. The fear did not stop but permeated everywhere. She told the man, "I think I'm pregnant." He organized the raid against her.

On nights when my mother and father talked about their life back home, sometimes they mentioned an "outcast table" whose business they still seemed to be settling, their voices tight. In a commensal tradition, where food is precious, the powerful older people made wrongdoers eat alone. Instead of letting them start separate new lives like the Japanese, who could become samurais and geishas, the Chinese family, faces averted but eyes glowering sideways, hung on to the offenders and fed them leftovers. My aunt must have lived in the same house as my parents and eaten at an outcast table. My mother spoke about the raid as if she had seen it, when she and my aunt, a daughter-in-law to a different household, should not have been living together at all. Daughters-in-law lived with their husbands' parents, not their own; a synonym for marriage in Chinese is "taking a daughter-in-law." Her husband's parents could have sold her, mortgaged her, stoned her. But they had sent her back to her own mother and father, a mysterious act hinting at disgraces not told me. Perhaps they had thrown her out to deflect the avengers.

She was the only daughter; her four brothers went with her father, husband, and uncles "out on the road" and for some years became western men. When the goods were divided among the family, three of the brothers took land, and the youngest, my father, chose an education. After my grandparents gave their daughter away to her husband's family, they had dispensed all the adventure and all the property. They expected her alone to keep the traditional ways, which her brothers, now among the barbarians, could fumble without detection. The heavy, deep-rooted women were to maintain the past against the flood, safe for returning. But the rare urge west had fixed upon our family, and so my aunt crossed boundaries not delineated in space.

The work of preservation demands that the feelings playing about in one's guts not be turned into action. Just watch their passing like cherry blossoms. But perhaps my aunt, my forerunner, caught in a slow life, let dreams grow and fade and after some months or years went toward what persisted. Fear at the enormities of the forbidden kept her desires delicate, wire and bone. She looked at a man because she liked the way the hair was tucked behind his ears, or she liked the question-mark line of a long torso curving at the shoulder and straight at the hip. For warm eyes or a soft voice or a slow walk—that's all—a few hairs, a line, a brightness, a sound, a pace, she gave up family. She offered us up for a charm that vanished with tiredness, a pigtail that didn't toss when the wind died. Why, the wrong lighting could erase the dearest thing about him.

It could very well have been, however, that my aunt did not take subtle enjoyment of her friend, but, a wild woman, kept rollicking company. Imagining her free with sex doesn't fit, though. I don't know any women like that, or men either. Unless I see her life branching into mine, she gives me no ancestral help.

To sustain her being in love, she often worked at herself in the mirror, guessing at the colors and shapes that would interest him, changing them frequently in order to hit on the right combination. She wanted him to look back.

On a farm near the sea, a woman who tended her appearance reaped a reputation for eccentricity. All the married women blunt-cut their hair in flaps about their ears or pulled it back in tight buns. No nonsense. Neither style blew easily into heart-catching tangles. And at their weddings they displayed themselves in their long hair for the last time. "It brushed the backs of my knees," my mother tells me. "It was braided, and even so, it brushed the backs of my knees."

At the mirror my aunt combed individuality into her bob. A bun could have been contrived to escape into black streamers blowing in the wind or in quiet wisps about her face, but only the older women in our picture album wear buns. She brushed her hair back from her forehead, tucking the flaps behind her ears. She looped a piece of thread, knotted into a circle between her index fingers and thumbs, and ran the double strand across her forehead. When she closed her fingers as if she were making a pair of shadow geese bite, the string twisted together catching the little hairs. Then she pulled the thread away from her skin, ripping the hairs out neatly, her eyes watering from the needles of pain. Opening her fingers, she cleaned the thread, then rolled it along her hairline and the tops of her eyebrows. My mother did the same to me and my sisters and herself. I used to believe that the expression "caught by the short hairs" meant a captive held with a depilatory string. It especially hurt at the temples, but my mother said we were lucky we didn't have to have our feet bound when we were seven. Sisters used to sit on their beds and cry together, she said, as their mothers or their slaves removed the bandages for a few minutes each night and let the blood gush back into their veins. I hope that the man my aunt loved appreciated a smooth brow, that he wasn't just a tits-and-ass man.

Once my aunt found a freckle on her chin, at a spot that the almanac said predestined her for unhappiness. She dug it out with a hot needle and washed the wound with peroxide.

More attention to her looks than these pullings of hairs and pickings at spots would have caused gossip among the villagers. They owned work clothes and good clothes, and they wore good clothes for feasting the new seasons. But since a woman combing her hair hexes beginnings, my aunt rarely found an occasion to look her best. Women looked like great sea snails—the corded wood, babies, and laundry they carried were the whorls on their backs. The Chinese did not admire a bent back; goddesses and warriors stood straight. Still there must have been a marvelous freeing of beauty when a worker laid down her burden and stretched and arched.

Such commonplace loveliness, however, was not enough for my aunt. She dreamed of a lover for the fifteen days of New Year's, the time for families to exchange visits, money, and food. She plied her secret comb. And sure enough she cursed the year, the family, the village, and herself.

Even as her hair lured her imminent lover, many other men looked at her. Uncles, cousins, nephews, brothers would have looked, too, had they been home between journeys. Perhaps they had already been restraining their curiosity, and they left, fearful that their glances, like a field of nesting birds, might be startled and caught. Poverty hurt, and that was their first reason for leaving. But another, final reason for leaving the crowded house was the never-said.

She may have been unusually beloved, the precious only daughter, spoiled and mirror gazing because of the affection the family lavished on her. When her husband left, they welcomed the chance to take her back from the in-laws; she could live like the little daughter for just a while longer. There are stories that my grandfather was different from other people, "crazy ever since the little Jap bayoneted him in the head." He used to put his naked penis on the dinner table, laughing. And one day he brought home a baby girl, wrapped up inside his brown western-style greatcoat. He had traded one of his sons, probably my father, the youngest, for her. My grandmother made him trade back. When he finally got a daughter of his own, he doted on her. They must have all loved her, except perhaps my father, the only brother who never went back to China, having once been traded for a girl.

Brothers and sisters, newly men and women, had to efface their sexual color and present plain miens. Disturbing hair and eyes, a smile like no other, threatened the ideal of five generations living under one roof. To focus blurs, people shouted face to face and yelled from room to room. The immigrants I know have loud voices, unmodulated to American tones even after years away from the village where they called their friendships out across the fields. I have not been able to stop my mother's screams in public libraries or over telephones. Walking erect (knees straight, toes pointed forward, not pigeon-toed, which is Chinese-feminine) and speaking in an inaudible voice, I have tried to turn myself American-feminine. Chinese communication was loud, public. Only sick people had to whisper. But at the dinner table, where the family members came nearest one another, no one could talk, not the outcasts nor any eaters. Every word that falls from the mouth is a coin lost. Silently they gave and accepted food with both hands. A preoccupied child who took his bowl with one hand got a sideways glare. A complete moment of total attention is due everyone alike. Children and lovers have no singularity here, but my aunt used a secret voice, a separate attentiveness.

She kept the man's name to herself throughout her labor and dying; she did not accuse him that he be punished with her. To save her inseminator's name she gave silent birth.

He may have been somebody in her own household, but intercourse with a man outside the family would have been no less abhorrent. All the village were kinsmen, and the titles shouted in loud country voices never let kinship be forgotten. Any man within visiting distance would have been neutralized as a lover—"brother," "younger brother," "older brother"—one hundred and fifteen relationship titles. Parents researched birth charts probably not so much to assure good fortune as to circumvent incest in a population that has but one hundred surnames. Everybody has eight million relatives. How useless then sexual mannerisms, how dangerous.

As if it came from an atavism deeper than fear, I used to add "brother" silently to boys' names. It hexed the boys, who would or would not ask me to dance, and made them less scary and as familiar and deserving of benevolence as girls.

But, of course, I hexed myself also—no dates. I should have stood up, both arms waving, and shouted out across libraries, "Hey, you! Love me back." I had no idea, though, how to make attraction selective, how to control its direction and magnitude. If I made myself American-pretty so that the five or six Chinese boys in the class fell in love with me, everyone else—the Caucasian, Negro, and Japanese boys—would too. Sisterliness, dignified and honorable, made much more sense.

Attraction eludes control so stubbornly that whole societies designed to organize relationships among people cannot keep order, not even when they bind people to one another from childhood and raise them together. Among the very poor and the wealthy, brothers married their adopted sisters, like doves. Our family allowed some romance, paying adult brides' prices and providing dowries so that their sons and daughters could marry strangers. Marriage promises to turn strangers into friendly relatives—a nation of siblings.

In the village structure, spirits shimmered among the live creatures, balanced and held in equilibrium by time and land. But one human being flaring up into violence could open up a black hole, a maelstrom that pulled in the sky. The frightened villagers, who depended on one another to maintain the real, went to my aunt to show her a personal, physical representation of the break she had made in the "roundness." Misallying couples snapped off the future, which was to be embodied in true offspring. The villagers punished her for acting as if she could have a private life, secret and apart from them.

If my aunt had betrayed the family at a time of large grain yields and peace, when many boys were born, and wings were being built on many houses, perhaps she might have escaped such severe punishment. But the men—hungry, greedy, tired of planting in dry soil—had been forced to leave the village in order to send food-money home. There were ghost plagues, bandit plagues, wars with the Japanese, floods. My Chinese brother and sister had died of an unknown sickness. Adultery, perhaps only a mistake during good times, became a crime when the village needed food.

The round moon cakes and round doorways, the round tables of graduated sizes that fit one roundness inside another, round windows and rice bowls—these talismans had lost their power to warn this family of the law: a family must be whole, faithfully keeping the descent line by having sons to feed the old and the dead, who in turn look after the family. The villagers came to show my aunt and her lover-in-hiding a broken house. The villagers were speeding up the circling of events because she was too shortsighted to see that her infidelity had already harmed the village, that waves of consequences would return unpredictably, sometimes in disguise, as now, to hurt her. This roundness had to be made coin-sized so that she would see its circumference: punish her at the birth of her baby. Awaken her to the inexorable. People who refused fatalism because they could invent small resources insisted on culpability. Deny accidents and wrest fault from the stars.

After the villagers left, their lanterns now scattering in various directions toward home, the family broke their silence and cursed her. "Aiaa, we're going to die. Death is coming. Death is coming Look what you've done. You've killed us. Ghost! Dead ghost! Ghost! You've never been born." She ran out into the fields, far enough from the house so that she could no longer hear their voices, and pressed herself against the earth, her own land no more. When she felt the birth coming, she thought that she had been hurt. Her body seized together. "They've hurt me too much," she thought. "This is gall, and it will kill me." With forehead and knees against the earth, her body convulsed and then relaxed. She turned on her back, lay on the ground. The black well of sky and stars went out and out and out forever; her body and her complexity seemed to disappear. She was one of the stars, a bright dot in blackness, without home, without a companion, in eternal cold and silence. An agoraphobia rose in her, speeding higher and higher, bigger and bigger; she would not be able to contain it; there would be no end to fear.

Flayed, unprotected against space, she felt pain return, focusing her body. This pain chilled her—a cold, steady kind of surface pain. Inside, spasmodically, the other pain, the pain of the child, heated her. For hours she lay on the ground, alternately body and space. Sometimes a vision of normal comfort obliterated reality: she saw the family in the evening gambling at the dinner table, the young people massaging their elders' backs. She saw them congratulating one another, high joy on the mornings the rice shoots came up. When these pictures burst, the stars drew yet further apart. Black space opened.

She got to her feet to fight better and remembered that old-fashioned women gave birth in their pigsties to fool the jealous, pain-dealing gods, who do not snatch piglets. Before the next spasms could stop her, she ran to the pigsty, each step a rushing out into emptiness. She climbed over the fence and knelt in the dirt. It was good to have a fence enclosing her, a tribal person alone.

Laboring, this woman who had carried her child as a foreign growth that sickened her every day, expelled it at last. She reached down to touch the hot, wet, moving mass, surely smaller than anything human, and could feel that it was human after all—fingers, toes, nails, nose. She pulled it up on to her belly, and it lay curled there, butt in the air, feet precisely tucked one under the other. She opened her loose shirt and buttoned the child inside. After resting, it squirmed and thrashed and she pushed it up to her breast. It turned its head this way and that until it found her nipple. There, it made little snuffling noises. She clenched her teeth at its preciousness, lovely as a young calf, a piglet, a little dog.

She may have gone to the pigsty as a last act of responsibility: she would protect this child as she had protected its father. It would look after her soul, leaving supplies on her grave. But how would this tiny child without family find her grave when there would be no marker for her anywhere, neither in the earth nor the family hall? No one would give her a family hall name. She had taken the child with her into the wastes. At its birth the two of them had felt the same raw pain of separation, a wound that only the family pressing tight could close. A child with no descent line would not soften her life but only trail after her, ghostlike, begging her to give it purpose. At dawn the villagers on their way to the fields would stand around the fence and look.

Full of milk, the little ghost slept. When it awoke, she hardened her breasts against the milk that crying loosens. Toward morning she picked up the baby and walked to the well.

Carrying the baby to the well shows loving. Otherwise abandon it. Turn its face into the mud. Mothers who love their children take them along. It was probably a girl; there is some hope of forgiveness for boys.

"Don't tell anyone you had an aunt. Your father does not want to hear her name. She has never been born." I have believed that sex was unspeakable and words so strong and fathers so frail that "aunt" would do my father mysterious harm. I have thought that my family, having settled among immigrants who had also been their neighbors in the ancestral land, needed to clean their name, and a wrong word would incite the kinspeople even here. But there is more to this silence: they want me to participate in her punishment. And I have.

In the twenty years since I heard this story I have not asked for details nor said my aunt's name; I do not know it. People who can comfort the dead can also chase after them to hurt them further—a reverse ancestor worship. The real punishment was not the raid swiftly inflicted by the villagers, but the family's deliberately forgetting her. Her betrayal so maddened them, they saw to it that she would suffer forever, even after death. Always hungry, always needing, she would have to beg food from other ghosts, snatch and steal it from those whose living descendants give them gifts. She would have to fight the ghosts massed at crossroads for the buns a few thoughtful citizens leave to decoy her away from village and home so that the ancestral spirits could feast unharassed. At peace, they could act like gods, not ghosts, their descent lines providing them with paper suits and dresses, spirit money, paper houses, paper automobiles, chicken, meat, and rice into eternity—essences delivered up in smoke and flames, steam and incense rising from each rice bowl. In an attempt to make the Chinese care for people outside the family, Chairman Mao encourages us now to give our paper replicas to the spirits of outstanding soldiers and workers, no matter whose ancestors they may be. My aunt remains forever hungry. Goods are not distributed evenly among the dead.

My aunt haunts me—her ghost drawn to me because now, after fifty years of neglect, I alone devote pages of paper to her, though not origamied into houses and clothes. I do not think she always means me well. I am telling on her, and she was a spite suicide, drowning herself in the drinking water. The Chinese are always very frightened of the drowned one, whose weeping ghost, wet hair hanging and skin bloated, waits silently by the water to pull down a substitute.

Postreading Writing Assignments

Option 1: What does the narrator "do" with the story her mother tells her? How does she add to, redefine, and reinterpret the story of her aunt?

Option 2: Why does Kingston's mother choose to tell this particular story—what does the story imply? Why does Kingston find this story significant—why does she alone "devote pages of paper" to her aunt?

Extended Writing Assignments

Option 3: Think back to a story your family shared with you when you were young. What was the purpose of telling you the story; was it to teach you a lesson, to share family history, to enable you to feel a sense of belonging with part of your past, or to entertain you? Use Kingston's example in telling a family story. Kingston does not just retell what her mother told her; she extends her mother's project. This assignment asks you to do something similar. Choose one story from your past that you remember as especially significant. Use Kingston's story as your model. Notice how Kingston begins with the story her mother tells her but goes on to build her own story and to discuss the ways this story has affected her twenty years after having heard it. Do something similar in your essay: begin with a family story, redefine it from your own point of view, add details that may have been left out, imagine scenarios that you were not told about, and discuss the significance that this story holds for you as an adult.

Option 4:

> Carrying the baby to the well shows loving. Otherwise abandon it. Turn its face into the mud. Mothers who love their children take them along. It was probably a girl; there is some hope of forgiveness for boys.
>
> (page 256)

Write an essay exploring the implications of the preceding passage. There are many issues and questions you might consider as you write: How is this story particularly about women and issues women face? Why is it that the family cannot speak this aunt's name—what does it do to call the aunt "No Name Woman"? How does this story shape Kingston's ideas of being a woman? How does it influence her mother's ideas of womanhood? What does this text tell you about life for women in 1924 China? Look closely at what Kingston does with this story. Does she use it the way her mother intended her to use it, or does she create her own sense and meaning of its importance?

Use the preceding passage as a way to explore the underlying meanings woven throughout the many stories in this text.

Forging Connections

Option 5: Read or reread Harriet Jacobs's "Flight and a Safe Retreat" after reading "No Name Woman." In what ways are these texts about ownership of women's bodies, of children, and of people's lives? How can the aunt in "No Name Woman" be compared with Harriet Jacobs—is the aunt enslaved? Write an essay looking closely at the life of Jacobs (whose story she tells us herself) and the life of Kingston's aunt (whose story is filtered through many voices). What can you say about these two women? They lived in different places and in different circumstances, and they chose different ways to subvert those in power over them. How does one story add to your understanding of the other? Do close readings of both stories, and then present an analysis of each woman's experience in light of the other.

Jonathan Kozol

THE SAVAGE INEQUALITIES OF PUBLIC EDUCATION IN NEW YORK

In 1967 Jonathan Kozol published Death at an Early Age, *a book about poor children in Boston's public schools. Still in his twenties and an obscure teacher in one of those schools, Kozol went on to win the National Book Award for his first book and became one of the most eloquent advocates for children in America.* Savage Inequalities, *from which this selection is taken, is an examination of our public education in the United States. Kozol lives near Boston and continues to visit schools and talk with teachers.*

Prereading Journal Questions

1. Read or reread the headnote; after noting that Kozol wrote a book titled *Death at an Early Age* about poor children in Boston's schools, what issues do you imagine Kozol explores in *Savage Inequalities*?
2. *Death at an Early Age* was published in 1967; *Savage Inequalities* was published in 1991. What was taking place in America's schools in the 1960s? What has changed since then? What kinds of inequalities do you think Kozol found to write about in 1991?

Reading tip: Imagine, as you read, that you are listening to Kozol speaking to a group—he is sharing this text with an audience. Who is his intended audience? What does he hope to accomplish? Be sure to see yourself as part of this audience; participate in a dialogue with Kozol and other audience members.

In a country where there is no distinction of class," Lord Acton wrote of the United States 130 years ago, "a child is not born to the station of its parents, but with an indefinite claim to all the prizes that can be won by thought and labor. It is in conformity with the theory of equality . . . to give as near as possible to every youth an equal state in life." Americans, he said, "are unwilling that any should be deprived in childhood of the means of competition."

It is hard to read these words today without a sense of irony and sadness. Denial of "the means of competition" is perhaps the single most consistent outcome of the education offered to poor children in the schools of our large cities; and nowhere is this pattern of denial more explicit or more absolute than in the public schools of New York City.

Average expenditures per pupil in the city of New York in 1987 were some $5,500. In the highest spending suburbs of New York (Great Neck or Manhasset, for example, on Long Island) funding levels rose above $11,000, with the highest districts in the state at $15,000. "Why . . . ," asks the city's Board of Education, "should our students receive less" than do "similar students" who live elsewhere? "The inequity is clear."

But the inequality to which these words refer goes even further than the school board may be eager to reveal. "It is perhaps the supreme irony," says the nonprofit Community Service Society of New York, that "the same Board of Education which perceives so clearly the inequities" of funding between separate towns and cities "is perpetuating similar inequities" right in New York. And, in comment on the Board of Education's final statement—"the inequity is clear"—the CSS observes, "New York City's poorest . . . districts could adopt that eloquent statement with few changes."

New York City's public schools are subdivided into 32 school districts. District 10 encompasses a large part of the Bronx but is, effectively, two separate districts. One of these districts, Riverdale, is in the northwest section of the Bronx. Home to many of the city's most sophisticated and well-educated families, its elementary schools have relatively few low-income students. The other section, to the south and east, is poor and heavily nonwhite.

The contrast between public schools in each of these two neighborhoods is obvious to any visitor. At Public School 24 in Riverdale, the principal speaks enthusiastically of his teaching staff. At Public School 79, serving poorer children to the south, the principal says that he is forced to take the "tenth-best" teachers. "I thank God they're still breathing," he remarks of those from whom he must select his teachers.

Some years ago, District 10 received an allocation for computers. The local board decided to give each elementary school an equal number of computers, even though the schools in Riverdale had smaller classes and far fewer students. When it was pointed out that schools in Riverdale, as a result, had twice the number of computers in proportion to their student populations as the schools in the poor neighborhoods, the chairman of the local board replied, "What is fair is what is determined . . . to be fair."

The superintendent of District 10, Fred Goldberg, tells the *New York Times* that "every effort" is made "to distribute resources equitably." He speculates that some gap might exist because some of the poorer schools need to use funds earmarked for computers to buy basic supplies like pens and paper. Asked about the differences in teachers noted by the principals, he says there are no differences, then adds that next year he'll begin a program to improve the quality of teachers in the poorer schools. Questioned about differences in physical appearances between the richer and the poorer schools, he says, "I think it's demographics."

Sometimes a school principal, whatever his background or his politics, looks into the faces of the children in his school and offers a disarming statement that cuts through official ambiguity. "These are the kids most in need," says Edward Flanery, the principal of one of the low-income schools, "and they get the worst teachers." For children of diverse needs in his overcrowded rooms, he says, "you need an outstanding teacher. And what do you get? You get the worst."

In order to find Public School 261 in District 10, a visitor is told to look for a mortician's office. The funeral home, which faces Jerome Avenue in the North Bronx, is easy to identify by its green awning. The school is next door, in a former roller-skating rink. No sign identifies the building as a school. A metal awning frame without an awning supports a flagpole, but there is no flag.

In the street in front of the school there is an elevated public transit line. Heavy traffic fills the street. The existence of the school is virtually concealed within this crowded city block.

In a vestibule between the outer and inner glass doors of the school there is a sign with these words: "All children are capable of learning."

Beyond the inner doors a guard is seated. The lobby is long and narrow. The ceiling is low. There are no windows. All the teachers that I see at first are middle-aged white women. The principal, who is also a white woman, tells me that the school's "capacity" is 900 but that there are 1,300 children here. The size of classes for fifth and sixth grade children in New York, she says, is "capped" at 32, but she says that class size in the school goes "up to 34." (I later see classes, however, as large as 37.) Classes for younger children, she goes on, are "capped at 25," but a school can go above this limit if it puts an extra adult in the room. Lack of space, she says, prevents the school from operating a prekindergarten program.

I ask the principal where her children go to school. They are enrolled in private school, she says.

"Lunchtime is a challenge for us," she explains. "Limited space obliges us to do it in three shifts, 450 children at a time."

Textbooks are scarce and children have to share their social studies books. The principal says there is one full-time pupil counselor and another who is here two days a week: a ratio of 930 children to one counselor. The carpets are patched and sometimes taped together to conceal an open space. "I could use some new rugs," she observes.

To make up for the building's lack of windows and the crowded feeling that results, the staff puts plants and fish tanks in the corridors. Some of the plants are flourishing. Two boys, released from class, are in a corridor beside a tank, their noses pressed against the glass. A school of pinkish fish inside the tank are darting back and forth. Farther down the corridor a small Hispanic girl is watering the plants.

Two first grade classes share a single room without a window, divided only by a blackboard. Four kindergartens and a sixth grade class of Spanish-speaking children have been packed into a single room in which, again, there is no window. A second grade bilingual class of 37 children has its own room but again there is no window.

By eleven o'clock, the lunchroom is already packed with appetite and life. The kids line up to get their meals, then eat them in ten minutes. After that, with no place they can go to play, they sit and wait until it's time to line up and go back to class.

On the second floor I visit four classes taking place within another undivided space. The room has a low ceiling. File cabinets and movable blackboards give a small degree of isolation to each class. Again, there are no windows.

The library is a tiny, windowless and claustrophobic room. I count approximately 700 books. Seeing no reference books, I ask a teacher if encyclopedias and other reference books are kept in classrooms.

"We don't have encyclopedias in classrooms," she replies. "That is for the suburbs."

The school, I am told, has 26 computers for its 1,300 children. There is one small gym and children get one period, and sometimes two, each week. Recess, however, is not possible because there is no playground. "Head Start," the principal says, "scarcely exists in District 10. We have no space."

The school, I am told, is 90 percent black and Hispanic; the other 10 percent are Asian, white or Middle Eastern.

In a sixth grade social studies class the walls are bare of words or decorations. There seems to be no ventilation system, or, if one exists, it isn't working.

The class discusses the Nile River and the Fertile Crescent.

The teacher, in a droning voice: "How is it useful that these civilizations developed close to rivers?"

A child, in a good loud voice: "What kind of question is that?"

In my notes I find these words: "An uncomfortable feeling—being in a building with no windows. There are metal ducts across the room. Do they give air? I feel asphyxiated. . . ."

On the top floor of the school, a sixth grade of 30 children shares a room with 29 bilingual second graders. Because of the high class size there is an assistant with each teacher. This means that 59 children and four grown-ups—63 in all—must share a room that, in a suburban school, would hold no more than 20 children and one teacher. There are, at least, some outside windows in this room—it is the only room with windows in the school—and the room has a high ceiling. It is a relief to see some daylight.

I return to see the kindergarten classes on the ground floor and feel stifled once again by lack of air and the low ceiling. Nearly 120 children and adults are doing what they can to make the best of things: 80 children in four kindergarten classes, 30 children in the sixth grade class, and about eight grown-ups who are aides and teachers. The kindergarten children sitting on the worn rug, which is patched with tape, look up at me and turn their heads to follow me as I walk past them.

As I leave the school, a sixth grade teacher stops to talk. I ask her, "Is there air conditioning in warmer weather?"

Teachers, while inside the building, are reluctant to give answers to this kind of question. Outside, on the sidewalk, she is less constrained: "I had an awful room last year. In the winter it was 56 degrees. In the summer it was up to 90. It was sweltering."

I ask her, "Do the children ever comment on the building?"

"They don't say," she answers, "but they know."

I ask her if they see it as a racial message.

"All these children see TV," she says. "They know what suburban schools are like. Then they look around them at their school. This was a roller-rink, you know. . . . They don't comment on it but you see it in their eyes. They understand."

On the following morning I visit P.S. 79, another elementary school in the same district. "We work under difficult circumstances," says the principal, James Carter, who is black. "The school was built to hold one thousand students. We have 1,550. We are badly overcrowded. We need smaller classes but, to do this, we would need more space. I can't add five teachers. I would have no place to put them."

Some experts, I observe, believe that class size isn't a real issue. He dismisses this abruptly. "It doesn't take a genius to discover that you learn more in a smaller class. I have to bus some 60 kindergarten children elsewhere, since I have no space for them. When they return next year, where do I put them?

"I can't set up a computer lab. I have no room. I had to put a class into the library. I have no librarian. There are two gymnasiums upstairs but they cannot be used for sports. We hold more classes there. It's unfair to measure us against the suburbs. They have 17 to 20 children in a class. Average class size in this school is 30.

"The school is 29 percent black, 70 percent Hispanic. Few of these kids get Head Start. There is no space in the district. Of 200 kindergarten children, 50 maybe get some kind of preschool."

I ask him how much difference preschool makes.

"Those who get it do appreciably better. I can't overestimate its impact but, as I have said, we have no space."

The school tracks children by ability, he says. "There are five to seven levels in each grade. The highest level is equivalent to 'gifted' but it's not a full-scale gifted program. We don't have the funds. We have no science room. The science teachers carry their equipment with them."

We sit and talk within the nurse's room. The window is broken. There are two holes in the ceiling. About a quarter of the ceiling has been patched and covered with a plastic garbage bag.

"Ideal class size for these kids would be 15 to 20. Will these children ever get what white kids in the suburbs take for granted? I don't think so. If you ask me why, I'd have to speak of race and social class. I don't think the powers that be in New York City understand, or want to understand, that if they do not give these children a sufficient education to lead healthy and productive lives, we will be their victims later on. We'll pay the price someday—in violence, in economic costs. I despair of making this appeal in any terms but these. You cannot issue an appeal to conscience in New York today. The fair-play argument won't be accepted. So you speak of violence and hope that it will scare the city into action."

While we talk, three children who look six or seven years old come to the door and ask to see the nurse, who isn't in the school today. One of the children, a Puerto Rican girl, looks haggard. "I have a pain in my tooth," she says. The principal says, "The nurse is out. Why don't you call your mother?" The child says, "My mother doesn't have a phone." The principal sighs. "Then go back to your class." When she leaves, the principal is angry. "It's amazing to me that these children ever make it with the obstacles they face. Many *do* care and they *do* try, but there's a feeling of despair. The parents of these children want the same things for their children that the parents in the suburbs want. Drugs are not the cause of this. They are the symptom. Nonetheless, they're used by people in the suburbs and rich people in Manhattan as another reason to keep children of poor people at a distance."

I ask him, "Will white children and black children ever go to school together in New York?"

"I don't see it," he replies. "I just don't think it's going to happen. It's a dream. I simply do not see white folks in Riverdale agreeing to cross-bus with kids like these. A few, maybe. Very few. I don't think I'll live to see it happen."

I ask him whether race is the decisive factor. Many experts, I observe, believe that wealth is more important in determining these inequalities.

"This," he says—and sweeps his hand around him at the room, the garbage bag, the ceiling—"would not happen to white children."

In a kindergarten class the children sit cross-legged on a carpet in a space between two walls of books. Their 26 faces are turned up to watch their teacher, an elderly black woman. A little boy who sits beside me is involved in trying to tie bows in his shoelaces. The children sing a song: "Lift Every Voice." On the wall are these handwritten words: "Beautiful, also, are the souls of my people."

In a very small room on the fourth floor, 52 people in two classes do their best to teach and learn. Both are first grade classes. One, I am informed, is "low ability." The other is bilingual.

"The room is barely large enough for one class," says the principal.

The room is 25 by 50 feet. There are 26 first graders and two adults on the left, 22 others and two adults on the right. On the wall there is the picture of a small white child, circled by a Valentine, and a Gainsborough painting of a child in a formal dress.

"We are handicapped by scarcity," one of the teachers says. "One fifth of these children may be at grade level by the year's end."

A boy who may be seven years old climbs on my lap without an invitation and removes my glasses. He studies my face and runs his fingers through my hair. "You have nice hair," he says. I ask him where he lives and he replies, "Times Square Hotel," which is a homeless shelter in Manhattan.

I ask him how he gets here.

"With my father. On the train," he says.

"How long does it take?"

"It takes an hour and a half."

I ask him when he leaves his home.

"My mother wakes me up at five o'clock."

"When do you leave?"

"Six-thirty."

I ask him how he gets back to Times Square.

"My father comes to get me after school."

From my notes: "He rides the train three hours every day in order to attend this segregated school. It would be a shorter ride to Riverdale. There are rapid shuttle-vans that make that trip in only 20 minutes. Why not let him go to school right in Manhattan, for that matter?"

At three o'clock the nurse arrives to do her recordkeeping. She tells me she is here three days a week. "The public hospital we use for an emergency is called North Central. It's not a hospital that I will use if I am given any choice. Clinics in the private hospitals are far more likely to be staffed by an experienced physician."

She hesitates a bit as I take out my pen, but then goes on: "I'll give you an example. A little girl I saw last week in school was trembling and shaking and could not control the motions of her arms. I was concerned and called her home. Her mother came right up to school and took her to North Central. The intern concluded that the child was upset by 'family matters'—nothing more—that there was nothing wrong with her. The mother was offended by the diagnosis. She did not appreciate his words or his assumptions. The truth is, there was nothing wrong at home. She brought the child back to school. I thought that she was ill. I told her mother, 'Go to Montefiore.' It's a private hospital, and well respected. She took my advice, thank God. It turned out that the child had a neurological disorder. She is now in treatment.

"This is the kind of thing our children face. Am I saying that the city underserves this population? You can draw your own conclusions."

Out on the street, it takes a full half hour to flag down a cab. Taxi drivers in New York are sometimes disconcertingly direct in what they say. When they are contemptuous of poor black people, their contempt is unadorned. When they're sympathetic and compassionate, their observations often go right to the heart of things. "Oh . . . they neglect these children," says the driver. "They leave them in the streets and slums to live and die." We stop at a light. Outside the window of the taxi, aimless men are standing in a semicircle while another man is working on his car. Old four-story buildings with their windows boarded, cracked or missing are on every side.

I ask the driver where he's from. He says Afghanistan. Turning in his seat, he gestures at the street and shrugs. "If you don't, as an American, begin to give these kids the kind of education that you give the kids of Donald Trump, you're asking for disaster."

Two months later, on a day in May, I visit an elementary school in Riverdale. The dogwoods and magnolias on the lawn in front of P.S. 24 are in full blossom on the day I visit. There is a well-tended park across the street, another larger park three blocks away. To the left of the school is a playground for small children, with an innovative jungle gym, a slide and several climbing toys. Behind the school there are two playing fields for older kids. The grass around the school is neatly trimmed.

The neighborhood around the school, by no means the richest part of Riverdale, is nonetheless expensive and quite beautiful. Residences in the area—some of which are large, free-standing houses, others condominiums in solid red-brick buildings—sell for prices in the region of $400,000; but some of the larger Tudor houses on the winding and tree-shaded streets close to the school can cost up to $1 million. The excellence of P.S. 24, according to the principal, adds to the value of these homes. Advertisements in the *New York Times* will frequently inform prospective buyers that a house is "in the neighborhood of P.S. 24."

The school serves 825 children in the kindergarten through sixth grade. This is approximately half the student population crowded into P.S. 79, where 1,550 children fill a space intended for 1,000, and a great deal smaller than the 1,300 children packed into the former skating rink; but the principal of P.S. 24, a capable and energetic man named David Rothstein, still regards it as excessive for an elementary school.

The school is integrated in the strict sense that the middle- and upper-middle-class white children here do occupy a building that contains some Asian and Hispanic and black children; but there is little integration in the classrooms since the vast majority of the Hispanic and black children are assigned to "special" classes on the basis of evaluations that have classified them "EMR"—"educable mentally retarded"—or else, in the worst of cases, "TMR"—"trainable mentally retarded."

I ask the principal if any of his students qualify for free-lunch programs. "About 130 do," he says. "Perhaps another 35 receive their lunches at reduced price. Most of these kids are in the special classes. They do not come from this neighborhood."

The very few nonwhite children that one sees in mainstream classes tend to be Japanese or else of other Asian origins. Riverdale, I learn, has been the residence of choice for many years to members of the diplomatic corps.

The school therefore contains effectively two separate schools: one of about 130 children, most of whom are poor, Hispanic, black, assigned to one of the 12 special classes; the other of some 700 mainstream students, almost all of whom are white or Asian.

There is a third track also—this one for the students who are labeled "talented" or "gifted." This is termed a "pull-out" program since the children who are so identified remain in mainstream classrooms but are taken out for certain periods each week to be provided with intensive and, in my opinion, excellent instruction in some areas of reasoning and logic often known as "higher-order skills" in the contemporary jargon of the public schools. Children identified as "gifted" are admitted to this program in first grade and, in most cases, will remain there for six years. Even here, however, there are two tracks of the gifted. The regular gifted classes are provided with only one semester of this specialized instruction yearly. Those very few children, on the other hand, who are identified as showing the most promise are assigned, beginning in the third grade, to a program that receives a full-year regimen.

In one such class, containing ten intensely verbal and impressive fourth grade children, nine are white and one is Asian. The "special" class I enter first, by way of contrast, has twelve children of whom only one is white and none is Asian. These racial breakdowns prove to be predictive of the schoolwide pattern.

In a classroom for the gifted on the first floor of the school, I ask a child what the class is doing. "Logic and syllogisms," she replies. The room is fitted with a planetarium. The principal says that all the elementary schools in District 10 were given the same planetariums ten years ago but that certain schools, because of overcrowding, have been forced to give them up. At P.S. 261, according to my notes, there was a domelike space that had been built to hold a planetarium, but the planetarium had been removed to free up space for the small library collection. P.S. 24, in contrast, has a spacious library that holds almost 8,000 books. The windows are decorated with attractive, brightly colored curtains and look out on flowering trees. The principal says that it's inadequate, but it appears spectacular to me after the cubicle that holds a meager 700 books within the former skating rink.

The district can't afford librarians, the principal says, but P.S. 24, unlike the poorer schools of District 10, can draw on educated parent volunteers who staff the room in shifts three days a week. A parent organization also raises independent funds to buy materials, including books, and will soon be running a fund raiser to enhance the library's collection.

In a large and sunny first grade classroom that I enter next, I see 23 children, all of whom are white or Asian. In another first grade, there are 22 white children and two others who are Japanese.

There is a computer in each class. Every classroom also has a modern fitted sink.

In a second grade class of 22 children, there are two black children and three Asian children. Again, there is a sink and a computer. A sixth grade social studies class has only one black child. The children have an in-class research area that holds some up-to-date resources. A set of encyclopedias (World Book, 1985) is in a rack beside a window. The children are doing a Spanish language lesson when I enter. Foreign languages begin in sixth grade at the school, but Spanish is offered also to the kindergarten children. As in every room at P.S. 24, the window shades are clean and new, the floor is neatly tiled in gray and green, and there is not a single light bulb missing.

Walking next into a special class, I see twelve children. One is white. Eleven are black. There are no Asian children. The room is half the size of mainstream classrooms. "Because of overcrowding," says the principal, "we have had to split these rooms in half." There is no computer and no sink.

I enter another special class. Of seven children, five are black, one is Hispanic, one is white. A little black boy with a large head sits in the far corner and is gazing at the ceiling.

"Placement of these kids," the principal explains, "can usually be traced to neurological damage."

In my notes: "How could so many of these children be brain-damaged?"

Next door to the special class is a woodworking shop. "This shop is only for the special classes," says the principal. The children learn to punch in time cards at the door, he says, in order to prepare them for employment.

The fourth grade gifted class, in which I spend the last part of the day, is humming with excitement. "I start with these children in the first grade," says the teacher. "We pull them out of mainstream classes on the basis of their test results and other factors such as the opinion of their teachers. Out of this group, beginning in third grade, I pull out the ones who show the most potential, and they enter classes such as this one."

The curriculum they follow, she explains, "emphasizes critical thinking, reasoning and logic." The planetarium, for instance, is employed not simply for the study of the universe as it exists. "Children also are designing their own galaxies," the teacher says.

A little girl sitting around a table with her classmates speaks with perfect poise: "My name is Susan. We are in the fourth grade gifted program."

I ask them what they're doing and a child says, "My name is Laurie and we're doing problem-solving."

A rather tall, good-natured boy who is half-standing at the table tells me that his name is David. "One thing that we do," he says, "is logical thinking. Some problems, we find, have more than one good answer. We need to learn not simply to be logical in our own thinking but to show respect for someone else's logic even when an answer may be technically incorrect."

When I ask him to explain this, he goes on, "A person who gives an answer that is not 'correct' may nonetheless have done some interesting thinking that we should examine. 'Wrong' answers may be more useful to examine than correct ones."

I ask the children if reasoning and logic are innate or if they're things that you can learn.

"You know some things to start with when you enter school," Susan says. "But we also learn some things that other children don't."

I ask her to explain this.

"We know certain things that other kids don't know because we're *taught* them."

She has braces on her teeth. Her long brown hair falls almost to her waist. Her loose white T-shirt has the word TRI-LOGIC on the front. She tells me that Tri-Logic is her father's firm.

Laurie elaborates on the same point: "Some things you know. Some kinds of logic are inside of you to start with. There are other things that someone needs to teach you."

David expands on what the other two have said: "Everyone can think and speak in logical ways unless they have a mental problem. What this program does is bring us to a higher form of logic."

The class is writing a new "Bill of Rights." The children already know the U.S. Bill of Rights and they explain its first four items to me with precision. What they are examining today, they tell me, is the very *concept* of a "right." Then they will create their own compendium of rights according to their own analysis and definition. Along one wall of the classroom, opposite the planetarium, are seven Apple II computers on which children have developed rather subtle color animations that express the themes—of greed and domination, for example—that they also have described in writing.

"This is an upwardly mobile group," the teacher later says. "They have exposure to whatever New York City has available. Their parents may take them to the theater, to museums. . . ."

In my notes: "Six girls, four boys. Nine white, one Chinese. I am glad they have this class. But what about the others? Aren't there ten black children in the school who could enjoy this also?"

The teacher gives me a newspaper written, edited and computer-printed by her sixth grade gifted class. The children, she tells me, are provided with a link to kids in Europe for transmission of news stories.

A science story by one student asks if scientists have ever falsified their research. "Gergor Mendel," the sixth grader writes; "the Austrian monk who founded the science of genetics, published papers on his work with peas that some experts say were statistically too good to be true. Isaac Newton, who formulated the law of gravitation, relied on unseemly mathematical sleight of hand in his calculations. . . . Galileo Galilei, founder of modern scientific method, wrote about experiments that were so difficult to duplicate that colleagues doubted he had done them."

Another item in the paper, also by a sixth grade student, is less esoteric: "The Don Cossacks dance company, from Russia, is visiting the United States. The last time it toured America was 1976. . . . The Don Cossacks will be in New York City for two weeks at the Neil Simon Theater. Don't miss it!"

The tone is breezy—and so confident! That phrase—"Don't miss it!"—speaks a volume about life in Riverdale.

"What makes a good school?" asks the principal when we are talking later on. "The building and teachers are part of it, of course. But it isn't just the building and the teachers. Our kids come from good families and the neighborhood is good. In a three-block area we have a public library, a park, a junior high. . . . Our typical sixth grader reads at eighth grade level." In a quieter voice he says, "I see how hard my colleagues work in schools like P.S. 79. You have children in those neighborhoods who live in virtual hell. They enter school five years behind. What do they get?" Then, as he spreads his hands out on his desk, he says: "I have to ask myself why there should be an elementary school in District 10 with fifteen hundred children. Why should there be an elementary school within a skating rink? Why should the Board of Ed allow this? This is not the way that things should be."

Postreading Writing Assignments

Option 1: Explore the word "inequality" as it is used in Kozol's essay. Which inequalities do you see as truly "savage"?

Option 2: Education can be seen as a microcosm of our society. What, then, is Kozol's essay telling us about American society—a society that allows certain groups of children to attend schools in such states of decay?

Option 3: What is Kozol saying here about economics, about the dramatic differences between upper, middle, and lower socioeconomic groups and the education that each group receives? In what ways is this a "moral" or an "ethical" issue? Who is responsible for these inequalities?

Extended Writing Assignments

Option 4:

> "Ideal class size for these kids would be 15 to 20. Will these children ever get what white kids in the suburbs take for granted? I don't think so. If you ask me why, I'd have to speak of race and social class. I don't think the powers that be in New York City understand, or want to understand, that if they do not give these children a sufficient education to lead healthy and productive lives, we will be their victims later on. We'll pay the price someday—in violence, in economic costs."
>
> (page 264)

Part One: Write Kozol a one- to two-page letter responding and reacting to his essay. In this letter, explore the emotions evoked by his piece, what struck you most as you read, and ask him any questions that came up during your reading of this work.

Part Two: Much of what Kozol says may be difficult for you to believe; although you may have experienced inequalities in education, many of us cannot imagine surviving the kinds of conditions that Kozol describes. Even so, you probably have encountered different kinds of situations that you feel to be examples of educational inequalities. Using Kozol's essay as a way of framing your own encounters in education, write an essay in which you explore what you feel to be the most significant inequalities apparent in today's educational system. Use your own experiences as well as those described by Kozol. One way to use Kozol effectively here might be to use his essay as a way to support your own assertions. Your examples do not have to be as "savage" as the ones he describes; however, you should justify in what ways the scenarios you describe qualify as inequalities.

Option 5: Is Kozol writing this text to incite action? If so, who is most likely to respond—negatively and/or positively? You might play the devil's advocate here and examine where you are reading Kozol's essay "against the grain." Where do you most clearly see gaps between Kozol's *intentions* and his *execution* of these intentions? What do these limitations suggest? If you were able to identify closely with this essay, you might also want to look at where you read "with the grain." Write an essay in which you present a close reading of Kozol; depending on the reading you created, this can be an exploration of reading *with the grain, against the grain,* or a combination of both with and against.

Forging Connections

Option 6: Read or reread Lynn Smith's essay "Minorities: Alienation and Failure in Academia." Smith examines the "pull of two worlds." What does it mean to live in two worlds, and why does this pull create problems for certain students trying to succeed in academic life? Write an essay in which you explore the idea of living between two worlds: the world of home and the world of academia. Use examples from Kozol and Smith to define, explore, and present the challenges of living in two worlds. If appropriate, use examples from your own life as well. Do you agree with each writer regarding the challenges he or she points out? Why or why not?

Nancy Mairs

CARNAL ACTS

Nancy Mairs writes of the unspoken issues that others are afraid to address. She writes in a direct manner of her battle with multiple sclerosis, her relationships, and her determination to experience life. Mairs is a feminist writer known for her poetry, memoirs, and essays. This selection is from Mairs's autobiography Carnal Acts.

Prereading Journal Questions

1. Describe what you believe to be true about people with physical disabilities: their perception of having a disability; the way they are seen and treated by nondisabled people; and their role in our world. Note any biases that you think individuals with disabilities face.
2. What does the term "finding one's voice" suggest to you? How does your "voice" as a writer differ from your other kinds of voices?
3. If you were to become "disabled" by an accident or illness, how do you imagine that your life would change?

Reading tip: Keep in mind that Mairs is writing this essay, in part, in response to a given request: "[Please] talk on how you cope with your M.S. disability, and also how you discovered your voice as a writer." As you read, look at the ways Mairs moves through many topics of discussion, yet still remains focused, in one sense or another, on addressing or attempting to address these complex subjects.

Inviting me to speak at her small liberal-arts college during Women's Week, a young woman set me a task: "We would be pleased," she wrote, "if you could talk on how you cope with your M.S. disability, and also how you discovered your voice as a writer." Oh, Lord, I thought in dismay, how am I going to pull this one off? How can I yoke two such disparate subjects into a coherent presentation, without doing violence to one, or the other, or both, or myself? This is going to take some fancy footwork, and my feet scarcely carry out the basic steps, let alone anything elaborate.

To make matters worse, the assumption underlying each of her questions struck me as suspect. To ask *how* I cope with multiple sclerosis suggests that I *do* cope. Now, "to cope," *Webster's Third* tells me, is "to face or encounter and to find necessary expedients to overcome problems and difficulties." In these terms, I have to confess, I don't feel like much of a coper. I'm likely to deal with my problems and difficulties by squawking and flapping around like that hysterical chicken who was convinced the sky was falling. Never mind that in my case the sky really *is* falling. In response to a clonk on the head, regardless of its origin, one might comport oneself with a grace and courtesy I generally lack.

As for "finding" my voice, the implication is that it was at one time lost or missing. But I don't think it ever was. Ask my mother, who will tell you a little wearily that I was speaking full sentences by the time I was a year old and could never be silenced again. As for its being a writer's voice, it seems to have become one early on. Ask Mother again. At the age of eight I rewrote the Trojan War, she will say, and what Nestor was about to do to Helen at the end doesn't bear discussion in polite company.

Faced with these uncertainties, I took my own teacherly advice, something, I must confess, I don't always do. "If an idea is giving you trouble," I tell my writing students, "put it on the back burner and let it simmer while you do something else. Go to the movies. Reread a stack of old love letters. Sit in your history class and take detailed notes on the Teapot Dome scandal. If you've got your idea in mind, it will go on cooking at some level no matter what else you're doing." "I've had an idea for my documented essay on the back burner," one of my students once scribbled in her journal, "and I think it's just boiled over!"

I can't claim to have reached such a flash point. But in the weeks I've had the themes "disability" and "voice" sitting around in my head, they seem to have converged on their own, without my having to wrench them together and bind them with hoops of tough rhetoric. They *are* related, indeed interdependent, with an intimacy that has for some reason remained, until now, submerged below the surface of my attention. Forced to juxtapose them, I yank them out of the depths, a little startled to discover how they were intertwined down there out of sight. This kind of discovery can unnerve you at first. You feel like a giant hand that, pulling two swimmers out of the water, two separate heads bobbling on the iridescent swells, finds the two bodies below, legs coiled around each other, in an ecstasy of copulation. You don't quite know where to turn your eyes.

Perhaps the place to start illuminating this erotic connection between who I am and how I speak lies in history. I have known that I have multiple sclerosis for about seventeen years now, though the disease probably started long before. The hypothesis is that the disease process, in which the protective covering of the nerves in the brain and spinal cord is eaten away and replaced by scar tissue, "hard patches," is caused by an autoimmune reaction to a slow-acting virus. Research suggests that I was infected by this virus, which no one has ever seen and which therefore, technically, doesn't even "exist," between the ages of four and fifteen. In effect, living with this mysterious mechanism feels like having your present self, and the past selves it embodies, haunted by a capricious and meanspirited ghost, unseen except for its footprints, which trips you even when you're watching where you're going, knocks glassware out of your hand, squeezes the urine out of your bladder before you reach the bathroom, and weights your whole body with a weariness no amount of rest can relieve. An alien invader must be at work. But of course it's not. It's your own body. That is, it's you.

This, for me, has been the most difficult aspect of adjusting to a chronic incurable degenerative disease: the fact that it has rammed my "self" straight back into the body I had been trained to believe it could, through high-minded acts and aspirations, rise above. The Western tradition of distinguishing the body from the mind and/or the soul is so ancient as to have become part of our collective unconscious, if one is inclined to believe in such a noumenon, or at least to have become an unquestioned element in the social instruction we impose upon infants from birth, in much the same way we inculcate, without reflection, the gender distinctions "female" and "male." I *have* a body you are likely to say if you talk about embodiment at all; you don't say, I *am* a body. A body is a separate entity possessable by the "I"; the "I" and the body aren't, as the copula would make them, grammatically indistinguishable.

To widen the rift between the self and the body, we treat our bodies as subordinates, inferior in moral status. Open association with them shames us. In fact, we treat our bodies with very much the same distance and ambivalence woman have traditionally received from men in our culture. Sometimes this treatment is benevolent, even respectful, but all too often it is tainted by outright sadism. I think of the bodybuilding regimens that have become popular in the last decade or so, with the complicated vacillations they reflect between self-worship and self-degradation: joggers and aerobic dancers and weightlifters all beating the bodies into shape. "No pain, no gain," the saying goes. "Feel the burn." Bodies get treated like wayward women who have to be shown who's boss, even if it means slapping them around a little. I'm not for a moment opposing rugged exercise here. I'm simply questioning the spirit in which it is often undertaken.

Since, as Hélène Cixous points out in her essay on women and writing, "Sorties,"* thought has always worked "through dual, hierarchical oppositions" the mind/body split cannot possibly be innocent. The utterance of an "I" immediately calls into being its opposite, the "not-I," Western discourse being unequipped to conceive "that which is neither 'I' nor 'not-I,'" "that which is both 'I' and 'not-I,'" or some other permutation which language doesn't permit me to speak. The "not-I" is, by definition, other. And we've never been too fond of the other. We prefer the same. We tend to ascribe to the other those qualities we prefer not to associate with our selves: it is the hidden, the dark, the secret, the shameful. Thus, when the "I" takes possession of the body, it makes the body into an other, direct object of a transitive verb, with all the other's repudiated and potentially dangerous qualities.

At the least, then, the body had best be viewed with suspicion. And a woman's body is particularly suspect, since so much of it is in fact hidden, dark, secret, carried about on the inside where, even with the aid of a speculum, one can never perceive all of it in the plain light of day, a graspable whole. I, for one, have never understood why anyone would want to carry all that delicate stuff around on the outside. It would make you awfully anxious, I should think, put you constantly on the defensive, create a kind of siege mentality that viewed all other beings, even your own kind, as threats to be warded off with spears and guns and atomic missiles. And you'd never get to experience that inward dreaming that comes when your flesh surrounds all your treasures, holding them close, like a sturdy shuttered house. Be my personal skepticism as it may, however, as a cultural woman I bear just as much shame as any woman for my dark, enfolded secrets. Let the word for my external genitals tell the tale: my pudendum, from the Latin infinitive meaning "to be ashamed."

It's bad enough to carry your genitals like a sealed envelope bearing the cipher that, once unlocked, might loose the chaotic flood of female pleasure—*jouissance,* the French call it—upon the world-of-the-same. But I have an additional reason to feel shame for my body, less explicitly connected with its sexuality: it is a crippled

*In *The Newly Born Woman,* translated by Betsy Wing (Minneapolis: University of Minnesota Press, 1986).

body. Thus it is doubly other, not merely by the homo-sexual standards of patriarchal culture but by the standards of physical desirability erected for every body in our world. Men, who are by definition exonerated from shame in sexual terms (this doesn't mean that an individual man might not experience sexual shame, of course; remember that I'm talking in general about discourse, not folks), may—more likely must—experience bodily shame if they are crippled. I won't presume to speak about the details of their experience, however. I don't know enough. I'll just go on telling what it's like to be a crippled woman, trusting that, since we're fellow creatures who've been living together for some thousands of years now, much of my experience will resonate with theirs.

I was never a beautiful woman, and for that reason I've spent most of my life (together with probably at least 95 percent of the female population of the United States) suffering from the shame of falling short of an unattainable standard. The ideal woman of my generation was . . . perky, I think you'd say, rather than gorgeous. Blond hair pulled into a bouncing ponytail. Wide blue eyes, a turned-up nose with maybe a scattering of golden freckles across it, a small mouth with full lips over straight white teeth. Her breasts were large but well harnessed high on her chest; her tiny waist flared to hips just wide enough to give the crinolines under her circle skirt a starting outward push. In terms of personality, she was outgoing, even bubbly, not pensive or mysterious. Her milieu was the front fender of a white Corvette convertible, surrounded by teasing crewcuts, dressed in black flats, a sissy blouse, and the letter sweater of the Corvette owner. Needless to say, she never missed a prom.

Ten years or so later, when I first noticed the symptoms that would be diagnosed as MS, I was probably looking my best. Not beautiful still, but the ideal had shifted enough so that my flat chest and narrow hips gave me an elegantly attenuated shape, set off by a thick mass of long, straight, shining hair. I had terrific legs, long and shapely, revealed nearly to the pudendum by the fashionable miniskirts and hot pants I adopted with more enthusiasm than delicacy of taste. Not surprisingly, I suppose, during this time I involved myself in several pretty torrid love affairs.

The beginning of MS wasn't too bad. The first symptom, besides the pernicious fatigue that had begun to devour me, was "foot drop," the inability to raise my left foot at the ankle. As a consequence, I'd started to limp, but I could still wear high heels, and a bit of a limp might seem more intriguing than repulsive. After a few months, when the doctor suggested a cane, a crippled friend gave me quite an elegant wood-and-silver one, which I carried with a fair amount of panache. The real blow to my self-image came when I had to get a brace. As braces go, it's not bad: lightweight plastic molded to my foot and leg, fitting down into an ordinary shoe and secured around my calf by a Velcro strap. It reduces my limp and, more important, the danger of tripping and falling. But it meant the end of high heels. And it's ugly. Not as ugly as I think it is, I gather, but still pretty ugly. It signified for me, and perhaps still does, the permanence and irreversibility of my condition. The brace makes my MS concrete and forces me to wear it on the outside. As soon as I strapped the brace on, I climbed into trousers and stayed there (though not in the same trousers, of course). The idea of going around with my bare brace hanging out seemed almost as indecent as exposing my breasts. Not until 1984, soon after I won the Western States Book Award for poetry, did I put on a skirt short enough to reveal my plasticized leg. The connection between winning a writing award and baring my brace is not merely fortuitous; being affirmed as a writer really did embolden me. Since then, I've grown so accustomed to wearing skirts that I don't think about my brace any more than I think about my cane. I've incorporated them, I suppose: made them, in their necessity, insensate but fundamental parts of my body.

Meanwhile, I had to adjust to the most outward and visible sign of all, a three-wheeled electric scooter called an Amigo. This lessens my fatigue and increases my range terrifically, but it also shouts out to the world, "Here is a woman who can't stand on her own two feet." At the same time, paradoxically, it renders me invisible, reducing me to the height of a seven-year-old, with a child's attendant low status. "Would she like smoking or nonsmoking?" the gate agent assigning me a seat asks the friend traveling with me. In crowds I see nothing but buttocks. I can tell you the name of every type of designer jeans ever sold. The wearers, eyes front, trip over me and fall across my handlebars into my lap. "Hey!" I want to shout to the lofty world. "Down here! There's a person down here!" But I'm not, by their standards, quite a person anymore.

My self-esteem diminishes further as age and illness strip from me the features that made me, for a brief while anyway, a good-looking, even sexy, young woman. No more long, bounding strides: I shuffle along with the timid gait I remember observing, with pity and impatience, in the little old ladies at Boston's Symphony Hall on Friday afternoons. No more lithe, girlish figure: my belly sags from the loss of muscle tone, which also creates all kinds of intestinal disruptions, hopelessly humiliating in a society in which excretory functions remain strictly unspeakable. No more sex, either, if society had its way. The sexuality of the disabled so repulses most people that you can hardly get a doctor, let alone a member of the general population, to consider the issues it raises. Cripples simply aren't supposed to Want It, much less Do It. Fortunately, I've got a husband with a strong libido and a weak sense of social propriety, or else I'd find myself perforce practicing a vow of chastity I never cared to take.

Afflicted by the general shame of having a body at all, and the specific shame of having one weakened and misshapen by disease, I ought not to be able to hold my head up in public. And yet I've gotten into the habit of holding my head up in public, sometimes under excruciating circumstances. Recently, for instance, I had to give a reading at the University of Arizona. Having smashed three of my front teeth in a fall onto the concrete floor of my screened porch, I was in the process of getting them crowned, and the temporary crowns flew out during dinner right before the reading. What to do? I wanted, of course, to rush home and hide till the dental office opened the next morning. But I couldn't very well break my word at this last moment. So, looking like Hansel and Gretel's witch, and lisping worse than the Wife of Bath, I got up on stage and read. Somehow, over the years, I've learned how to set shame aside and do what I have to do.

Here, I think, is where my "voice" comes in. Because, in spite of my demurral at the beginning, I do in fact cope with my disability at least some of the time. And I do so, I think, by speaking about it, and about the whole experience of being a body, specifically a female body, out loud, in a clear, level tone that drowns out the frantic whispers of my mother, my grandmothers, all the other trainers of wayward childish tongues: "Sssh! Sssh! Nice girls don't talk like that. Don't mention sweat. Don't mention menstrual blood. Don't ask what your grandfather does on his business trips. Don't laugh so loud. You sound like a loon. Keep your voice down. Don't tell. Don't tell. Don't tell." Speaking out loud is an antidote to shame. I want to distinguish clearly here between "shame," as I'm using the word, and "guilt" and "embarrassment," which, though equally painful, are not similarly poisonous. Guilt arises from performing a forbidden act or failing to perform a required one. In either case, the guilty person can, through reparation, erase the offense and start fresh. Embarrassment, less opprobrious though not necessarily less distressing, is generally caused by acting in a socially stupid or awkward way. When I trip and sprawl in public, when I wet myself, when my front teeth fly out, I feel horribly embarrassed, but, like the pain of childbirth, the sensation blurs and dissolves in time. If it didn't, every child would be an only child, and no one would set foot in public after the onset of puberty, when embarrassment erupts like a geyser and bathes one's whole life in its bitter stream. Shame may attach itself to guilt or embarrassment, complicating their resolution, but it is not the same emotion. I feel guilt or embarrassment for something I've done; shame, for who I am. I may stop doing bad or stupid things, but I can't stop being. How then can I help but be ashamed? Of the three conditions, this is the one that cracks and stifles my voice.

I can subvert its power, I've found, by acknowledging who I am, shame and all, and, in doing so, raising what was hidden, dark, secret about my life into the plain light of shared human experience. What we aren't permitted to utter holds us, each isolated from every other, in a kind of solipsistic thrall. Without any way to check our reality against anyone else's, we assume that our fears and shortcomings are ours alone. One of the strangest consequences of publishing a collection of personal essays called *Plaintext* has been the steady trickle of letters and telephone calls saying essentially, in a tone of unmistakable relief, "Oh, me too! Me too!" It's as though the part I thought was solo has turned out to be a chorus. But none of us was singing loud enough for the others to hear.

Singing loud enough demands a particular kind of voice, I think. And I was wrong to suggest, at the beginning, that I've always had my voice. I have indeed always had *a* voice, but it wasn't *this* voice, the one with which I could call up and transform my hidden self from a naughty girl into a woman talking directly to others like herself. Recently, in the process of writing a new book, a memoir entitled *Remembering the Bone House,* I've had occasion to read some of my early writing, from college, high school, even junior high. It's not an experience I recommend to anyone susceptible to shame. Not that the writing was all that bad. I was surprised at how competent a lot of it was. Here was a writer who already knew precisely how the language worked. But the voice . . . oh, the voice was all wrong: maudlin, rhapsodic, breaking here and there into little shrieks, almost, you might say, hysterical. It was a voice that had shucked off its own body, its own homely life of Cheerios for breakfast and seventy pages of Chaucer to read before the exam on Tuesday and a planter's wart growing painfully on the ball of its foot, and reeled now wraithlike through the air, seeking incarnation only as the heroine who enacts her doomed love for the tall, dark, mysterious stranger. If it didn't get that part, it wouldn't play at all.

Among all these overheated and vaporous imaginings, I must have retained some shred of sense, because I stopped writing prose entirely, except for scholarly papers, for nearly twenty years. I even forgot, not exactly that I had written prose, but at least what kind of prose it was. So when I needed to take up the process again, I could start almost fresh, using the vocal range I'd gotten used to in years of asking the waiter in the Greek restaurant for an extra anchovy on my salad, congratulating the puppy on making a puddle outside rather than inside the patio door, pondering with my daughter the vagaries of female orgasm, saying goodbye to my husband, and hello, and goodbye, and hello. This new voice—thoughtful, affectionate, often amused—was essential because what I needed to write about when I returned to prose was an attempt I'd made not long before to kill myself, and suicide simply refuses to be spoken of authentically in high-flown romantic language. It's too ugly. Too shameful. Too strictly a bodily event. And, yes, too funny as well, though people are sometimes shocked to find humor shoved up against suicide. They don't like the incongruity. But let's face it, life (real life, I mean, not the edited-for-television version) is a cacophonous affair from start to finish. I might have wanted to portray my suicidal self as a languishing maiden, too exquisitely sensitive to sustain life's wounding pressures on her soul. (I didn't want to, as a matter of fact, but I might have.) The truth remained, regardless of my desires, that when my husband lugged me into the emergency room, my hair matted, my face swollen and gray, my nightgown streaked with blood and urine, I was no frail and tender spirit. I was a body, and one in a hell of a mess.

I "should" have kept quiet about that experience. I know the rules of polite discourse. I should have kept my shame, and the nearly lethal sense of isolation and alienation it brought, to myself. And I might have, except for something the psychiatrist in the emergency room had told my husband. "You might as well take her home," he said. "If she wants to kill herself, she'll do it no matter how many precautions we take. They always do." *They* always do. I was one of "them," whoever they were. I was, in this context anyway, not singular, not aberrant, but typical. I think it was this sense of commonality with others I didn't even know, a sense of being returned somehow, in spite of my appalling act, to the human family, that urged me to write that first essay, not merely speaking out but calling out, perhaps. "Here's the way I am," it said. "How about you?" And the answer came, as I've said: "Me too! Me too!"

This has been the kind of work I've continued to do: to scrutinize the details of my own experience and to report what I see, and what I think about what I see, as lucidly and accurately as possible. But because feminine experience has been immemorially devalued and repressed, I continue to find this task terrifying. "Every woman has known the torture of beginning to speak aloud," Cixous writes, "heart beating as if to break, occasionally falling into loss of language, ground and language slipping out from under her, because for woman speaking—even just opening her mouth—in public is something rash, a transgression."

The voice I summon up wants to crack, to whisper, to trail back into silence. "I'm sorry to have nothing more than this to say," it wants to apologize. "I shouldn't be taking up your time. I've never fought in a war, or even in a schoolyard free-for-all. I've never tried to see who could piss farthest up the barn wall. I've never even been to a whorehouse. All the important formative experiences have passed me by. I was raped once. I've borne two children. Milk trickling out of my breasts, blood trickling from between my legs. You don't want to hear about it. Sometimes I'm too scared to leave my house. Not scared *of* anything, just scared: mouth dry, bowels writhing. When the fear got really bad, they locked me up for six months, but that was years ago. I'm getting old now. Misshapen, too. I don't blame you if you can't get it up. No one could possibly desire a body like this. It's not your fault. It's mine. Forgive me. I didn't mean to start crying. I'm sorry . . . sorry . . . sorry. . . ."

An easy solace to the anxiety of speaking aloud: this slow subsidence beneath the waves of shame, back into what Cixous calls "this body that has been worse than confiscated, a body replaced with a disturbing stranger, sick or dead, who so often is a bad influence, the cause and place of inhibitions. By censuring the body," she goes on, "breath and speech are censored at the same time." But I am not going back, not going under one more time. To do so would demonstrate a failure of nerve far worse than the depredations of MS have caused. Paradoxically, losing one sort of nerve has given me another. No one is going to take my breath away. No one is going to leave me speechless. To be silent is to comply with the standard of feminine grace. But my crippled body already violates all notions of feminine grace. What more have I got to lose? I've gone beyond shame. I'm shameless, you might say. You know, as in "shameless hussy"? A woman with her bare brace and her tongue hanging out.

I've "found" my voice, then, just where it ought to have been, in the body-warmed breath escaping my lungs and throat. Forced by the exigencies of physical disease to embrace my self in the flesh, I couldn't write bodiless prose. The voice is the creature of the body that produces it. I speak as a crippled woman. At the same time, in the utterance I redeem both "cripple" and "woman" from the shameful silences by which I have often felt surrounded, contained, set apart; I give myself permission to live openly among others, to reach out for them, stroke them with fingers and sighs. No body, no voice; no voice, no body. That's what I know in my bones.

Postreading Writing Assignments

Option 1: Mairs quotes liberally here from Hélène Cixous: what do these quotes add to Mairs's exploration of self? How does she define herself in Cixous's terms?

Option 2: While addressing the issue of "voice," Mairs also focuses on "body" and disability: why does Mairs see these ideas as interrelated? Explore the connections between body, voice, and writing.

Option 3: Where are you reading Mairs "with" or "against" the grain? What would you like to say back to her after reading this piece about her life? Write this essay in the form of a letter as you respond to and question Mairs.

Extended Writing Assignments

Option 4:

> [Wearing] the brace makes my MS concrete and forces me to wear it on the outside. As soon as I strapped the brace on, I climbed into trousers and stayed there (though not in the same trousers, of course). The idea of going around with my bare brace hanging out seemed almost as indecent as exposing my breasts. Not until 1984, soon after I won the Western States Book Award for poetry, did I put on a skirt short enough to reveal my plasticized leg. The connection between winning a writing award and baring my brace is not merely fortuitous; being affirmed as a writer really did embolden me. Since then, I've grown so accustomed to wearing skirts that I don't think about my brace any more than I think about my cane. I've incorporated them, I suppose: made them, in their necessity, insensate but fundamental parts of my body.
>
> (page 279)

What does Mairs want us to learn about her life, about the lives of women? Explore the preceding passage from the selection in context of the entire essay. Why is it that Mairs sees a connection between her writing and her "body"? What does she tell us about the role that writing plays in her life and her role as a writer? As you examine Mairs's work, look closely at what she is telling us about women: the values placed on women's bodies; the ways in which "feminine experience has been immemorially devalued and repressed"; and the ways Mairs has been able to "cope" with a body that is disabled in certain ways. There are many ways to approach writing this essay: looking at what our society says about women and women's bodies; exploring the connections between valuing one's body and one's work; examining writing as a way to value one's self in other areas of life; and being a woman with a physical disability in a society that demands women's bodies to look a certain way. Choose one or two issues you find significant: how does Mairs address each of these issues, and how do you address them?

Option 5: Follow Mairs's example, and address the following question in your essay: How do you cope with ______________, and how are you discovering your voice as a writer? You fill in the blank here: how do you cope with having a "disability," or with being an "outsider" in some way, or with being male/female or a member of a particular ethnic group, or being a college student perhaps away from home for the first time, or with a particular relationship? Is there a connection between the issue with which you are "coping" (or attempting to cope) and what you are doing to "find" or develop a voice as a writer? If so, what is the connection? Frame your autobiographical exploration in light of what Mairs is doing. One way for you to use Mairs's text as a model might be to reflect on your role as a writer. How is it difficult to tell your own story? How is it empowering? How much are you considering your audience as you write? The objective here is not merely to retell your own story but also to resee and redefine it after reading Mairs.

Forging Connections

Option 6:

> "We're going to have to control your tongue," the dentist says, pulling out all the metal from my mouth. Silver bits plop and tinkle into the basin. My mouth is a motherlode.
>
> The dentist is cleaning out my roots. I get a whiff of the stench when I gasp. "I can't cap that tooth yet, you're still draining," he says.
>
> "We're going to have to do something about your tongue," I hear the anger rising in his voice. My tongue keeps pushing out the wads of cotton, pushing out the drills, the long thin needles. "I've never seen anything as strong or as stubborn," he says. And I think, how do you tame a wild tongue, train it to be quiet, how do you bridle and saddle it? How do you make it lie down?
>
> (Azaldua, page 119)

Read or reread Anzaldúa's essay "How to Tame a Wild Tongue." Mairs and Anzaldúa are both writing about (among other things, of course) "silencing": traditions of silencing that particularly affect women. Although Anzaldúa looks specifically at the silencing of Spanish, her work might be seen as complementing Mairs.

Write an essay in which you read Mairs's text and experience through Anzaldúa's lens. How might Anzaldúa read Mairs? Can Mairs be seen as writing from the "Borderlands," from outside a dominant discourse? How might Anzaldúa read Mairs against the grain? Anzaldúa, after all, is looking at a specific kind of silencing: would she see Mairs as fitting her definitions of people who are silenced? Do you think that Mairs or Anzaldúa would want you to tame your tongue as you write this? Be sure to allow room for your reading and interpretations.

Barbara Mellix

FROM OUTSIDE, IN

Barbara Mellix, who grew up in Greeleyville, South Carolina, has an M.F.A in creative writing and teaches composition and fiction at the University of Pittsburgh at Greensburg. In the following essay, Mellix discusses the different forms of English that are part of her life.

Prereading Journal Questions

1. Read the headnote, and use it to formulate some predictions about her essay. What kind of writing do you expect from her?
2. How do you speak differently at home than you do in other situations, for example, at school, at work, or with friends?
3. Mellix discusses the relationship between "language" and "power." How do you imagine that language and power might be related?

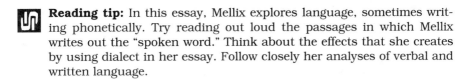

Reading tip: In this essay, Mellix explores language, sometimes writing phonetically. Try reading out loud the passages in which Mellix writes out the "spoken word." Think about the effects that she creates by using dialect in her essay. Follow closely her analyses of verbal and written language.

Two years ago, when I started writing this paper, trying to bring order out of chaos, my ten-year-old daughter was suffering from an acute attack of boredom. She drifted in and out of the room complaining that she had nothing to do, no one to "be with" because none of her friends were at home. Patiently I explained that I was working on something special and needed peace and quiet, and I suggested that she paint, read, or work with her computer. None of these interested her. Finally, she pulled up a chair to my desk and watched me, now and then heaving long, loud sighs. After two or three minutes (nine or ten sighs), I lost my patience. "Looka here, Allie," I said, "you too old for this kinda carryin' on. I done told you this is important. You wronger than dirt to be in here haggin' me like this and you know it. Now git on outta here and leave me off before I put my foot all the way down."

I was at home, alone with my family, and my daughter understood that this way of speaking was appropriate in that context. She knew, as a matter of fact, that it was almost inevitable; when I get angry at home, I speak some of my finest, most cherished black English. Had I been speaking to my daughter in this manner in certain other environments, she would have been shocked and probably worried that I had taken leave of my sense of propriety.

Like my children, I grew up speaking what I considered two distinctly different languages—black English and standard English (or as I thought of them then, the ordinary everyday speech of "country" coloreds and "proper" English)—and in the process of acquiring these languages, I developed an understanding of when, where, and how to use them. But unlike my children, I grew up in a world that was primarily black. My friends, neighbors, minister, teachers—almost everybody I associated with every day—were black. And we spoke to one another in our own special language: *That sho is a pretty dress you got on. If she don' soon leave me off I'm gon tell her head a mess. I was so mad I could' a pissed a blue nail. He all the time trying to low-rate somebody. Ain't that just about the nastiest thing you ever set ears on?*

Then there were the "others," the "proper" blacks, transplanted relatives and one-time friends who came home from the city for weddings, funerals, and vacations. And the whites. To these we spoke standard English. "Ain't?" my mother would yell at me when I used the term in the presence of "others." "You *know* better than that." And I would hang my head in shame and say the "proper" word.

I remember one summer sitting in my grandmother's house in Greeleyville, South Carolina, when it was full of the chatter of city relatives who were home on vacation. My parents sat quietly, only now and then volunteering a comment or answering a question. My mother's face took on a strained expression when she spoke. I could see that she was being careful to say just the right words in just the right way. Her voice sounded thick, muffled. And when she finished speaking, she would lapse into silence, her proper smile on her face. My father was more articulate, more aggressive. He spoke quickly, his words sharp and clear. But he held his proud head higher, a signal that he, too, was uncomfortable. My sisters and brothers and I stared at our aunts, uncles, and cousins, speaking only when prompted. Even then, we hesitated, formed our sentences in our minds, then spoke softly, shyly.

My parents looked small and anxious during those occasions, and I waited impatiently for our leave-taking when we would mock our relatives the moment we were out of their hearing. "Reeely," we would say to one another, flexing our wrists and rolling our eyes, "how dooo you stan' this heat? Chile, it just tooo hy*ooo*-mid for words." Our relatives had made us feel "country," and this was our way of regaining pride in ourselves while getting a little revenge in the bargain. The words bubbled in our throats and rolled across our tongues, a balming.

As a child I felt this same doubleness in uptown Greeleyville where the whites lived. "Ain't that a pretty dress you're wearing!" Toby, the town policeman, said to me one day when I was fifteen. "Thank you very much," I replied, my voice barely audible in my own ears. The words felt wrong in my mouth, rigid, foreign. It was not that I had never spoken that phrase before—it was common in black English, too—but I was extremely conscious that this was an occasion for proper English. I had taken out my English and put it on as I did my church clothes, and I felt as if I were wearing my Sunday best in the middle of the week. It did not matter that Toby had not spoken grammatically correct English. He was white and could speak as he wished. I had something to prove. Toby did not.

Speaking standard English to whites was our way of demonstrating that we knew their language and could use it. Speaking it to standard-English-speaking blacks was our way of showing them that we, as well as they, could "put on airs." But when we spoke standard English, we acknowledged (to ourselves and to others—but primarily to ourselves) that our customary way of speaking was inferior. We felt foolish, embarrassed, somehow diminished because we were ashamed to be our real selves. We were reserved, shy in the presence of those who owned and/or spoke *the* language.

My parents never set aside time to drill us in standard English. Their forms of instruction were less formal. When my father was feeling particularly expansive, he would regale us with tales of his exploits in the outside world. In almost flawless English, complete with dialogue and flavored with gestures and embellishment, he told us about his attempt to get a haircut at a white barbershop; his refusal to acknowledge one of the town merchants until the man addressed him as "Mister"; the time he refused to step off the sidewalk uptown to let some whites pass; his airplane trip to New York City (to visit a sick relative) during which the stewardesses and porters—recognizing that he was a "gentleman"—addressed him as "Sir." I did not realize then—nor, I think, did my father—that he was teaching us, among other things, standard English and the relationship between language and power.

My mother's approach was different. Often, when one of us said, "I'm gon wash off my feet," she would say, "And what will you walk on if you wash them off!" Everyone would laugh at the victim of my mother's "proper" mood. But it was different when one of us children was in a proper mood. "You think you are so superior," I said to my oldest sister one day when we were arguing and she was winning. "Superior!" my sister mocked. "You mean I am acting 'biggidy'?" My sisters and brothers sniggered, then joined in teasing me. Finally, my mother said, "Leave your sister alone. There's nothing wrong with using proper English." There was a half-smile on her face. I had gotten "uppity," had "put on airs" for no good reason. I was at home, alone with the family, and I hadn't been prompted by one of my mother's proper moods. But there was also a proud light in my mother's eyes; her children were learning English very well.

Not until years later, as a college student, did I begin to understand our ambivalence toward English, our scorn of it, our need to master it, to own and be owned by it—an ambivalence that extended to the public-school classroom. In our school, where there were no whites, my teachers taught standard English but used black English to do it. When my grammar-school teachers wanted us to write, for example, they usually said something like, "I want y'all to write five sentences that make a statement. Anybody git done before the rest can color." It was probably almost those exact words that led me to write these sentences in 1953 when I was in the second grade:

> The white clouds are pretty.
> There are only 15 people in our room.
> We will go to gym.
> We have a new poster.
> We may go out doors.

Second grade came after "Little First" and "Big First," so by then I knew the implied rules that accompanied all writing assignments. Writing was an occasion for proper English. I was not to write in the way we spoke to one another: The white clouds pretty; There ain't but 15 people in our room; We going to gym; We got a new poster; We can go out in the yard. Rather I was to use the language of "other": clouds *are,* there *are,* we *will,* we *have,* we *may.*

My sentences were short, rigid, perfunctory, like the letters my mother wrote to relatives:

> Dear Papa,
>
> How are you? How is Mattie? Fine I hope. We are fine. We will come to see you Sunday. Cousin Ned will give us a ride.
>
> Love,
>
> Daughter

The language was not ours. It was something from outside us, something we used for special occasions.

But my coloring on the other side of that second-grade paper is different. I drew three hearts and a sun. The sun has a smiling face that radiates and envelops everything it touches. And although the sun and its world are enclosed in a circle, the colors I used—red, blue, green, purple, orange, yellow, black—indicate that I was less restricted with drawing and coloring than I was with writing standard English. My valentines were not just red. My sun was not just a yellow ball in the sky.

By the time I reached the twelfth grade, speaking and writing standard English had taken on new importance. Each year, about half of the newly graduated seniors of our school moved to large cities—particularly in the North—to live with relatives and find work. Our English teacher constantly corrected our grammar: "Not 'ain't,' but 'isn't.'" We seldom wrote papers, and even those few were usually plot summaries of short stories. When our teacher returned the papers, she usually lectured on the importance of using standard English: "I *am;* you *are;* he, she, or it *is,*" she would say, writing on the chalkboard as she spoke. "How you gon git a job talking about 'I is,' or 'I isn't' or 'I ain't'?"

In Pittsburgh, where I moved after graduation, I watched my aunt and uncle—who had always spoken standard English when in Greeleyville—switch from black English to standard English to a mixture of the two, according to where they were or who they were with. At home and with certain close relatives, friends, and neighbors, they spoke black English. With those less close, they spoke a mixture. In public and with strangers, they generally spoke standard English.

In time, I learned to speak standard English with ease and to switch smoothly from black to standard or a mixture, and back again. But no matter where I was, no matter what the situation or occasion, I continued to write as I had in school:

Dear Mommie,

How are you? How is everybody else? Fine I hope. I am fine. So are Aunt and Uncle. Tell everyone I said hello. I will write again soon.

Love,

Barbara

At work, at a health insurance company, I learned to write letters to customers. I studied form letters and letters written by co-workers, memorizing the phrases and the ways in which they were used. I dictated:

> Thank you for your letter of January 5. We have made the changes in your coverage you requested. Your new premium will be $150 every three months. We are pleased to have been of service to you.

In a sense, I was proud of the letters I wrote for the company: they were proof of my ability to survive in the city, the outside world—an indication of my growing mastery of English. But they also indicate that writing was still mechanical for me, something that didn't require much thought.

Reading also became a more significant part of my life during those early years in Pittsburgh. I had always liked reading, but now I devoted more and more of my spare time to it. I read romances, popular novels. Looking back, I realize that the books I liked best were simple, unambiguous: good versus bad and right versus wrong with right rewarded and wrong punished, mysteries unraveled and all set right in the end. It was how I remembered life in Greeleyville.

Of course I was romanticizing. Life in Greeleyville had not been so very uncomplicated. Back there I had been—first as a child, then as a young woman with limited experience in the outside world—living in a relatively closed-in society. But there were implicit and explicit principles that guided our way of life and shaped our relationships with one another and the people outside—principles that a newcomer would find elusive and baffling. In Pittsburgh, I had matured, become more experienced: I had worked at three different jobs, associated with a wider range of people, married, had children. This new environment with different prescripts for living required that I speak standard English much of the time, and slowly, imperceptibly, I had ceased seeing a sharp distinction between myself and "others." Reading romances and mysteries, characterized by dichotomy, was a way of shying away from change, from the person I was becoming.

But that other part of me—that part which took great pride in my ability to hold a job writing business letters—was increasingly drawn to the new developments in my life and the attending possibilities, opportunities for even greater change. If I could write letters for a nationally known business, could I not also do something better, more challenging, more important? Could I not, perhaps, go to college and become a school teacher? For years, afraid and a little embarrassed, I did no more than imagine this different me, this possible me. But sixteen years after coming north, when my younger daughter entered kindergarten, I found myself unable—or unwilling—to resist the lure of possibility. I enrolled in my first college course: Basic Writing, at the University of Pittsburgh.

For the first time in my life, I was required to write extensively about myself. Using the most formal English at my command, I wrote these sentences near the beginning of the term:

> One of my duties as a homemaker is simply picking up after others. A day seldom passes that I don't search for a mislaid toy, book, or gym shoe, etc. I change the Ty-D-Bol, fight "ring around the collar," and keep our laundry smelling "April fresh." Occasionally, I settle arguments between my children and suggest things to do when they're bored. Taking telephone messages for my oldest daughter is my newest (and sometimes most aggravating) chore. Hanging the toilet paper roll is my most insignificant.

My concern was to use "appropriate" language, to sound as if I belonged in a college classroom. But I felt separate from the language—as if it did not and could not belong to me. I couldn't think and feel genuinely in that language, couldn't make it express what I thought and felt about being a housewife. A part of me resented, among other things, being judged by such things as the appearance of my family's laundry and toilet bowl, but in that language I could only imagine and write about a conventional housewife.

For the most part, the remainder of the term was a period of adjustment, a time of trying to find my bearing as a student in college composition class, to learn to shut out my black English whenever I composed, and to prevent it from creeping into my formulations; a time for trying to grasp the language of the classroom and reproduce it in my prose; for trying to talk about myself in that language, reach others through it. Each experience of writing was like standing naked and revealing my imperfection, my "otherness." And each new assignment was another chance to make myself over in language, reshape myself, make myself "better" in my rapidly changing image of a student in a college composition class.

But writing became increasingly unmanageable as the term progressed, and by the end of the semester, my sentences sounded like this:

> My excitement was soon dampened, however, by what seemed like a small voice in the back of my head saying that I should be careful

> with my long awaited opportunity. I felt frustrated and this seemed to make it difficult to concentrate.

There is a poverty of language in these sentences. By this point, I knew that the clichéd language of my Housewife essay was unacceptable, and I generally recognized trite expressions. At the same time, I hadn't yet mastered the language of the classroom, hadn't yet come to see it as belonging to me. Most notable is the lifelessness of the prose, the apparent absence of a person behind the words. I wanted those sentences—and the rest of the essay—to convey the anguish of yearning to, at once, become something more and yet remain the same. I had the sensation of being split in two, part of me going into a future the other part didn't believe possible. As that person, the student writer at that moment, I was essentially mute. I could not—in the process of composing—use the language of the old me, yet I couldn't imagine myself in the language of "others."

I found this particularly discouraging because at midsemester I had been writing in a much different way. Note the language of this introduction to an essay I had written then, near the middle of the term:

> Pain is a constant companion to the people in "Footwork." Their jobs are physically damaging. Employers are insensitive to their feelings and in many cases add to their problems. The general public wounds them further by treating them with disgrace because of what they do for a living. Although the workers are as diverse as they are similar, there is a definite link between them. They suffer a great deal of abuse.

The voice here is stronger, more confident, appropriating terms like "physically damaging," "wounds them further," "insensitive," "diverse"—terms I couldn't have imagined using when writing about my own experience—and shaping them into sentences like "Although the workers are as diverse as they are similar, there is a definite link between them." And there is the sense of a personality behind the prose, someone who sympathizes with the workers. "The general public wounds them further by treating them with disgrace because of what they do for a living."

What caused these differences? I was, I believed, explaining other people's thoughts and feelings, and I was free to move about in the language of "others" so long as I was speaking of others. I was unaware that I was transforming into my best classroom language my own thoughts and feelings about people whose experiences and ways of speaking were in many ways similar to mine.

The following year, unable to turn back or to let go of what had become something of an obsession with language (and hoping to catch and hold the sense of control that had eluded me in Basic Writing), I enrolled in a research writing course. I spent most of the term learning how to prepare for and write a research paper. I chose sex education as my subject and spent hours in libraries, searching for information, reading, taking notes. Then (not without messiness and often-demoralizing frustration) I organized my information into categories, wrote a thesis statement, and composed my paper—a series of paraphrases and quotations spaced between carefully constructed transitions. The process and results felt artificial, but as I would later come to realize I was passing through a necessary stage. My sentences sounded like this:

> This reserve becomes understandable with examination of who the abusers are. In an overwhelming number of cases, they are people the victims know and trust. Family members, relatives, neighbors and close family friends commit seventy-five percent of all reported sex crimes against children, and parents, parent substitutes and relatives are the offenders in thirty to eighty percent of all reported cases.[12] While assault by strangers does occur, it is less common, and is usually a single episode.[13] But abuse by family members, relatives and acquaintances may continue for an extended period of time. In cases of incest, for example, children are abused repeatedly for an average of eight years.[14] In such cases, "the use of physical force is rarely necessary because of the child's trusting, dependent relationship with the offender. The child's cooperation is often facilitated by the adult's position of dominance, an offer of material goods, a threat of physical violence, or a misrepresentation of moral standards."[15]

The completed paper gave me a sense of profound satisfaction, and I read it often after my professor returned it. I know now that what I was pleased with was the language I used and the professional voice it helped me maintain. "Use better words," my teacher had snapped at me one day after reading the notes I'd begun accumulating from my research, and slowly I began taking on the language of my sources. In my next set of notes, I used the word "vacillating"; my professor applauded. And by the time I composed the final draft, I felt at ease with terms like "overwhelming number of cases," "single episode," and "reserve," and I shaped them into sentences similar to those of my "expert" sources.

If I were writing the paper today, I would of course do some things differently. Rather than open with an anecdote—as my teacher suggested—I would begin simply with a quotation that caught my interest as I was researching my paper (and which I scribbled, without its source, in the margin of my notebook): "Truth does not do so much good in the world as the semblance of truth does evil." The quotation felt right because it captured what was for me the central idea of my paper—and expressed it in a way I would like to have said it. The anecdote, a hypothetical situation I invented to conform to the information in the paper, felt forced and insincere because it represented—to a great degree—my teacher's understanding of the essay, her idea of what in it was most significant. Improving upon my previous experiences with writing, I was beginning to think and feel in the language I used, to find my own voice in it, to sense that how one speaks influences how one means. But I was not yet secure enough, comfortable enough with the language to trust my intuition.

Now that I know that to seek knowledge, freedom, and autonomy means always to be in the concentrated process of becoming—always to be venturing into new territory, feeling one's way at first, then getting one's balance, negotiating, accommodating, discovering one's self in ways that previously defined "others"—I sometimes get tired. And I ask myself why I keep on participating in this highbrow form of violence, this slamming against perplexity. But there is no real futility in the question, no hint of that part of the old me who stood outside standard English, hugging to herself a disabling mistrust of language she thought could not represent a person with her history and experience. Rather, the question represents a person who feels the consequence of her education, the weight of her possibilities as a teacher and writer and human being, a voice in society. And I would not change that person, would not give back the good burden that accompanies my growing expertise, my increasing power to shape myself in language and share that self with "others."

"To speak," says Frantz Fanon, "means to be in a position to use a certain syntax, to grasp the morphology of this or that language, but it means above all to assume a culture, to support the weight of a civilization."[1] To write means to do the same, but in a more profound sense. However, Fanon also says that to achieve

[1] Black Skin, White Masks (1952; rpt. New York: Grove Press, 1967).

mastery means to "get" in a position of power, to "grasp," to "assume." This, I have learned both as a student and subsequently as a teacher, can involve tremendous emotional and psychological conflict for those attempting to master academic discourse. Although as a beginning student writer I had a fairly good grasp of ordinary spoken English and was proficient at what Labov calls "code-switching" (and what John Baugh in *Black Street Speech* terms "style shifting"), when I came face to face with the demands of academic writing, I grew increasingly self-conscious, constantly aware of my status as a black and a speaker of one of the many black English vernaculars—a traditional outsider. For the first time, I experienced my sense of doubleness as something menacing, a built-in enemy. Whenever I turned inward for salvation, the balm so available during my childhood, I found instead this new fragmentation which spoke to me in many voices. It was the voice of my desire to prosper, but at the same time it spoke of what I had relinquished and could not regain: a safe way of being, a state of powerlessness which exempted me from responsibility for who I was and might be. And it accused me of betrayal, of turning away from blackness. To recover balance, I had to take on the language of the academy, the language of "others." And to do that, I had to learn to imagine myself a part of the culture of that language, and therefore someone free to manage that language, to take liberties with it. Writing and rewriting, practicing, experimenting, I came to comprehend more fully the generative power of language. I discovered—with the help of some especially sensitive teachers—that through writing one can continually bring new selves into being, each with new responsibilities and difficulties, but also with new possibilities. Remarkable power, indeed. I write and continually give birth to myself.

Postreading Writing Assignments

Option 1: Explore the ways Mellix uses language with her daughter and how Mellix herself experienced language as a child. What is significant about her experiences? What kinds of experiences is she providing for her daughter?

Option 2: This essay focuses on language. Throughout the essay, Mellix defines and discusses the uses of Standard English. Write an essay in which you do the following: define Standard English as Mellix uses it and as you understand it; then go on to explore the kinds of situations in which the use of Standard English is an issue.

Option 3: Discuss your own experiences with Standard English and other dialects you use. In what contexts do you find yourself using Standard English? How have you learned when Standard English is expected and when other forms of English or other languages are acceptable?

Extended Writing Assignments

Option 4: At the end of her essay, Mellix says, "I discovered—with the help of some especially sensitive teachers—that through writing one can continually bring new selves into being, each with new responsibilities and difficulties, but also with new possibilities." Write an essay in which you explore Mellix's ideas about writing. Use Mellix's essay and your own experience with writing to consider how writing can enable people to "bring new selves into being."

Option 5: When Mellix was a child, she learned that Standard English brought power. Her parents, other relatives, and her experiences away from home emphasized this sense of power. The end of her essay suggests that writing can also bring power. Write an essay exploring the issues of power and language—written and spoken language. Interpret your experiences with languages, and use them to analyze Mellix's claims.

Forging Connections

Option 6: Read or reread Richard Rodriguez's essay "Aria." Rodriguez also writes about language as he discusses his struggles with reconciling two languages, English and Spanish. Write an essay interpreting the ways in which Mellix and Rodriguez each define, understand, and struggle with "public" and "private" languages. As you explore the two essays, work to create your own point of view regarding language and power. To help you guide your essay, consider the following questions: What major issues are raised in each essay? Where and in what ways do Rodriguez and Mellix present contradictory views? How does each essay address issues of language and power? Include a discussion of your own experiences in addition to your analysis of both essays.

Richard Rodriguez

ARIA

Richard Rodriguez, in his autobiography Hunger of Memory, *examines his life as a schoolchild, a university scholar, and a son. Rodriguez says of his text, "This is what matters to me; the story of the scholarship boy who returns home one summer from college to discover bewildering silence, facing his parents. This is my story. An American story." In* Hunger of Memory, *from which the selection is taken, Rodriguez explores education, language, family, and assimilation. He was graduated from Stanford and Columbia Universities and did graduate work at the Warburg Institute and the University of California, Berkeley. He currently lives in San Francisco, where he works as a writer and lecturer.*

Prereading Journal Questions

1. Define the terms "assimilation" and "acculturation." After defining these terms, make some predictions regarding Rodriguez's essay.
2. Explore the quote in the preceding headnote. What might Rodriguez mean by the term "Scholarship Boy," and why might such a student return home from college to discover "bewildering silence"?

Reading tip: Rodriguez writes his story, occasionally stopping to explore educational issues. As you read, you may find his story more interesting than his discussion of education; however, try pulling all the pieces of his essay together to analyze what he is saying about his education and what his arguments are about education in general.

I grew up victim to a disabling confusion. As I grew fluent in English, I no longer could speak Spanish with confidence. I continued to understand spoken Spanish. And in high school, I learned how to read and write Spanish. But for many years I could not pronounce it. A powerful guilt blocked my spoken words; an essential glue was missing whenever I'd try to connect words to form sentences. I would be unable to break a barrier of sound, to speak freely. I would speak, or try to speak, Spanish, and I would manage to utter halting, hiccuping sounds that betrayed my unease.

When relatives and Spanish-speaking friends of my parents came to the house, my brother and sisters seemed reticent to use Spanish, but at least they managed to say a few necessary words before being excused. I never managed so gracefully. I was cursed with guilt. Each time I'd hear myself addressed in Spanish, I would be unable to respond with any success. I'd know the words I wanted to say, but I couldn't manage to say them. I would try to speak, but everything I said seemed to me horribly anglicized. My mouth would not form the words right. My jaw would tremble. After a phrase or two, I'd cough up a warm, silvery sound. And stop.

It surprised my listeners to hear me. They'd lower their heads, better to grasp what I was trying to say. They would repeat their questions in gentle, affectionate voices. But by then I would answer in English. No, no, they would say, we want you to speak to us in Spanish. *('. . . en español.')* But I couldn't do it. *Pocho* then they called me. Sometimes playfully, teasingly, using the tender diminutive—*mi pochito.* Sometimes not so playfully, mockingly, *Pocho.* (A Spanish dictionary defines that word as an adjective meaning 'colorless' or 'bland.' But I heard it as a noun, naming the Mexican-American who, in becoming an American, forgets his native society.) '¡*Pocho*!' the lady in the Mexican food store muttered, shaking her head. I looked up to the counter where red and green peppers were strung like Christmas tree lights and saw the frowning face of the stranger. My mother laughed somewhere behind me. (She said that her children didn't want to practice 'our Spanish' after they started going to school.) My mother's smiling voice made me suspect that the lady who faced me was not really angry at me. But, searching her face, I couldn't find the hint of a smile.

Embarrassed, my parents would regularly need to explain their children's inability to speak flowing Spanish during those years. My mother met the wrath of her brother, her only brother, when he came up from Mexico one summer with his family. He saw his nieces and nephews for the very first time. After listening to me, he looked away and said what a disgrace it was that I couldn't speak Spanish, '*su proprio idioma.*' He made that remark to my mother; I noticed, however, that he stared at my father.

I clearly remember one other visitor from those years. A long-time friend of my father from San Francisco would come to stay with us for several days in late August. He tood great interest in me after he realized that I couldn't answer his questions in Spanish. He would grab me as I started to leave the kitchen. He would ask me something. Usually he wouldn't bother to wait for my mumbled response. Knowingly, he'd murmur: '*¿Ay Pocho, Pocho, adónde vas?*' And he would press his thumbs into the upper part of my arms, making me squirm with currents of pain. Dumbly, I'd stand there, waiting for his wife to notice us, for her to call him off with a benign smile. I'd giggle, hoping to deflate the tension between us, pretending that I hadn't seen the glittering scorn in his glance.

I remember that man now, but seek no revenge in this telling. I recount such incidents only because they suggest the fierce power Spanish had for many people I met at home; the way Spanish was associated with closeness. Most of those people who called me a *pocho* could have spoken English to me. But they would not. They seemed to think that Spanish was the only language we could use, that Spanish alone permitted our close association. (Such persons are vulnerable always to the ghetto merchant and the politician who have learned the value of speaking their clients' family language to gain immediate trust.) For my part, I felt that I had somehow committed a sin of betrayal by learning English. But betrayal against whom? Not against visitors to the house exactly. No, I felt that I had betrayed my immediate family. I *knew* that my parents had encouraged me to learn English. I *knew* that I had turned to English only with angry reluctance. But once I spoke English with ease, I came to *feel* guilty. (This guilt defied logic.) I felt that I had shattered the intimate bond that had once held the family close. This original sin against my family told whenever anyone addressed me in Spanish and I responded, confounded.

But even during those years of guilt, I was coming to sense certain consoling truths about language and intimacy. I remember playing with a freind in the backyard one day, when my grandmother appeared at the window. Her face was stern with suspicion when she saw the boy (the *gringo*) I was with. In Spanish she called out to me, sounding the whistle of her ancient breath. My companion looked up and watched her intently as she lowered the window and moved, still visible, behind the light curtain, watching us both. He wanted to know what she had said. I started to tell him, to say—to translate her Spanish words into English. The problem was, however, that though I knew how to translate exactly *what* she had told me, I realized that any translation would distort the deepest meaning of her message: It had been directed only to me. This messge of intimacy could never be translated because it was not *in* the words she had used but passed *through* them. So any translation would have seemed wrong; her words would have been stripped of an essential meaning. Finally, I decided not to tell my friend anything. I told him that I didn't hear all she had said.

This insight unfolded in time. Making more and more friends outside my house, I began to distinguish intimate voices speaking through *English.* I'd listen at times to a close friend's confidential tone or secretive whisper. Even more remarkable were those instances when, for no special reason apparently, I'd become conscious of the fact that my companion was speaking only to me. I'd marvel just hearing his voice. It was a stunning event: to be able to break through his words, to be able to hear this voice of the other, to realize that it was directed only to me. After such moments of intimacy outside the house, I began to trust hearing intimacy conveyed through my family's English. Voices at home at last punctured sad confusion. I'd hear myself addressed as an intimate at home once again. Such moments were never as raucous with sound as past times had been when we had had 'private' Spanish to use. (Our English-sounding house was never to be as noisy as our Spanish-speaking house had been.) Intimate moments were usually soft moments of sound. My mother was in the dining room while I did my homework nearby. And she looked over at me. Smiled. Said something—her words said nothing very important. But her voice sounded to tell me (*We are together*) I was her son.

(*Richard!*)

Intimacy thus continued at home; intimacy was not stilled by English. It is true that I would never forget the great change of my life, the diminished occasions of intimacy. But there would also be times when I sensed the deepest truth about language; and intimacy: *Intimacy is not created by a praticular language: it is created by intimates.* The great change in my life was not linguistic but social. If, after becoming a successful student, I no longer heard intimate voices as often as I had earlier, it was not because I spoke English rather than Spanish. It was because I used public language for most of the day. I moved easily at last, a citizen in a crowded city of words.

This boy became a man. In private now, alone, I brood over language and intimacy—the great themes of my past. In public I expect most of the faces I meet to be the faces of strangers. (How do you do?) If meetings are quick and impersonal, they have been efficiently managed. I rush past the sounds of voices attending only to the words addressed to me. Voices seem planed to an even surface of sound, soundless. A business associate speaks in a deep baritone, but I pass through the timbre to attend to his words. The crazy man who sells me a newspaper every night mumbles something crazy, but I have time only to pretend that I have heard him say hello. Accented versions of English make little impression on me. In the rush-hour crowd a Japanese tourist asks me a question, and I inch past his accent to concentrate on what he is saying. The Eastern European immigrant in a neighborhood delicatessen speaks to me through a marinade of sounds, but I respond to his words. I note for only a second the Texas accent of the telephone operator or the Mississippi accent of the man who lives in the apartment below me.

My city seems silent until some ghetto black teenagers board the bus I am on. Because I do not take their presence for granted, I listen to the sounds of their voices. Of all the accented versions of English I hear in a day, I hear theirs most intently. They are *the* sounds of an outsider. They annoy me for being loud—so self-sufficient and unconcerned by my presence. Yet for the same reason they seem to me glamorous. (A romantic gesture against public acceptance.) Listening to their shouted laughter, I realize my own quiet. Their voices enclose my isolation. I feel envious, envious of their brazen intimacy.

I warn myself away from such envy, however. I remember the black political activists who have argued in favor of using black English in schools. (Their argument varies only slightly from that made by foreign-language bilingualists.) I have heard 'radical' linguists make the point that black English is a complex and intricate version of English. And I do not doubt it. But neither do I think that black English should be a language of public instruction. What makes black English inappropriate in classrooms is not something *in* the language. It is rather what lower-class speakers make of it. Just as Spanish would have been a dangerous language for me to have used at the start of my education, so black English would be a dangerous language to use in the schooling of teenagers for whom it reenforces feelings of public separateness.

This seems to me an obvious point. But one that needs to be made. In recent years there have been attempts to make the language of the alien public language. 'Bilingual education, two ways to understand . . . ,' television and radio commercials glibly announce. Proponents of bilingual education are careful to say that they want students to acquire good schooling. Their argument goes something like this: Children permitted to use their family language in school will not be so alienated and will be better able to match the progress of English-speaking children in the crucial first months of instruction. (Increasingly confident of their abilities, such children will be more inclined to apply themselves to their studies in the future.) But then the bilingualists claim another, very different goal. They say that children who use their family language in school will retain a sense of their individuality—their ethnic heritage and cultural ties. Supporters of bilingual education thus want it both ways. They propose bilingual schooling as a way of helping students acquire the skills of the classroom crucial for public success. But they likewise insist that bilingual instruction will give students a sense of their identity apart from the public.

Behind this screen there gleams an astonishing promise: One can become a public person while still remaining a private person. At the very same time one can be both! There need be no tension between the self in the crowd and the self apart from the crowd! Who would not want to believe such an idea? Who can be surprised that the scheme has won the support of many middle-class Americans? If the barrio or ghetto child can retain his separateness even while being publicly educated, then it is almost possible to believe that there is no private cost to be paid for public success. Such is the consolation offered by any of the current bilingual schemes. Consider, for example, the bilingual voters' ballot. In some American cities one can cast a ballot printed in several languages. Such a document implies that a person can exercise that most public of rights—the right to vote—while still keeping apart, unassimilated from public life.

It is not enough to say that these schemes are foolish and certainly doomed. Middle-class supporters of public bilingualism toy with the confusion of those Americans who cannot speak standard English as well as they can. Bilingual enthusiasts, moreover, sin against intimacy. An Hispanic-American writer tells me, 'I will never give up my family language; I would as soon give up my soul.' Thus he holds to his chest a skein of words, as though it were the source of his family ties. He credits to language what he should credit to family members. A convenient mistake. For as long as he holds on to words, he can ignore how much else has changed in his life.

It has happened before. In earlier decades, persons newly successful and ambitious for social mobility similarly seized upon certain 'family words.' Working-class men attempting political power took to calling one another 'brother.' By so doing they escaped oppressive public isolation and were able to unite with many others like themselves. But they paid a price for this union. It was a public union they forged. The word they coined to address one another could never be the sound (*brother*) exchanged by two in intimate greeting. In the union hall the word 'brother' became a vague metaphor; with repetition a weak echo of the intimate sound. Context forced the change. Context could not be overruled. Context will always guard the realm of the intimate from public misuse.

Today nonwhite Americans call 'brother' to strangers. And white feminists refer to their mass union of 'sisters.' And white middle-class teenagers continue to prove the importance of context as they try to ignore it. They seize upon the idioms of the black ghetto. But their attempt to appropriate such expressions invariably changes the words. As it becomes a public expression, the ghetto idiom loses its sound—its message of public separateness and strident intimacy. It becomes with public repetition a series of words, increasingly lifeless.

The mystery remains: intimate utterance. The communication of intimacy passes through the word to enliven its sound. But it cannot be held by the word. Cannot be clutched or ever quoted. It is too fluid. It depends not on word but on person.

My grandmother!

She stood among my other relations mocking me when I no longer spoke Spanish. '*Pocho*,' she said. But then it made no difference. (She'd laugh.) Our relationship continued. Language was never its source. She was a woman in her eighties during the first decade of my life. A mysterious woman to me, my only living grandparent. A woman of Mexico. The woman in long black dresses that reached down to her shoes. My one relative who spoke no word of English. She had no interest in *gringo* society. She remained completely aloof from the public. Protected by her daughters. Protected even by me when we went to Safeway together and I acted as her translator. Eccentric woman. Soft. Hard.

When my family visited my aunt's house in San Francisco, my grandmother searched for me among my many cousins. She'd chase them away. Pinching her granddaughters, she'd warn them all away from me. Then she'd take me to her room, where she had prepared for my coming. There would be a chair next to the bed. A dusty jellied candy nearby. And a copy of *Life en Español* for me to examine. 'There,' she'd say. I'd sit there content. A boy of eight. *Pocho*. Her favorite. I'd sift through the pictures of earthquake-destroyed Latin American cities and blond-wigged Mexican movie stars. And all the while I'd listen to the sound of my grandmother's voice. She'd pace round the room, searching through closets and drawers, telling me stories of her life. Her past. They were stories so familiar to me that I couldn't remember the first time I'd heard them. I'd look up sometimes to listen. Other times she'd look over at me. But she never seemed to expect a response. Sometimes I'd smile or nod. (I understood exactly what she was saying.) But it never seemed to matter to her one way or another. It was enough I was there. The words she spoke were almost irrelevant to that fact—the sounds she made. Content.

The mystery remained: intimate utterance.

I learn little about language and intimacy listening to those social activists who propose using one's family language in public life. Listening to songs on the radio, or hearing a great voice at the opera, or overhearing the woman downstairs singing to herself at an open window, I learn much more. Singers celebrate the human voice. Their lyrics are words. But animated by voice those words are subsumed into sounds. I listen with excitement as the words yield their enormous power to sound—though the words are never totally obliterated. In most songs the drama or tension results from the fact that the singer moves between word (sense) and note (song). At one moment the song simply 'says' something. At another moment the voice stretches out the words—the heart cannot contain!—and the voice moves toward pure sound. Words take flight.

Singing out words, the singer suggests an experience of sound most intensely mine at intimate moments. Literally, most songs are about love. (Lost love; celebrations of loving; pleas.) By simply being occasions when sound escapes word, however, songs put me in mind of the most intimate moments of my life.

Finally, among all types of song, it is the song created by lyric poets that I find most compelling. There is no other public occasion of sound so important for me. Written poems exist on a page, at first glance, as a mere collection of words. And yet, despite this, without musical accompaniment, the poet leads me to hear the sounds of the words that I read. As song, the poem passes between sound and sense, never belonging for long to one realm or the other. As public artifact, the poem can never duplicate intimate sound. But by imitating such sound, the poem helps me recall the intimate times of my life. I read in my room—alone—and grow conscious of being alone, sounding my voice, in search of another. The poem serves then as a memory device. It forces remembrance. And refreshes. It reminds me of the possibility of escaping public words, the possibility that awaits me in meeting the intimate.

The poems I read are not nonsense poems. But I read them for reasons which, I imagine, are similar to those that make children play with meaningless rhyme. I have watched them before: I have noticed the way children create private languages to keep away the adult; I have heard their chanting riddles that go nowhere in logic but harken back to some kingdom of sound; I have watched them listen to intricate nonsense rhymes, and I have noted their wonder. I was never such a child. Until I was six years old, I remained in a magical realm of sound. I didn't need to remember that realm because it was present to me. But then the screen door shut behind me as I left home for school. At last I began my movement toward words. On the other side of initial sadness would come the realization that intimacy cannot be held. With time would come the knowledge that intimacy must finally pass.

I would dishonor those I have loved and those I love now to claim anything else. I would dishonor our closeness by holding on to a particular language and calling it my family language. Intimacy is not trapped within words. It passes through words. It passes. The truth is that intimates leave the room. Doors close. Faces move away from the window. Time passes. Voices recede into the dark. Death finally quiets the voice. And there is no way to deny it. No way to stand in the crowd, uttering one's family language.

The last time I saw my grandmother I was nine years old. I can tell you some of the things she said to me as I stood by her bed. I cannot, however, quote the message of intimacy she conveyed with her voice. She laughed, holding my hand. Her voice illuminated disjointed memories as it passed them again. She remembered her husband, his green eyes, the magic name of Narciso. His early death. She remembered the farm in Mexico. The eucalyptus nearby. (Its scent, she remembered, like incense.) She remembered the family cow, the bell round its neck heard miles away. A dog. She remembered working as a seamstress. How she'd leave her daughters and son for long hours to go into Guadalajara to work. And how my mother would come running toward her in the sun—her bright yellow dress—to see her return. '*Mmmaaammmmááá*,' the old lady mimicked her daughter (my mother) to her son. She laughed. There was the snap of a cough. An aunt came into the room and told me it was time I should leave. 'You can see her tomorrow,' she promised. And so I kissed my grandmother's cracked face. And the last thing I saw was her thin, oddly youthful thigh, as my aunt rearranged the sheet on the bed.

At the funeral parlor a few days after, I knelt with my relatives during the rosary. Among their voices but silent, I traced, then lost, the sounds of individual aunts in the surge of the common prayer. And I heard at that moment what I have since heard often again—the sounds the women in my family make when they are praying in sadness. When I went up to look at my grandmother, I saw her through the haze of a veil draped over the lid of the casket. Her face appeared calm—but distant and unyielding to love. It was not the face I remembered seeing most often. It was the face she made in public when the clerk at Safeway asked her some question and I would have to respond. It was her public face the mortician had designed with his dubious art.

Postreading Writing Assignments

Option 1: What is your response to Rodriguez's struggle with public and private language? What do you want to say back to Rodriguez after reading this text?

Option 2: Write a response exploring Rodriguez's views of affirmative action and bilingual education. Define and analyze his views on these two issues. Do you agree or disagree with Rodriguez? Why? Structure your arguments carefully as you present your own perspectives.

Extended Writing Assignments

Option 3: Write an essay that presents your experiences with public and private language as well as Rodriguez's experiences. Use your own experiences with education and language to "test" Rodriguez's claims. You will first need clearly to define Rodriguez's claims. Where do your experiences support or undermine Rodriguez's assertions? This essay should present both a with and against the grain reading of Rodriguez's text.

Option 4: Write an essay exploring your "story" of childhood literacy, starting school, and the changes that education brought to your life. What conclusions about education can you draw based on your story? How does your story compare with Rodriguez's?

Forging Connections

Option 5: Read or reread Barbara Mellix's "From Outside, In." Write an essay interpreting the ways in which Mellix and Rodriguez each define, understand, and struggle with "public" and "private" languages. As you explore the two essays, work to create your own point of view regarding language and power. To help you guide your essay, consider the following questions: What major issues are raised in each essay? Where and in what ways do Rodriguez and Mellix present contradictory views? How does each essay address issues of language and power? Include a discussion of your own experiences in addition to your analysis of both essays.

Option 6: Read or reread Gloria Anzaldúa's "How to Tame a Wild Tongue." For this assignment, write a dialogue between Rodriguez and Anzaldúa. What do you imagine these two writers would say to one another? You will be the writer/interviewer. Set up a situation (a talk show or newspaper interview) in which you ask both writers questions and then develop their responses. You will guide the conversation. As each author responds, you need to imagine their ways of thinking and ways of speaking; explore how these two people would interact with each other and with you. As the writer, you should include your evaluations and conclusions.

Lynn Smith

MINORITIES: ALIENATION AND FAILURE IN ACADEMIA

Lynn Smith's investigative report first appeared in 1988 as a lead story in the Los Angeles Times.

Prereading Journal Questions

1. The title of this text provides a lot of information. What assumptions does the title, "Minorities: Alienation and Failure in Academia," lead you to develop before you begin reading?
2. What do you believe constitutes "minority" status in academia?
3. Why might some students be more "at-risk" for failure in college than others? What factors contribute to success or failure for students pursuing a college degree?

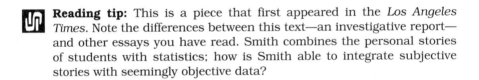

Reading tip: This is a piece that first appeared in the *Los Angeles Times*. Note the differences between this text—an investigative report—and other essays you have read. Smith combines the personal stories of students with statistics; how is Smith able to integrate subjective stories with seemingly objective data?

The night he left East Los Angeles for Harvard, George Sanchez recalled, his parents took him to the local church to be blessed by the priest.

"They had no way of knowing what they were sending me off to. I didn't know." Within the next few hours, Sanchez took his first plane ride, to Boston, and his first taxi, to the ivy-covered walls of Cambridge. There, also for the first time, he would come to realize he is a Latino.

"I knew I had Mexican parents," said Sanchez, 28, who had attended St. Paul's High School, a predominantly Anglo Catholic school in Santa Fe Springs. "I thought of myself as an all-American kid in some ways."

"All of a sudden I got to Harvard and realized what all-American meant and it wasn't me."

Others Concur

The distance from the nation's barrios and ghettos to the rumpled sophistication of its elite universities can be far greater than the mileage traveled—as other, higher profile cases have pointed out.

Jose Luis Razo, a straight-A scholar-athlete from Servite High School, a private school in Anaheim, said he never fit in during his two years at Harvard. "No one understood me," said Razo, 20, a Mexican immigrant whose wrist carries the tattoo of a homeboy, a local. He is scheduled to go on trial Jan. 12 charged with several armed robberies allegedly committed in Los Angeles and Orange counties during his college breaks.

Similarly, Edmund E. Perry, an honors graduate from Phillips Exeter Academy who had received a full scholarship to Stanford University, seemed to have turned education into a ticket out of Harlem and poverty. But his friends said he struggled with perceived racism at the famous Eastern prep school. Two years ago, Perry, then 17, was shot and killed during what police say was an attempt to mug a New York detective.

Pull of Two Worlds

These extreme cases, baffling to outsiders, may be explained by highly individual problems rooted in home life or emotional makeup. Yet the two young men—both bright and ambitious—also felt the pull of two worlds and the alienation of belonging to neither. It is a "sink or swim" feeling that many minority students—even the most successful—say they share.

"It's incredibly unfair. They admit them and expect them to muddle on through," said Catherine J. Kissee-Sandoval, 26, a Yale graduate from Los Angeles and the first Chicana Rhodes Scholar, who wrote a 1986 study on Latinos in the Ivy League.

She said even academic deficiencies are easier to overcome than homesickness and alienation. "After the first or second years and you learn to write papers and analyze, that part becomes easier. . . . The problems are more difficult when you're dealing with personal and social factors relating to issues of race and culture and ethnicity," she said.

Michele Denise DeCouteau, a black Rhodes Scholar–elect from UC Berkeley, said, "Recruitment is half the work. To finish the commitment, they [university administrators] should concentrate on retention."

"[Black] students who come here are prepared. They have the qualifications to do the work," said DeCouteau, an engineering student. "However, social, cultural and ethnic issues can sort of chip away at your self-esteem. Very subtle psychological factors can interfere with how you perceive your ability to do your schoolwork and how others perceive your ability to do your schoolwork."

DeCouteau's father is a conductor with the San Francisco Ballet and her mother is an educational psychologist. She had no financial worries, but DeCouteau said she shared common experiences with more disadvantaged minorities and relied heavily on two university programs, the Minority Engineering Program and the Professional Development Program for minorities.

"Minority students are something of an island. It's important to know you're not the only one. It's tremendous knowing there are people you can go to in terms of a psychological boost, to get back your perspective and keep you from falling into a hole of despair and self doubt."

Improved minority support programs, more hiring of black faculty members and a grievance board to investigate allegations of racism were among demands this fall of UC Berkeley's African Students Assn. Black students criticized university administrators for not responding to their special problems.

Lack of a sense of community, as well as academic problems, accounted for alarming dropout rates for black students, a UC Berkeley task force reported last year. At Berkeley, 73% of black and Hispanic students drop out, contrasted with 35% for all students combined.

Mia Barber, a junior, said she was ready to transfer to Howard University, a predominantly black institution in Washington, as a result of racial incidents last spring at a co-op residence. Friends in the African Students Assn. encouraged her to stay, she said.

Abe Ruelas, project director of Casa Joaquin Murrieta, a private residential program for Latino students attending UC Berkeley, said poor Latinos feel guilty for pursuing academics rather than earning money for the family. Some students have sent some of their financial aid money home to their struggling families, he said.

"Even here at Cal, a progressive school, a lot of people try to remain committed to the [old] community in the process of going through school," said Armando Mejia, a UC Berkeley student and Nicaraguan immigrant from Echo Park. "Once you achieve, you achieve on selfish grounds. You start to forget where you come from.

Many become disillusioned. They say, 'What is the point? What am I doing? I'm not doing anything for my people. My people are still jobless.'

"Some say, 'I'll just go back.'"

Graduation Statistics

Of students entering the nation's two- and four-year colleges intending to obtain a bachelor's degree in 1971, only 40% of the Latino students had graduated by 1980 compared to 51% of the black students and 56% of the Anglo students, said Alexander Astin, director of UCLA's Higher Education Research Institute and author of "Minorities in American Higher Education."

(National retention rates for Asians are not available, Astin said, and he did not include Asians in his study because they are not an under-represented minority. For example, 16% of the students in the University of California system are Asian, more than double their percentage of the nation's general population.)

At UCLA, 36% of black and Latino freshmen entering in 1979 had graduated within five years contrasted with 59% of Anglos and 60% of Asians, according to Paula Lutomirsky, director of information management at UCLA.

Retention rates are improving for all students at UCLA, she said, but the improvement for under-represented groups in recent years has been dramatic, particularly in the first year, she said.

"In the fall of '79, we lost 26% of the under-represented freshmen after the first year. Now, we're only losing 13%," she said. She attributed the change to better prepared students and the benefits of UCLA's Academic Advancement Program, which offers tutoring and counseling.

Despite such gains, shifting demographics make the retention problem crucial, said Assemblyman John Vasconcellos (D-Santa Clara), who chairs the Joint Legislative Committee for review of the state's master plan for higher education. "By the year 2000 there will be no majority and by the year 2030, the majority will be from the Latino population," he said.

"Latinos are dropping out of high school at a 50% rate and not finishing college at a further diminished rate. It's a formula for disaster" in both human and economic costs, he said.

Contributing to the problem are fewer financial grants from the federal government, lackluster commitment to recruiting minority students, faculty and staff, and parents who are uninvolved in their children's education, minority advocates said.

Meanwhile, college recruitment officers said they are competing for what they see as a limited number of qualified minority high school graduates. "We all want to boost our minority numbers," said Jane Gutman, director of the Western Regional Office of the University of Pennsylvania, one of the eight Ivy League schools.

"It's one thing to have the numbers, to say, 'Oh, I have a certain amount of minority students,' but another to say I have enough support to get them through, correct counseling and to have minority faculty members," said Sanchez, the son of Mexican immigrants who graduated from both Harvard and Stanford and will teach history at Princeton next fall.

"Undergraduate students from working-class backgrounds, predominantly Mexican-American backgrounds, see people on campus they most relate to are not the faculty and staff, but gardeners and kitchen help which are highly represented," Sanchez said.

Others said they have been discouraged by racial stereotyping and racism.

Affirmative Action

Nearly all Chicano students have a story about a first-year English composition professor who doubts they have written the paper they turned in, said Alfred Ramirez, who grew up in East Los Angeles, graduated from Columbia College and now manages Inroads Los Angeles, a career training and development organization for minorities in business and technology. Simply asking the question can make a student well up with discouragement and disillusionment, he said.

"Often what you get is that the majority of the faculty and other majority students expect all minorities are there on waivers of standards. They expect [minorities] are all 'affirmative action' admissions and do not expect them to do well. There is that Pygmalion effect of prophecy fulfillment," said Sara Melendez of the American Council on Education.

Programs to identify and admit under-represented minorities began in earnest in 1968 after the death of Dr. Martin Luther King Jr. The influx of minorities admitted to predominantly white institutions through affirmative action programs peaked in 1976, but since then the numbers of black college students have been declining and the numbers of Latinos and American Indians, though increasing, have not kept pace with their growth in the general population, according to the American Council on Education.

In the 1978 Bakke decision, the U.S. Supreme Court struck down special hiring and admissions quotas to reach parity, but allowed admissions criteria that used race and ethnic background as a decisive factor for otherwise qualified students. Except for athletes, admission requirements are not waived, a council spokesman said. Even though students admitted under flexible criteria to the Ivy League may have SAT scores as low as 1,000, they are not considered unqualified, he said.

But flexible admissions have backfired for some who believe they resulted in feelings of tokenism and self-doubt—even among minorities with high scores and middle-class backgrounds.

A 1980 study by a Harvard student-faculty staff committee on race relations reported that 69% of black students agreed that admissions policies that are thought to favor minorities generally often create doubt about their academic ability.

Nearly every black student feels rage at one time or another over perceived racism or discrimination by the institution, said Francis Terrell, a black psychology professor at North Texas State University. One of his black students wanted to hit a professor who he believed had given him a lower grade because of racial prejudice, Terrell said.

Terrell said he used relaxation techniques to calm the student. But when some angry students visit his office "they are in such a rage there's not really much you can do. A lot of students cannot be appeased. And they will quit school."

A high achiever with a 3.8 grade point average and participant in extracurricular activities, Lucky Gutierrez, 23, a graduate of the predominantly Latino Roosevelt High School in Los Angeles, said he had been heavily courted by colleges, particularly by student recruiters from the Ivy League. He chose Stanford.

Like Sanchez, he said he immediately became painfully aware of his ethnicity. The first quarter, a classmate from the East Coast called him a "spic." Campus police followed and questioned him and another Latino student when they drove together on campus.

When classmates spent winter vacations skiing in Aspen, he went home to East Los Angeles.

Gutierrez, whose grandparents came from Mexico and who does not speak Spanish, suddenly became an activist. At the end of his sophomore year, he was voted the Most Likely to Lead a Third World Revolution. At the end of his junior year, he took a year off to sort out questions of identity and belonging.

This year, Stanford students citing "institutional racism and underlying prejudice" have pushed for better conditions for campus minorities. Last spring, in response to student demands, Stanford redesigned its required Western Culture class to incorporate more contributions from Third World countries and women.

Students on the university's Committee of Minority Affairs also say they want an increase in minority undergraduate and graduate admissions as well as more minority professors and administrators.

But controversy has dogged three ethnic theme dormitories—where 50% of the residents are black, Mexican-American or Asian. The dorms sponsor ethnic-oriented educational, social and cultural programs and aim to "let people know we care about them and respond to their needs and we want them to become part of the general student body," said Michael L. Jackson, associate dean of students for campus affairs. Critics, however, argue that the houses only foster segregation.

Stanford is now 35% minority, Jackson said. "What does that mean 30 years from now? Who will be the majority, who will be the minority? We don't know."

As a private institution, Stanford counts on its alumni for support and new ideas, he said. "If that base is 35% minority, you damn well better make sure they have a good experience and believe in Stanford if you want them to give back and contribute to the institution."

Stanford's overall attrition rate is about 10%, with minorities only slightly higher, he said.

At UC Berkeley, racism "is more subtle now," said student Barber. "Black people don't have dogs sicked on them. But it's things that are said, professors' actions, things that happen in your living situation that affect you mentally, as opposed to physically."

During the last two years, UC Berkeley officials have identified black retention as a serious problem, and agreed to form a grievance board for allegations of racism. Chancellor Ira Michael Heyman has stated that improved opportunities for minority students is his highest priority this year.

In one private program at UC Berkeley, Latino alumni have sponsored a residential program which aims to strengthen Chicano identity as well as shore up academic and social skills.

Backers of Casa Joaquin Murrieta hope to develop leaders from selected low-income students with computer and study skills workshops, stress management seminars and a "supportive cultural environment." In the living room is a mural depicting the Chicano struggle. Richards are called Ricardos, Joes are called Joses.

"By denying culture, you lose some of your best basis for success. That's what makes you who you are," said Ruelas, who directs the 40-student co-ed house. "I don't buy into having to abandon [ethnic] culture to succeed in American society."

Residents are allowed to stay two years. With that beginning, 90% graduate compared with 50% of the Latinos at UC Berkeley, Ruelas said.

"When you're in a situation that forces you to deny who you are, you have to wear who you are in defiance. It leads to violence. Whereas when you are accepted as you are, there's no problem."

The goal of assimilating into the mainstream of society for student minorities is a throwback to "the dark ages," he said.

Like most college administrators, Harvard officials said they believe they are morally obligated to offer minority students support. But—as at Stanford—they debate whether the forms of support foster integration or segregation.

At Harvard, students are required to live on campus in houses where employees are available to offer advice and guidance. A Bureau of Study Counsel also offers a range of services from academic support to personal counseling for all students.

Minority students are encouraged to use counseling centers but no special counseling is provided because "we don't want to start with the assumption that all minorities need it," said L. Fred Jewett, dean of students at Harvard College.

When he was a Harvard student, Sanchez lobbied for Chicano studies and a minority cultural center. He said he ran into "a fairly traditional attitude that students should come and work things out. . . . It partly comes from an attitude: Minority students are here to enrich the rest of the campus."

Officials rejected student demands for the cultural center in favor of a Foundation on Race Relations that was to present minority culture as a whole, he said. "It's a fine idea, but it doesn't replace the need for a minority cultural center, which can give added support and provide a nucleus for interaction," he said.

"Harvard fears a certain amount of separatism," he said. At the same time, he said, "It's almost impossible to go to a place like Harvard and be a separatist. Why go to Harvard—the heart of Anglo-American power?"

Harvard in particular is known as an effective recruiter—cited as a model for minority admissions by the Supreme Court in the Bakke decision.

Like many colleges, Harvard does not necessarily waive standards for disadvantaged minorities but rather uses race and ethnic background (as well as special talents, alumni interests and achievements) as tipping factors for otherwise qualified students, officials said.

At least 75% of Harvard's under-represented minority students graduate, compared to an overall graduation rate "in the low to mid-90%," Jewett said.

Last fall, a new assistant dean for minority affairs, a Puerto Rican, started work at Harvard. "Clearly, we're trying to make up for the fact there are not as many [minority] people on the staff as we would like," Jewett said. But the decision to create the position was not made in reaction to the Razo case, he said.

Harvard officials wonder "whether there are things we might have done which would have prevented" Jose Razo's troubles, Jewett said. "We're not absolutely sure how much Harvard contributed or didn't contribute to it. . . . We haven't found readily identifiable cause-and-effect factors."

Razo may have sought counseling for academic problems, but his problem was not academic, he said. Razo had not developed the sort of personal relationships that most students need to ease their transition, Jewett said.

Razo has voluntarily withdrawn from Harvard, and a final decision on whether he may return will be made later, Jewett said. Razo, who is in the Orange County Jail, declined to be interviewed for this story.

"The thing we haven't done is indict a whole program of admissions and a whole group of people because of a single incident."

Jewett fears that observers will conclude that minority students with disadvantaged backgrounds cannot succeed at college. In fact at Harvard, "Hundreds of minority students have come here over the years and done well," Jewett said. "Many of them have had transition problems and have gone on to become successful doctors, lawyers and teachers.

"In making admissions decisions, we try to pick people that have the strength, resiliency and growth potential and we try hard with our counseling and support resources to get through the transition period and complete their studies."

Harvard takes no risk in admitting students with credentials at the edge of acceptability, he said. "The only person taking the risk is the student," Jewett said. "The institution is not particularly shaken if an individual doesn't succeed. . . . We have to be careful that *they're* not taking too great a risk."

Those who have succeeded without elaborate institutional support say they managed to balance the values of academia, the mainstream society, with those of their community and their own families.

"It takes character," said Rhodes Scholar Kissee-Sandoval. "Sometimes when I listen to my uncle who works at Sinclair Paints, I realize there are so many types of wisdom other than academic wisdom."

"Your life has to represent a bridge," Sanchez said. "Part of me is always remaining connected to my parents. The other part to the larger society. In a small way, my presence can change that world."

Postreading Writing Assignments

Option 1: Look back at your response to prereading question number two. How does your definition of "minority" compare with Smith's definition? Can factors other than race or ethnicity contribute to "minority" status?

Option 2: Explore Smith's use of the idea "being pulled between two worlds." How does this idea relate to minorities in academia? Analyze the following quotation from Smith's essay in your essay:

> The distance from the nation's barrios and ghettos to the rumpled sophistication of its elite universities can be far greater than the mileage traveled. . . .
>
> (page 311)

Option 3: As you read Smith's essay against the grain, where do you find yourself challenging or questioning her assertions?

Extended Writing Assignments

Option 4: As you respond to Smith's essay, look closely at the personal histories she provides. What do these histories tell you about the students' backgrounds and about our education system? Does anyone believe that our society provides an equal playing field when it comes to education? Write an essay in which you examine what it means to be a "minority" in academia, and explore whether such status alone determines academic success or failure. Consider the following questions: What factors, race and ethnicity not being exclusive here, lead to minority status? What obstacles must a "minority" student overcome to "succeed" in academia? Are these obstacles different from what "nonminority" (you will need to specify whom you see as nonminority) students face?

Option 5: Write your own investigative report on the conditions of any group of students who you feel are "marginalized" at your college, students who are struggling to work within "two worlds," the worlds of home and school. Identify what makes this group a "minority"; you will want to follow Smith's example of citing personal histories (be sure to get permission from the people whom you discuss), statistics (visit your college's Retention Center or Academic Advising Center), and your own story if applicable. Imagine that you will present this report to a college task force that is working to improve conditions for marginalized students: what can you tell this group about improving conditions in academia for those students whose stories you tell?

Forging Connections

Option 6: Read or reread Maya Angelou's essay "Graduation." What is each writer saying here about the role of society and society's expectations? From the two readings, what problems do you see occurring when a society imposes limits on certain groups of students, telling them what they can and cannot achieve? Write an essay in which you examine the different kinds of "tracking," placement, and imposed limitations Angelou and Smith discuss: it would be beneficial to your project to include a discussion of one specific moment from your own education, a moment when you have been tracked or limited in some way.

Part Four

Thematic Writing Assignments

SECTION I. EQUAL EDUCATION: IS EDUCATION FAIR TO EVERYONE?

Jonathan Kozol, "Savage Inequalities of Public Education in New York"
Lynn Smith, "Minorities: Alienation and Failure in Academia"
Maya Angelou, "Graduation"
bell hooks, "keeping close to home: class and education"

These readings examine the many and varied inequalities some see as inherent in the education systems of the United States. Kozol provides graphic testimony to the inequalities he found in America's schools, inequalities based largely on the socioeconomic status of children's parents. Smith provides a scholarly look at the challenges "minority" students face in academia. Angelou provides a different perspective; in this excerpt from her autobiography, she confronts the low expectations of others. hooks provides a discussion of maintaining ties between her public and private life. Through these readings and the thematic writing assignments, you will be exploring, defining, and redefining your own key experiences in education. Although some of what you read may be difficult for you to relate to (or difficult to read with the grain), try to read with an open mind; be willing, as you read, to see others' perspectives and to find ways to connect what you read with what you already believe to be true. As you work through these texts, reading them with and against the grain, place yourself at the center of the discussions. You are someone with something valuable to say here—an expert, an authority; assert that authority as you write in response to these texts.

Writing Assignment 1

Jonathan Kozol, "Savage Inequalities of Public Education in New York"

Part One: Write Kozol a one- to two-page letter responding and reacting to his essay. In this letter, explore the emotions evoked by his piece, what struck you most as you read, and ask him any questions that came up during your reading of this work.

Part Two: Much of what Kozol says may be difficult for you to believe; although you may have experienced inequalities in education, many of us cannot imagine surviving the kinds of conditions that Kozol describes. Even so, you probably have encountered different kinds of situations that you feel to be examples of educational inequalities. Using Kozol's essay as a way of framing your own encounters in education, write an essay in which you explore what you feel to be the most significant inequalities apparent in today's educational system. Use your own experiences as well as those described by Kozol.

Writing Assignment 2

Lynn Smith, "Minorities: Alienation and Failure in Academia"
Jonathan Kozol, "Savage Inequalities of Public Education in New York"

Smith examines the "pull of two worlds." What does it mean to live in two worlds, and why does this pull create problems for certain students trying to succeed in academic life? Write an essay in which you explore the idea of living between two worlds: the world of home and the world of academia. Use examples from Kozol and Smith to define, explore, and present the challenges of living in two worlds. If appropriate, use examples from your own life as well. Do you agree with each writer regarding the challenges he or she points out? Why, or why not?

Writing Assignment 3

Maya Angelou, "Graduation"
Lynn Smith, "Minorities: Alienation and Failure in Academia"

Review Smith's essay and her use of the term "Pygmalion effect." Write an essay focusing on the idea of expectations and self-fulfilling prophecy. Use Smith's essay as a way of "reading" Angelou's experience. What might Smith say to Angelou regarding her encounter with Mr. Donleavy? How might Smith use Angelou's example in her essay as a way further to support her arguments regarding minorities and their role in academia? This essay can be written as an actual dialogue—create a scenario in which Angelou, Smith, and you engage in a conversation in which Angelou's education is the focal point.

Writing Assignment 4

bell hooks, "keeping close to home: class and education"
Lynn Smith, "Minorities: Alienation and Failure in Academia"
Maya Angelou, "Graduation"
Jonathan Kozol, "Savage Inequalities of Public Education in New York"

This assignment is your chance to reflect upon the reading and writing you have completed this term. After examining education from this many perspectives, you now need to make some assertions of your own. Drawing upon the works you have read, create a project that you see as important to education. After reading hooks's essay, how might you want to revise your earlier projects? How does hooks support or challenge arguments posed by the other writers? While hooks's essay might become the focus of this assignment, you will want to include a discussion of the work you have already completed.

SECTION II. THE POWER OF LANGUAGE

Richard Rodriguez, "Aria"
bell hooks, "keeping close to home: class and education"
Barbara Mellix, "From Outside, In"
Gloria Anzaldúa, "How to Tame a Wild Tongue"

Each of these texts presents discourse about the power of language and the ways in which language can be used to include or exclude people from various discourse communities. Each of the essays examines the use of "public" and "private" languages. Rodriguez explores connections between language and intimacy; he also argues against bilingual education. hooks provides a different perspective; indeed, in her essay she provides direct rebuttal to Rodriguez's arguments against bilingual education. She also explores maintaining family ties in the midst of academic and professional success. Mellix discusses her use of "cherished" black English and her journey into "academic" English. She also looks at the transforming power of writing. Anzaldúa's text will prove problematic. She writes in the many discourses of her life: Spanish, English, Tex-Mex, and Spanglish. Her essay is a powerful testimony to what happens when others try to "tame [her] wild tongue."

Writing Assignment 1

Richard Rodriguez, "Aria"

Write an essay that presents your experiences with public and private language as well as Rodriguez's experiences. Use your own experiences with education and language to "test" Rodriguez's claim. Where do your experiences support or undermine Rodriguez's assertions? This essay should present both a with and an against the grain reading of Rodriguez's text.

Writing Assignment 2

bell hooks, "keeping close to home: class and education"
Richard Rodriguez, "Aria"

> Many white people enthusiastically supported Richard Rodriguez's vehement contention in his autobiography, *Hunger of Memory*, that attempts to maintain ties with his Chicano background impeded his progress, that he had to sever ties with community and kin to succeed at Stanford and in the larger world, that family language, in his case Spanish, had to be made secondary or discarded. (hooks, page 226)

Reread Richard Rodriguez's "Aria," an excerpt from *Hunger of Memory*, from hooks's perspective. Create a dialogue between hooks, Rodriguez, and yourself in which you define and explore both writers' ideologies. This should be more than a comparison/contrast essay; you should go beyond simply agreeing with one writer while disagreeing with the other. Rather, you should explore each writer's ideas from a number of perspectives—present a with/against the grain reading of each piece. One way to approach this assignment is to create a believable setting in which the three of you meet and discuss issues of race, class, and language. (Perhaps the setting could be a talk show where you are the host, and hooks and Rodriguez are your guests; you write the transcript.) Your perspective should be important to both hooks and Rodriguez as they are both, at times, writing about students who are in some ways like you. Be sure to allow equal time and space to hooks, Rodriguez, and yourself, since all three of you have powerful views that deserve to be heard and explored.

Writing Assignment 3

Barbara Mellix, "From Outside, In"
Richard Rodriguez, "Aria"
bell hooks, "keeping close to home: class and education"

When Mellix was a child, she learned that Standard English brought power. Her parents, other relatives, and her experiences away from home emphasized this sense of power. The end of her essay suggests that writing can also bring power. Write an essay exploring the issues of power and language—written and spoken language. Interpret your experiences with languages, and use them to analyze Mellix's claims. Then examine in what ways Mellix's arguments support or dispute the claims of hooks and Rodriguez.

Writing Assignment 4

Gloria Anzaldúa, "How to Tame a Wild Tongue"
Richard Rodriguez, "Aria"
bell hooks, "keeping close to home: class and education"
Barbara Mellix, "From Outside, In"

Choose one of your completed essays to revise in light of Anzaldúa's text. What can you add or change after reading Anzaldúa's perspective? She most clearly conflicts with Rodriguez, but what can you say about hooks and Mellix now that you have read all four essays? As you revise writing assignment 1, 2, or 3, consider focusing on language and power; what do each of the essays suggest about the correlation between language and power? This response should go beyond summarizing each of the texts. You need to develop and support your own point of view as you discuss Anzaldúa and the other texts you have read.

SECTION III. DEFINING LITERACY: WHOSE AGENDA HITS THE MARK?

Richard Rodriguez, "Aria"
bell hooks, "keeping close to home: class and education"
Frederick Douglass, "The Pathway from Slavery to Freedom"
E. D. Hirsch Jr., "The Decline of Teaching Cultural Literacy"

These readings provide varied definitions of literacy and education. Rodriguez explores connections between language and intimacy; he also argues against bilingual education. hooks provides a different perspective; indeed, in her essay she provides direct rebuttal to Rodriguez's arguments against bilingual education. She also explores maintaining family ties in the midst of academic and professional success. Douglass, in this excerpt from his autobiographical writings, discusses the consequences that he, as a slave, was willing to face in order to learn how to read and write. E. D. Hirsch Jr., in this excerpt from his book *Cultural Literacy*, discusses assimilation, acculturation, and his belief that American schoolchildren need to learn a curriculum based on "shared knowledge" and national culture. As you write in response to these readings, you will be asked to see ideas from each writer's perspective, to redefine some of your own experiences, to read one text from another writer's perspective, and to develop your own strong readings of each essay. You may find yourself identifying closely with one writer and reacting strongly against another; remember to read each text closely, trying to see through each writer's lens, understanding her or his point of view, before moving to an "against the grain" reading.

Writing Assignment 1

Richard Rodriguez, "Aria"

In many ways this is a story about becoming educated, literate. Write an essay in which you look closely at the paths Rodriguez takes in his pursuit of higher learning. Address Rodriguez's definition of literacy and his experiences with public and private language. Summarize Rodriguez's arguments in your attempt to understand his perspective. This assignment is asking you to do a "with the grain" reading of Rodriguez's experience. If you find yourself reading "against" Rodriguez, this assignment may pose some problems for you. You will, in a subsequent assignment, be given the opportunity to challenge Rodriguez's assertions; for now, though, look through his lens as you seek to understand his perspectives on language, learning, and literacy.

Writing Assignment 2

bell hooks, "keeping close to home: class and education"
Richard Rodriguez, "Aria"

> . . . the use of a language and style of presentation that alienates most folks who are not also academically trained reinforces the notion that the academic world is separate from real life, that everyday world where we constantly adjust our language and behavior to meet diverse needs. The academic setting is separate only when we work to make it so. It is a false dichotomy which suggests that academics and/or intellectuals can only speak to one another, that we cannot hope to speak with the masses. (hooks, page 223)

As you begin drafting your essay for this assignment, reread Rodriguez's essay using hooks's lens, her perspective. Create a dialogue between hooks, Rodriguez, and yourself in which you define and explore both writers' ideologies regarding language, literacy, and higher education. This should be more than a comparison/contrast essay; in other words, you should go beyond simply agreeing with one writer, while disagreeing with the other. Rather, you should explore each writer's ideas from a number of perspectives—present a with/against the grain reading of each piece. One way to approach this assignment is to create a believable setting in which the three of you meet and discuss the different ways that each writer defines and understands literacy, education, and the consequences of becoming educated. You might frame this response as a news show where you are the host, and hooks and Rodriguez are your guests; you write the transcript. Your perspective should be important to both hooks and Rodriguez, as they are both, at times, writing about students who are in some ways like you. Be sure to allow equal time and space to hooks, Rodriguez, and yourself, as all three of you have powerful views that deserve to be heard and explored.

Writing Assignment 3

Frederick Douglass, "The Pathway from Slavery to Freedom"

At one point Douglass says, "I would at times feel that learning to read had been a curse rather than a blessing. . . . I envied my fellow-slaves for their stupidity." Look closely at the ways in which Douglass learns to read and write—the prices he is willing to pay to become literate. Why is literacy—reading and writing—so powerful here? In the essay, Mr. Auld (upon discovering that Mrs. Auld is teaching Douglass to read) tells his wife, "Learning would *spoil* the best nigger in the world. . . . If you teach [Douglass] . . . how to read, there would be no keeping him. It would forever unfit him to be a slave." Write an essay interpreting, analyzing, and exploring the power of literacy as it is presented in this text. Include Douglass's perspective, Mr. Auld's ideas, and your own reading of Douglass's experience. Your essay might focus on any of the following issues: Douglass's reasons for wanting to be literate, the slave-owner's reasons for wanting slaves to remain illiterate, or the ways in which Douglass came to see his literacy as both a blessing and a curse.

Writing Assignment 4

E. D. Hirsch Jr., "The Decline of Teaching Cultural Literacy"
Frederick Douglass, "The Pathway from Slavery to Freedom"

E. D. Hirsch in his essay "The Decline of Teaching Cultural Literacy" argues for teaching children about the "information that Americans share." After reading Hirsch's essay, reread Frederick Douglass's narrative. Where might Douglass's slave narrative fit into Hirsch's idea of "shared literacy"? Hirsch mentions Douglass as a person whom all culturally literate Americans should know; why would Hirsch feel this way? What is Douglass doing here that Hirsch sees as contributing to "cultural literacy"? Define Douglass's account through the lens of E. D. Hirsch. What might Hirsch do with this text—what might Hirsch's critics say about his inclusion of Douglass? Write an essay in which you explore Douglass from Hirsch's point of view; then examine what you have to say about Hirsch, Douglass, and cultural literacy.

Writing Assignment 5

E. D. Hirsch Jr., "The Decline of Teaching Cultural Literacy"
Richard Rodriguez, "Aria"
bell hooks, "keeping close to home: class and education"
Frederick Douglass, "The Pathway from Slavery to Freedom"

Define the ways in which Hirsch uses the terms "acculturation" and "assimilation"; then redefine the terms according to Rodriguez, hooks, and Douglass. What does Hirsch's argument add to your understanding of one of the other three writers? Create a project in which you revise sections of your earlier essays now that you have read Hirsch. What are the key issues each writer is discussing, and how does Hirsch's essay give you a new way to discuss issues of language, literacy, culture, and assimilation?

You will likely find other issues on your own that you feel are significant to your project. As you look for ways to forge connections between these texts, extend the work you began in earlier essays.

SECTION IV. READING PEOPLE'S STORIES: WHY SHOULD WE CARE?

Nancy Mairs, "Carnal Acts"
Harriet Jacobs, "Flight and a Safe Retreat"
Black Elk (as told through John G. Neihardt), "Grandmother's Land"
Frederick Douglass, "The Pathway from Slavery to Freedom"

These autobiographical essays offer glimpses into each writer's life. Are their stories important or worthwhile? Why do people write autobiographies? What do they believe they have to offer their readers? In addition to reading these texts as "stories," you will find that these texts also offer you insight into the act of writing, the empowering quality of writing, and being aware of one's audience.

Nancy Mairs writes about being a woman, finding a written voice and the ways in which her writing empowers her in all areas of life, and "coping" with disability. Harriet Jacobs's narrative explores issues surrounding slavery from a woman's perspective. Black Elk (a holy man of the Oglala Sioux) tells the stories that he does not want to have buried with him, to John G. Neihardt. Frederick Douglass discusses his experiences with learning to read and write as a slave. As you read and respond to each writer's story, keep the following question in mind: does the act of telling one's story empower the writer, the reader, or both?

Writing Assignment 1

Nancy Mairs, "Carnal Acts"

> [Wearing] the brace makes my MS concrete and forces me to wear it on the outside. As soon as I strapped the brace on, I climbed into trousers and stayed there (though not in the same trousers, of course). The idea of going around with my bare brace hanging out seemed almost as indecent as exposing my breasts. Not until 1984, soon after I won the Western States Book Award for poetry, did I put on a skirt short enough to reveal my plasticized leg. The connection between winning a writing award and baring my brace is not merely fortuitous; being affirmed as a writer really did embolden me. Since then, I've grown so accustomed to wearing skirts that I don't think about my brace any more than I

> think about my cane. I've incorporated them, I suppose: made them, in their necessity, insensate but fundamental parts of my body. (Mairs, page 279)

What does Mairs want us to learn about her life, about the lives of women? Explore the preceding passage in the context of the entire essay. Why is it that Mairs sees a connection between her writing and her "body"? What does she tell us about the role that writing plays in her life? As you examine Mairs's work, look closely at what she is telling us about women: the values placed on women's bodies; the ways in which "feminine experience has been immemorially devalued and repressed"; and the ways Mairs has been able to "cope" with a body that is disabled in certain ways. There are many ways to approach writing this essay: looking at what our society says about women and women's bodies; exploring the connections between valuing one's body and one's work; examining writing as a way to value one's self in other areas of life; and being a woman with a physical disability in a society that demands women's bodies look a certain way. Choose one or two issues you find significant: how does Mairs address each of these issues, and how do you address them?

Writing Assignment 2

Harriet Jacobs, "Flight and a Safe Retreat"

This assignment requires you to do some outside reading. Find one or two standard history textbooks that address any aspect of slavery. What issues do these texts introduce? Whose point of view is emphasized? Do the accounts provide personal stories or general information? After reading these texts, reread Jacobs's narrative. Is her account different? Where is her focus, emphasis? How do you explain the differences? You might also consider the idea of "audience." Jacobs is conscious of her audience: mostly white middle-upper-class women in the north. In what ways does consciousness of her audience influence her writing? Who is the audience for the textbooks? If you had read only the textbook accounts of slavery, what does Jacobs's story add to your understanding of slavery?

You are looking here specifically at how Jacobs's story adds a new or different dimension to your understanding of slavery and how consciousness of one's audience affects the ways in which one writes.

Ultimately, you should respond to the question in the title of this Thematic Writing Assignment: Why should we care? Why should we, people in the twenty-first century read an autobiography of a slave girl? What does she have to teach us about slavery, writing, and/or surviving?

Writing Assignment 3

Nancy Mairs, "Carnal Acts"
Harriet Jacobs, "Flight and a Safe Retreat"

After reading Mairs and Jacobs, follow Mairs's example and address the following question: How do you cope with ____________, and how are you discovering your voice as a writer? You fill in the blank here: how do you cope with having a "disability," or with being an "outsider" in some way, or with being male/female or a member of a particular ethnic group, or being a college student perhaps away from home for the first time, or with a particular relationship? Is there a connection between the issue with which you are "coping" (or attempting to cope) and what you are doing to "find" or develop a voice as a writer? If so, what is the connection? Frame your autobiographical exploration in light of what Mairs is doing. You might also use Jacobs's text as a model here. Jacobs is also revealing her voice as a writer, and is, in a sense, discussing how she coped or survived slavery. Although Jacobs and Mairs are writing about very different kinds of issues, look for places in both texts that you can model as you tell your own story. One way for you to use their texts as a model might be to reflect on your role as a writer. How is it difficult to tell your own story? How is it empowering? How much are you considering your audience as you write?

Writing Assignment 4

Black Elk, as told through John G. Neihardt, "Grandmother's Land"

Black Elk told John Neihardt during one of his visits, "There is so much to teach you. What I know was given to me for men and it is true and it is beautiful. Soon I shall be under the grass and it will be lost. You were sent to save it, and you must come back so that I can teach you." In telling one's story, choosing which stories to include or exclude is crucial. Choose a moment from your life that you feel is true and beautiful—a piece of your life that you do not want to be lost when you are "under the grass." Choose your moment carefully; use Black Elk's text as a frame for your own story. Look to his allusions, what he helps his readers to understand and what we must try to understand on our own. Consider what you want your audience to know about you, your family, the moment in history you are describing, and why your story is one worth reading.

Writing Assignment 5

Harriet Jacobs, "Flight and a Safe Retreat"
Frederick Douglass, "The Pathway from Slavery to Freedom"

Douglass and Jacobs are both writing "slave narratives." After reading these two texts, what differences do you notice in the way that Jacobs and Douglass tell their stories—what aspects of slavery does each one emphasize? Other than the fact that these are both narratives about slavery, are there any other similarities? Read Jacobs's text from Douglass's perspective and vice versa. What might Douglass say to Jacobs about her experience? How is Jacobs's experience indicative of her gender as well as her ethnicity? What do you imagine Jacobs saying in response to Douglass's text? Write an essay in which you define and interpret the differences between the story that each writer chooses to tell and the different ways in which each tells it.

Writing Assignment 6

Nancy Mairs, "Carnal Acts"
Harriet Jacobs, "Flight and a Safe Retreat"
Black Elk (as told through John G. Neihardt), "Grandmother's Land"
Frederick Douglass, "The Pathway from Slavery to Freedom"

All of the essays in this thematic unit are written by people who are outside a "dominant discourse"; Nancy Mairs writes as a woman with a disability, Harriet Jacobs as a female slave, Black Elk as a Native American, and Frederick Douglass as a male slave. What do the voices of these writers share? Does each writer share in some way the struggles of the others? The voices of these writers and people like them are often dismissed, marginalized; did reading their stories affect you? Do you care about their lives? Should you care?

Write an essay interpreting and exploring the implications of the stories you have been told and what these essays say to you about the role of a writer and/or storyteller. After reading them, can you answer the question "Why should we care about people's autobiographies?" What if you do not care? Examine why the writer chose to tell the story; what did he or she hope to accomplish? For this project, look closely at specific moments of each text—how are these stories similar, and how do they differ? Ultimately, who is empowered by stories such as these, the storyteller, the reader, or both?

SECTION V. WOMEN'S BODIES: WOMEN'S LIVES

Maxine Hong Kingston, "No Name Woman"
Harriet Jacobs, "Flight and a Safe Retreat"
Nancy Mairs, "Carnal Acts"
Paula Gunn Allen, "Where I Come From Is Like This"
Michael Dorris, "The Broken Cord"

These essays explore the idea of women's bodies and "ownership" of women. Each text presents a different perspective of how we view women and how society determines in some ways what women should look like and act like. Kingston's story is a retelling of a family story about her aunt and the reason that the family cannot speak her aunt's name. Jacobs's text exemplifies the idea of "ownership" as she presents her story of being a female slave. Mairs writes about being a woman, finding a written voice and the ways in which her writing empowers her in all areas of life, and "coping" with a disabled body in a culture that "demands" women look a certain way. Allen presents "tribal" views of Native American women and explores the ways in which women come to define and redefine themselves. Dorris's text may appear to be out of place here. Dorris is a man, yet he is writing about an issue that very much affects both men and women and ownership of women's bodies. He explores the issue of Fetal Alcohol Syndrome (FAS). Should a woman's right to "drink" while pregnant overshadow the rights of an unborn child to be born without FAS? There are no easy answers here, but there are many powerful stories and complex ideas to consider.

Prereading Journal Assignment

Before beginning this series of essays, write a journal response examining the ways in which our society defines women. Look for magazine ads, television commercials, magazines geared to a female audience, books, and any other sources you can find to present a comprehensive look at how women are labeled, defined, and categorized in American society. Also discuss the ways in which your culture (or any group of which you are a member) defines women. What do these definitions suggest? Do we live with sexism in our "modern" society, or have we "come a long way"?

Writing Assignment 1

Maxine Hong Kingston, "No Name Woman"

> Carrying the baby to the well shows loving. Otherwise abandon it. Turn its face into the mud. Mothers who love their children take them along. It was probably a girl; there is some hope of forgiveness for boys. (Kingston, page 256)

Write an essay exploring the implications of the preceding passage. There are many issues and questions you might consider as you write: How is this story particularly about women and issues that women face? Why is it that the family cannot speak this aunt's name—what does it do to call the aunt "No Name Woman"? How does this story shape Kingston's ideas of being a woman? How does it influence her mother's ideas of womanhood? What does this text tell you about life for women in 1924 China? Look closely at what Kingston does with this story. Does she use it the way her mother intended her to use it, or does she create her own sense and meaning of its importance? Focus on two or three of the preceding questions to explore the underlying meanings woven throughout the many stories in this text.

Writing Assignment 2

Harriet Jacobs, "Flight and a Safe Retreat"
Maxine Hong Kingston, "No Name Woman"

Reread Maxine Hong Kingston's "No Name Woman" after reading Jacobs's essay. In what ways are these texts about ownership of women's bodies, of children, and of people's lives? How can the aunt in "No Name Woman" be compared with Harriet Jacobs—is the aunt enslaved? Write an essay looking closely at the life of Jacobs (whose story she tells us herself) and the life of Kingston's aunt (whose story is filtered through many voices). What can you say about these two women? They lived in different places and different circumstances, and they chose different ways to subvert those in power over them. How does one story add to your understanding of the other? Do close readings of both stories, and then present an analysis of each woman's experience in light of the other.

Writing Assignment 3

Nancy Mairs, "Carnal Acts"

> [Wearing] the brace makes my MS concrete and forces me to wear it on the outside. As soon as I strapped the brace on, I climbed into trousers and stayed there (though not in the same trousers, of course). The idea of going around with my bare brace hanging out seemed almost as indecent as exposing my breasts. Not until 1984, soon after I won the Western States Book Award for poetry, did I put on a skirt short enough to reveal my plasticized leg. The connection between winning a writing award and baring my brace is not merely fortuitous; being affirmed as a writer really did embolden me. Since then, I've grown so accustomed to wearing skirts that I don't think about my brace any more than I think about my cane. I've incorporated them, I suppose: made them, in their necessity, insensate but fundamental parts of my body. (Mairs, page 279)

What does Mairs want us to learn about her life, about the lives of women? Explore the preceding passage in the context of the entire essay. Why is it that Mairs sees a connection between her writing and her "body"? What does she tell us about the role that writing plays in her life and her role as a writer? As you examine Mairs's work, look closely at what she is telling us about women: the values placed on women's bodies; the ways in which "feminine experience has been immemorially devalued and repressed"; and the ways Mairs has been able to "cope" with a body that is disabled in certain ways.

There are many ways to approach writing this essay: looking at what our society says about women and women's bodies; exploring the connections between valuing one's body and one's work; examining writing as a way to value one's self in other areas of life; and being a woman with a physical disability in a society that demands women's bodies look a certain way. Choose one or two issues you find significant: how does Mairs address each of these issues, and how do you address them?

Writing Assignment 4

Paula Gunn Allen, "Where I Come From Is Like This"
Nancy Mairs, "Carnal Acts"

Both Mairs and Allen are exploring ways in which women are attempting to "redefine" themselves. Write an essay in which you explore the definitions presented by both Allen and Mairs. What does it mean to redefine one's "self"? Go on in your essay to discuss how you define yourself. If you are male, how does your culture define males? How are you attempting to define yourself within this definition? If you are female, how does your culture define females, and how are you defining yourself? Use the texts you have read as models for your own essay. Compare your way of defining yourself with Allen's and Mairs's exploration of "self."

Writing Assignment 5

Michael Dorris, "The Broken Cord"
Paula Gunn Allen, "Where I Come From Is Like This"

Reread Paula Gunn Allen's essay after reading Dorris's text. Both Dorris and Allen are Native American writers exploring issues that involve Native American women. What are the differences between the two essays? What are the similarities? What do you imagine these two writers might have to say to one another? Write an essay discussing these two texts and the implications that both have for Native American women. It would also be interesting to discuss the role of Native American men and nonnative peoples. What role do Allen and Dorris see such groups playing? What role do you see for these groups?

Note: The term "Native American" does not distinguish between the hundreds of different tribes and cultures. It is used here to differentiate between indigenous and nonindigenous peoples.

Writing Assignment 6

Michael Dorris, "The Broken Cord"
Harriet Jacobs, "Flight and a Safe Retreat"
Maxine Hong Kingston, "No Name Woman"
Nancy Mairs, "Carnal Acts"
Paula Gunn Allen, "Where I Come From Is Like This"

Review your response to the prereading journal question, and take this as an opportunity to "revise" yourself. You have now read five texts about the lives and bodies of women. Use key moments from all five texts to revise your prereading response. Choose a focus for your essay—something you feel compelled to write about after exploring these issues. Your own sense of what is important should guide your last essay. Review your earlier essays for ideas of what to explore further.

SECTION VI. FICTION WRITERS: DO THESE STORIES REFLECT OR DEFINE SOCIETY AND CULTURE?

Margaret Atwood, "Rape Fantasies"
Gabriel García Márquez, "The Handsomest Drowned Man in the World"
Susan Glaspell, *Trifles*
Ernest Hemingway, "Hills Like White Elephants"

One of the intriguing aspects of fiction is that it tells us about ourselves. If a reader takes the time to investigate beyond the entertainment of a story, she or he may be rewarded by discovering rich insights not only into the story but also into the society or culture out of which the story grew. This section explores four diverse short stories. As you read and then write about these stories, you will be looking to discover or uncover the commentaries that they provide about society and culture.

Writing Assignment 1

Margaret Atwood, "Rape Fantasies"

We can read "Rape Fantasies" as an exploration into a person's mind. Fiction often explores human issues and does the following: tells us what it means to be human, explores the world around us, and gives us insight into ourselves. Write an essay in which you present this story as a text that reveals something about being human. What does this text expose about being human and about storytelling? Look closely at the stories that the narrator tells, and explore the stories she repeats about her friends' fantasies. What does the narrator reveal through the stories and her comments about the stories?

Writing Assignment 2

Gabriel García Márquez, "The Handsomest Drowned Man in the World"

Discuss the importance of myth and storytelling in your own family or culture. Does your family or culture share a story similar to "The

Handsomest Drowned Man in the World"? Write an essay in which you explore and interpret a "myth" or story that played a vital role in your family or culture. You will need to "tell" the story, discuss the context in which you learned the story (who usually told it), analyze what the storyteller hoped you might gain from hearing or learning this story, and discuss ways in which this particular story influenced your beliefs and understanding about the world.

Writing Assignment 3

Margaret Atwood, "Rape Fantasies"
Gabriel García Márquez, "The Handsomest Drowned Man in the World"

What do both these stories tell us about being "human"? Do the stories reflect certain needs or wants of humans? Use specific moments from each story to explore what each text reveals about the nature of humans.

Writing Assignment 4

Susan Glaspell, *Trifles*

The gender issues in this play surface early and become key to the entire plot. Notice the ways in which the men and the women treat one another in this play. Write an essay exploring the gender issues apparent in this play that most interest you; for example, you might explore any of the following questions: How do the men respond to the women? Is this response important in the play? Do the men underestimate the women? Do the women take advantage of the men's attitude toward them? Finally, explore whether or not we still hold any of these attitudes toward women today, or have we "come a long way"? Does the play reflect certain attitudes about men and women that still play out in today's society?

Writing Assignment 5

Ernest Hemingway, "Hills Like White Elephants"
Susan Glaspell, *Trifles*

Both "Hills Like White Elephants" and *Trifles* present men and women talking around and past each other. Write an essay analyzing the ways that each story presents men and women talking and interacting. Consider the following questions: Are the men and the women in both stories misunderstanding one another? How so? Do you think that the men and the women are "choosing" to misunderstand one another? Both texts deal with deception. Who is deceiving whom in each story? Explore specific sections of dialogue from both texts to come to your own understanding of gender issues presented in *Trifles* and "Hills Like White Elephants."

Writing Assignment 6

Margaret Atwood, "Rape Fantasies"
Gabriel García Márquez, "The Handsomest Drowned Man in the World"
Susan Glaspell, *Trifles*
Ernest Hemingway, "Hills Like White Elephants"

Now that you have read these four texts and written extensively, what claims can you make about fiction and the ways in which fiction can (or cannot) define or reflect society? Use key moments from each text to support your claims.

SECTION VII. WAYS OF TELLING: DOES GENDER SHAPE REALITY?

Richard Rodriguez, "Aria"; and Gloria Anzaldúa, "How to Tame a Wild Tongue"
Frederick Douglass, "The Pathway from Slavery to Freedom"; and Harriet Jacobs, "Flight and a Safe Retreat"
E. D. Hirsch Jr., "The Decline of Teaching Cultural Literacy"; and bell hooks, "keeping close to home: class and education"

Does gender affect and shape the way people view the world? As you read these texts, notice the ways in which the men and the women tell different stories and how the stories are told differently. Watch for patterns that emerge within the stories, think of ways to categorize each writer's text, and try to establish criteria for ordering and labeling the texts. While gender can be one issue to keep in mind as you interpret and analyze these texts, think of other factors (such as ethnicity, socioeconomic level, and political ideology) that also influence the way that one comes to define reality.

Writing Assignment 1

Gloria Anzaldúa, "How to Tame a Wild Tongue"; and Richard Rodriguez, "Aria"

Richard Rodriguez emphasizes his struggle over public and private language. He presents compelling reasons to see language the way he does. Although you may not have experienced the dichotomy that he has between your public and private selves, you can still read with the grain to try to gain a sense of his point of view. Gloria Anzaldúa presents a very different perspective from that of Rodriguez. As you read these two conflicting accounts of language and public and private identity, what do you imagine these two writers might say to one another? Do you see their gender as playing a role in how they interpret and define reality? How so? You will need to develop certain criteria for your discussion—how can you support assertions that Rodriguez believes a certain way because he is a man, and Anzaldúa because she is a woman? You will probably want to avoid making sweeping generalizations; rather, you want to use specific moments from these two texts, these two writers, to interpret, explore, and analyze the different ways Rodriguez and Anzaldúa define language and life.

Writing Assignment 2

Frederick Douglass, "The Pathway from Slavery to Freedom"; and Harriet Jacobs, "Flight and a Safe Retreat"

Douglass and Jacobs are both writing "slave narratives." After reading these two texts, what differences do you notice in the way that Jacobs and Douglass tell their stories—what aspects of slavery does each one emphasize? Other than the fact that these are both narratives about slavery, are there any other similarities? Read Jacobs's text from Douglass's perspective, and Douglass's from Jacobs's point of view. What might Douglass say to Jacobs about her experience? How is Jacobs's experience indicative of her gender as well as her ethnicity? What do you imagine Jacobs saying in response to Douglass's text? Write an essay in which you define and interpret the differences between the story that each writer chooses to tell and the different ways in which each tells it.

Writing Assignment 3

E. D. Hirsch Jr., "The Decline of Teaching Cultural Literacy"; and bell hooks, "keeping close to home: class and education"

What does hooks have to say about the intimate and varied connections between social class, language, and education? Can one maintain ties to a particular social class (one that is not part of the dominant culture) and still succeed in mainstream "American" life? As you prepare to write your essay, you will want to pose some questions in Hirsch's name. For example, how do you think Hirsch would view "maintaining ties" to one's community? Would he see it as necessary, or would he point out problems and difficulties in handling a balancing act as described by hooks? What are the benefits, drawbacks, and sacrifices in maintaining such a lifestyle? Is there one right answer or solution to this dilemma? Is this a personal issue, or does society have a moral obligation to value social, racial, and cultural diversity?

One way to frame this essay would be to assume the persona of bell hooks; your job is to write E. D. Hirsch a letter responding to his essay on cultural literacy. You will need to capture hooks's written voice and to use words and sentences that seem to fit with your idea of her. Then assume the persona of Hirsch, and write hooks a response. Imagine what these two strong-minded individuals would have to say to one another. Where do you see them reading one another, with or against the grain?

Writing Assignment 4

Richard Rodriguez, "Aria"; and Gloria Anzaldúa, "How to Tame a Wild Tongue"
Frederick Douglass, "The Pathway from Slavery to Freedom"; and Harriet Jacobs, "Flight and a Safe Retreat"
E. D. Hirsch Jr., "The Decline of Teaching Cultural Literacy"; and bell hooks, "keeping close to home: class and education"

Now that you have read six diverse essays, write a response examining an issue that you feel deserves further analysis. You need to develop a clear controlling idea, one that you can develop and support with specific examples from the texts that you have read and the essays that you have already written. There are no limitations for this assignment; thus, you need to have a clear idea of your "project." Write your own assignment, and clearly define what you hope to accomplish with this essay. Extend the work that you have already begun in writing assignments 1, 2, and 3.